The Ecuador Reader

THE LATIN AMERICA READERS

A series edited by Robin Kirk and Orin Starn

Also in this series:

THE

ECUADOR

READER

HISTORY, CULTURE, POLITICS

Edited by Carlos de la Torre and Steve Striffler

DUKE UNIVERSITY PRESS   *Durham and London*   2008

© 2008 Duke University Press
All rights reserved
Printed in the United States of America on acid-free paper ∞
Typeset in Monotype Dante by Achorn International
Library of Congress Cataloging-in-Publication Data appear
on the last printed page of this book.

Contents

IV   Global Currents   189

V   Domination and Struggle   277

VI   Cultures and Identities Redefined   337

Acknowledgments

We thank the people who shared their ideas and helped guide the direction of this book. Special thanks go to all those who suggested or made particular contributions, translated or edited individual selections, and otherwise helped in the difficult task of putting this volume together. We would like to particularly thank Wilfrido Corral and Mayté Chiriboga for all their help. For financial support, we are deeply indebted to the P. Huber Hanes Publication Fund through Duke University Press. Valerie Millholland, at Duke University Press, provided invaluable guidance and was amazingly patient throughout the process. Miriam Angress provided crucial assistance at every stage. We thank them both.

Ecuador

Introduction

For many living outside Latin America, Ecuador is not on the geographic or imaginative map. Colombia, Ecuador's northern neighbor, is well known and misrepresented as the land of violent narcotraffickers and happy coffee farmers (à la Juan Valdez). Peru, to the south, seems reduced in popular imagination to a source of raw coca or as a mystical land whose Andean mountains (Machu Picchu) and Amazonian jungle are waiting to be discovered by adventurous travelers. For better or worse, fragmentary images, stereotypes, and fantasies about Ecuador are less readily available.

Among outsiders who do have an image of Ecuador, the country is generally seen as relatively peaceful, easy to get around in, and possessing spectacular beauty in both human (i.e., indigenous people with colorful clothes and weavings) and natural forms (i.e., the Andes, Amazon, and Galápagos Islands). These images are due in part to something akin to globalization. Ecuador has emerged as a major tourist destination in the past two decades, and indigenous weavers and musicians now travel to Europe and the United States to market their goods, and themselves. Foreign travelers come to Ecuador, more and more Ecuadorians visit other countries, and Ecuadorians are one of the fastest-growing immigrant groups in the United States and Spain. For the mainstream media, Ecuador is a small—but important—oil producer whose economic and political crises warrant an occasional article. Even for Latin American scholars, Ecuador is—along with Paraguay and Uruguay—often the South American country they know least about.

This anthology offers a deeper understanding of Ecuador. Here, the reader has exposure to histories of colonial grave robbers, lawsuits, collections of poems, biographies, art and music, speeches, beauty pageants, novel excerpts, essays, letters, and even recipes. To be sure, we are not the first to offer a more complex understanding of Ecuador. Ecuadorians—indigenous people, Afro-Ecuadorians, whites, and mestizos, men and women, poor and rich, Catholics and Protestants—have been doing this for generations in an attempt to carve out a more autonomous space in a wider world whose broad contours they do not fully control. This struggle has ranged from attempts to prevent Spanish conquerors from looting indigenous graves, to contemporary efforts to force International Monetary Fund (IMF) officials to understand the impact of structural adjustment policies. In varying ways, we hope that each of the chapters in this anthology contributes to a more complex understanding of Ecuador's past, present, and future.

Choosing material for the *Ecuador Reader* was a difficult task. We were challenged by two desires. First, because Ecuador itself is so diverse, we wanted to provide the reader with a wide array of material in terms of topic, approach, historical period, region, perspective, and especially form (poems, recipes, speeches, etc.). Some may argue that we sacrificed depth for breadth. This may be true, but we would argue that a deeper understanding of Ecuador requires an appreciation of the country's diversity. Second, we wanted to offer readers the chance to hear what Ecuadorians have to say about their country and its place in the world. Few Ecuadorians, from novelists and artists to scholars and politicians, reach American audiences in the United States and Europe. This is partly a problem of translation, but also a result of the unequal nature of cultural production. Here we include scholars and social commentators such as Andrés Guerrero and Felipe Burbano de Lara; political figures as diverse as Nina Pacari and José María Velasco Ibarra; poets and fiction writers such as Maria Fernanda Espinosa, Javier Vásconez, Iván Oñate, and Pablo Palacio; and viewpoints ranging from that of journalist Pablo Cuvi to that of holocaust survivor Salomon Isacovici.

Together, these contributions present a diverse set of perspectives on the country's past and present, from Velasco Ibarra, Ecuador's ultimate populist and five-time president, to Pancho Jaime, a political satirist; from Julio Jaramillo, a popular singer from the twentieth century to (anonymous) indigenous women artists producing ceramics in the 1500s through the present day; from the poems of Afro-Colombians to the fiction of vanguardist Pablo Palacio, masterfully translated and introduced by Wilfrido Corral; from market women to beauty queens.

To complement these perspectives, we have also drawn from some of the best writing on Ecuador by outsiders. Frank Salomon, a senior ethnohistorian who has been working in the region for decades, provides a wonderful account of how an indigenous group with non-Inca origins came to see themselves as definitively Incan. Rob Rachowiecki, the leading author of travel guides on Ecuador, traces the fascination with the Andes from the 1700s to the present day. In separate pieces on very different geographic regions, Suzana Sawyer and Steve Striffler explore the less than exemplary behavior of U.S. corporations in Ecuador. Jean Muteba Rahier chronicles the emergence and controversy surrounding the country's first black Miss Ecuador. Brad D. Jokisch and David Kyle follow Ecuadorians as more and more of them find themselves living in the United States and Europe.

As diverse as the stories and protagonists in this volume are, certain themes recur with some regularity, perhaps none more important than the struggle for recognition and justice by some of Ecuador's most marginalized groups. Their oppressors, including Spanish colonizers and their elite descendants, missionaries, multinational corporations, and even tourists, have come in almost as many shapes and sizes as their forms of expression and resistance—ranging from rebellion, migration, and political organizing; to satire, deception, and artistic production.

The resulting volume is not simply cross-disciplinary. It communicates through radically different genres and fields. For those with little prior knowledge of Ecuador, we hope the collection provides a broad introduction to a country rich in diversity, while at the same time challenging readers to learn more about the regions, traditions, and time periods that this volume encompasses. For those with more previous experience in the region, we suspect—in part because we are victims of this ourselves—that most students, scholars, and commentators tend to read fairly narrowly. It is hard to do otherwise in this era of specialization. Our belief, however, is that the breadth of this anthology will enrich those of us who are often forced to limit our reading to certain fields or topics. In compiling this collection, the editors, one living in Ecuador, the other in Arkansas, have benefited in this way. Poets, fiction writers, musicians, and artists have a lot to teach historians, social scientists, and journalists who "know" Ecuadorian society. At the same time, artists and other professionals can learn a lot from those who spend years, even decades, studying archives, communities, and political events.

We had no problem finding quality material for this volume. Our difficulty, rather, was deciding what to exclude or abridge. When choosing among similar contributions, we felt certain ones somehow "fit" better, an admittedly subjective and difficult process. *The Ecuador Reader* covers a lot of territory, but it is not "complete" in any sense of the word. The suggested readings at the end of the book, which attempt to remedy this shortcoming, do not provide an exhaustive list of material. We hope that this volume will serve as an exciting point of departure, not the definitive last word.

The sections are organized, in some cases quite loosely, both in chronological and thematic order. Parts I ("Conquest and Colonial Rule") and II ("A New Nation") cover an exceptionally long period, from prior to the arrival of the Spanish in the late 1400s, through colonialism and independence in the early 1800s, and finally into Ecuador's full integration into the world economy during the late 1800s and early 1900s. Some contributions, such as Sherwin K. Bryant's research on slavery in the colonial period, explore little-known aspects of Ecuador's rich history. Others, such as Blanca Muratorio's work on missionaries in the Amazon and Ronn Pineo's research into the rise of cocoa production along Ecuador's coast, examine better-known processes and events that have shaped the country. Andrés Guerrero, A. Kim Clark, and Ronn Pineo show the contested meanings of liberalism. The next four parts—"The Rise of the Popular," "Global Currents," "Domination and Struggle," "Cultures and Identities Redefined"—move the reader through twentieth century.

These have been turbulent times. Despite substantial oil reserves, productive land, a booming tourist industry, and a political climate that has often made it the envy of its northern and southern neighbors, Ecuador has been among South America's poorest nations. It has been particularly vulnerable to virtually all of the problems that have plagued Latin America as a whole. Partially incorporated into the Inca Empire at the time of the Conquest, Ecuador was unevenly conquered by the Spanish during the 1500s and occupied a relatively marginal position throughout the colonial period. The country limped into independence during the first half of the 1800s, and by the end of the century its development and insertion into the world economy was—like much of Latin America's—driven by the export of a single commodity. The expansion of cacao stimulated the development of the coastal plain and exacerbated regional differences between, on the one hand, a highland/hacienda economy dominated by Conservative landlords and, on the other, an export-based plantation economy controlled by Liberal elites in the coast. This regional divide has been a defining feature of the country's twentieth-century social, political, and economic landscape. The cacao economy collapsed in the 1920s, and for the rest of the pre–World War II period the country was largely ungovernable; neither coastal nor highland elites were able to rule, and the central government changed hands over twenty times from the early 1920s until the late 1940s. This period also saw increasing popular organization and the development of modern mass politics associated with Velasco's populism. Populist rhetoric created a powerful opposition between the noble pueblo, or people, and the evil oligarchy, which in turn contributed to mass mobilization and the integration of previously excluded Ecuadorians into the political system. From this moment, democracy in Ecuador has been more about the occupation of public spaces than the respect of liberal procedures and institutions.

The postwar period has been equally tumultuous. The banana boom of the 1950s ushered in a period of relative political stability, but ultimately exacerbated the country's dependence on basic exports—a process that reached its zenith during the oil boom of the 1970s. The postwar political climate has seen just about everything Latin American, including populist demagogues, military dictatorships, the semilegal removal of democratically elected presidents, and widespread political corruption; a powerful indigenous movement, the destruction of the rainforest, and uncontrolled urbanization and growing migration to the United States and Europe. A halfhearted attempt at industrialization was followed by a renewed (and more profound) dependence on exports, neoliberal structural adjustment, and spiraling debt (the worst per capita in the region). The country's currency was recently pegged to (and effectively replaced by) the U.S. dollar, a symbolic recognition that Ecuadorians have only tenuous control over their country's future. If the 1980s was the "lost decade," the subsequent period has not been any better for the majority of Ecuadorians. For many, the country is not only once again ungovernable; it is simply unlivable.

Conflict has been a hallmark of Ecuadorian history, and this volume examines power and privilege as well as marginal spaces and perspectives. Indigenous groups, as well as slaves brought from Africa and their descendants, challenged missionaries, colonizers, and masters even before Ecuador became a nation-state. At times such challenges took the form of open rebellion; at others it meant learning from and embracing aspects of Spanish culture and economy. Independence and Ecuador's growing dependence on exports—cacao, bananas, oil, shrimp, textiles, and so on—exacerbated conflict by further expanding the gap between rich and poor. This in turn produced not only popular movements (from labor, women, and indigenous groups to name a few), but populists such a Velasco Ibarra, singers such as Julio Jaramillo, and political commentators such as Pancho Jaime.

Ecuador's indigenous peoples and Afro-Ecuadorians have seen their communities fragmented, their lands destroyed, and their cultures marginalized and ridiculed. They also, by the 1990s, had produced the largest indigenous movement in the region and a number of vibrant Afro-Ecuadorian organizations. Ethnic domination in the highlands was institutionalized by the hacienda system. Hacienda owners controlled most of the land and used literacy requirements to exclude indigenous peasants from the vote until 1979! Agrarian reform in the 1960s and 1970s brought an end to this institution and created political spaces that were eagerly embraced by indigenous, Afro-Ecuadorian, and peasant organizations.

Indeed, the emergence of ethnic movements was undoubtedly the most significant event in Ecuador during the 1990s. In 1986, after a prolonged period of organization, indigenous nationalities of the three main regions created the Confederación de Nacionalidades Indígenas de Ecuador (CONAIE—Confederation of Indigenous Nationalities of Ecuador). This organization led mobilizations and "uprisings" in July 1990, April 1992, June 1994, January and February 1997, and January 2000 and January 2001. However, CONAIE is not the sole representative of the indigenous movement. Indigenous evangelicals, for example, have their own organization, the Federación de Indígenas

Evangélicos del Ecuador (FEINE—the Federation of Indigenous Evangelicals of Ecuador), and a political party (Amauta Jatari, later renamed Amauta
Yuyay) that has participated in elections since 1998.

Indigenous communities, organizations, and movements have periodically
blocked major roads and carried out long—and highly publicized—marches
to present their demands in Quito and other urban centers. The same groups
have been at the forefront of opposition to structural adjustment policies, and
have prevented the full implementation of IMF policies. They have also incorporated ethnic claims such as bilingual education, and the change of national
identity from mestizo to multinational. Indigenous-led protests were even
prominent in the removal of three elected presidents from office: Abdalá
Bucaram in February 1997, Jorge Jamil Mahuad in January 2000, and Lucio
Gutiérrez in April 2005.

Remarkably, indigenous protests have met with little state repression.
State officials, including presidents with different ideological orientations,
have entered into national dialogues and have accepted some indigenous
claims. The Constitution of 1998, for instance, incorporated collective rights
and has changed the character of the nation to multinational. CONAIE has directed bilingual education programs targeted at indigenous people, and has
participated with the government and the World Bank in the first major ethnodevelopment project in the Americas. In addition, indigenous nationalities
of the Amazon were legally recognized by the state as the owners of more
than a million hectares of land. Although Afro-Ecuadorians have not had the
same visibility as indigenous people, the number of black organizations mul-
tiplied in the 1990s. The state and the World Bank have included them in
ethnodevelopment projects, and Afro-Ecuadorians are demanding the creation of *palenques* (settlements) in their "ancestral" territories in the northern
province of Esmeraldas.

Whatever else can be said about these conflicts—and at times that have
been quite brutal—they have not resulted in the genocides, mass disappear-
ances, and "Dirty Wars" that have characterized much of Latin America
(though random violence and crime do appear to be increasing in Ecuador's
major urban areas). The relatively low level of state repression is explained in
part by the weakness of a highly fragmented Ecuadorian elite. But it is also due
to the unwillingness of the armed forces to massacre fellow citizens. On this
note, the rest of the region perhaps has something to learn from Ecuador.

Ultimately, then, what we hope the reader comes away with is a better understanding of how Ecuadorians have attempted to make their world. They
have neither shaped it as they please—or necessarily with pure motives and
intentions—nor have they sat by and waited for global events to overtake
them. Faced with considerable obstacles, including a particularly difficult

present characterized by growing poverty and economic crisis, Ecuadorians continue to chart independent—though often contradictory—visions of the future. The country remains plagued by rigid hierarchies deeply engrained in both culture and economy, but at the same time it is clear we are no longer in the colonial period. Indigenous people, peasants, women, students, workers, and other folks have dismantled the older order of noble and serf, hacendado and peon. Ecuador has been profoundly democratized by popular struggles. The relative openness of the political system and the unwillingness of elites to repress have created a favorable environment for popular challenges. Yet the risk of destroying liberal democratic institutions is a constant threat. Democracy without social equality and amidst constant economic turmoil is precarious. The challenge of further democratizing Ecuadorian culture and society remains.

Portrait, no date.
(Anonymous photo,
courtesy of Taller Visual)

I

Conquest and Colonial Rule

Documenting Ecuador's past is not an easy endeavor. The people who inhabited what is now Ecuador prior to the arrival of the Spanish in 1534 did not use the written word. In the case of pre-Conquest cultures, historians and archaeologists have been left with either material culture—such as paintings, ceramics, and ruins—which in the case of Ecuador lacks the scale (and scholarly attention) of Latin America's more famous archaeological findings, or have depended on chroniclers of the Conquest itself. Most chroniclers were Spanish, some worked through interpreters, all had agendas, and even the most well meaning lacked the cultural knowledge to understand much of what they were witnessing.

This endeavor is further complicated by the peripheral and diverse nature of what would become Ecuador. Prior to the Inca Conquest, numerous indigenous groups—relatively isolated from one another and living outside the control of a unifying state or ruler—inhabited the coastal lowlands, the Sierra, and parts of the Amazon. The Inca Tupac Yupanqui did not conquer the southern provinces of Ecuador until 1480, when further advancement was stopped by indigenous resistance. His son, Huayna Capac, pushed the Inca Conquest farther north, but many groups in the coastal lowlands and Amazon were never conquered. Ecuador's incorporation into the Inca Empire lasted less than fifty years and never succeeded in imposing a uniform language, religion, or set of political and economic institutions. Inca rule in the north was thus much shorter and less than intense than in Peru. To equate pre-Spanish Ecuador with "the Inca," then, is to misunderstand the diversity and history of indigenous peoples in the region.

The late and uneven arrival of the Incas was in large part a product of geography. In the southern Andes of Peru and Bolivia, where higher elevations, lower temperatures, and a dryer climate limit food production, indigenous peoples were forced to develop methods of food preservation and storage. Such an endeavor required significant political organization, state systems, roads, and other forms of physical and social infrastructure. The northern Andes of Ecuador, by contrast—with lower elevations, higher temperatures, and constant humidity—permitted year-round crop production, thereby eliminating the need for highly developed systems of political organization.

What emerged in the northern Andes, then, were small-scale chiefdoms, each with its own language and customs, and each comprising numerous villages that ranged in size from several dozen to several thousand people. Prior to the arrival of the Incas in the late 1400s, the northern region between southern Colombia and Quito was dominated by the Pastos, Caras, and Panzaleos. Ecuador's central Andes were populated by the Puruha and Cañaris. Conflicts between these groups were endemic, but no one nation was dominant.

This native population produced an abundance of agricultural goods—including corn, beans, peas, squash, quinoa, and potatoes—while establishing systems of trade for goods such as cotton, chili peppers, and coca that were grown at lower elevations. Ultimately, it was this natural wealth that attracted the Inca and contributed to their success in conquering the region. Topa Inca, heir to Pachacuti Inca, first defeated the Cañaris during the last part of the fifteenth century and used their capital—Tomebamba—as a launching-off point for future expeditions. Historical sources lack much in the way of detail, but chroniclers suggest that the Incas' military victories were hard fought, often requiring multiple expeditions and, in the case of lowland regions to the east and west, ending largely in failure.

Once in "control" of a region and people, the Incas attempted to secure their rule by relocating a large percentage of the native population while importing more loyal subjects from the southern Andes. Aside from this population reshuffling, the Inca left community relations largely intact, preferring to utilize local leaders—caciques—to maintain control and siphon off tribute. Caciques who lacked sufficient loyalty were replaced; communities that did not submit were often brutalized.[1]

The first contact between subjects of the Inca and explorers from Spain led by Francisco Pizarro reportedly took place off the coast of Ecuador in 1527. Spanish subjugation of the Andean region has become the stuff of myths, but the speed of the initial military conquest was remarkable and made possible by the fact that the Inca had laid the groundwork. They had centralized political control over a region that extended from central Chile to southern Colombia. To be sure, when the Spanish finally arrived in the northern Andes in 1534, they found a diverse array of populations whose assimilation into the Inca Empire had been partial and uneven (especially in terms of language, religious practices, customs, etc.). Yet, the Incas had succeeded in establishing political control over an area larger than the Roman Empire, appointing loyal officials throughout the Andes who implemented policies emanating from Cuzco. The system of political organization created by the Inca facilitated the Spanish takeover.

It was Francisco Pizarro's lieutenant, Sebastián de Belalcázar, who orchestrated the campaign into the northern sector of the Inca Empire during 1533 and 1534. He and 200 men battled through the Ecuadorian highlands, allied themselves with the Cañari, and subjugated the area around Riobamba. The Spanish founded their first settlement, San Francisco de Quito, toward the end of 1534 and continued the military campaign from there. Some communities welcomed the end of Inca rule and submitted to Spanish authority; other resisted; still others found some middle ground. Unable to find much in the way of precious metals, the initial conquerors became frustrated, abused local populations, abandoned towns almost as soon as they founded them, and otherwise left an unenviable legacy.

The Spanish did not disappear, however. New conquerors replaced old ones, bringing with them monks, priests, nuns, soldiers, and fortune seekers who established a permanent Spanish presence in Quito and a number of other towns by the end of the sixteenth century. Within a hundred years, by the end of the seventeenth century, Quito had a population of 25,000 and boasted some of the continent's most magnificent churches, convents, monasteries, works of art, and educational institutions. The coastal region of Ecuador remained relatively undeveloped, though Guayaquil became the shipyard of South America and one of the continent's most important ports.

By 1563, Quito was the seat of the Royal Audiencia of Quito, a territory much larger than present-day Ecuador. It remained under the jurisdiction of either the Viceroyalty of New Castile (Peru) or the Viceroyalty of New Granada (Colombia), but as an *audiencia* was able to deal directly with Madrid on many matters. *Encomiendas*—a grant of rights to collect tribute from a carefully defined indigenous population—were given by the Crown to those Spaniards it wanted to reward and who could be trusted to run the empire. The value of a particular encomienda was not so much in the amount of land one controlled but in the number of Indians. The *encomendero* was to care for and convert "his" Indians to Catholicism; in exchange they would provide him with agricultural services, cultivate his land, and provide labor for textile mills, mines, and other projects. This system would last in some form throughout the colonial period, challenged as much by the decimation of the indigenous population by disease and abuse as by periodic political uprising.

This is not to say Ecuador was devoid of political rebellion or interesting characters. The push for independence from Spain was foreshadowed by a series of major Indian uprisings that shook the highlands in the late 1700s (particularly around Latacunga and Riobamba). They never reached the scale of similar insurrections in Peru, but their demands—the overthrow of Spanish rule and the end of elite dominance in the countryside—threatened the entire social structure, which in turn motivated pro-Independence elites to take action.

One of the most fascinating historical figures of the period was Francisco Eugenio de Santa Cruz y Espejo. Born in 1747 to an Indian father and mulatto mother, Eugenio de Santa Cruz y Espejo was one of Ecuador's earliest scholars, a serious doctor, and a political heretic. He was also considered America's first journalist and writer of fame. He was persecuted, imprisoned, and exiled for political ideas that he never wrote down, but spread by word of mouth. He advocated emancipation from Spain, democratic government, and nationalization of the clergy. He died a Spanish subject in 1795 in a dungeon, but came to represent a future independent from Spain.

An interesting contemporary of Eugenio was Juan de Velasco, one of South America's early historians. Born in Riobamba in 1727, de Velasco was educated in Quito and Lima, entered the Jesuit Order, and was the chair of theology at the University of San Marcos in Lima. He would eventually flee to Italy after the Jesuits were expelled from the Spanish Empire in 1767, and he died there in 1819. It was during this time that he gave us the History of the Kingdom of Quito in South America, a remarkable account of pre-Columbian and colonial Quito that was not published until well into the nineteenth century (and not widely studied until translated into French in 1840). Although his work has been criticized for historical inaccuracies, de Velasco has earned his place as the first scholar to deal seriously with the indigenous population while trying to create the myth of the Creole nation. In stressing the value of the Americas (and its equality with Europe), he lent justification to the creation of an independent Ecuadorian state. For some he may well be considered Ecuador's first historian while for others the creator of nationalist myths.[2]

Finally, there is Manuela Sáenz, the "Libertadora del Libertador," perhaps most famously known as Simón Bolívar's lover, but deservedly recognized as an important revolutionary in her own right and as one of Latin America's earliest fighters for women's rights. One of Latin America's most important female figures, Sáenz was born in Quito in 1797, educated in a convent, and then married off to an English merchant. Well connected in political circles, she became involved in the movement for independence from Spain (first in Peru and then Ecuador). In 1822, after leaving her husband, she met Bolívar in Quito and supported him (once helping save his life), the push for independence, and women's rights until his death in 1830 (after which in 1833 she was effectively exiled from Ecuador and died in poverty in a small town in Peru). With Bolívar out of the picture, the dream of uniting the northern republics of South America into a single nation-state evaporated. Ecuador declared independence, becoming a nation-state in the same year of Bolívar's death in 1830.

Notes

1. For brief and readable overviews of pre-Columbian society, the Spanish Conquest, and the colonial period, see Suzanne Austin Alchon, *Native Society and Disease in Colonial Ecuador* (Cambridge: Cambridge University Press, 1991); Lilo Linke, *Ecuador: Country of Contrasts* (London: Oxford University Press, 1960); David W. Schodt, *Ecuador: An Andean Enigma* (Boulder, Colo.: Westview, 1987). Alchon's is also a wonderful case study of the impact of disease on colonial Ecuador. For a detailed treatment of pre-Columbian society, Frank Salomon's *Native Lords of Quito in the Age of the Incas: The Political Economy of North-Andean Chiefdoms* (Cambridge: Cambridge University Press, 1986) is a good place to begin. Also see the remarkably comprehensive, multivolume, *Nueva historia del Ecuador* (Quito: Corporación Editora Nacional 1983–95), edited by Enrique Ayala Mora.

2. Marc Becker, *"Indigenismo* and Indian Movements in Twentieth-Century Ecuador," paper presented at the 1995 meeting of the Latin American Studies Association, Sheraton Hotel, Washington, 28–30 September 1995.

Ecuador's Pre-Columbian Past

Tamara Bray

Given its unique geographical position on the South American continent, Ecuador has often been referred to as an "Intermediate Area," a kind of gateway between the two "great" centers of civilization in the Americas: the central Andes (Inca) and Mesoamerica (Aztecs and Maya). Rarely, however, has this region been approached as an important site of indigenous cultural achievement in its own right. The archaeologist Tamara Bray argues that greater insights are gained by adopting a locally grounded perspective that sees Ecuador's position as a crossroads not as a limitation, but as a source of innovation. It is, after all, in the coast of Ecuador where we find some of the earliest evidence for agriculture and pottery production in the hemisphere. The Ecuadorian littoral was also the main source of the highly prized thorny oyster (Spondylus princeps), an essential element of Andean ritual as early as 5,000 years ago and a key component in extensive interregional trade networks. Rather than ask why the complex societies of this region failed to evolve into full-fledged states, as many have, perhaps it is more interesting to consider how they resisted the rise of the state.

Valdivia and the Origins of Pottery in the New World

The appearance of pottery in the archaeological record has long been considered a key indicator of sedentary village life and the momentous shift to food production. Though exceptions do exist, and there is no direct cause-and-effect relation, ceramic technology is generally found to be associated with agriculturally based sedentary societies rather than mobile hunting and gathering groups. When Valdivia (Valdivia culture is defined by archaeologists as the beginnings of settlement life in Ecuador between 3500 and 1500 BC) pottery was first identified through archaeological excavations on the Santa Elena peninsula of Ecuador, its early age and technological sophistication created a stir within the scientific community. Radiocarbon methods dated the lowest levels of the Valdivia occupation to 3100 BCE, making the 5,000-year-old Valdivia pottery, for a time, the earliest known in South America. Valdivia culture was quickly hailed as the progenitor of New World pottery production and the hemispheric birthplace of the Neolithic Revolution.

The claims for cultural precociousness, however, had to be fitted to the general understanding of the Intermediate Area as peripheral to the primary centers of New World civilization. Resulting attempts to do so made Valdivia the focal point of considerable controversy and debate.

The Valdivia cultural tradition was first identified by the archaeologist Emilio Estrada in the mid-1950s and since then has been the focus of much scholarly research. While Valdivia sites are found throughout southwestern Ecuador, only a few have been intensively studied. Excavations at the Valdivia site of Real Alto indicate that it was occupied for a period of nearly 2,000 years. During this time, it evolved from a small village with houses organized around a central open space into a segregated ceremonial complex. While the population of Real Alto seems to have declined through time from an estimated maximum of 1,500 people around 2200 BCE, there appears to have been a corresponding increase in the ritual importance of the site as evidenced by the construction of a pair of large earthen mounds in the central plaza and the material remains associated. In Valdivia culture, maize agriculture, public feasting, the ritual renewal of sacred features, and elaborate burials seem to have been important components in the transformation from egalitarian to socially stratified, complex society that occurred on the Santa Elena peninsula during the early Formative period.[1]

The pottery that helps define this period is some of the earliest known in the Western Hemisphere. Valdivia ceramics are technologically sophisticated and quite distinctive. The tradition is characterized by the use of red-slip and incised decoration. The vessel shapes, which include globular-bodied jars with medium tall necks, squat vessels with short necks, and simple hemispherical bowls (figure 1), are remarkably standardized. Also of interest is the fact that a relatively high proportion of Valdivia pottery is decorated, suggesting more of an emphasis on serving, as opposed to cooking and storage, vessels. A variety of decorative techniques, including excision, broad-line incision, rocker-stamping (a decorative technique to create pattern impressions in clay vessel), combing, embossing, finger-grooving, and appliqué, were employed in the embellishment of Valdivia wares.

Beyond the pottery, probably no other element of the Valdivia assemblage has received as much attention as the famed "Venus" figurines (figure 2). The Valdivia figurine tradition is the earliest form of such artistic expression in the New World. These ubiquitous artifacts are almost exclusively female, with their tiny faces dwarfed by massive and elaborate coiffures. They are found in large numbers in refuse deposits at Valdivia sites and were regularly broken or otherwise mutilated before being discarded with the rest of the household trash. While the function of these objects is not entirely clear, they were almost certainly involved in some type of ceremonial activity. Because of their

Figure 1. Valdivia bowl with excised decoration. (Photo by author)

overtly feminine form, Valdivia figurines were initially interpreted as fertility cult objects. Other interpretations have focused on their possible role in curing ceremonies, ecstatic shamanism, and female life-cycle rituals.

Valdivia ceramics seem to appear on the scene as a fully developed technology. There is no evidence of the kind of experimental fumbling one might expect to see prior to reaching such a level of technical proficiency. Similarly, the high degree of standardization, the clearly demarcated categories of vessel shapes, and the fact that no local antecedents are readily identifiable—not to mention the geographical problem of being found in the Intermediate Area— seem to have contributed to a certain unease among scholars as to what to make of Valdivia. How could one account for the precocious development of pottery in a presumed cultural backwater? Of the several hypotheses regarding the possible origins of Valdivia that were advanced to try to explain the perceived anomaly, one stands out as particularly radical.

This was the theory of accidental transpacific contact between Japan and Ecuador developed by the original Valdivia scholars, Emilio Estrada, Betty Meggers, and Clifford Evans. Proposing that the essential elements of Valdivia culture derived from Neolithic Japan, they published and doggedly promoted their theory of wayward Jomon fisherman adrift at sea for months until finally beaching on the shores of Ecuador whereupon they bequeathed their knowledge of ceramic production to contemporary local residents.² Their hypothesis of transoceanic contact was based on perceived similarities between

Figure 2.
Valdivia female figurine.
National Museum of the
American Indian, Smithsonian
Institution. (Photo by author)

Valdivia and Jomon pottery, knowledge of ocean currents, and, I would argue, an implicit bias against the capabilities and talents of the peoples of the Intermediate Area.

More recent finds of ancient pottery in South America that predate Valdivia, as well as more critical thinking about the arguments put forth by Estrada, Meggers, and Evans and the comparative methods they employed, has led to the general discounting of the explanation of transoceanic diffusion for the early appearance of pottery on Ecuador's coast. The Jomon theory, however, serves as an important example of the way in which disciplinary frameworks, in this case the one underpinning our model of the rise of civilization in the Western Hemisphere, affects the interpretation of scientific data. The fact that the Formative period inhabitants of Ecuador's Santa Elena peninsula, as well as contemporary groups in Colombia, were some of the earliest innovators of ceramic technology and agricultural production in the

New World is still important and challenges the standard models of pre-Columbian culture history.

Spondylus and Long-Distance Trade

In Andean studies, approaches to understanding ancient political economy have long been dominated by the vertical archipelago model. Originally formulated by the ethnohistorian John Murra in the 1960s, the model describes an approach to interzonal articulation that emphasizes economic self-sufficiency and direct access to resources at the expense of territorial contiguity and as opposed to a reliance on trade and exchange. Encompassing the notion of ecological complementarity, the verticality model sketches the way in which Andean communities attempted to ensure direct access to a variety of nonlocal resources through the deployment of permanent colonies to different, vertically arrayed ecozones. Families dispatched to the different production zones formed discrete enclaves in territories that were often multiethnic. These colonists retained membership in their original home communities and maintained close contact through kin obligations and economic transactions. The movement of goods within this system was based on relations of reciprocity and redistribution. It is important to note that this model was developed through an analysis of ethnohistoric accounts pertaining to several ethnic groups from the south-central Andes.

The verticality model stands in sharp contrast to other systems of regional economic integration emphasizing specialized production and formal exchange such as found in many other parts of the world. The general embrace of the verticality model by Andean scholars has arguably had the effect of inscribing it as an ancient, deeply ingrained, and widespread Andean cultural pattern. Its overwhelming dominance also seems to have diminished interest in exploring evidence for other modes of interzonal articulation in the Andes. Interestingly, key evidence for alternative models of economic integration, such as long-distance trade, is to be found not in the presumed centers of cultural development but at the margins, for example, in the Intermediate Area.

Many theories about the evolution of social complexity give interregional interaction and exotic commodity procurement a central role. Evidence from Ecuador leaves little doubt that exchange relations and long-distance trade were important facets of the political economy in this region. The historical depth and widespread occurrence of *Spondylus* in the archaeological record suggest the critical importance of this resource to ancient Andean social, economic, and religious life. The fact that the habitat of this shell is restricted to the equatorial waters of Ecuador and the Intermediate Area implicates this

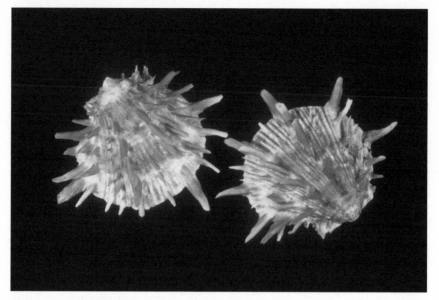

Figure 3. *Spondylus princeps shells.* (Photo by author)

region as key to our understanding of Andean political economy and the development of core cultural features.

Throughout Andean prehistory, *Spondylus* shell appears to have been one of the most essential elements of ritual activity. *Spondylus* is the genus name of the thorny oyster—a large, spectacular, and brightly colored bivalve equipped with impressive spines (figure 3, above). The native habitat of the shell is the warm equatorial waters of the eastern Pacific where it is found at depths ranging from twenty-five to sixty meters. The southernmost extension of *Spondylus* is the Gulf of Guayaquil, Ecuador. Like cowrie shells and *Dentalium* in other parts of the world, *Spondylus* was highly valued both for its sacred nature and as a source of raw material for bead and jewelry manufacture. Given the depths at which the mollusk is naturally found, the harvesting of *Spondylus* on any kind of regular basis could only have been accomplished by skilled divers.

Archaeological evidence consisting of finds of cut shell at the Early Formative site of Real Alto indicates that *Spondylus* was likely being circulated as a trade item as early as 3000 BCE. The distribution and significance of *Spondylus* gradually increase through time, as indicated by finds from slightly later Preceramic period sites on the Peruvian coast as well as early sites in the eastern Andean foothills. During the Early Horizon period, beginning around 800 BCE, demand for *Spondylus* increases dramatically throughout the Andean region and its sacred nature is codified in Chavin religious art. From this point forward, *Spondylus* shell becomes an indispensable element of ceremonial of-ferings and an important symbol of elite status. It is found in archaeological contexts throughout the Andes in both its natural state (either whole or pow-dered) and as the raw material of items of personal adornment such as beads, pendants, ear spools, and figurines.

Ethnohistoric sources enhance our understanding of the role of *Spondylus* in pre-Columbian societies of the Andes. It is clear that this shell was a funda-mental component of petitions made to the *huacas* (deities) for rain and good harvests throughout the highlands. The Inca made offerings of *mullu*, the Quechua term for *Spondylus*, at springs when requesting adequate rainfall for crops. The shell was also generally recognized as the appropriate "food of the gods"; failure to provide it could incur the supreme displeasure of the deities. Such was its importance that the Inca named a special labor tribute category *mullu chasqui camayoq*, which designated certain tributaries as responsible for ensuring that Inca temples and huacas had adequate supplies of *Spondylus* on hand at all times.

Given the profound sacred, ceremonial, and economic importance of *Spon-dylus*, control over its procurement and distribution would have been highly consequential. As the southernmost extension of the native habitat of this shell correlates with the littoral zone of Ecuador, it is logical to assume that the coastal cultures of this region were key players and principal beneficiaries of the *Spondylus* demand. The ability to control access to this critical cultural input undoubtedly would have conferred significant economic wealth and political power. Both ethnohistoric and archaeological evidence suggest that *Spondylus* was a principal component in a network of long-distance exchange and that the Ecuadorian coast was a central link in this system, which stretched from far southern Peru to the west coast of Mexico.

The earliest source of written information on long-distance trade and *Spondylus* dates to 1525 and comments upon a chance encounter between the ship of Bartolomé Ruiz, chief navigator on Pizarro's second expedition, and a large balsa raft off the coast of Ecuador. The raft was heavily laden with trade goods, and the indigenous merchants on board were reportedly on a trading expedition to acquire more *Spondylus* from neighbors to the north. Other early documentary evidence of maritime commerce published by María Rostworowski indicates that coastal residents of the Chincha valley in Peru traded as far north as the coast of Ecuador and may have been engaged in the exchange of copper for *Spondylus*.[3]

Equally important in the northern equatorial highlands were overland trade and exchange networks. Much has been written about the specialized long-distance traders, known as *mindaláes*, who functioned as personal emis-saries of local rulers and trafficked in goods of high prestige and unit value such as bone and shell beads, coca, gold, feathers, and woven goods. Explicit comparisons have been made between the mindaláes of Ecuador and the *pochteca* of Mexico, the latter being a guild of specialized long-distance traders that worked for the Aztec state. Like the pochteca, the mindaláes formed their own separate corporate body, living in a distinct sector of the home community. They apparently did not pay regular tribute like other commoners but rather served as special envoys. In addition to obtaining exotic goods for their political sponsors, mindaláes also seem to have functioned at times as political agents and spies for their lords.[4]

The evidence from Ecuador indicates that other potentially earlier and equally important forms of economic integration existed in the pre-Columbian Andes in addition to the vertical archipelago model. As previously noted, many theories accord long-distance exchange and the ability to obtain exotic goods primary importance in the rise of social complexity. There is little doubt that long-distance trade was an important facet of the political economy of the northern Andes. The importance of interregional exchange from very early on may well have contributed to the precocious development of complex social forms in Ecuador and the Intermediate Area. The archaeological evidence also suggests that rather than being peripheral to the mainstream trajectory of cultural development in the Andes, Ecuadorian polities, with their control over and probable promotion of the *Spondylus* trade, were likely key players in the shaping of Andean cultural expression.

The Caranqui-Cayambe Confederation

The combination of small-scale with complex stratified organization was a hallmark of northern Andean polities during the late prehistoric period. The highly stratified nature of these societies found its material expression in the construction of large truncated pyramidal mounds known locally as *tolas* (figure 4). The distribution of these monumental earthworks is coterminous with the limits of ethnic Caranqui territory and serves to physically define the extent of Caranqui-Cayambe influence. On the basis of archaeological survey work and the study of aerial photographs, investigators have identified nearly 100 mound sites in Caranqui territory. Most are found within a twenty-kilometer radius of Mt. Imbabura in the vicinity of the modern towns of Ibarra and Otavalo in the northern highlands of Ecuador at elevations between 2,200 and 3,000 meters above sea level. As noted by geographers, this is the optimal altitudinal zone for maize production.

While the number of mounds per site varies greatly, ranging from one or two at the smallest centers to 150 at the largest known site, of Zuleta (figure 5), the majority have between 20 and 50 such features. The two basic types of

Figure 4. Ramped pyramidal mound at the site of Cochasqui. (Photo by author)

mounds in this region are hemispherical and trapezoidal. The hemispherical mounds tend to predate the quadrilateral ones, with the construction of the latter thought to signal fundamental changes in sociopolitical organization. Archaeological investigations indicate that the construction of hemispherical mounds was an established practice in the northern highlands by at least 700 CE. Quadrilateral mounds, and particularly those with ramps, were a relatively late development within Caranqui territory (1250–1425 CE). The impressive site of Cochasqui, located about seventy kilometers northeast of Quito, remains the best studied mound site in the northern equatorial Andes.[5]

Archaeologists divide the mounds of this region into four basic categories: large and small hemispherical tolas, quadrilateral mounds (in the form of truncated pyramids), and quadrilateral mounds with ramps. The smaller hemispherical mounds, which range from three to six meters in diameter and one to two meters tall, are generally believed to represent funerary mounds. The larger hemispherical tolas can exceed thirty meters in diameter and reach five meters in height. Domestic refuse and occupational surfaces found in association with these suggest their probable function as house mounds. The quadrilateral mounds can reach sizes of up to eighty meters on a side and heights of eight meters or more. To date, no functional differences have been recognized between the ramped versus nonramped pyramidal mounds. These have often been interpreted as ceremonial in nature, though it is also generally agreed that they served as house platforms for elite residences.

Figure 5. Overview of mounds at the site of Zuleta. (Photo by author)

In early historic references to the polities of this region, chroniclers often used the term *cacicazgo*, which approximates the notion of chiefdom, to describe them. Each cacicazgo was composed of numerous villages, or *llacta*. The ethnohistorian Frank Salomon states that a llacta may be defined as "a group of persons sharing hereditary rights over certain factors of production (particular lands, the labor of certain people, specific tools and infrastructures), and recognizing as a political authority a privileged member of their own number."[6] The political authority of each llacta would be the equivalent of a chief, and the head of the most important llacta would also be recognized as the head of the larger cacicazgo. Each headman was entitled to several wives and a certain amount of labor from his subjects, who, among other things, were required to work the chief's fields, assist in the construction of his residence, carry firewood, and act as house servants. The headman also controlled access to exotic goods through the sponsorship of the long-distance trade specialists known as mindaláes.

The degree of political organization observed within this region has frequently been discussed as a consequence of the Inca threat and the need to unite for defensive purposes. Others have argued, however, that the powerful regional confederation the Inca sought to subdue was not constituted as an ad hoc response to imperial invasion but rather what had attracted the Cuzqueños to this region in the first place. Historic sources report that it took seventeen long years of warfare for the Inca to finally defeat the Caranqui-

Cayambe confederation and that Inca domination of the region was subsequently cut short by the Spanish invasion.

Ample evidence exists to suggest that the cacicazgos of this region, including the Caranquis, Cayambes, Otavaleños, Cochasquis, and Pimampiros, to name but a few of the best known, were highly stable and successful political entities that produced surplus, had considerable wealth, and participated in a complex web of strategic interactions with neighboring groups. The decentralized nature of the regional political economic organization depended on a variety of creative social strategies that simultaneously reinforced the autonomous standing of the polities and fostered critical alliances. Such strategies included the development of trade partnerships, the arrangement of outside marriages, the reciprocal exchange of children, the hosting of feasts, and espionage.

The typical approach to the study of pre-Columbian societies in the Intermediate Area has focused on the question of why we do not see the development of full-fledged states in this region. Rather than view the northern Andean cacicazgos as interesting and important polities in their own right, the tendency has been to treat them as entities somehow frozen in their culture's evolutionary tracks. To further our understanding of Andean forms of sociopolitical organization, it is important to overcome the presupposition that northern Andean chiefdoms were truncated states that never reached their full evolutionary potential. More interesting is to consider how the societies of this region managed to resist the rise of the state and imperial incursion for such a long period. Investigating the late prehistoric era cacicazgos of northern Ecuador in terms of their own unique development and cultural achievements presents new ways of modeling social complexity in the Andes. The political landscape of the northern highlands during the late prehispanic period emphasizes the possibilities of multiple bases of power and influence and offers us alternative ways of theorizing cultural complexity as possibly other than hierarchical in nature.

In sum, the archaeological record of the Intermediate Area shows the pre-Columbian cultures of this region to have been donors rather than recipients of important cultural developments. To move beyond the traditional view of this region as epiphenomenal to the high civilizations that developed in nuclear Central and South America opens the door to a richer understanding of ancient Andean societies. The precocious developments noted in Ecuador suggest that this region is key to our formulations of pre-Columbian culture history. The fact that Ecuador was a major conduit of cultural exchange from earliest times is reflected in the deep and varied record of the country's prehistory.

Notes

1. For more information on the site of Real Alto and Valdivia culture, see Donald Lathrap, Jorge Marcos, and James Zeidler, "Real Alto: An Ancient Ceremonial Center," *Archaeology Magazine* 30 (1977): 2–13.

2. For further details on the transpacific hypothesis of Valdivia origins, see Emilio Estrada and Betty Meggers, "A Complex of Traits of Probable Transpacific Origin on the Coast of Ecuador," *American Anthropologist* 63 (1961): 913–39; and Betty Meggers, Clifford Evans, and Emilio Estrada, *Early Formative Period of Coastal Ecuador: The Valdivia and Machalilla Phases* (Washington, D.C.: Smithsonian Institution Press, 1965).

3. See, for example, María Rostworowski, *Etnia y Sociedad: Costa Peruana Prehispanica* (Lima: Instituto de Estudios Peruanos, 1977).

4. For additional information on mindaláes, see Frank Salomon, *Native Lords of Quito in the Age of the Incas* (Cambridge: Cambridge University Press, 1986), and "A North Andean Status Trader Complex under Inka Rule," *Ethnohistory* 34 (1987): 63–77; and Joanne Rappaport, "Relaciones de intercambio en el Sur de Nariño," *Museo del Oro Boletín*, 22 (1988): 33–52.

5. For more information on the site of Cochasqui, see Udo Oberem, ed., *Cochasqui: Estudios arqueológicos*, 3 vols. (Otavalo, Ecuador: Colección Pendoneros, Instituto Otavaleño de Antropología, 1981), and Udo Oberem and Wolfgang Wurster, *Excavaciones en Cochasqui, Ecuador 1964–1965* (Mainz am Rhein, Germany: Verlag Philipp von Zabern, 1989). For a regional view of mound sites in the Caranqui northern highlands, see J. Stephen Athens, *El proceso evolutivo en las sociedades complejas y la ocupación del período Tardío-Cara en los Andes Septentrionales del Ecuador* (Otavalo, Ecuador: Colección Pendoneros, Instituto Otavaleño de Antropología, 1980).

6. Salomon, *Native Lords of Quito in the Age of the Incas*, 45.

Ancestors, Grave Robbers, and the Possible Antecedents of Cañari "Inca-ism"

Frank Salomon

The Incas arrived in what came to be Ecuador in the late 1400s and occupied the region for less than fifty years prior to the arrival of the Spanish and the end of the Inca empire. As a result, indigenous groups in the northern Andes were not only relatively independent of the Inca in terms of language and culture at the time of the Spanish Conquest, but in many cases had openly opposed and resisted Inca rule. Such divisions help explain Spanish success in conquering the region. In this essay, anthropologist and ethnohistorian Frank Salomon explores the fascinating phenomenon of what he calls "Inca-ism"—the tendency for contemporary indigenous groups of decidedly non-Inca origins to define themselves as descendants of the Incas.

The Americas offer striking examples of divergence between historians' definitions of peoples and their own idea of their place in a world of change. This essay concerns a single such phenomenon, namely, the fact that many Andean peoples known on firm ethnohistoric and archaeological grounds to be of non-Inca origin and anti-Inca political antecedents nonetheless define themselves as the descendants of Incas. Indeed today they adopt Inca genealogy as the very banner of their collective legitimacy, a phenomenon one could reasonably call "Inca-ism" since it usually has the overt, ideological tone we associate with the suffix *-ism*.

The emergence of "Inca-ism" involves a wholesale reversal of "self" and "other" in genealogical terms. A more fundamental process than "structural amnesia," as Africanists call the forgetting of no-longer relevant ancestors, is involved. "Inca-ism" implies a wholesale reorganization of collective memory. This is important. "Inca-ism" has formed the ideological backbone of political movements that profoundly affected the evolution of the overall colonially dominated society, notably but not only during the great eighteenth-century rebellions. It is still a powerful motif today in Quechua movements of revitalization or ethnic mobilization.

The people in question are the Cañari of the modern south Ecuadorian high-lands.[1] Their documented antecedents and archaeological remains demonstrate an undisputedly non-Inca origin. Indeed the Cañari figure in historical research as the very archetype of anti-Inca activism. But the Cañari of today, indifferent to the historians' history, define themselves as the descendants of Incas:

> The peasants of Juncal even today consider themselves to be descendants of the Incas . . ."Inca," to the modern Juncaleños, means on the one hand a bygone epoch, and on the other, appears as a special attribute of the culture heroes above-mentioned.[2] But at the same time, in a more general sense, it includes all the Indians of the Peruvian highlands, of the whole Andean cordillera, and in a historic sense, it includes all the humans who existed on the continent. For this reason the Cañaris were Incas until they were conquered by the Spanish, and they take no notice of the fact that in the thousand years prior to the brief Inca dominion, they had an independent Cañari culture, with a language of its own. They first became Cañaris on being conquered by the Spanish . . . in regard to the Spanish conquest they say that a person called Anticristo appeared and told the Incas that they would now have to bury themselves with their gold treasures, their maize beer jugs, etc.

"Inca-ism" along these lines appears to have arisen independently in many populations. This essay deals only with a single episode in the period of its apparent genesis, and the analysis of the episode is only intended to suggest the type of experience contributing to it. Neither the evidence nor the interpretation is to be taken as an "origin myth." The central contention is that Spanish and creole assaults on ancestral burials (tombs, mummy caves, etc., varying by cultural group), which took place steadily from the conquest to the present, have joined the process of interethnic encounter inextricably with the reconceptualization of relations between living and dead aboriginal people. The conquerors as much as the conquered are principals in the problem. The process by which their awareness of the Cañaris changed, in itself modified the conditions of Cañari thinking and becomes a part of the Cañari story.

The events described here come to light through the trial of a Spanish official accused of cheating the colonial treasury on the value of treasure robbed from native tombs.[3] They occurred in 1563, at a crucial juncture in the evolution of relations between Andean peoples and the Spanish, and are understandable only in the context of that period.

Cañaris, Incas, and Spaniards

The Incas attacked the Cañari people and, after overcoming long resistance, conquered them, only about sixty years before the Spanish invasion (that is, circa AD 1475). But Cañaris continued to suffer more under Tawantinsuyu[4] than virtually any other group, and antipathy to Incas was to endure. Inca ideology stereotyped the Cañaris as extremely rustic and violent people. The Inca state consistently recruited them to do the dirty work of repression and coercion, and contingents of Cañari "police troops" were located at most Inca administrative centers, including Cuzco. Cañaris of suspect loyalty were forcibly transplanted to remote zones more often than most other groups. In colonial Quechua (for example, in the famous colonial Quechua play *Ollantay*), the term *kañari* was used as a byword for ignobility.

Just before the Spanish invasion, Cañari troops suffered disproportionately in a dynastic war between two would-be Inca kings, which was fought fiercely in Cañari terrain. One of the contenders, Atawalpa Inka, inflicted an atrocious revenge on Cañari noncombatants suspected of siding with his opponent. All of these circumstances make it easy to understand why at least one Cañari lord, Vilcachumlay, greeted the invading Spaniards as prospective saviors from the ravages of Inka oppression and warfare, and offered alliance.

Cañari society did not react uniformly to the invasion crisis, but a substantial part of Cañari armed might went over to the Spanish and formed a crucial support in the earliest phases of the war against Tawantinsuyu. The alliance with the Cañari belonged to the short-lived but immensely important chapter of "Hispano-Andean alliances," which also brought the Spanish into common cause with the Chachapoya, the Wanka, and some groups near Quito. During the initial period of Spanish hegemony, the tiny European minority depended on negotiated ties with lords of non-Inca groups to mobilize labor and arms, organize tribute, and supply subsistence goods. Cañari troops enabled the Spanish to withstand the Inca sieges of Cuzco and Lima. For a few years the weakness of Crown authority and fluid political conditions created a setting in which local lords flourished and even in part recovered their pre-Inca autonomy.

Such arrangements, however, proved fragile, and the 1560s saw them break down. Rising numbers of Spaniards were by then acquiring means to coerce even large native formations. They acquired a motive to do so in the insatiable demand for mine labor, and soon after, weaving labor to clothe freezing miners. Crown authority established in the La Gasca era put decisions about tribute almost wholly in Spanish hands. Non-Inca lords found it necessary to switch strategies, relying increasingly on litigation, on the holding of native magistracies, and on initiatives in the monetarized market to make good their legally recognized standing as "natural" rulers of natives. By 1563, the record (incomplete as it is) no longer shows any special favor toward Cañari because of their service during the invasion years. The Spanish of the former Inca center Tumipampa, renamed Cuenca, recognized Cañari native lords, but do not seem to have taken notice of the Cañari "nation" (*nación, linaje*, etc.) as anything apart from other members of the lumped-together category "Indians."

Amid these large problems, Spanish grave-robbing and the pillaging of other holy places were probably only one among many factors aggravating ethnic frictions. The Spanish grouped all places of Andean worship under the term *huaca* (Quechua *wak'a*, "shrine"), including graves, temples, mummy caves, abandoned ceremonial centers, etc. The desecration and pillaging of huacas began in the first moments of the invasion and continues unabated to the present. In the 1560s, Spanish law treated the buried treasure of pagan antiquity as being virtually equivalent to raw mineral gold (an intriguing clue to the culture/nature antithesis as then understood). The legal procedure for looting was the same as for staking a mining claim; prospective looters had merely to declare what remains they intended to sack, and obtain a license whose terms included a requirement to pay the royal fifth of any precious metal found.

How hard native society took this injury is not clear. In later times, for which we have detailed records about Spanish campaigns to find and burn mummified ancestors, it is clear that Andeans felt deeply outraged and humiliated. The Spanish of the 1560s, however, with the exception of a few ethnologically minded researchers, did not understand that the Andeans regarded their ancestors as ever-present mediators between human and superhuman society, and as living personages requiring respect and reciprocity. The fact that early assaults on the dead were undertaken for the sake of gold and not as a part of "extirpation" campaigns against Andean religion was presumably of no comfort to the victims.

The Looters' Expedition to Jatun Cañar, 1563

In 1563 a Spaniard of Cuenca, Martín Bueno, spoke to Father Juan de Valladares about a rich tomb in the Cañari country. Valladares, whose lifelong avocation for the sacking of huacas occupied him for over forty years, went to Quito and invited Licenciado Juan de Salazar to join in the looting of what he called "a *huaca* and hidden cache in which there are over a million in gold and emeralds" (CVG primera serie Vol. 30:568).

Bueno's confidant Juan Salazar de Villasante, an almost ideal-type sixteenth-century personality, was an acute and forceful *oidor* (member of the Audiencia, or governing council) whose personal failings—compulsive gambling, inability to hide his disdain for the indoor life of lawyers and officials, and a terrifying streak of impulsive brutality—repeatedly brought him into disrepute and controversy. He wrote an early geographical report on the Quito area and attempted a forced resettlement of Quito-area natives which foreshadowed the Toledan *reducciones*. Partly to satisfy his love of hunting and fishing, he spent much time in the native countryside. As a result, although he treated Indians with more than usual brutality, he also possessed a more than usually detailed knowledge of the varied cultures that had recently come under Spanish dominion. This knowledge was to prove crucial in the chapter which Martín Bueno's report opened.

Two of Salazar's political cronies, Francisco Venegas and Andrés Moreno, insisted on joining in, a request Valladares could not safely deny. Shortly the four set out southward accompanied by some of Moreno's black slaves. While they were resting in Riobamba, two more Spaniards of the Quito political elite, Gaspar Ruiz and Alonso de Peñafiel, wangled a part in the expedition.

On arriving in the Cañari country, Salazar made camp at a place then known as "the *tambos* of Jatun Cañar"[5] or as "New Jatun Cañar," possibly the same as the modern town of Cañar or the village of Honorato Vásquez. The followers stayed there while Valladares and Moreno went ahead to Cuenca. The Cuenca party apparently had the triple purpose of bringing back Martín Bueno as guide, of officializing the "registration of the huaca" to obtain a looting permit, and of recruiting informants and native laborers.

The "registration" (made, presumably, under Martín Bueno's guidance) reveals a Cuencano's idea about which prehispanic structures might be expected to contain treasure. The sites registered were, in the looters' words:

First, below the Red Way-Station (*tambo bermejo*), on the slope where the road to Caray descends toward the river, [a site] which is a hill that dominates the slope descending downward.

Item, another hill which is above the Red Way-Station, from which Martín Muñoz pitched a large stone that used to be balanced on the said hill down the hill; [the site is] on the said hill which is where Antón de la Calle and Martín Muñoz and the said Father Juan de Valladares went about four or five months ago, more or less.

Item, the Way-Station of the Serpent, which they have declared, and which is next to where there is a small tank of water in which the Inca used to wash himself.

Item, a lake which is on the right hand along the road to Quito, higher up from the said Way-Station of the Serpent.

Item, a hill which is next to the farmstead of Alonso García de Orellana, on the other side of the Tarquisque River, over there on the far side of the City of Cuenca, toward the mines, on the left side, on the other bank of the river as has been said.

Item, they said that they have likewise registered already the Royal Way-Stations of the said city of Cuenca, toward the riverbanks. (CVG primera serie Vol. 30:492)

Evidently the treasure-hunters were thinking of specifically Inca remains. This is evident in the mention of the "tank . . . in which the Inca washed," and also in the phrase "Red Way-Station."

When researching his 1878 *Estudio Histórico sobre los Cañares*, Federico González Suárez could still observe at the ruins of Ingapirca "interior walls of the way-stations . . . covered with a type of stucco, with a reddish earthen substance, of which many traces remain. It seems therefore that the interior of this building was painted, like the palace which Atahualpa occupied in Cajamarca according to Jérez." Jérez does in fact refer to a "red plaster." This, then, could have been the "red way-station." The "hills" the looters registered were probably taken to be Inca places of worship; a balanced hilltop rock would be a likely Inca shrine site, and toppling the rock a characteristic Spanish act of desecration.

Heading back to where Salazar de Villasante awaited them, the Cuenca party recruited or coerced the cooperation of a Cañari native lord named Don Juan Gualtavizna, ruler of Guangara[6] (CVG primera serie Vol. 31:656). Don Juan said he was aware of no huaca and instead advised the Spaniards to consult "an old Indian woman called Doña María who is a native of the land," omitting to tell them that María was his own grandmother (CVG primera serie Vol. 30:744–45).

María was staying at the time in "some huts (*tiendas*) called Cerepus" near the "Way-Station of Jatun Cañar." On seeing Don Juan a prisoner of the looters, she agreed to accompany them and confessed that "she had in former times heard her ancestors say that ancient chieftains and an Indian woman" were buried nearby. She also said she had heard that "at the time of their burial, they had put into the earth gold and silver and copper hatchets and bead-wealth (*chaquira*) of gold and red and white bone." *Chaquira* often denoted beads of drilled Spondylus-shell lip, a highly esteemed offering to deities. It is possible that "red and white bone" means Spondylus; Spondylus is found in large amounts in Cerro Narrío and other Cañar areas offering burial sites (Collier and Murra 1943), and its colors include red and white as well as purple. But the term *chaquira* also included metal bead–wealth, especially very small seedlike beads of gold, silver, *tumbaga* (copper-gold alloy), etc. (CVG primera serie Vol. 30:756).

During this encounter, more Spanish grave-robbers joined the group: Pedro Muñoz el Mozo, son of Pedro Muñoz Ricos Saltos, who held the *encomienda* of many Cañari natives; and Antón de la Calle, another Cuenca

Spaniard active in looting tombs of the area. De la Calle was occupied at the time in digging another nearby grave, that of a native leader remembered as "Xerber" or "Captain Xeyver" (CVG primera serie Vol. 31:157).

From "New Jatun Cañar," Salazar de Villasante's group then headed for the place Martín Bueno pointed out, "one league away . . . at the site of Old Atuncañar, next to a fortress" (CVG primera serie Vol. 31:234–42). This site was almost certainly the so-called "fortress" of Ingapirca, today the most spectacular Inca monument of the northern Andes. According to the Indians who followed the expedition and later gave testimony, Salazar de Villasante at this time promised to pay for their labor. There, "next to a river near where there used to be a strongpoint and a fortress," Salazar de Villasante dug stubbornly for three days. This was the place Martín Bueno thought to be "the *huacas* and tombs of Guayna Capac." But despite the help of thirty, native laborers, the three days' digging brought up nothing (CVG primera ser Vol. 30:567, Vol. 31:656).

When no hope of finding anything remained, Salazar de Villasante later recalled, "I and all the others realized that he (Martín Bueno) was a fraud and we did not dig any more there" (CVG primera serie Vol. 30:569). At this moment Salazar took a decisive step. He turned from the known "Inca" remains and became interested in other burials. He had observed them from the roadside, but they had not figured in the plans of Valladares and Muñoz:

> About two crossbow-shots from there (i.e., from the failed excavation), there were some burials like those which are in cemeteries in Spain, very clearly visible, and sunken from the waters. Passing by them, I asked the said Indians if these burials contained gold, and they said no, that they were burials of *yanga* (Quechua: "ordinary") Indians, poor people. When I importuned them to tell me the truth, an old Indian woman said I might dig one which she pointed out, and if I found nothing in it, then I should not bother to dig any of the others.

Probably the old Indian woman hoped to put the looters off the trail by steering them to what she guessed was a poor burial. The Spaniards from Cuenca were unable to believe such remains, different from their stereotype of a rich "Inca" site, could be anything but poor. Father Valladares and the Cuenca group working at the grave of Captain Xeyver laughed at Salazar de Villasante, saying "that it was to dig in vain, because they had opened some trenches through those graves more than a year ago, and they had left them because there was nothing, and they even showed me the trenches" (CVG primera serie Vol. 30:569). Father Valladares ridiculed Salazar de Villasante, remarking "I wouldn't give this old breviary for what Your Mercy will get out of all the graves there are around here." Salazar replied, "I want to see what there is in each of them, and spend my money if I care to" (cvg primera serie Vol. 31:237).

Salazar's stubborn curiosity about these tombs surprised those who knew the Cañari region well, for, in the words of Diego Barroso:

> Many people had set out to dig the kind of huacas mentioned in the question in other parts of that district, but they left them. [The witness] has heard that Licenciado Salazar put a lot of energy into it and showed a lot of stubbornness in wanting to see those tombs. And [the witness] had never heard that there would be any gold to find in such tombs, because in Cuenca it was the common opinion that one would find nothing . . . This witness saw the tombs in question and they were clearly visible and all the people who went by there saw them, because they were raised over the ground in mounds of earth, and everybody believed they were graves of poor Indians.

Undeterred by this opinion, Salazar dug one of the "pits" (*hoyos*) "until he hit the hard part" (*lo tiesto*). As the old lady had guessed, he found no treasure in it. Neither did he find any in the next two or three. But on the fourth or fifth try, "a little golden hatchet (*hachuela*) turned up." Salazar de Villasante later testified, "on seeing that, I dedicated myself to digging until I chanced on the tomb from which I took out all the gold I melted down in Cuenca." Other witnesses, however, agreed that Salazar de Villasante removed much more gold than he showed to the Cuenca authorities, and that at least the fourth and fifth of the six "pits" he opened contained treasure.

The Grave Wealth of a Cañari Tomb

The eyewitnesses did not agree on the value of the grave wealth, but it must have been immense. The lowest estimate was 1,200 pesos and the highest 3,000 pesos. These sums are comparable with the annual value of tribute income from any of the major encomiendas of the time.

The testimony also affords a valuable clue to the content of wealthy Cañari graves and to the circulation of native wealth objects in a larger context. In alphabetical order, the items named were

> *Bars (Barretillas) of copper*: Mentioned once by a single hearsay witness.
> *Chagualas of gold*: Mentioned by one eyewitness. The term *chagual* means a small button of polished gold. They appear to have served as objects of ostentation in ceremonious exchange.
> *Chaouira of gold and "red and white bone"*: Mentioned by ten eyewitnesses, and described variously as to material. Small beads of pierced *Spondylus* shell, of gold, and of alloyed metals were used in many parts of the

northern Andes as a form of concentrated value; in the north, in fact, their quasi-monetary use seems to overshadow the ritual uses of *Spondylus* common in the south.

Diadems of gold: Mentioned by one eyewitness. A diadem of hammered gold or alloy with a gold plume was an insignia of native lords' status in the Ecuadorian Andes; González Suárez excavated one in the Cañar country.

"Hatchets of copper": Mentioned by ten eyewitnesses. The amount found is variously described as "over a thousand," "a quantity of eight hundred," "something like six hundred." One hearsay witness guessed at 2,300. The presence of buried hatchets in such remarkable numbers makes it virtually certain that they constituted a form of symbolic wealth. Grave wealth was sent to the afterlife for use, but clearly one does not need hundreds of axes to cut anything in this life or the next. It is much more likely that they were sent to be used as innumerable axes were apparently used among the living, that is, as coinage. Holm (1966–67) has archaeologically demonstrated the widespread presence in Ecuador of small copper hatchets, produced in varying "denominations" and sometimes arranged in decimalized packets for burial.

"Hatchet of gold": Mentioned twice by Salazar de Villasante and described as "of low-purity gold," possibly meaning tumbaga. The object described would presumably be a "money axe" of high rank.

Ear spools of gold: Mentioned by two eyewitnesses. Ear spools were a sign of Inca rank, but were also used by many non-Inca peoples.

Patens of gold: Mentioned by two eyewitnesses; may refer to shallowly convex pectorals common in wealthy Ecuadorian tombs.

Plumes (Penachos) of gold: One eyewitness saw a gold plume as part of the treasure Salazar de Villasante sent to Quito. Metal plumes were used in headgear as insignia of high political rank among aborigines.

Earrings (Zarcillos) of gold: Mentioned by Salazar as small treasures which he meant to keep as ornaments for his daughter's hairdo.

Apart from these items, ten eyewitnesses mentioned different kinds of metal objects not described except as being of "gold of low purity," "good gold," or "gold over silver."

There is little doubt that the tombs sacked were of Cañari and not Inca origin. The witnesses described them as consisting of deep shafts, three or four times the height of a person, with a hardened vault containing the dead at the bottom. The graves were marked on the surface by depressions where water entering the shaft fill had caused the vault to cave in, and also perhaps covered by monoliths.[7] The description of Salazar de Villasante's site matches a description of the custom for burying Cañari chiefs some twenty years later: "Making a very deep vault in the center of the earth, they used to bury a native lord." It also accords with the more generally north-Andean custom of shaft-tomb burial, practiced to and beyond the farthest Inca frontier. "Shaft-and-chamber burials" have been found around Quito and far into Colombia, beyond the Inca frontiers. At the bottom of the shaft, they contain one or more dome-shaped rooms well furnished with the utensils and luxuries of a home. Indeed they were homes for the ancestors; their appearance in modern reconstructions is cozy and domestic. The witnesses' mention of a woman interred with the lord she had served conforms to the north-Andean, but non-Inca, custom of "co-burial" as part of the "provisioning" the home of the dead. Some such tombs included pipes through which the living could pour beverages for the refreshment of their underground kin.

After the find, Salazar de Villasante behaved spitefully as well as illegally toward his companions. In order to avoid paying the royal fifth due on pagan treasure, he hid the smaller treasures in his saddlebags. He refused to share the find with the other Spanish looters, charging that they had been of no help in finding it.

Toward Don Juan Gualtavizna and the other Cañaris he showed the brutality that had made him politically controversial. When Gualtavizna asked some compensation for the help he had been coerced into giving, Salazar de Villasante "gave him many punches in the face, and kicks, and banged his head against the wall, and left him for dead." Gualtavizna's grandmother María also asked for restitution:

> She went to his [Salazar de Villasante's?] house, and for three days asked an Indian who was the said Licenciado Salazar's interpreter why he would not give her anything, since what they had removed from the huacas had belonged to her own brother. The said Licenciado asked the interpreter what she was saying, and when he had understood, he ordered her given a copper hatchet. The witness accepted it, and stooped to pick up another, saying "this one was part of my brother's provision." She took away the two hatchets, which she showed [to the court].

Considering the archaeological evidence, we may accept her claim that the dead were her own Cañari kin. Her behavior in accepting the two hatchets as compensation is of some interest, insofar as it suggests, first, that around 1560 Cañaris still considered hatchets a viable form of wealth, and second, that Cañari hatchets were not standardized currency (as coastal hatchets may have been), but had individuality of appearance sufficient to allow easy identification, and, unlike true moneys, derived part of their value from the personality of their owners.

It was the complaints of the defrauded Spanish looting partners which alerted treasury authorities in Cuenca to Salazar de Villasante's attempted tax evasion. The remainder of the trial concerns details of gold duties due the Crown. On August 1, 1565, Salazar de Villasante was found guilty.

Clues to the Transfiguring of Cañari Ancestry and Identity

The incident of Salazar de Villasante's grave robbery could not by itself have caused the massive shift of consciousness which turned the Incas from enemies to ancestors in Cañari folk history. But historical research gives us, through this incident, at least a vignette of the kind of experience that Cañaris underwent as the shift of folk-historical consciousness was beginning.

The reclassification in Spanish thought of the Cañaris as a people whose historical deposits bore gold came about as a result of several coinciding factors. First, Inca sites had by 1563 been largely exhausted; second, Spanish-Cañari relations had deteriorated to a point allowing more aggressive encroachment (e.g., the physical coercion of native nobles like Gualtavizna); and third, ethnographic knowledge was accumulating. The first two factors were necessary but not sufficient conditions. Because Cañari graves were evidently very deep and hard to open,[8] and because it was evidently not possible to tell rich ones from poor on surface inspection, even unbridled grave-robbers would not persevere unless they had reason to foresee a cache.

The probable reason why it took a traveler from Quito and the far north to break the Cuenca-district stereotype was that Quito-area Spaniards had come farther toward the discovery of non-Inca burial customs than had Cuenca-area Spaniards. Early losers in the race for Inca gold, they had gone after non-Inca treasures. Some, like Salazar de Villasante, were already expert by the 1560s in north-Andean cultures and familiar with the shaft-tomb burials of the region. By virtue of his empirical revision of folk-historical suppositions, Salazar de Villasante can claim title as a crooked but genuine forerunner of archaeology.

From the Cañari side, the attack on Cañari ancestors may have set into motion a process that the Inca state would not have allowed even if Cañaris had desired it, namely, the retrospective grafting of Cañari genealogy onto Inca descent. In order to understand how it occurred, one must remember that in Quechua thinking a dead person is considered to be present and active so long as he or she has physical existence. When the Cañari dead were taken from their tombs and exposed, broken and impoverished, they ceased to be rich, honored, and potent ancestors, and became dishonored, defeated, and disinherited ones. Neglected pre-Columbian ancestor mummies (*gentiles*) today form a class of hungry ghosts who pervasively haunt Quechua folklore in various regions. When the Spanish vandalized the Cañari dead and disposed of their bodies as garbage, they created a new common condition for Inca and non-Inca peoples alike, that of descendants of destroyed persons. Although natives of some Peruvian regions sought to defend their genealogical identities by devising special forms of reverence for destroyed ancestors (called "burned parents" in Quechua), others lost their cults. Aboriginal genealogies were altered to a status resembling orphanhood, the term for which (*wajcha*) is the Andean byword for misery.

Because Andean worshipers expressed the specificity of their group affiliations in terms of descent from specific, remote, and holy ancestors, the loss of ancestors was also damaging to the ritual foundations of ethnic boundary maintenance among natives. It is true that there were no "Indians" prior to the conquest, and that this lumping category arose in the simplifying process of the invaders' colonial administration. But it is also true that almost simultaneously with the spread of the term, many natives increasingly behaved like "Indians"—for example, in marrying and resettling across previously inviolate ethnic boundaries—and this long-running tendency also needs some explanation. Perhaps living as descendants of destroyed ancestors reduced the number of ritual obligations that bound individuals to a specific localized collective identity. Less definable in terms of localized genealogy, "Indians" were perhaps in their own eyes more conspicuously united in terms of remote descent from nonlocalized ancestors. All-inclusive, supralocal concepts such as "Inca" may have gained greater ideological salience even as their political potency waned.

Such a shift could not have occurred all at once, but it did not have to, because the processes propelling it were durable. The rise of "Inca-ism" probably occurred as a slow shift occurring at the margins of awareness while the drama of Spanish assault on local ancestors was performed thousands of times over in innumerable villages—first through grave robbing for gold, later through the "extirpation of idolatries," and in modern times via looting for the antiquities market, and even attacks on *gentil* mummies by Evangelical converts. Other factors also seem to have fostered a shift toward pro-Inca motifs in popular culture: the claims of urban Inca descent groups which achieved early prominence in colonial native politics, for example, were often Inca-based even when individuals had non-Inca names. Claims and titles based on Inca law had some usefulness as a defense against colonial abuses.

Seen from the very great distance at which we now stand, treasure-hunting appears the structural opposite of the cult of the dead: whereas the cult, propitiating ancestors, helped them propel reproduction forward and downward into particularity and the unique local group of the present, looting, by destroying ancestors, "retroduced" the genealogical link backward into the remote common origins of Andean humanity. Well-being and order receded into distant, central symbols—for example, the broken body of Inkarri—and folk history redefined the living as orphaned descendants of an all-engendering majesty.

Notes

For complete references and footnotes, please see a slightly longer version of this article in *Natives and Neighbors in South America: Anthropological Essays*, ed. Harald O. Skar and Frank Salomon (Göteborg: Göteborg Etnografika Museum, 1987), 207–32.

1. Approximately from the modern town of Alausí southward to the southern periphery of Cuenca (Incaic Tumipampa), including most of modern Cañar and Azuay Provinces.

2. I.e., those who subjugated nature and created the infrastructure of agriculture by such miraculous means as tethering the sun and lassoing the rivers.

3. The trial record is inserted as part of the documentation compiled for the *residencia*, or exit hearings, of the *oidor* Licenciado Juan de Salazar de Villasante, held in Quito, Cuenca, and Guayaquil in 1565. The originals are in the Archivo General de Indias. The copies used in this study belong to the Colección Vacas Galindo [cvg]. This collection was compiled in support of Ecuador's claims regarding its boundary dispute with Peru. The citations refer to Vacas Galindo's classification.

4. The Inca name for the Inca state, literally "Fourfold Domain."

5. From Quechua *tampu*, "way-station"; often refers to Inca facilities for lodging of caravans, armies, etc.

6. Guangara may be the place modern Ingapircanos call Guangra, located in the parish of Achupallas, or it may be Aguarongo Pamba in Honorato Vásquez parish.

7. Monoliths or grave steles may be what witnesses meant when saying the graves resembled Spanish ones. Perhaps they were thinking of horizontally laid gravestones.

8. The "trenches" cut by early, Cuenca-based looters had probably failed to reach the depth at which rich graves lay. One witness from Cuenca expressed himself as startled at the "bulldog stubbornness" with which Salazar persisted in digging to depths that seemed unpromising.

Building a Life in Colonial Quito:
José Jaime Ortiz, Architect and Entrepreneur

Susan V. Webster

By the late seventeenth century, the city of Quito had enjoyed nearly a hundred years of burgeoning prosperity and power. It boasted a wealth of monumental architecture, housing nearly twenty well-appointed monasteries, convents, parish churches, and chapels, and the numerous palaces and mansions of wealthy citizens lined the streets that radiated from the spacious central plaza. The imposing built environment of Quito was seen as a reflection and embodiment of its community through which the principal citizens sought to aggrandize and promote their status within the viceroyalty. Based on archival documents, Susan Webster's account of the life and times of a newly arrived Spanish architect in colonial Quito illustrates the extent to which fame and fortune could be attained by an enterprising and ambitious colonist, and the costs that could be involved in pursuing those desires. Indeed, the architect's career and fortunes parallel in some ways those of the city itself during the late seventeenth and early eighteenth centuries, rising on a crest of wealth and ambition, only to enter a decline from which it never recovered.

The brave man carves out his own fortune, and every man is the son of his own works.—Miguel de Cervantes, *Don Quixote*

[I want] only to build a church that will stand firm and perfect, looking always to the service of God and the permanence of the structure . . . [one that will] promote my status and be to my credit and that will leave a lasting memory of myself and my work for generations to come.—José Jaime Ortiz, 1699

Opportunity was likely uppermost in the minds of the many Spaniards who left their homeland on an arduous journey to an uncertain future in the colonial Americas. The promise of this "New World" held out abundant opportunities to reinvent oneself, to build a new life, and to find fame and fortune on a new frontier. Not all who undertook the journey were successful in realizing such dreams, but some prospered and even attained lasting fame.

One of these dreamers was a thirty-eight-year-old Spanish architect named José Jaime Ortiz, who arrived in the city of Quito in 1694. Ortiz had sailed from Spain to Cartagena, and was traveling overland to Lima in search of promising architectural commissions. He arrived in Quito at an auspicious time, for the city was still enjoying a golden age of prosperity and growth that was reflected in the expansion of its monumental architecture and urban fabric. Ortiz's arrival, in fact, was doubly auspicious, for there were at that time no professional architects active in the city, and the Confraternity of the Most Holy Sacrament was desperately in need of an expert to design and construct its new church. The confraternity, composed of the most elite and powerful citizens of Quito, offered Ortiz the impressive amount of 4,500 pesos and an annual stipend for the duration of the work, thereby convincing him to stay and accept the commission.

This was the first great challenge of Ortiz's new career, for the church was to be built alongside the cathedral atop one of the deepest of the ravines that traversed the city. The architect labored for more than two years just to set the foundations, some at a depth of more than fifty feet, into the living rock of the crevasse. Over the next decade, the magnificent Church of El Sagrario rose atop the ravine as a monumental testament to the architect's skill, sweat, and tenacity (figure 1).

The rectangular three-aisled plan of El Sagrario is novel in that the crossing, crowned by a high dome, bisects the nave at almost the midsection, creating an unusual type of centralized plan (figure 2). This virtual centering of the dome may have served to protect it by equalizing its weight with respect to the buttressed walls, given the precarious site and the frequent seismic movements in the city. Another novel feature was the construction material of the soaring vaults (figure 3), which were composed of lightweight pumice stone that was transported by cargoes of mules from Latacunga, some sixty miles to the south. The impressive dome of the church, capped by a gigantic gilded monstrance, towered above the neighboring cathedral and was visible from all sectors of the city, and the imposing facade was adorned with additional symbols of the illustrious patrons, the Confraternity of the Most Holy Sacrament. Upon its completion, El Sagrario served as the cathedral parish in the heart of the city and quickly became the church of Quito's elite; everyone who was anyone was baptized, married, and buried there, and its architectural forms were imitated throughout the remainder of the eighteenth century. Chroniclers' and travelers' accounts from the eighteenth and nineteenth centuries never fail to single out El Sagrario and marvel at its opulence and grandeur.

With his peninsular background, his authoritative knowledge of architectural practices, and his remarkable success in the construction of the Church

Figure 1.
José Jaime Ortiz, Church
of El Sagrario, 1694–1715.
(Photo by author)

of El Sagrario, Ortiz achieved immediate renown in the city. In 1695, the city
fathers named him *arquitecto mayor* (master architect), and awarded him a
prestigious post overseeing municipal buildings and works, including the
consolidation and construction of several bridges and the city infrastructure
and waterworks. His fortunes were further increased when a great earthquake struck the city in 1698, and the widespread damage resulted in a del-
uge of commissions. In 1700, while still hard at work on El Sagrario, Ortiz
signed a lucrative contract to reconstruct the Church of La Merced from its
foundations, receiving nearly twice the sum he had obtained for that of El
Sagrario. The Mercedarian friars were clearly impressed by Ortiz's work for
the confraternity, for they requested that he build the pillars, crossing, and
dome of their new church in imitation of those of El Sagrario. The spectacular church that Ortiz began to design and construct for the Mercedarians further increased his stature, and commissions began arriving in rapid succession
(figures 4 and 5).

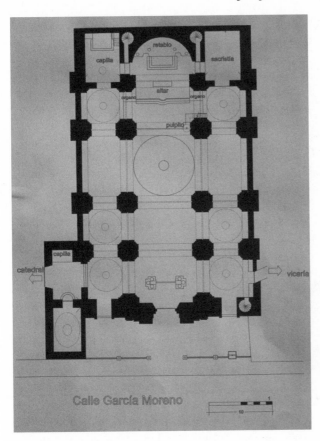

Figure 2.
Church of El
Sagrario, plan.
(Photo by author)

Business was booming, and Ortiz held a virtual monopoly on the building trade. The enterprising architect was able to reap the benefits of multiple, simultaneous commissions by organizing and training teams of builders and craftsmen to carry out his plans for each building while he moved from one site to the other, supervising the constructions. As these buildings rose, he was awarded numerous architectural commissions over the following years. Between 1700 and 1707, Ortiz took on a total of nine major architectural projects, including the Church of La Merced, the main cloister of the Convent of the Immaculate Conception, the facades of the Church of Santa Catalina (figure 6), the tower of the Church of Santo Domingo (figure 7), and the Arches of Santa Elena, in addition to the mansions of several principal citizens. He also constructed his own houses and architectural workshop in the parish of San Marcos, and began to train a generation of local builders and artisans in the professional practices of his craft.

Figure 3.
Church of El
Sagrario, interior.
(Photo by author)

Within a few years of his arrival, Ortiz had carved out a place for himself as an active and important member of the community. Unlike the majority of peninsular Spaniards, who took up residence in the urban centers of the Americas, Ortiz did not choose to marry into the local elite. However, in addition to a well-appointed home, he also established a family. In 1703 the bachelor Ortiz adopted two young orphans, María Tomasa and María Bernarda, whom he began to raise from infancy. He also developed a series of close friendships with resident Spaniards, with whom he collaborated in a variety of business ventures. Clearly, these were fruitful and satisfying times for the architect—his star was on the rise.

As his fortunes increased, Ortiz embarked on a remarkable entrepreneurial career; more than eighty individual contracts document his extensive business ventures, including investments in real estate, rental properties, mortgages, the slave market, the art market, transatlantic trade, textile workshops, a hat workshop, and gold mines. Ortiz was indeed an enterprising, ambitious, and at times ruthless businessman who capitalized on his abilities and maximized his resources in search of glory and prosperity; indeed, the record demonstrates that when it came to business, he was not a humble man. And he

Figure 4. José Jaime Ortiz, Church of La Merced, constructed 1701–37 (reconstructed). (Photo by Hernán Navarrete)

likely made more than a few enemies in the course of his business ventures, just as his architectural successes undoubtedly made him the envy of many. In fact, his enterprising spirit and rapid successes may have rankled the local elite, especially the Creoles, who generally viewed outsiders, and particularly peninsular Spaniards, as threats to their power and prestige.

At times his lofty ambitions and self-importance brought him into conflict with his patrons, his associates, and the local authorities, and Ortiz frequently used the legal system to his advantage in the same way that he mustered his abilities and resources. Within his first few years in Quito, he was involved in several lengthy lawsuits, some of which he himself pursued, others that were lodged against him. The first notable example involved a lawsuit that Ortiz imposed on the confraternity that had first commissioned him to build its church.

After toiling for nearly three years to excavate and set the foundations for El Sagrario, Ortiz sued the confraternity, accusing it of fraud for not informing him of the extent of the work required to build the church on the site of the ravine, demanding additional compensation for his efforts. Playing on his peninsular status and the "innocence" it conferred, Ortiz argued that the confraternity had taken advantage of him "as a newcomer and a foreigner." The

Figure 5.
Church of La Merced,
interior. (Photo by
Hernán Navarrete)

confraternity, in turn, accused Ortiz of fraud for not having advised it from
the beginning of the enormous costs that would be involved, claiming that
Ortiz, as a professional architect, should have recognized the inherent problems with the site. When the confraternity threatened to annul the contract
and hire someone else to finish the job, Ortiz and his lawyer responded with
horror and dismay, demanding that "no other person should be permitted
to take over the construction because there is no other person in the entire
city who is remotely skilled in this art and they would ruin the arches and
the vaults that are yet to be built and the church would be rendered imperfect and without grace, which are of the utmost importance to Ortiz . . . and
such an act would result in the discredit of Ortiz and terrible damage to the
church." It is clear that the architect saw the Church of El Sagrario as his mag-
num opus, and he was not about to let it fall into other hands.

Ultimately, the court ruled in favor of the confraternity; however, Ortiz
continued work on the church with an increased annual stipend. This was his

Figure 6.
José Jaime Ortiz, principal
facade of the Church of
Santa Catalina, 1702–12.
(Photo by author)

first experience as an "outsider" coming up against the city's powerful and insular legal community and the equally wealthy, powerful, and predominantly Creole membership of the Confraternity of the Most Holy Sacrament. The local colonial power structure zealously protected its own members and interests, and Ortiz possessed neither the familial connections nor the financial power to buck the system. In the end, however, all parties wanted Ortiz to build the church, including the architect himself, for it was clearly in everyone's greater interests to enhance the splendor and magnificence of the confraternity, the community, and the city.

Ortiz's appetite for fortune and adventure ultimately led him on an ill-fated expedition to locate Inca gold and *huacas* (Inca "idols" or sacred sites) that were reportedly hidden in a deep ravine atop the volcano Pichincha that towers over the city of Quito. Rumors of this hidden treasure had circulated in the city for decades, and Ortiz was clearly not one to pass up such an exciting and potentially profitable opportunity. Although the details of this expedition

Figure 7.
José Jaime Ortiz, tower
of the Church of Santo
Domingo, 1705–6
(reconstructed). (Photo
by author)

read like something straight out of a novel, they are in fact recounted in the
testimony of numerous witnesses in a lengthy criminal proceeding that was
lodged against the architect upon his return.

At dawn on the morning of 14 April 1707, Ortiz set out to climb Pichincha, accompanied by five Spanish and Creole colleagues, two native serfs,
his black slave, a Dominican friar, and several mules laden with tents and
provisions. The friar came equipped with an ample supply of holy water to
ward off the "demonic apparitions" that were said to have been experienced
by those who had scaled the volcano. According to the witnesses, the party
would be able to locate the spot in the ravine where the gold and huacas were
hidden because "it was marked by the bones of an Indian woman who had
been hit by lightning."

After reaching the summit, the serfs set up the tents while the others dispersed along the edges of a deep ravine, searching for clues to the location of
the treasure. Suddenly and without warning, a pounding hailstorm moved in,

and, one by one, the expedition members scrambled back to the tents, freezing and bedraggled. By nightfall, the group realized that one of their members had not returned: Francisco Fons, a minister of the Real Audiencia of Quito. The serfs were sent out to search for the missing man, bearing lit candles in each hand. All witnesses testified that on this night there was a total lunar eclipse. The serfs shouted the man's name and, when he failed to respond, they placed the lit candles in the fallen hail outside the tents in order to direct Fons should he near the location. After a fruitless search the following morning, the group decided to return to Quito in order to mount a more extensive search party.

Upon their report to the authorities in Quito, the expedition members were immediately imprisoned in the Royal Jail, where they were manacled hand and foot. Charges of murder were pressed by the missing man's wife, Francisca de Torres Pizarro, who was a member of one of Quito's oldest and most powerful families. Search parties were organized and combed the area over a period of several weeks, but no viable sign of the missing man was ever found. At this point, the court placed the architect's properties and belongings under embargo, and the criminal trial proceeded with extensive testimony of witnesses, which dragged on for months.

During this time, the incarcerated architect and his companions were subjected to repeated torture in order to extract confessions, their suffering compounded by the freezing and unsanitary conditions of the prison. By early September, after nearly five months of incarceration and torture, the architect's health was broken. In a letter written to the court, Ortiz's lawyer pleaded for the release of his client, stating that the architect was deathly ill, had not changed clothing since his incarceration, had not been able to stand on his feet in two months, and was in grave danger of losing his life if these conditions persisted. Still, more witnesses were brought in, the proceedings continued, and the architect remained in prison.

On the 17 September, the court finally recommended that the accused be absolved of any crime, and they were released from prison near the end of the month. In a separate notarial document, dated 7 October, Ortiz granted power of attorney to one of his Spanish colleagues, Antonio Mateus—a friend, business associate, and member of the ill-fated expedition—to execute his last will and testament. This document proved to be timely, as the architect died early the following day, 8 October 1707. Within a year, Ortiz's houses, workshops, and estates were sold at public auction; his young children were again placed in an orphanage; and his architectural projects were taken over by others. Despite, and more likely because of, his many impressive successes and contributions to the community, Ortiz ultimately remained an outsider, subject to the envy, suspicion, and protectionism of powerful local and Creole interests.

The adventurous and enterprising spirit that had first brought the architect to the New World marked his life and death in Quito. A venturesome search for buried treasure with a group of colleagues resulted in the architect's tragic loss of freedom, property, and ultimately his life. Yet in the thirteen years that Ortiz lived in Quito, he realized fame and fortune and built an enviable life for himself. At the time of his death, Ortiz possessed his house and workshop, a large block of rental properties, two textile factories, a hat factory, and a hacienda outside the city. He lived to see the completion of the magnificent Church of El Sagrario, and although several of his other architectural commissions remained incomplete at the time of his death, his designs were carried out by the teams of craftsmen and artisans that he had trained.

Remarkably, within a few decades Ortiz's name as an architect was all but lost from the historical record. Later histories of Quito attributed the design and construction of the Church of El Sagrario to another architect, and his authorship of other buildings remained unrecognized. It was not until the late twentieth century that documents attesting to Ortiz's authorship of El Sagrario and other buildings were finally recovered from the local archives. It is not clear how Ortiz's name and fame could be so easily and so thoroughly consigned to oblivion for nearly three centuries; however, local interests may have determined that the architect's presence in Quito was best forgotten.

In a curious parallel, the years immediately following the architect's death marked the beginning of an extended economic decline for the city of Quito—one from which it never fully recovered. During the economic stagnation and crisis of the eighteenth century, the demise of the textile industry—the backbone of the local economy—combined with the effects of agricultural failures, epidemics, and the subsequent loss of labor to transform the once thriving city into a relatively isolated, impoverished provincial backwater. Although work proceeded on buildings already under construction in the city, no new major architectural projects were undertaken for the rest of the century.

What remains today from the glory days of the seventeenth century and early eighteenth are the monumental colonial buildings whose grandeur and opulence speak eloquently of an era of prosperity, the final splendid examples of which were constructed by an enterprising immigrant architect who arrived just in time to capitalize on the city's last wave of eminence. It is particularly noteworthy that unlike the majority of other churches in Quito, the architecture of El Sagrario has never succumbed to the many earthquakes that have ravaged the city over the centuries. It stands today just as José Jaime Ortiz hoped and planned that it would: a solid, monumental testament to his talents and abilities.

Note

For a broader discussion and more extensive citations, please see Susan V. Webster, *Arquitectura y empresa en el Quito colonial: José Jaime Ortiz, Alarife Mayor* (Quito: Abya- Yala, 2002); Webster, "The Architect and the Construction of the Church of El Sagrario in Quito," *Colonial Latin American Review* 11, no. 1 (2002): 71–87.

Finding Freedom: Slavery in Colonial Ecuador

Sherwin K. Bryant

Colonial Ecuador was not known as a slave society. In fact, slaves represented a minor fraction of the total labor force. They were less a source of wealth than a reflection of status. Nevertheless, as the historian Sherwin Bryant shows, slaves became an increasingly important source of both labor and conflict after 1700. More important, the institution as a whole provides a unique window into colonial society.

In the year 1703, the freedom suit of Juana Rica, an alleged "mulata" slave from the town of Cuenca, reached the docket of Quito's highest court—the *audiencia*. The case featured Juana, her two daughters, her grandchildren, and great-grandchildren. Their claim included testimony from expected individuals, such as her son-in-laws, and those not ordinarily expected, such as local elites. The stakes were high. Given that slave status followed the condition of the mother, the freedom of four generations hung in the balance of Juana's sole claim. Juana and her family argued that they were all free because they were the descendants of Juana's grandmother, a free black woman by the name of Ana Rica, who had lived and worked as a free domestic in the village of Zaruma. She had lived and worked in the home of a mestiza by the name of Francisca Calderón. During this time, she gave birth to a daughter named Magdalena—Juana Rica's mother. Since Ana Rica had been a free woman, her daughter Magdalena and granddaughter, Juana, and all subsequent descendants should have enjoyed free status. But freedom was difficult to acquire and sometimes difficult to maintain.

In this case, or as Juana and her children told it, the family status came into doubt when Magdalena moved away from Zaruma, where her free status was recognized publicly. It all occurred when Pedro Pesantes, an itinerant merchant took Magdalena (who would latter give birth to Juana Rica) from Zaruma to the town of Cuenca. There, Magdalena was to live in an elite home and work as a hired domestic just as her mother, Ana Rica, had many years before. Ana Rica had consented to Magdalena's move to Cuenca, and even had occasion to travel to Cuenca and visit Magdalena. In Cuenca, Ana

Rica found Magdalena in the home of Doña Magdalena de Espinosa. During the visit, Ana observed that Doña Magdalena was treating her daughter well. Young Magdalena was well dressed and fed, and appeared to be in a good situation as a free woman of color. But by 1703, many years had passed and Magdalena's descendants—Juana and her children—were not faring quite as well. Somehow, over the years they came to be understood falsely as the property of two elite sisters, Doña María de Zúniga and Doña Juliana Espinosa Montero, who now sought to separate the family through sale.

At times, the lines between hired servitude and slavery could seem confusingly similar on the surface. Those legally enslaved could live out experiences that made them *appear* free. Juana Rica's mother, Magdalena, could have been a slave or a hired servant. In either case, she might have achieved a level of authority and autonomy in an elite home, enjoying increased levels of mobility that allowed her to move about the town of Cuenca for the benefit of the family home. With greater control over her time, she might have worked selling goods in Cuenca's market, thereby feeding, clothing, and caring for herself and her daughter, Ana Rica. While slaveholders were legally responsible for feeding, clothing, and instructing the enslaved as would "good fathers," most sought to delegate the responsibilities of mastery to their chattel. Allowing slave laborers increased mobility and the opportunity to earn money outside the home facilitated the operation of the house while undercutting the costs of slave ownership.

Still, such arrangements had their drawbacks. Allowing a slave woman such as Magdalena or her daughter, Juana, to enjoy range of movement and responsibility could cause her to appear as *though* they were free women. But while appearances can be deceiving, the story told by Juana and her children might have been true. Magdalena might have been the free daughter of a free black domestic from the town of Zaruma, but found her free status questioned once in Cuenca and away from those who knew her true position. Still, their case seems to have risen and fallen on the notion that they had lived *as* free people, free people who were *known* by everyone to be free.

While the documentary trail ends before revealing the ultimate outcome of the Rica family saga, this case opens a window into the existence and importance of slavery in colonial Ecuador while showcasing some of the ways that the enslaved worked to wrest freedom, or in some instances a mere modicum of autonomy, from those who sought mastery over them. Although customary law allowed slave laborers to purchase their freedom in colonial Ecuador, as this essay will show, obtaining and maintaining free status were not accomplished easily. A reading of civil lawsuits over freedom from the period demonstrates that freedom was at once available to the enslaved, and yet rather *elusive*. Looking through the prism of the judicial system, a system that often checked and even undermined master authority, we can begin to see the precarious and vicious nature of slave life in Spanish American slave societies. One pernicious element to this experience was the simultaneous availability and *elusiveness* of freedom.

Much has been made of the opportunities that slave laborers throughout Spanish American enjoyed under the law. Indeed, laws governing slavery in Spanish America provided slave laborers with a range of opportunities and a few rights. As Christian subjects, slave laborers had the right to the sacraments, including marriage, and thereby a right to a conjugal life (*vida maridable*). Civil law provided slaves with the right to denounce cruel masters before local courts for gross mistreatment (*sevicia*). Once a cruel master was denounced, officials launched an investigation in order to evaluate the merits of the claim. If warranted, the case would then be set for trial, which could take years including appeals. Masters found guilty of gross mistreatment usually suffered the penalty of having their slaves confiscated and sold to a new owner presumed to be more benevolent.

One might argue that while legal principles (whether customary or codified) allowed slaves many more opportunities, denouncing masters for gross mistreatment (sevicia) and access to the sacraments were slaves' only legally codified *rights*. In addition to these codified rights, slaves enjoyed a range of customary legal opportunities, many of which developed over time as the institution grew and in response to changing conditions and realties wrought by slaves, masters, and the colonial state. And while a great many slaves purchased their freedom and/or that of their children, or acquired it through special arrangements with a master, freedom was a premium that masters often guarded tenaciously. After all, ceding freedom was in fact relinquishing property, property that held expansive value in colonial Ecuador.

The Ana Rica case, cited at the beginning of this essay, opens a window into the complex process of labor enlistment in colonial Ecuador. Similar to elites in other Spanish American colonies, colonial elites employed a multi-varied system of labor organization, including *encomienda* charges (entrusted indigenous laborers), *yanaconas* (indigenous servants), wage labor, and African slavery in all of its guises. Among these labor forms, slavery was in many ways the most malleable to temporal and environmental realities. Defined legally as chattel, slave laborers could be forced to move at an owner's whim; forced to remain at various, and often, distant work sites; and apprenticed, leased, and mortgaged, or sold to stave off economic hardships. And given their expensive price tag (some 400 pesos for an able-bodied woman), it is no wonder the claims of Juana Rica and family members cited at the beginning did not go unanswered.

Contests over freedom often followed the death of a master, usually because a master had promised a slave or slaves their freedom at some future date but while the master was alive, or because the owner had left orders to free slaves upon the owner's death. In other instances, the need to claim free status emerged because the passing of slave ownership from testator to heir could often bring changes that transgressed prior arrangements between master and slave. Upon a master's death, slaves who had lived *as though* they were free might be sold as heirs sought to benefit fully from their inheritance. Whereas purchasing or claiming freedom might not have been an urgent matter before, it could prove essential with the passing of a master. This seems to have been the case in the lawsuit that began this essay.

As the recent heirs of their mother's estate, Doñas María and Juliana Espinosa insisted that the claims of the Juana and her descendants were absurd. For the Espinosas, the point was simple. The Espinosas asserted that their family had owned Juana and her family for years. Now, it was time to sell members of this extended family. Around this same time, they had sold some of Juana's relatives, including a mulato named Bernardo to Cristóval de Raíz, of Cuenca, and a mulata, named Gregoria, to Don Diego Ruiz de Roxas, of Latacunga. They had also sold another mulata—Agustina—along with a slave named Bernardo to their brother, Maestro Benito Montero, a priest in the city of Quito. But Bernardo had managed to escape his captors and return to the city of Cuenca before he could be resold.

This spate of sales points to the fact that the eighteenth century was a moment of significant expansion in slaveholding throughout the audiencia of Quito. Enslaved Africans and their descendants had long been a mainstay of Guayaquil's urban economy, and continued to be in demand there. But with the increasing diversification of the north-central highland economy, before predicated solely upon the *obraje* complex (textile production), elites turned increasingly to African slave laborers, employing slaves on their estates and within the more urbanized districts. As elites sought to cash in their investments in slaves, the threatened disruption of enslaved families and communities provoked a range of responses in enslaved and would-be free people, including incidents of flight and resistance, and in some cases increased efforts to gain freedom. For the Espinosas, Juana and her descendants were merely crafty slave laborers who sought to thwart their right to dispose as they pleased of the property that they had rightfully inherited.

In short, the Espinosas sought to show that they were slaveholders who knew the travails of maintaining and managing slaves, and that Juana and her clan represented merely the most recent challenge to their authority as rights-bearing slaveholders. They had maintained, disposed of, profited from the sale of, and suffered the consequences of owning slaves. Consequently, this court case was the most recent challenge they had faced in seeking to liquidate and benefit from the estate of their now deceased mother, of which Ana and her family members belonged.

Persisting in their claim, Juana and her family argued that they had lived as free people. They had not received any day wages as slaves; neither had they received any sort of maintenance from Doñas María, Juliana, or their family. Furthermore, they argued, "We have tended our own gardens in order to feed and maintain ourselves and our children." For Juana and her descendants, slave status had to be demonstrated through the proper treatment and management of one's property. Implicit in their arguments about the way that they had *lived as* free people was the notion that slave ownership brought obligations that the doñas had never met. In Quito, as in other Spanish American slave societies, those who claimed mastery tacitly acknowledged the rights *and* obligations to punish, protect, educate, convert, and dispose of human property through sale or ad hoc arrangements. If Juana and her children could not clearly demonstrate their pedigree, and thereby their free status, the Espinosa sisters could not demonstrate their mastery, or so Juana and her descendants insisted. If they were not free, they had certainly lived as free people, and this for them was cause for granting free status and protection from the threat of further separating the family.

While stopping short of invoking the term *honor*, this family clearly sought to demonstrate that they were not only free, but honorable, industrious subjects, and by extension that the doñas were dishonorable owners who had failed to provide for their would-be slaves. The statement implied that slave ownership could, or should be lost, forfeited, based on not meeting obligations. While such an assertion ran afoul of the law, which only suggests that slaves were entitled to a new and presumably more benevolent owner, it was a reflexive strategy meant to highlight the way that Juana and her children had lived on their own *as* free people. The might-be slaves brought several witnesses to help substantiate their claims, ranging from other blacks, both slave and free, to whites and Indians. Each argued that they knew various aspects of the history as told by this family to be true. Several of the witnesses even argued that the ancestor, Ana Rica, was the daughter of an indigenous woman.

The defendants—Doñas María and Juliana—continued to bring forth evidence in support of their case. During the course of the trial they produced the following: bills of sales, documenting that they had indeed sold some of Juana's family members; the will and testament of their brother, to whom they had sold a couple of the relatives; a will of their mother leaving slaves to them by the name of Magdalena and Ana; and a statement from the Zaruma parish which claimed that Magdalena had been born the daughter of Ana, who was the slave of Beatriz [not Francisca] Calderón.

Nevertheless, Juana and her family members pressed ahead, basing their claims not only upon the corroboration of their account of their lineage, but also upon the very constitution and viability of their familial union. Mother testified for daughter while husband testified for wife and mother-in-law. Ultimately, however, they sought to convey a larger, and perhaps more notable, picture. Even if their story was to be viewed as mere family folklore supported only by a barrage of hearsay, their larger message was undeniable. They were *the* model free black family, who loved and supported one another, adhering doggedly to the laws of the land. They were an honorable family whose members had inherited and earned their freedom. After all, they had not lived as slaves; neither had they received support from their alleged owners. Rather, they were victims of generational wrongs, and now it was up to the high court to correct the injustices of a bygone era. One wonders if Juana and her family were claiming a kind of model citizenry similar to a *merito* and *servicio*, and thereby sought a reward for past service. In this case, their service might be to society, or the compliance with expected social norms, unlike those who absconded, or who otherwise disrupted the public peace. What is clear, however, is their claim to have lived "habitually" as free persons, undertaking the costs of caring for themselves in food, clothing, and shelter. To limit their ability to continue do so now would ignore the ways that their would-be owners had skirted the financial responsibility of holding slaves, thereby robbing Juana and her children of the freedom that they had now earned.

By the end of the documentary trail Juan and her family appear no closer to freedom than when the case began. Cases such as Juana's showcase both the difficulty of acquiring freedom and the legal maneuvering that those who would be free undertook in order to acquire free status.

The case of Prudencio Correa, an enslaved "pardo" (person of mixed ancestry, often refers to free "colored" population) from Quito, offers another view of the search for freedom in colonial Quito, illustrating the tenuous nature of free status. Prudencio petitioned for his freedom, claiming his parents had been free, and "had baptized him in the faith." In so doing, he bolstered his bona fide claim as a Christian and a legitimate member of society—an insider—in contrast to those who sought illegitimate or antisocial recourse. Prudencio sought to nullify the recent sale of his person on two accounts: (1) his actual free status from birth, and (2) the cruelties he had suffered at the hands of the purchaser.

Prudencio's would-be owners, Doñas Bernarda de Ariniga y Margarita de Sambrano, argued, however, that not only was Prudencio their slave, but that he had been "born and raised" in their home as the son of Gerónima Correa, an enslaved woman who had another child, a daughter named Gertrudis.

According to these two elite women, Prudencio's mother sought her freedom some years earlier, but could not find anyone to help in the matter. The doñas were also careful to point out that they had inherited this family as the heirs of Bernada Pérez, the daughter of their great-grandmother, Magdalena Pérez, arguing, moreover, that their great-grandmother had owned both Prudencio's grandmother, and his great-grandmother as well. Nevertheless, Prudencio continued to appeal to the justices, complaining that his owner, Don Jaime Ortiz had information about his freedom, which would nullify the sale "of his person." According to Prudencio, "el maestro Sebastián de Araujo clérgio Presvítero" falsely stated that he was a slave and forged documents to state that his father and mother did not present him to the faith in baptism. Prudencio explained:

> Proceeding maliciously he [Fray Sebastián1] turned over [a false] writ of sale to don Jaime Ortiz, architect of this city [Quito], who has committed a grave crime because he has sold a free person which is against one to give attention to such evil and grant the said sale without bringing in someone who could protest this falsely-placed slavery, and without bringing in anything [such as] information that has not been considered [which might] resolve my case [or demonstrating that] I am free, and as I have been as such in the city of Loja and in [my] travels to this city.

To bolster his case, Prudencio cited the bodily harm that he had endured at the hands of Ortiz, he stated:

> Yesterday, Thursday, which makes 14 days of the current [month] around seven at night, the manager of the house of don Jaime Joseph de Ortiz requested to keep me inside the obraje (textile mill), dragging me into it; I leaned against a staff which I had, and for this the said, don Joseph, knocked the staff out of my hand. He gave me many blows to the body and luckily I am [not] totally crushed, after which he took a strip of leather and gave me cruel lashes, leaving me defenseless and at risk [of losing] my life because my chest, arms, and back are swollen with marks so prominent and in order to use my right as it suits me. . . . I ask and plead [that you] circulate [this] petition [in order] that an attorney might receive my case, for heaven's sake given the beating, marks, and the swelling place me in the local jail while you determine the case of my freedom I will be in [the] said jail, and moreover, [because] he has assaulted me and will [assault me], and nevertheless the said has in times past knocked my wife down as she carried the petitions to the Audiencia, don't be malicious.

The investigation of Prudencio's case continued until 3 August 1703, when the justices of the audiencia ruled in favor of the alleged masters. And while

Prudencio filed appeals, protesting that he was being treated maliciously, when the document ended he was no closer to his freedom than when he began the process, as his case seemed to drag on in appeal after appeal. But while those who would be free deployed allegations of gross mistreatment to highlight the need for judicial inquiry, suffering abuse was not a precondition of free status; nor did it lead to the granting free status. At best, the proper demonstration of gross mistreatment could compel judges to grant a slave the opportunity to search for a new master ("papel para buscar un Nuevo amo"), who might prove more benevolent. Such denouncements were efforts for slave litigants to acquire a second-best option. Physical evidence in the form of a writ of freedom or the proper baptism registry were the surest, if still dubious, methods of proving free status.

Acquiring free status even proved difficult for those who could marshal physical evidence that showed they were entitled to a writ of *libertad*. Yet, even here those who sought freedom could find themselves on shifting ground. Free black siblings such as Leonardo and Francisca Valuarte of Latacunga knew perhaps all too well. Leonardo testified,

> Here in the local jail at the behest of Maestro Fray Andrés de Araujo of the Dominican Order, and I am [not] his slave, being free or as I am and not a subject of servitude as it states in the authentic clauses of the testament that I presented to him with every solemnity . . . which supports executing the [said clause] of María de Valuarte y Aguilar, now deceased, returning me [to my] original [state].

During the proceedings Leonardo's and Francisca's father, Juan Valuerte, a property or citizen of Quito and resident of Latacunga, testified that Doña María Valuarte had freed both his children in two clauses of her last will and testament. In addition to bringing a number of witnesses to corroborate their testimony, they produced a copy of Doña María's 1681 will, which stated that both children (at the time eight and ten years of age respectively) "should not be sold under any circumstances, but should enjoy the same freedoms that any other free person enjoyed." Leonardo's and Francisca's case did not hinge solely upon the validity of María's will, however. Like many others they further bolstered claims of free status with allegations of gross mistreatment. Their case offers, therefore, more than another comment on the challenges of acquiring freedom. It showcases the cruelties that characterized servitude in a place like colonial Ecuador.

Francisca, like many women of color, presented her case, saying

> Now I am in the house of *depósita* [practice of being placed or deposited at any institution such as a convent for disciplinary reasons]. I generally serve

the table of the captain don Gregorio Matheos and he has given me over 100 lashes and has pulled out my hair and I have learned of his vile [plan] to dispatch me to Barbacoas not observing the law.

Apparently, Francisca's testimony was used to further demonstrate the injustice meted out to them. Not only had they been forced illegally into bondage; Gregorio had denied them the basic rights accorded even to slaves. Moreover, Gregorio was threatening to send her to one of the worse places for a Quiteña captive—Barbacoas, a gold-mining region on Quito's northern frontier known for its sweltering heat, venomous snakes, and the most horrible treatment of enslaved laborers.

Gregorio argued, however, that he had purchased Francisca legally and contended that he knew nothing of the previous owner (Doña María Valuerte). He insisted, moreover, that Francisca should be made to return with him or present documents substantiating her claims, something that was impossible from Gregorio's perspective, given that he knew that he had a bill of sale, documenting that he purchased her for 350 pesos from General de la Cavallería Don Feliz de Luna in Ibarra on 16 May 1706. The court, however, found in favor of Leonardo and Francisca, declaring them free and all sales null and void, saying nothing of Don Gregorio's 350 pesos. Leonardo's and Francisca's saving grace was the will, the legal document that proved the postmortem communication of free status by the deceased.

Two years later, in a case similar to that of Leonardo and Francisca, freed black Antonio Botín cited his free status based on his deceased master's last will and testament. Antonio Botín, described in the documents as "negro libre residente de Quito," requested to have a "certified statement of freedom." Antonio was the former slave of the now deceased Doña Michaela de Ayala (widow of the president of San Nicolas del Palenque, Don Augustin Botín) who had issued him his freedom in the presence of Don Pedro Antonio de Ribera, *teniente de corregidor*. The problem occurred because she had failed to sign the will and testament (por falta del sellado y para en ningún tiempo ni lugar) prior to her passing. After a lengthy trial and investigation Botín was awarded a certified *carta de libertad*. Of these examples of successful cases, many more were unsuccessful. Deathbed manumissions were fairly common, indeed one of the principle avenues to freedom. But as these cases show, in most instances free status had to be earned *and* protected—no easy feat.

For enslaved women, the process of seeking freedom could be a double-edged sword; those women who earned enough money to purchase their freedom were assumed to be prostitutes or thieves, and those women in loving relationships with men, who desired to purchase their freedom, also risked being viewed as prostitutes, inherently dishonored and untrustworthy.

Since the master-slave relationship was fundamentally coercive, the very nature of the relationship meant that anytime a woman entered into an agreement with a man to "purchase her freedom" (which in fact meant purchasing the slave, male or female), she was vulnerable to her new owner's advances and demands (sexual or otherwise).

This is the picture that Juana Antonia Márquez painted when giving her deposition in the lawsuit she filed against her owner, Francisco Antonio de Aveldebeas. On 8 August 1754, Juana testified that she had just received word that Francisco was leaving for Guayaquil "early in the morning of the following day." His departure would disrupt and perhaps jeopardize her pending lawsuit aimed at acquiring her freedom. Juana testified that she and Francisco had had an arrangement, or more precisely a relationship, one that extended back some five years. In 1749, she had agreed to enter into an "illicit relationship" (*amistad ilísita*) with Francisco in exchange for him purchasing her freedom from captain Don Juachin DeSoto Mayor for 370 pesos. And, while Francisco had indeed purchased her, five years had passed in which he had not granted Juana her freedom. Juana contended:

> it has been my obligation, without giving him my hand (marrying him), the affliction [or forced sex continually] until he impregnated me with his baby boy, who lives [and is] four years of age, and as in all that I have reported as I said, I have served [him] not only in this city [Quito] but as far as the city of Guayaquil with my person and my mother per the contract that I made owing me the writ of freedom, and in the city of Guayaquil, there [were] many potential purchasers, not only as a servant but also in order to take me, or enter with me into the holy state of matrimony, and in such cases don Francisco prevented me, saying many times that I did not have the freedom to marry (in this case that she was not free to marry, insinuating that she was married or possessed some other moral impediment) to make such an arrangement, and these proposals were not two or three times, but many more, thus in the city of Guayaquil, las Bodegas y Esuaranda, but also in the city of Quito.

She stated, moreover, that throughout their illicit affair Francisco mistreated her:

> Not only with blows but with an instrument in his hand as in all that I demonstrate I have only endured all of this to obtain my freedom, and not all of the abuses that I [have endured] have been solely [at the hand] of my master, but also his brother-in-law, don Juan Romero, who tried to kill me when I had been violated [in order] to extract the aforementioned for which I add also that [he caused] me to miscarry another child—also the

result of the rapes (*maltratos*) of don Francisco—of one month and fifteen days pregnant.

According to Juana, she had paid a hefty price for her freedom, a price that included her body, her time, her opportunities at meaningful, desirable, and church-sanctioned relationships, the death of an unborn fetus, and the use of her mother's time. Juana entered into this arrangement expecting to give of herself and her resources for a limited time in exchange for her freedom. Her owner, Francisco, claimed, however, that he had not purchased Juana under any such pretenses; nor had he committed any of the alleged crimes. Rather, he claimed that his sister—Juana Abeldebeas—had requested that he purchase Juana, and he had obliged. Francisco's attorney, Carlos de Larrayos, insisted that the claims brought by the enslaved woman were unfair, and constituted a misrepresentation of the truth, imploring the court to seek the truth by investigating these claims.

In an apparent effort to neutralize Juana, they requested that she be placed in depósito in the Santa Catherina Monastery. Once Juana was placed in the custody of the monastery, Larrayos moved to have the case thrown out. He claimed that around the time when Juana would have conceived Juachín Phelipe (the living child), Francisco was in Panama and therefore the young child could not be his. Furthermore, since he had never made such an agreement, the case lacked merit and should be thrown out.

Yet, much to the chagrin of Larrayos, the justices found that the case warranted a trial, and ordered both sides to develop their cases and present them. While Juana was *depositada* in the monastery, her lawyer (Phelipe Victorio de Miranda, *procurador* [public defender] *de los* [*pobres*]) continued to build and argue her case. Miranda insisted among other things that shortly after Juana gave birth to Juachín Phelipe, Francisco went to Panama City, leaving Juana in the care of the Dominican priest Fray Santiago de Jesús for several weeks while he traveled to Panama. Miranda argued, moreover, that this "illicit friendship" between Juana and Francisco continued upon Francisco's return while in the home of Francisco's aunt. The couple had made one trip to the coastal city of Guayaquil along the way, but upon their second day, Francisco carried Juana's mother—Gertrudis de la Cruz ("morena libre," a free person of color)—to serve him and assist with laundry and other household chores in the city of Guayaquil, in the Bodega de Babaoyo, and in the town of Guaranda. Thereafter, Francisco placed Juana in the house of his brother-in-law because it was "known publicly" that he could no longer keep her in the city of Guayaquil because his wife had learned of the relationship and of the "excesses that he had committed with his own slave." "If he brought Juana there," Miranda argued, "that would cause a scandal." Therefore, Francisco chose to leave Juana in his brother-in-law's house. It was during this stay, Miranda argued, that Francisco's brother-in-law also abused Juana.

Juana and her attorney developed a considerable cadre of witnesses, many of them women of all classes and hues. María Petrona Sotomayor, for example, testified on Juana's behalf, stating that she met Juana when she and Francisco were occupying a rented room in the home of Miguel Sotomayor. She testified that Francisco did not treat Juana like his slave, but "like his lady" ("sino como su dama") with whom he had "business" ("con quien tenía comercio"). According to María, Francisco had Juana stay in the same room where he slept. On various occasions she noticed that in the mornings and in the evenings, Juana got out of the same bed as Francisco, "with whom she slept and recognized with much love."

Several other witnesses came forth testifying essentially to the same account, many of them arguing that the relationship between Juana and Francisco was "public and notorious" ("público y notorio en la oha ciudad de Guayaquil") in the city of Guayaquil. One witness, Juan Bezerra Chabarría, said that he had knowledge of the same, noting that Juana sojourned at his house in the parish of San Marcos on various occasions and that on at least one of these occasions, Chabarría witnessed Francisco searching for Juana. Upon finding her, Chabarría stated that Francisco:

> Mistreated her with words, and actions, and the witness did not know what the motive was, and only learned from a conversation with Juana, that she was the slave of the said don Francisco, and was his lover, and had a son by him in illicit friendship and that he wanted to take her to the city of Guayaquil and being with her he promised to give her 50 pesos and with these she could work and search out her life and with which to increase her freedom and move out of the enslaved condition (*esclavitud*) that she possessed.

Another witness, Bernarda Muños Chamorro, testified that she and Juana worked in the home of Señora Leonora. According to Bernarda, Francisco proposed that Señora Leonora hold Juana hostage in the room where Juana and Francisco had lived together previously. While Leonora never agreed to this, Bernarda testified that Juana and Francisco did share a room, explaining that Francisco had Juana "for his friend which has been public and notorious just like it is also known that he had offered her freedom like this witness has heard on various occasions from his mouth." In addition, Bernarda noted that Juana suffered because she lacked "various necessities, enduring hunger and many bouts of mistreatment."

As a result, the witness saw that Juana took occasion to hide in the home of Señor Thobar. When this occurred, Bernada noted, Don Francisco sent

Doña Luisa Amaya to look for Juana and to promise her that she would receive her freedom in exchange for returning. But rather than return with Doña Amaya, Juana caused a scene, recounting openly the escapades of herself and Francisco, all while screaming through the door of the house where she hid. Bernarda alleged that during this exchange Juana insisted that she would not return until Francisco provided her with a carta de libertad plus fifty pesos. Several other witnesses would testify in support of Bernarda's claims, each claiming to have witnessed or heard about Juana's now infamous performance.

As the trial ensued Francisco's lawyer came forth on several occasions, complaining that Juana should be confined to Convent de Santa Martha, insisting that it was not legal for her to be walking the streets and plazas while in protective custody. He continued to prolong the case, filing complaints that stated, among other things, that he had not received all of the "autos"—evidence, testimonies, and the like—in order that he might review them before the trial.

Entering her body and physical state as evidence, Juana and her lawyer called upon the testimony of Fray Jasinto Gauisandes, a local priest who had cared for Juana at the behest of her master Francisco. Fray Jasinto claimed that Juana fell into his care because of abuses she had suffered at the hand of her master. He explained,

> [Juana] suffered from pain in her body as a result of an object that her master used to beat her because the night before he had been in a bar . . . enjoying himself with some of his acquaintances, but he needed the said mulata to be treated in order that she might travel to Quito as he did the third day of my having the confessed (Juana); and I did not receive notice that she had another accident; neither that she might miscarry from this bout of sickness.

Francisco's attorney, de Larrayos, countered, basing his case upon two fundamental points: First, the case lacked merit and should be thrown out. Two, they sought to demonstrate the absurdity of Juana's claims; they did so by denying the sexual relationship, the paternity of Juana's child (or children), and the alleged pretences under which he purchased Juana. Calling upon several witnesses, de Larrayos argued Francisco had never engaged in such an illicit affair: Francisco was traveling in Panama at the time of the child's conception, and could not have impregnated Juana. Evidence of this fact, de Larrayos claimed, lay in Francisco's view that the child did not resemble Francisco ("ni en color, ni en fisonomía"), but reflected, rather, the likeness of one Manuel Nicolás, a free black tailor from Quito (a man witnesses claimed to have seen leaving Juana's quarters on several mornings).

The defense continued its simultaneous attack upon Juana's reputation and the validity of her claims, charging that she had a pattern of making outlandish accusations against former masters. When Francisco purchased her, he argued, she was in depósito, looking for a new master after having leveled similar claims against her former owner. Her reputation as an incorrigible, bellicose prostitute was so notorious, Francisco contended, that when he tried to sell her, he found that no one wanted to purchase her, even from as far away as Guayaquil.

Eventually, the president of the audiencia rendered a verdict, declaring

I find that the said María Juana Antonia has not proven the said promise (*como probar le convino*), and that her master proved *en bastante forma* (in fine form) his exception and defense. And in conformity I must order and [therefore] order that the said mulata be returned (*restituida*) to the dominion and esclavitud of her master understanding that only for the effect because she is not to be returned to his service, not to his house, neither to his custody due to the danger of sin and for the scandal that he had caused, the said don Francisco Antonio de Aveldebeas with the said concubinage with his own slave to whom he was obligated to give good doctrine and example, I apply the fine of 50 pesos.

Although Juana failed to receive her freedom, the court had granted her thirty days to secure a new owner. While this was hardly the verdict she sought, the justices had accorded her with a measure of mercy, a signal to the merits of her case. She continued to appeal her case to the justices' sense of fairness and compassion, requesting three additional months to find a new master or the money to purchase her freedom. In the end her owner's fine of fifty pesos had been forgiven, and her appeals largely ignored.

By 1754, when María Juan Antonia's case reached the docket of the high court, slaves had been living and working in the region of modern Ecuador for approximately 220 years. They had worked for nearly two centuries to acquire their freedom in colonial Quito. Working as individuals, family units, siblings, lovers, and acquaintances, their struggle was not one to overthrow the system of slavery, but one for individual freedom and autonomy. Arriving first with the conquistadors, the early arrivals occupied a complex range of positions in the colonial society. At least two, Juan (*negro*) and Anton (*de color negro*) were listed among the founders of the "Inka city" at its renaming for Saint Francis in 1534. In those early years blacks held the position of town crier, and master of weights and measures, even as the first arrivals from "Guinea" made their way to the region's gold mines of Zaruma, the shipyards of Guayaquil, and the farms and estates of Riobamba, Ambato, and Latacunga. Here, as in other parts of Spanish America, Africans and their descendants constituted a critical element in Spanish conquest and colonization efforts. Consequently, as Spaniards settled towns such as Loja and Cuenca, Africans were part of the conquering and settlement parties. Building the colonial regime that would become "Spanish America" was predicated as much upon African slavery and the contributions of free blacks as it was upon Spain and its colonial bureaucracy. Here, as in many other aspects, colonial Ecuador proved no exception.

Likewise, here as in other places, enslaved Africans and their descendants had access to free status. Freedom was indeed a legally sanctioned ideal, tempered by other legal preferences (namely, property rights) and therefore both available and elusive. With this understanding those who would be free had to take on a subtle and understated methodology. Similar to places such as colonial New Spain, most slaves in colonial Ecuador came by freedom through special arrangements with slaveholders. The process or series of negotiations that produced free status were intimate (if not sexual) and, therefore, often hidden from the historical record. Consequently, many of the challenges that slaves faced in acquiring their freedom often remain outside of the reach of contemporary historians. Yet, a comprehensive look at the document record reveals that slaves desired freedom and they pursued it whenever possible. Often, they found creative ways of acquiring it. It was available and yet elusive, everywhere and nowhere. The achievement of free status for oneself or a loved one was often the outgrowth of a life's work quite literally. And as these cases have shown, holding on to that free status was often just as arduous. In colonial Ecuador most slaves lived out their lives in bondage while a significant and slow-growing population of free blacks developed over the colonial era. Slave status was often a fluid construct, one to be negotiated between slaveholder and enslaved. Free blacks could find their material circumstances proved little better, if not worse than those of a slave. And legally enslaved individuals could sometimes live *as though* they were "free." Indeed, the qualitative distinction between slave and free was often just as elusive as free status. At the very least, however, free status meant that one could not be sold at a master's whim, or as a result of mortgage default or the need to settle the debts of a deceased owner's estate. Finding freedom meant avoiding these pitfalls and gaining increased autonomy over one's body, an attainment that evaded many even as it rewarded some.

Note

This essay is based primarily on research done in the Archivo Nacional del Ecuador (Quito). It draws heavily upon records in the section of that archive entitled "Sección Esclavos," which contains a range of civil court cases involving slaveholders suing one another over slave ownership, accurate valuation of slaves (redhibition, warranty guaranteeing value of slave) as well as cases involving slaves suing masters for gross mistreatment (*sevicia*). Included therein, also, are the legal petitions of enslaved and free people suing slaveholders for free status and/or manumission. All of the cases found in Sección Esclavos are civil court cases that were appealed to the region's highest colonial court (*audiencia*). A complete list of references is available from the author.

Throughout the essay, both parentheses and brackets are used by the author for interpolations in quotations of Spanish translations. Brackets are used to insert wording that seems to have been accidentally omitted in the original. Parentheses are used to insert translations from Spanish to English or vice versa, and to clarify the identity of individuals whose names are incomplete in the original.

A Battle of Wills: Inventing Chiefly Legitimacy in the Colonial North Andes

Karen Vieira Powers

Surrounded by five snow-covered volcanoes, the spectacle of Riobamba's landscape can be matched only by the political dramas that its indigenous peoples have created and performed for centuries. From 1450 to the present, the region has been subject to successive invasions and colonization schemes, first by the Inca, then by the Spaniards, and more recently by Ecuadorian national agrarian capitalists. The demographic and political upheavals that ensued defy cultural survival, yet Riobamba's ethnic groups are among the largest and most cohesive in contemporary Ecuador. Known among members of the dominant culture as vivos *(sharp, cunning), the region's native peoples have met these challenges by developing their individual and collective imaginations as well as their political and theatrical skills. Anthropologist Karen Vieira Powers examines these strategies through a fascinating reading of colonial wills.*

When the Spaniards arrived in Riobamba in 1534, they encountered a highly atomized political scenario. With the Spanish conquest of the Inca, the area's indigenous inhabitants were first polarized into aboriginal Puruhuayes and Inca *mitmaq* (colonists), and then further fragmented on both sides into constellations of small, independent groups. According to most scholars of the northern Andes, this political decentralization was characteristic of pre-Incaic Ecuador and resurged after the Incaic veneer was lifted. The political infighting, both between and inside these small units, that must have been suppressed by Cuzco, resurfaced as Inca-appointed and -demoted leaders, both mitmaq and puruha, all vied for position in the new political configurations of yet another invasive force—the Spaniards. This left the local indigenous leadership disunited and its legitimacy in serious question throughout the early-colonial period.

The Spaniards, already familiar with larger, more politically centralized ethnic groups in the southern Andes, attempted to apply what they thought they knew of that model in the northern Andes. Their centralizing administrative reorganization, especially of the Riobamba region, was therefore akin to forcing square pegs into round holes and unleashed centuries-long hostilities both within and between indigenous communities and between the Indian republic and the Spanish regime. For this reason, the *corregimiento* of Riobamba, in the *audiencia* of Quito, is especially interesting for studying the institution of the colonial *cacicazgo* (indigenous rulership) and attendant issues of chiefly legitimacy. Perhaps nowhere in the viceroyalty of Peru was there as much need for "invention" in order to fit local realities to colonial imperatives. And perhaps nowhere in Riobamba was there a chiefly lineage more adept at "inventing" themselves than the Duchiselas of the town of Yaruquíes (see Duchisela genealogy on page 70).

An examination of the Duchiselas' rise to local and regional power is especially timely since they have recently become the "darlings" of Ecuadorian nationalist histories—belated *indigenista* and/or integrationist attempts to construct a national identity in the present through the "imagined community" of a glorified indigenous past. The Duchisela lineage plays a crucial role in this modern construction, where it is placed at the pinnacle of a chiefly hierarchy composing a "Kingdom of Quito" that is both pre-Hispanic and pre-Incaic—that is, pre-Peruvian to "patriotic" Ecuadorians recently embroiled in a border war with their neighbors to the south. What I seek here is not the truth or the lie, but rather how the historical actors, the Duchiselas in this case, were "made." The main sources for this drama derive from a late-eighteenth-century suit over the cacicazgo of Yaruquíes in which seven testaments of members of the Duchisela lineage are presented as evidence.[1] The wills range from that of don Juan Duchisela (the elder) in 1605 to that of his grandson, don Manuel, in 1769, providing a century and a half of clues about the imagination and shrewd political maneuvers that went into the "making" of the Duchisela cacicazgo and the "inventing" of the family's legitimacy. This chapter is composed of three vignettes extracted from the Duchisela wills that narrate, in theatrical form, the lived experiences of the Duchisela family under colonial rule.

"A Battle of Wills": A Family Drama in Three Acts

ACT I. WOOING LEGITIMACY: A COLONIAL LOVE(?) STORY

It is the year 1605 and the community of Yaruquíes has now passed through decades of unrelenting epidemic disease. At the age of thirty-five, don Juan Duchisela has just lost his third wife and is himself ill enough to write a last will and testament. As the cacique dictates his will to don Juan Paguay, the Indian scribe, a colorful life story unfolds that is in vivid contrast to the pervasive misery that must have enveloped the town during prolonged periods

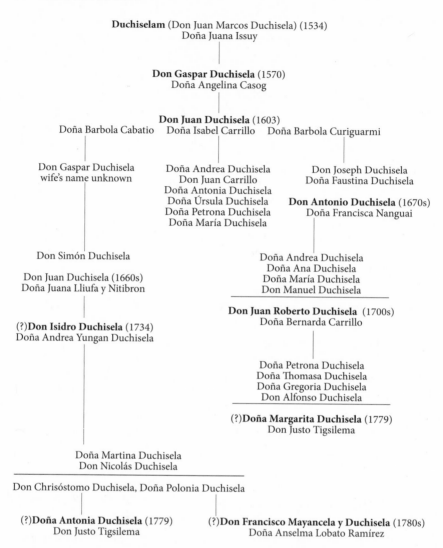

Duchiselam (Don Juan Marcos Duchisela) (1534)
Doña Juana Issuy

Don Gaspar Duchisela (1570)
Doña Angelina Casog

Don Juan Duchisela (1603)
Doña Barbola Cabatio   Doña Isabel Carrillo   Doña Barbola Curiguarmi

Don Gaspar Duchisela   Doña Andrea Duchisela   Don Joseph Duchisela
wife's name unknown   Don Juan Carrillo   Doña Faustina Duchisela
                                Doña Antonia Duchisela
                                Doña Úrsula Duchisela   **Don Antonio Duchisela** (1670s)
                                Doña Petrona Duchisela   Doña Francisca Nanguai
                                Doña María Duchisela

Don Simón Duchisela   Doña Andrea Duchisela
                                               Doña Ana Duchisela
Don Juan Duchisela (1660s)   Doña María Duchisela
Doña Juana Lliufa y Nitibron   Don Manuel Duchisela

                                               Don Juan Roberto Duchisela (1700s)
(?)**Don Isidro Duchisela** (1734)   Doña Bernarda Carrillo
Doña Andrea Yungan Duchisela

                                               Doña Petrona Duchisela
                                               Doña Thomasa Duchisela
                                               Doña Gregoria Duchisela
                                               Don Alfonso Duchisela

                                               (?)**Doña Margarita Duchisela** (1779)
                                               Don Justo Tigsilema

                        Doña Martina Duchisela
                        Don Nicolás Duchisela

Don Chrisóstomo Duchisela, Doña Polonia Duchisela

(?)**Doña Antonia Duchisela** (1779)   (?)**Don Francisco Mayancela y Duchisela** (1780s)
Don Justo Tigsilema   Doña Anselma Lobato Ramírez

Duchisela genealogy. Note: Names in boldface type are those of persons who were appointed as caciques of Yaruquíes; names preceded by a question mark are persons whose
legitimacy was questioned in litigation. Names of issue do not always appear in birth
order, owing to design flow of family tree, and dates that appear alongside chiefly names
represent the first mention as cacique of the town.

of sickness. It is a story filled with philandering, strategic liaisons, internecine
conflicts, and extortion. Among the main characters are a mestiza lover, a
prodigal son, a favored son, and six illegitimate children.

As a young man, don Juan has a son with his lover, doña Barbola Cabatio,
whom he marries three years after the boy's birth, thereby legitimating him.

This son, don Gaspar Duchisela, would so bitterly disappoint his father that don Juan would later dispossess him not only of the cacicazgo but of any share in the family's considerable assets. Disenchantment with his original family begins early on, for the whole time that he is married to doña Barbola, don Juan carries on an illicit affair with doña Isabel Carrillo. The union of this powerful Indian cacique and wealthy mestiza lover produces six illegitimate children and an awesome family fortune. Upon doña Barbola's death, don Juan marries doña Isabel but refuses to legitimate her children, probably because they are mestizos and will not legally have rights to the cacicazgo.

From what we know of doña Isabel Carrillo, she is a veritable world-beater. Not only has she inherited properties from a presumably Spanish father, but according to don Juan's will, she has amassed considerable wealth in money and land from her own hard work and industry ("de su propio trabajo e industria"). She finances don Gaspar Duchisela's (don Juan's first son) stint as *alcalde mayor* in the city of Quito, where he is said to have racked up two thousand pesos of debt. She is also especially adept at buying up lands in ecological zones that yield highly sought after products. As we shall see shortly, the efforts of this shrewd mestiza businesswoman will play a pivotal role in the survival of the Duchisela cacicazgo and in the invention and maintenance of the family's chiefly legitimacy. It is enough to make one wonder about the texture of their love affair and subsequent marriage. Was she in love with him? Why else would a wealthy mestiza have an affair and six illegitimate children with an Indian, even if he was a cacique? Considering Spanish America's race-based social hierarchy, women like doña Isabel usually aspired to marry, and to marry "whiter," or at least "wealthier." Was he in love with her? This is a more difficult question to answer, especially in view of his attempts to maneuver her assets into his will.

By 1605, doña Isabel has died and don Juan has already married and buried his third wife. With doña Barbola Curiguarmi, don Juan has three children—don Antonio, don Joseph, and doña Faustina—this time all of them legitimate. His decision to step over his firstborn son, don Gaspar Duchisela, and name the twelve-year-old don Antonio as his successor in the cacicazgo is not only a stunning rebuke to don Gaspar and his sons but is so unfathomable that his descendants would describe it as a family mystery for generations to come. To add fuel to the fire, he names his illegitimate mestizo son, don Juan Carrillo, to administer the cacicazgo until don Antonio comes of age. He then proceeds to distribute the majority of his assets to his three legitimate children with doña Barbola Curiguarmi, his last wife. In the 1605 will, many of these assets, especially lands, were doña Isabel's but appear as his own, and the two-thousand-peso debt his son owed her has been forgotten.

Unlike his unfortunate spouses, don Juan bounces back from his illness and lives a long life. In 1655, at the age of ninety, we find him making amendments to his will. Apparently, during the ensuing years he is either badgered by doña Isabel's children or has suffered from a guilty conscience about the incorporation of Carrillo resources into his cacicazgo. In this codicil, he makes arrangements to pay his illegitimate children for the two-thousand-peso loss—a change of heart that will later lead to bitter fraternal strife. He also admits that doña Isabel wrote a will naming all her properties, but he "suspects" that it has been lost. He then rearranges the distribution to compensate her six children for at least those lands that belonged to her before their marriage. This still leaves considerable properties in his and his heirs' names, which will be carried on as part of the Duchisela cacicazgo. And when, in 1685, don Antonio Duchisela, his heir, finally writes his last will and testament, he succeeds in incorporating into the cacicazgo even some of the lands that were designated by this father, don Juan, as part of the Carrillo estate—this by claiming doña Isabel as his mother, when he is clearly the son of doña Barbola Curiguarmi, don Juan's third wife. More than eighty years later, in 1769, doña Isabel's private lands still appear as part of the cacicazgo in the last will and testament of don Antonio's son, don Manuel Duchisela. Evidently, a protracted love affair and subsequent marriage with a wealthy mestiza was quite a strategic liaison and translated into a political instrument of chiefly legitimacy across generations.

ACT II. SPORTING LEGITIMACY: THE STORY
OF THE PRODIGAL SON

It is 1655 in the town of Yaruquíes, and don Juan Duchisela the elder, now on his deathbed, asks his lifelong friend, Sargento Juan de Guadalupe, to draw closer. He implores him to honor the friendship and love they have always shared by executing his will in a manner that will alleviate his conscience, and by fulfilling the special promise he made to him regarding this matter. The Indian scribe, don Juan Paguay, dutifully records these words, and only these words. It is clearly a secret promise.

Although the centuries since this mysterious scene have left no trace of evidence that would help us to unlock the secret of don Juan's heart, the historian/playwright suspects that it was about don Gaspar. Both the old man's will and his codicil take on a distinctive tone whenever he refers to his first-born son—an almost acerbic tone—a tone perhaps born of the contempt that a man of means and power might feel toward a son for whom he had wished great things, but who consistently failed him. Whatever the motive for his bitterness, it is evident that don Juan and his presumed successor had had a serious falling out.

There is something at once defensive and scolding about the way don Juan alludes to don Gaspar's less than exemplary history. He states repeatedly that he has already given don Gaspar his inheritance when he came of age, and that he owes him and his heirs nothing. Styling himself the generous though unappreciated father, he lists everything he ever gave his eldest son—two thousand pesos in silver, fancy clothes, fine furniture, houses, lands, and orchards—all of them described in the minutest detail. In the codicil, he enumerates all the debts that don Gaspar had incurred in Quito while he was the *alcalde de naturales* (administrator of indigenous people), a prestigious, but apparently costly, position. How had he spent two thousand pesos of doña Isabel's money on clothes, banquets, and other luxuries in a single year? Disgusted and ashamed, he feels compelled to pay his son's debts from his own assets in order to relieve his conscience and to account to God. He then warns that there might still be some lands out there that don Gaspar is using, but they are not his; he stipulates emphatically that he did not give those lands to him as possessions, but only loaned them to him. Indeed, don Gaspar Duchisela comes off as a spendthrift dandy; a talentless, irresponsible gadabout who has squandered part of the family fortune and whose wealthy mestiza stepmother naively paid the bill.

In the half century between his will and his codicil, don Juan Duchisela has had sufficient time for his resentments to accumulate toward a vengeful, draconian solution. He now names his and doña Isabel's illegitimate mestizo son, don Juan Carrillo, as one of the executors of his will, instructing him to take from his possessions the equivalent of the two thousand pesos that don Gaspar owed his mother. In addition, he arranges to pay doña Isabel's children for some of their mother's properties, which turn out to be the very lands he had originally given to don Gaspar as his inheritance when he came of age. Between these two moves and the bequeathing of the cacicazgo to don Antonio, don Gaspar Duchisela becomes the family's *desheredado* (disinherited one). The prodigal son, however, would not be the one to bear the onerous burden of this vindictive maneuver; it would, instead, be shouldered by don Gaspar's issue, the truly "unfortunate" don Juan and don Simón.

In fact, the life and death of don Juan the elder would leave a grievous legacy for the whole Duchisela family. His descendants from three separate marriages would engage in bitter internecine rivalries over both the cacicazgo and its assets for nearly two hundred years. The retaliatory acts and shifting alliances of this protracted battle scene begin immediately after don Juan the elder's death, when the seventeenth-century protagonists—don Antonio Duchisela, don Juan Carrillo, and don Juan Duchisela (don Gaspar's son)—come into collision over the political and economic control of the cacicazgo. Although don Juan the elder has named don Juan Carrillo to administer the cacicazgo until don Antonio came of age, his tenure in the position does not last long. Apparently, the old man had not counted on the meddlesome nature of Spanish colonial officials, who had an unshakeable belief in the concepts of legitimacy, primogeniture, and racial purity. Their sensibilities, no doubt, were offended by the specter of a mestizo bastard occupying the town's highest office. They instead appoint don Juan Duchisela, the firstborn son of don Gaspar—an event that is sure to have caused don Juan the elder to roll over in his grave.

The second don Juan Duchisela manages to maintain political power until his pending death but remains without rights to the family's economic resources. In his will of 1670 he speaks bitterly of the manner in which his grandfather summarily disowned his father, don Gaspar, ultimately resulting in his and his brother's complete disinheritance. But he reserves his most acrimonious accusations for don Juan Carrillo, who he says went about collecting his mother's two thousand pesos with such a vengeance that there was now nothing left of the Duchisela fortune. He portrays don Juan Carrillo as a greedy viper who usurped his position as executor of his grandfather's will to force payment of the two thousand pesos and then some. In the process, he sold the family finery and silver at public auction, rented lands and ranches at will, and seized all manner of livestock and other prized possessions. He then distributed the proceeds among his five sisters, leaving the legitimate heirs completely "destroyed." Don Gaspar's son reiterates several times that the Carrillos have been more than well paid for his father's debt to their mother, and warns Juan and his family not to demand anything further of his heirs. Of course, this is a gross exaggeration, considering that his successors in the cacicazgo retain many of doña Isabel's lands for generations to come. His portrayal of don Juan Carrillo is undoubtedly the distorted perception of a man who, through no fault of his own, is made to live out the consequences of his father's reckless behavior and his grandfather's vindictiveness—and what better scapegoat than a "bastard half-breed." As for the cacicazgo, don Juan Duchisela, eldest son of don Gaspar, dies without issue and names the favored don Antonio as his successor in fulfillment of his grandfather's wishes. And so, don Juan the elder's will, thought temporarily thwarted, is carried out.

ACT III. "FORGING" LEGITIMACY: THE IMPOSTER CACIQUES
As the *visitador* (royal inspector), don Juan Josep de Villalengua, travels along the flank of Chimborazo, the most dazzling of Riobamba's snow-covered volcanoes, he cannot imagine what political intrigues await him in Yaruquíes. The year is 1779 and he has been charged with conducting a royal inspection and census of the audiencia of Quito's Indian subjects; it is also the year that doña Antonia Duchisela, the town's *cacica* (female ruler), has died without

heirs. In the Riobamba region, as elsewhere in the audiencia, the untimely death of a ruler is always an occasion for the usual protagonists to dredge up bitter injustices of the past in multiple and protracted bids for power. Typically, descendants of the direct line, lateral lines, and female lines—as well as bastards and imposters—all vie for control of the cacicazgo, often supported by regional factions that cut across race and class. Litigation goes on interminably while the legal maneuvers, unorthodox practices, and downright deceptions used to wrest the prize are too numerous and varied to be recorded here. Yaruquíes is no exception, and a more experienced visitador would have braced himself for the inevitable.

Immediately upon the inception of the royal *visita* (inspection), one contender, don Francisco Xavier Mayancela y Duchisela, steps boldly forward to request possession of the cacicazgo of Yaruquíes. He claims he should rule by right of inheritance because he is a descendant of the direct line; he is, after all, the legitimate grandson of don Isidro Duchisela, who, in turn, claims to be the son of don Juan Duchisela, grandson of don Juan Duchisela the elder, and great-grandson of don Gaspar Duchisela, trunk of the chiefly line. The visitador Villalengua, following established procedures, then publishes the request with a warning that don Francisco will be granted the cacicazgo provided that no one with more right claims it.

At this juncture, the usual cast of characters predictably appears on stage. Doña Margarita Duchisela, followed by an entourage of supporters, comes to object. Indignant, she charges that don Francisco Mayancela y Duchisela is an imposter who has usurped the Duchisela surname. Her allegation focuses on the legitimacy of don Francisco's grandfather, don Isidro Duchisela, who she says was not the legitimate son of don Juan Duchisela, but a bastard to whom don Juan's wife, doña Juana Lliufa y Nitibron, gave birth after her husband's death. According to doña Margarita, don Isidro had not one drop of Duchisela blood. Others paint a more lurid scenario: that not only was he illegitimate, but also he was the progeny of an illicit love affair that the widow, doña Juana Lliufa, had with her husband's brother, don Simón.

What then ensues is a veritable "battle of wills," as doña Margarita, claiming to be the legitimate daughter of don Juan Roberto Duchisela, brings suit against don Francisco Mayancela for the cacicazgo of Yaruquíes. There is no end to surprises as the contenders and their respective factions present several of their ancestors' last wills and testaments to prove or disprove the legitimacy of the late don Isidro. From this bizarre parade of dead Duchiselas, the ingenuous don Francisco calls forth his grandfather to give witness to his legitimacy. There, in his will of 1758, don Isidro stated repeatedly (perhaps too repeatedly) that he was indeed, the legitimate son of don Juan Duchisela and doña Juana Lliufa y Nitibron, as well as the grandson and great-grandson of the original caciques of the town. Considering the almost sacrosanct nature of last wills and testaments, one would think that the presentation of such a legal instrument would be sufficient to truncate the proceedings. In a stunning reversal, however, doña Margarita presents two more wills, those of don Juan Duchisela (1670) and doña Juana Lliufa y Nitibron (1682), in which both declared that there had been no issue from their marriage. Furthermore, doña Juana stated explicitly that after her widowhood, God had seen fit to give her a son, don Isidro Lliufa y Nitibron. Doña Margarita's lawyer interjects here that not even don Isidro's mother had had the nerve to confuse his name with that of the Duchiselas, as he had so brashly done in his own will.

This unexpected turn of events leaves both don Francisco Mayancela and his lawyer abashed and prompts the latter to desist upon examination of the latest evidence. Doña Margarita now presses to receive costs and damages. To counter this, don Francisco's lawyer, still believing in the veracity of the opposition's evidence, charges that if his client had known about these wills and thus his real genealogy, he would never have pursued the case. Giving the story yet another twist, he accuses don Justo Tigsilema of hiding these wills from don Francisco and encouraging him to claim the cacicazgo. It turns out that don Justo is the widower of doña Antonia, the cacica who has just died; he has consequently been administering the cacicazgo for years and is apparently seeking a way to maintain influence. According to don Francisco's lawyer, however, he suddenly switches sides in the suit because he has conjured up a better way to ensure control—he simply marries doña Margarita, the plaintiff—a maneuver that would once again place him in direct administration of the cacicazgo should she win the case. It was at this point that he supposedly whipped out the two wills proving don Isidro's illegitimacy. Don Justo Tigsilema, of course, vehemently denies this and claims that he never had the wills in his possession to begin with and that he and doña Margarita had to round them up and even had to pay off a pawnbroker in Riobamba for one of them.

In the interim, however, don Francisco's lawyer comes up with a couple of new angles and requests that the case be reopened. First, he presents another will as evidence, that of don Juan Roberto Duchisela of 1734. Don Juan Roberto, a member of the direct line, was the *cacique principal* (paramount lord) and *gobernador* (Spanish-appointed ruler) of the town by right of inheritance from his father, don Antonio Duchisela. Don Antonio was the son of don Juan Duchisela the elder, but according to don Juan Roberto there was an irregularity in his father's succession. For some "unknown" reason, don Juan Duchisela the elder had passed over his firstborn son, don Gaspar Duchisela, to grant the cacicazgo to don Antonio, a younger son from his third marriage. In a stunning deathbed reversal, don Juan Roberto stated that because of the laws of primogeniture and *mayorazgo* [system of inheritance], the cacicazgo really belonged to the heirs of don Gaspar, the formerly disinherited branch of the family. He thus names don Isidro Duchisela, whom he described as don Gaspar's legitimate son, as his successor.

Second, don Francisco Mayancela's lawyer also claims that after more careful examination of the wills of don Juan Duchisela and doña Juana Lliufa y Nitibron, it is evident to him that they are forgeries and that the charges of his client's illegitimacy are completely false. He maintains that the handwriting of the two wills is not that of the seventeenth-century but that of the contemporary period. He also compares them to earlier documents written by the same scribe and signed by some of the same witnesses and points out that the writing and signatures are different. Evidently, don Isidro's bastard status has been trumped up by doña Margarita and her new consort through the creation of falsified legal instruments.

The plot now thickens as doña Margarita and don Justo respond by adding yet another intrigue to the scenario. They insist that don Juan Roberto made a big mistake in assuming don Isidro to be his legitimate cousin, as evidenced by the wills of don Juan Duchisela and doña Juana Lliufa. But even worse, he had allowed the parish priest to dupe him into believing this was so and to coerce him into inserting a completely erroneous, last-minute "confession" in his will. The priest, Dr. don Joseph de la Vega, they allege, had some interesting reasons of his own for this maneuver. It seems that he arranged a marriage between don Isidro and his favorite "maid" (probably his lover or his daughter) and then engineered the couple's takeover of the cacicazgo at the expense of the town's legitimate caciques. Don Isidro, supposedly a bastard who usurped the Duchisela name and possessed not a drop of Duchisela blood, did indeed become the cacique and even succeeded in passing the cacicazgo on to his granddaughter, the recently deceased doña Antonia.

As for the variations in handwriting and inconsistent signatures of the wills, the court examines the evidence carefully and moves that while the boldness of the letters varies, the characters all exhibit more or less the same formation, and so the wills cannot be proven to be forgeries. In the end, the Spanish administration, its decision resting on the damning evidence of illegitimacy contained in the two wills, names doña Margarita to the cacicazgo. And the "bastard" line of don Isidro supposedly passes into oblivion, but not really. Because "déjà vu" is the leitmotiv of north Andean succession stories, the audience will get to revisit this drama.

A few years later, doña Margarita Duchisela, cacica of Yaruquíes, dies without heirs. Once again the usual cast of characters appears on stage, don Francisco Mayancela y Duchisela among them. Now, don Alfonso Duchisela, legitimate grandson of don Juan Roberto Duchisela, assumes doña Margarita's former role and reenacts the challenge to don Francisco's legitimacy. This time the Spanish courts rule in favor of don Francisco Mayancela, the usurper of the previous case, leaving the audience to wonder whether "legitimacy" isn't just a battle of wills.

Notes

For complete references and bibliography, see Karen Vieira Powers's chapter in *Dead Give-aways: Indigenous Testaments of Colonial Mesoamerica America and the Andes*, ed. Susan Kellogg and Matthew Restall (Salt Lake City: University of Utah Press, 1998), 183–213.

1. ANQ Cacicazgos 38, 75, 1788. The wills and their dates are those of don Juan Duchisela the elder (1605 and 1655), don Juan Duchisela (1670), doña Juana Lliufa y Nitibron (1682), don Antonio Duchisela (1685), don Juan Roberto Duchisela (1734), don Isidro Duchisela (1758), and don Manuel Duchisela (1769). All subsequent data for Act 1 are culled from two eighteenth-century copies of the following document unless otherwise specified: "Testamento de don Juan Duchisela, 1605 y su codicilo, 1655," presented as evidence in ANQ Cacicazgos 38, 75, 1788: 8–21; and ANQ Cacicazgos 32, 52, 1754: 43v–69v. The combined study of both copies was necessary for a complete paleographic transcription and to determine authenticity.

Manuela Sáenz: *Americana* or *Quiteña?*

Sarah C. Chambers

Manuela Sáenz is best known as the colorful lover of independence leader Simón Bolívar. They met during his triumphal entry into Quito in 1822, but most of their relationship unfolded in either Peru or Colombia. Indeed although Sáenz was born and raised in Quito from 1797 to 1816, she spent most of her adult life outside of what was to become the nation of Ecuador. In 1817, she married British merchant James Thorne in Lima, and after Bolívar's death, she lived out her life in exile in the port of Paita, in northern Peru, from 1834 to 1856. So why is she included in The Ecuador Reader? *The easy answer is that national leaders tend to embrace those born within their borders who go on to gain fame, wherever that may take them. More important, as the letters reprinted below demonstrate, even from exile Sáenz participated in the politics of Ecuador of the 1830s and 1840s.*

Sáenz and Bolívar shared a passion both for each other (as the first letters demonstrate), as well as for the independence of America from Spain. He charged her with managing his personal correspondence and listened to her advice on the loyalties of other prominent figures. Her official position in the army allowed Sáenz to don a military uniform, and she was effective at rallying his troops. She even saved Bolívar from assassination attempts. Her actions sometimes won Bolívar's approval—he affectionately referred to her as *la loca* (the crazy one)—but sometimes went too far for his tastes, as when she staged a mock execution in effigy of his rival, Colombian vice-president Francisco de Paula Santander. Nonetheless, through the ups and downs of their relationship and after Bolívar's death in 1830, Sáenz's loyalty to him remained steadfast, and their names are inextricably intertwined in historical memory.[1]

Although Sáenz is virtually always considered in relationship to Bolívar, she had joined the conspiracies against Spain in Peru before meeting him, and she continued her activism after his death. Like Bolívar, Sáenz considered herself an "American" as she moved from Quito to Lima to Bogotá. By 1830, however, Bolívar had been forced out of power, and first Venezuela and then

Ecuador seceded from the Colombian confederation. In 1830, while residing in Bogotá, Sáenz rejected the label of "foreigner," asserting that "my country is the continent of America."² As a controversial woman associated with a now unpopular leader, however, Sáenz found herself expelled first from Colombia in 1833 and then from Ecuador in 1834. In her letter from Jamaica in 1834, Sáenz's strong character shines through as she defends the legality of her actions and denounces the enemies of Bolívar.

Adapting herself to the new national political context, Sáenz allied herself with General Juan José Flores, a former ally of Bolívar, who became the first president of an independent Ecuador. Flores and the civilian politician Vicente Rocafuerte were rivals until 1845, competing for power sometimes by the ballot box and at others by conspiracy and rebellion.³ Rocafuerte had banned Sáenz from residing in Ecuador, but her residence in Paita provided her an opportunity to gather intelligence on the activities there of both Peruvians and Ecuadorians and pass it on to Flores. Her correspondence with him reveals her growing national identity as Ecuadorian, her preference (like Bolívar's) for a strong presidency, and her defense of women's participation in the republic as loyal advisors not swayed by corruption or political partisanship.⁴ The letter of 1843 displays many of these characteristics: she indicates her connection to important political figures and her ability to judge their trustworthiness, and defends her interest in Ecuadorian politics. Although she appears to downplay the power of women, in the context of her life and all her letters, her reference to the importance of having both female and male friends highlights the usefulness of women's advice.

The final letter, from 1853, reveals that by the end of her life in the 1850s, her friends were mostly Ecuadorian and that she had come to identify herself in more national than continental terms. She thanked Roberto Ascásubi, who had been with her in Paita but had since returned to Quito, for helping her to recover her maternal inheritance and asked him to send her Ecuadorian-made nativity scenes so that she could spend Christmas Eve with friends "remembering the homeland."

Lima, 14 April 1825
A.S.E. [A Su Excelencia] General Simón Bolívar

Dear Sir,

I know that my only hope for happiness has departed with you. Why, then, have I let you slip from my arms like water that vanishes between my fingers? In my reflections I am more than convinced that you are the ideal lover, and your memory weighs on me all of the time.

I find that in engaging my caprices my feelings become submerged, but I cannot manage to fulfill myself, since it is you who I need; there is nothing that could compare with the force of my love. Buying perfumes, costly garments, or jewelry does not flatter my vanity. Only your words can do that. If you were to write me in small print on huge pages, I would be elated.

My labors never end, as I begin one and do not finish it before I have already begun another. I confess that I am restless and cannot manage to do anything. Tell me what I ought to do, since I can't do a single thing, and all due to your absence. If you were to tell me to come, I would go flying, as it were, to the ends of the earth!

Your poor and desperate friend,
Manuela

Huamachuco, 16 June 1824
A.S.E. the Liberator Simón Bolívar

My beloved Simón,

My love: The adverse conditions that present themselves in the path of the campaign that you plan to realize do not intimidate my womanhood. To the contrary, I challenge them. What do you think of me! Have you not always told me that I am more manly than any of your officers? From the heart I tell you: You will not have a more faithful comrade than I and not a single complaint will depart your lips that would have you regret the decision to accept me.

Will you take me with you? If so, I will go. This is not a rash decision, but one of esteem and of love for the independence [of America from Spain] (do not be jealous).

Always yours,
Manuela

I loved the Liberator; in death I honor him.

President of the Ecuadorian State
General Juan José Flores
Kingston, Jamaica, 6 May 1834

Señor:

I do hope that this arrives in your hands, as it comes from this island, and since even from Bogotá I wrote you many letters without the most minimal reply. Already it is apparent—my bad writing is well-known—and directed at you it will be worse; could you all believe that I was saying something political? I loved the Liberator; in death, I honor him and for this I am exiled by Santander. Believe me, my friend, as I protest you with my frank character, that I am innocent, all except for taking the Liberator's portrait from the castle of the plaza. Considering that no one else would do it, I believed that it was my duty, and this I do not regret; and assuming this offense, was there no Law of Amnesty passed by the Convention? Did I go beyond this law? They also say that my house was the meeting point for all of those dissidents. General, believe me that I was not living in some savannah in which those would have hid. Some friends of mine used to visit me: as it was unnecessary, I overlooked asking them if they were content or discontent [with Santander's government]; in any case, they would have said that I had poor manners. That I took part in the Sanctuary, señor, is a sizeable slander; I was in Guaduas, three days from Bogotá, and the act took place in Funza, near the capital; and what's more, I was bitten twice by a venomous snake; who knows, if I had been in good shape, maybe I would have just mounted my horse and left on account of my temper; of course, you do not ignore that a humble woman like me cannot do anything; but Santander does not think likewise; he grants me an imaginary quality, he says that I am capable of anything, and he is miserably mistaken; what I am is, with a bold character, the friend of my friends and the enemy of my enemies, and no one as much as that ungrateful man. But now I could not care less about him: There exists in my power your personal correspondence with the Liberator and I am making good use of it. It cost me a lot of work to save all of the papers from the year '30 and this is my property.[5] In order not to leave any doubts about the events of the past, I call on you on my behalf. You know how I conduct myself and I will carry this march to the grave, no matter how the slander may have insulted me. Time will justify me.

Now that I have bothered you with my complaints, let us move on to something even more bothersome. The little that I possess of my mother, señor, I owe it to the desire and interest that you took in my inheritance and it is not normal that I should lack this financial aid, as I left Quito in the year '27, leaving my hacienda to be rented at 600 pesos, since I pardoned Gómez for those 50. Señor, in all of this time I have not seen half of the inheritance; I have only drawn a thousand pesos for señora Juana Torres, and I do not even know if she received it; no matter how much I write Don Pedro, he does not answer me.

Desperate, I begged señor Modesto Larrea to sell the hacienda; and that same gentleman told me that it was bad to sell it and resolved not to. Señor, no one writes me; though granted that is partly fine with me. Señor, since you see me on this island alone and without my family, I believe that compassion and our old friendship will have you excuse me for calling your attention to my trifles; señor, you can command whomever and be served; while as for me, no one will even respond to me.

Write me at length, my General and friend; steal yourself a moment from your affairs; for your amiable wife I implore you, for your sweet children I beg you, and put me at the disposition of your wife; it could be that she might want something from this island.

I always recall our old friendship with delight, and in its name I ask that you should attend to me; then I will know that you remember your friend and acquaintance.

Manuela Sáenz

> *My documents of safe passage have not been able to reunite me with my affections most dear: my homeland and my friends.*
> *Paita, 7 September 1843*

Your Excellency Señor General President Don Juan José Flores
Quito
Entrusted to my brother and friend Señor General Santa Cruz
Señor General don Juan José Flores

My friend without equal:

How amiable and good you are with your friends! and as I am faithful and constant with you, you ought to be with me. A terrible denunciation from hell, dictated by Rocafuerte, has me far from my homeland and from my friends like you, and even worse is that the decree mandates that I never return to my patriotic land; as you know, my friend, it is easier to destroy something than to begin anew; an order took me from my country; and my documents of safe passage have not been able to reunite me with my affections most dear: my homeland and my friends.

Since this is not possible for me, believe me that near Paita or Lima I will always be the same Manuela that you met in '22. The tranquility of the country pleases me greatly. Nothing is more agreeable than tranquility.

The gentleman Monsalve is a good friend of yours and therefore of mine. We are in agreement, and thus I entrust that when you deign to write me, you should do it under the charge of this gentleman, so that the letters will assuredly arrive. He is a worthy subject and very refined; I did not know him before, but I am very satisfied with this gentleman now. You will have already seen in [an edition of the newspaper] "Comercio" what they say of him, but that is the work of don Juan Otoya, since it is he who has longed for the Consulate; he and others make use of Rocafuerte for their articles. Today Avedaño departs, but I do not send my correspondence with him, since the mail is better. Do me the favor of greeting General Santa Cruz and telling him to write me under the charge of señor Monsalve, and tell him that I did not write because I was very busy. Greet señor Pareja and tell him that I already sent him the letter of authorization, and he should let me know me if he has received it yet. The ex-counsel wrote again.[6] He sent you the papers, now he and Cárdenas can argue over who is the author. I am pleased to find out news from the South, but if the politics of a foreign country interest me, it is only for the relation that they have with the politics of my country and for my friends; and the rest of it has little or no importance for me. When I say that I am interested, understand that this interest does not pass beyond wishes and good intentions; since you ought to suppose that a humble woman can neither take up nor buy arms, and much less generate any political influence whatsoever; rather it is best to have friends, whether they be men or women; don't you think so?

I will be very grateful that you make the people who owe me to pay, as is the case with señora Gangotena and señora Benítez, don Ignacio and don Pedro Sanz and don Jacobo Gómez; therefore by you taking an interest in this matter and replacing Coronel Pareja, I do not doubt that I will emerge from my problems, which are not few. Dear friend, your best friend wishes you health.

Manuela Sáenz

> *My heart can still be moved,*
> *as the heart does not grow old.*
> *(From the original, unedited, property*
> *of Señora Alicia Coloma de Reed.)[7]*
> *Paita, 28 October 1853*

Señor Don Roberto Ascásubi,
My very beloved friend,

I send you greetings of the highest affection and I entrust you to pass them on to your whole family; my health is good, and to that end I believe that the pleasant company that I keep with your brother and my fellow countryman Pólit contributes quite a lot. When someone is treated pleasantly and sincerely, it warms the heart; so I ought to thank you, rather than you thanking me, since I do not do anything for this gentleman, although I do not lack good wishes. I confess that I wish that they would not leave Paita until they return to Quito. I knew of señor García before, but now I am very pleased to have spoken with him.

[I have] written you two letters, one to my señora Rosarito (I did not know they interrupted the communication). In my letters I gave you the most expressive thanks for your good works, which I repeat now, assuring you that they are preserved in my heart, which can still be moved, as the heart does not grow old.

To my friend señor García I say that he should tell you a few things and I implore you to manage my affairs as if they were your own, assured that for all that you do I will approve with gratitude. Withhold the money there; and for God's sake, get together for me a group of baskets and embroidered goods, lace cloth, etc. If it is possible for you, send to me quickly via Guayaquil the nativity scenes of *corozo*[8] in order to place them for the 24th of December [and] drink *rosero*[9] with my friends, in remembrance of the homeland.

There is no news of Flores's expedition, only rumors aimed at gaining attention. Until the final breath bids you and your sisters farewell, your friend *llacta huasi*[10] and assured servant,

Manuela Sáenz of Quito

Notes

Source for Bolivar letters: Aníbal Noguera Mendoza, ed., *Epistolarios: Bolívar y las damas, las damas y Bolívar* (Caracas: Editorial de la Presidencia de la República, 1983). Letters to Flores are from his presidential archive and were published in *Manuela Sáenz: Epistolario* (Quito Banco Central de Ecuador, 1986).

1. See the new English-language biography of Sáenz by Pamela S. Murray and Frederick B. Pike, *For Glory and Bolivar: The Remarkable Life of Manuela Sáenz* (Austin: University of Texas Press, 2008).

2. Letter of 1830, reprinted in Eduardo Posada, "La Libertadora," *Boletín de Historia y Antigüedades* (Bogotá) 15 (August 1925): 32.

3. Mark Van Aken, *King of the Night: Juan José Flores and Ecuador, 1824–1864* (Berkeley: University of California Press, 1989).

4. For a full analysis of her activities and correspondence in exile, see Sarah C. Chambers, "Republican Friendship: Manuela Sáenz Writes Women into the Nation, 1835–1856," *Hispanic American Historical Review* 81, no. 2 (2001): 225–57.

5. Manuela is not threatening Flores, but rather Santander.

6. The ex-counsel is Pedro Moncayo, a major figure in the Liberal opposition to Flores.

7. Luis Felipe Borja, "Epistolario de Manuela Sáenz," *Boletín de la Academia Nacional de la Historia* 29 (1946): 178–79.

8. Corozo is a vegetable from the coast of Ecuador.

9. Rosero is a traditional fruit drink from Quito.

10. In Kichwa, the most common of the indigenous languages of Ecuador, *llacta* means "land"; and *huasi* means "house" or "home"; therefore *amiga llacta huasi* would most nearly signify "friend of the homeland."

The State, Missionaries, and Native Consciousness in the Upper Amazon, 1767–1896

Blanca Muratorio

The indigenous people discussed by anthropologist Blanca Muratorio in this essay are the Napo Quichua, one of several indigenous nationalities of the Ecuadorian Upper Amazon. They call themselves Napo Runa or just Runa (human being). Muratorio looks at two historical traditions, oral and written, to interpret a century of socioeconomic and cultural life in this area of the Upper Amazon. Central to this story is the complex interaction between Jesuit missionaries and the indigenous people of the Amazon.

In 1830, Ecuador was proclaimed an independent republic, headed by Juan José Flores as its first president duly elected by a constituent assembly. This significant event did not have important repercussions in the Oriente until several years later. In this vast province, the century that elapsed from the expulsion of the Jesuits in 1767 until their return to the region in 1870, may be considered as a unity, both politically and economically. Throughout this period, the Napo Runa were subject to a venal civil administration which coveted the natives' tribute, and to a few ignorant and corrupt priests who visited the area from time to time. This situation prevailed even after 1830, for the Republican Government took no remedial steps. Instead, it created an administrative void in the Oriente because even the weak controls previously exercised by the royal bureaucracy vanished, and soldiers in search of fortune, traders, a few priests, and adventurers of all kinds "took over" the region. The state continued to draw surplus from the Indians in the form of tribute paid by them mainly in gold, equivalent to twelve pesos or six gold *castellanos*. Governors in the Oriente had relatively low salaries, which in Archidona they amply supplemented by the *repartos* (forced apportionments of goods) carried out at least twice a year. This practice consisted of forced sales of *tucuyo* (coarse cotton cloth made in the Sierra), thread, needles, and a large number of superfluous goods paid for with *pita* (agave) fiber and gold dust. Five *varas* (14 feet) of tucuyo were paid for with one gold castellano, or fourteen times their value. The Indians of Napotoa, Payamino, Aguano, Santa Rosa, and Suno were considered primarily "gold producers," and those of Archidona " pita producers."[1]

William Jameson estimates that around the 1850s, on completing his term in office a governor could have amassed a sum equivalent to some 6,000 to 8,000 pounds sterling; a "considerable fortune" in Ecuador at that time. When Jameson visited Archidona, the governor was an army lieutenant-colonel who had been sentenced to death for murder, but whose penalty had been commuted by the President of the Republic to banishment in the Napo for ten years.[2] Although he was but acting governor, at that time the position of Governor of the Oriente was generally bestowed on the "government's military friends." According to one observer, the entire region served "as a penitentiary for political criminals." Quiteños did not venture to visit the Oriente and the government was largely disinterested in the region. Private interests acted with de facto authority, thus depriving the Indians of all legal protection.

In 1847, Archidona was a small village where the governor was in residence. Ten years later, it had become a ghost town, and Tena was a new village where the Indians had just finished building the town hall. It is obvious that in the mid-nineteenth century, the juridical-political apparatus of government was absent from the Oriente. The few whites residing there could not survive without appropriating the Indians' surplus and without abusing their labor to extract gold and pita. It is not surprising, therefore, that one of the typical Indian defense strategies was to vanish from a village immediately upon the white authorities' decision to settle there. This also explains the governors' frequent changes of residence between Santa Rosa, Archidona, and Tena, mentioned in historical sources. In certain cases, the Indians' flight was preceded by acts of violence, such as the murder of a priest in Archidona and a governor in Puerto Napo. These actions, however, were only localized uprisings easily quelled by the whites. One of the outcomes of 300 years of Colonial domination was the destruction of the indigenous socio-political organization that had made possible the joint and coordinated action of the different ethnic groups, as evidenced by the 1578 Indian rebellion. Nevertheless, this protracted domination was never accepted as legitimate by the Napo Runa. Efforts to punish them provoked the same reaction they were intended to prevent: the Indians fled to their *tambus* (forest dwellings) located a walking distance of three or four days from the villages, returning only after three or four months when pressed by the need to obtain manufactured goods.

Cargo bearer in a trip to Archidona, anonymous painting.
(Courtesy of José Manuel Jijón y Caamaño)

Although the Indians did still pay the priests in gold, tobacco, and pita for prayers and weddings, they exhibited "great disdain" for religion, did not attend church, and showed no special respect for the secular priests. The church tried to justify its participation in appropriating the Indians' surplus by alleging its social duty to "civilize" them, and its religious mission to "evangelize" them. From the Napo Runa's point of view, the merits of these two ventures were not self-evident, but revealed instead the irrationality of the process of white domination: to ensure its legitimacy by destroying the culture and religion of the dominated group.

Contrary to what most historical sources suggest, the absence of an open and joint resistance during that period does not mean that the Napo Runa were totally subdued, or that they were unaware of being exploited. One of the forms taken by this resistance is expressed, for example, in a song sung by an Indian when handing over his *camarico* (mandatory gift of animals and food) to the priest: "Take this, we bring you our goods, the fruit of our labor and our sweat, stuff yourself, you crooked rascal."

Humor and irony in folk songs and dances as a form of protest against arbitrary power and authority are almost universal in peasant cultures, including the Andean. This irreverence, that sometimes can be perceived only in the tone of voice and in the accompanying facial expressions, is a subtle form of resistance, quite significant also in Rucuyaya Alonso's story, particularly when he speaks of the authorities and patrons.[3]

Flight into the forest to attain freedom—already called "emigration" by the whites in the mid-nineteenth century—and the Indians' lack of interest in being converted to Christianity, were two of the forms taken by Napo Runa resistance. This resistance became a serious problem for the government and

its representatives in the Oriente. In 1846, in an attempt to solve both problems, the National Congress was forced to exempt the Oriente Indians from
the "personal contribution." The text of the law exhibits some of the then
current misconceptions held by the national government regarding those
Indians, in comparison with the highland Indian peasants, with whom they
were more familiar. The law assumes that, if only that particular tribute
was removed, the Oriente Indians—including those not yet converted to
Christianity—would be easily settled.

In the Sierra, the peasants' sedentary nature, a high population density, the
expropriation of community lands by landowners, and the ready access to this
region by state and church representatives, were the major constraints to highland Indian resistance, which took different forms from those in the Oriente.
The political and economic control mechanisms wielded by the state could
not be extended there as easily as in the Sierra until well into the twentieth century. The Amazon region's inaccessibility and hostility to the white man were
instrumental in the relative freedom enjoyed by the Oriente Indians. For them,
the tropical forest was a familiar and safe environment, a refuge where they
could ensure both their own material and spiritual existence, and the valued
resources coveted by the whites to be exchanged for manufactured goods.

Only five months prior to the enactment of the exemption law, the Indian
authorities of Napo and Archidona brought a complaint before the Minister of the Interior through the Fiscal Agent. In a document dated June 13,
1846, they reported a long list of abuses and humiliations to which they were
subjected by the local political chiefs, including the obligation of providing
maintenance for those same political chiefs and their dependents. They also
demanded that the government take steps to put an end to all such abuses,
threatening otherwise to "abandon our villages and seek safe asylum in the
remotest sites of our vast and mountainous province." Furthermore, there
is evidence that they did not always pay the debts incurred through repartos, "When creditors reprimanded them for their debts, they would answer:
'Don't be upset, no one will turn you out. I'll pay you when the boy who was
born on top of this cotton cloth you gave me on credit, and who has aged it
while growing up, is able to work. It is he who must work and pay.'"

Moreover, in the Tena-Archidona area, the missionaries were never able
to consolidate their domination through the political and religious hierarchies associated with the fiesta system, comparable to that which developed
in the Sierra. On the one hand, the Oriente Indian communities were never
established on a sufficiently permanent basis to keep up with a regular cal-
endar of imposed religious festivities. On the other, the missionaries were
unable to maintain either the necessary continuity of their presence in the
region, or the spiritual control and native cooperation long enough to sustain

a fiesta system. Although the Spaniards did impose on the Indians a form of native hierarchy of religious authorities, by the eighteenth century these had become amalgamated with the civil native officials. None of the Napo Runa whom we questioned on the subject, nor the archival material mentioned *priostes* (sponsor of religious fiestas), or the rituals commonly associated with the fiesta system as having existed in the area since the mid-nineteenth century, the approximate time limit of the oral history tradition available to us.

From the point of view of the authorities and traders, the problem was that, despite their coercive power, the very nature of the extractive economy allowed the Indians a degree of freedom and self-determination that guaranteed neither the regularity nor the discipline of their labor. More drastic solutions were required in order to ensure such qualities in the Oriente Indian labor force. One of these solutions was provided by the experiment of a "theocratic government" in the Napo, under the tutelage of a conservative government in alliance with the missionaries of the Society of Jesus.

A Short-Lived Attempt at "Oriental Theocracy": God, Discipline and Development for the Indians. 1870–75

In the 1870s, García Moreno, then Conservative President of Ecuador, designed a relatively coherent government project to integrate the Oriente into a new national "order and progress" political regime. García Moreno's economic project aimed at modernizing the country by creating a communication infrastructure to mobilize the factors of production, do away with extreme economic regionalism, and create the possibilities for expansion of the domestic market and the conditions to profit from the new opportunities offered by the international market. In order to train the necessary labor force, García Moreno advocated technical and scientific education, founded the Polytechnic School, and hired European teachers, as well as doctors and lawyers, to upgrade university education. This modernization was made possible by the government's rationalization and centralization of fiscal revenue, and by its efforts to stabilize the bureaucracy. But all this development took place within an autocratic political program intended to create the required social peace by way of an arbitrary repressive system and the asphyxiating ideological tutelage of the Catholic Church. The Concordat between the Vatican and the Government of Ecuador, ratified in 1863, was a political pact whereby the church provided an ideological superstructure to "moralize" the country, to create "political cohesion," to control education and culture, and even the most routine aspects of people's lives.

The Oriente, which until then had remained almost beyond the reach of the government, plagued as it was by corrupt merchants and by Indian "paganism," provided García Moreno with an exemplary challenge to test his concept of economic development based on "moral regeneration." To this end, the president found his best allies in the Jesuits, and for the five years until his death, he assigned to them the role of legitimate representatives of the state in the Napo region. He therefore awarded them full powers as governors with authority to "take the necessary measures for order and appropriate civil and ecclesiastic government in that Province." This implied instituting and removing authorities, punishing crimes, opening up schools, and decreeing laws. García Moreno's interests coincided with those of the Jesuit missions on two essential points: to blaze trails facilitating the entry of missionaries and nuns, and to evangelize and settle the Indian population so as to transform it through all possible means, into a "trustworthy" labor force.

By securing a Jesuit governance in the Oriente, García Moreno did not intend to prohibit extractive activities or trade, but rather to regulate, control, and moralize them. The structural contradictions of this project, mainly in terms of the corrupt makeup of the merchant "bourgeoisie" in the Oriente and of its limited potential access to Indian labor, were evident soon after the Jesuits came into the area. The first decree issued by the Jesuit Vicar of the Oriente Province in 1879, stipulated the prohibition of selling on credit to the Indians, allowing them to pay their debts in cash, and the abolition of the liquor trade. Both measures set off a conflict between the interests of the Jesuits, as evangelizers and representatives of the state, and the interests of the traders and Indians, whose "alliance"—although occasional and precarious— turned out to be mutually advantageous at that point in time.

The major cause for the opposing interests between the merchants and the Jesuits lay in the conflicting demands of two different economies: one extractive and the other agricultural. Both economies confronted shortages of labor which, in the best of cases, was reluctant and evasive. The merchants granted *licencias*, or leaves, to the Indians exempting them from the *doctrinas* (evangelization strategy) so that they may engage in gold panning and scraping pita fiber. In addition, during that period the Tena-Archidona area was regularly visited by cinchona bark companies wanting to hire Indian families as labor. Osculati, as well as other historical sources, show that the Napo Runa were "infinitely jubilant" to accept these licencias. They preferred "paying" for their right to move freely into the forest, rather than submit to the permanent supervision of the white merchants. In sum, the social relations of production required by this extractive economy did not interfere with the social organization of the Napo Runa based on the *muntun* (kin group) as a productive unit, nor with their land-use rights, or with their residential patterns. The Indians maintained control over their subsistence production based on shifting horticulture and on periodic hunting, fishing, and gathering expeditions. Consequently, it was in defense of their own reproduction as a group that the Napo Runa made momentary "alliances" with the traders against the Jesuits. On the contrary, the missionaries wanted access to a "regular and disciplined" Indian labor force to build houses, convents, churches, and schools. Their final objective was the establishment of agricultural and livestock settlements, a goal wholly incompatible with the prevailing economic organization and worldview of the Napo Runa. The Jesuits defined the licencias as "those routines characteristic of the Yumbos, whose passion for their idle and independent forest life borders on a savage fanaticism." They also objected on the grounds that the abusive trade practiced by the whites against the interests of the Indians was "contrary to natural rights." Besides, the Indians' absences under the system of licencias deprived the mission of hands for work and of souls for indoctrination, reducing it to "uselessness." Further, in their ignorance and ideological repugnance of forest life, the Jesuits believed that the Napo Runa used their licencias only for "sprees," "drinking," and "mischief," for beyond their paternalistic tutelage, any freedom had by the Indians was considered profligacy.

The final outcome of this conflict between the missionaries, the merchants, and the Indians—loss of power by the Jesuits and their second expulsion from the area in 1896—was strongly influenced by the Indians' resistance to settle more or less permanently in villages, and to become a peasant or semi-proletarianized labor force. The other decisive factor was the invasion of the entire Amazon by industrial capitalism in search of rubber, a raw material produced mainly in this region from the late nineteenth century until approximately the first two decades of the twentieth century.

"Civilization" of the Labor Force

IDEOLOGICAL BASES

The ideological foundation of Jesuit economic strategy rested on three major premises: the "moralizing" nature of agriculture, the "civilizing" capacity of religion and, the concept that the Indians were "perpetual children" requiring the severe but paternalistic protection of the missionaries.

One of the Jesuits' favorite mottos was: "The sword and the plow behind the cross, not in front of it." In Napo, as they had in Paraguay, the Jesuits opposed armed violence because, according to them, it only served to "frighten away or irritate the savages." Hence, they defended their pacifist theocratic experiment with the conviction that "civilization without religion is absurd, and religion without ministers to teach it, is senseless." They saw in agriculture the "civilized" future of the Oriente, since it entailed settlements and villages, work performed on a regular basis, and the possibility of monitoring a labor force disciplined by doctrinas, unlike the extractive economy that allowed almost untrammeled Indian freedom.

The final aim of the Jesuits was to convert a hunting and gathering people into a European-style peasantry. Considering that the major obstacle against this purpose was the Indians' *tambus*, the Jesuits tried to turn them into farms. The Indians could go every day to their tambus for their jobs of planting and harvesting only if they returned regularly to their village homes, as required to meet any political or religious obligations. According to the missionaries, this pattern would make the Indians conform to the way "all peasants live in Europe and in the interior of the Republic." The majority of the Jesuits were of European origin, used to a society that had been a predominantly peasant one for hundreds of years, in which villages were the social core of the countryside and towns the hub of civilization. Consequently, it was almost impossible for them to understand the rationale of the Napo Runa's tropical forest economy and social organization. Xavier Albó argues that Jesuit "civilizing action" toward the Indians of Peru in the sixteenth and seventeenth centuries, which was similar to that followed by them in the Napo mission, suffered from a fundamental contradiction. On the one hand, the Jesuits wanted to maintain a rigid separation between Spaniards and Indians, while on the other, they adopted a Spanish-oriented model to acculturate them. This model assumed an underlying idea of religion and political order similar to that existing "in the towns of Castille."

The strategies used by the Jesuits to discipline the Indians as a labor force must be considered an integral part of the evangelization process, insofar as the missionaries thought of regular work as the best way to combat the original sin of "idleness." Supported by García Moreno, the Jesuits were determined to be, and actually acted as, the "natural defenders" of the Indians against the "abuses and swindles" they suffered at the hands of the merchants. One important mistake the Jesuits made about the situation in the Napo, however, was to assume that the abuses against the Indians were in many ways comparable to the slave hunts suffered by the Guaraní Indians. Even in the nineteenth century, Paraguay continued to be their missionary model, but it was not applicable in Tena-Archidona, where that ethnocidal practice of "recruiting" labor did not exist until the rubber boom era, and where the subsistence interests of the Napo Runa were, at the time we are discussing, better "protected" by the traders.

Another of the Jesuits' main errors in judgment was to overestimate the "ignorance and frankness of the unfortunate Indians," and consequently to establish a harsh system of corporal punishment justified by the need of the "fathers" to correct "perpetually child-like peoples" for their "laziness." The misconception of the Indians as beings incapable of reasoning, for whom punishment was "the only thing that moves them and excites their sensitivity and imagination," pervaded Jesuit evangelizing action, in both the first and second mission periods. In Jesuit sources the Napo Runa are portrayed as "lost and ignorant children" who, "being irrational," submit to the merchants' exploitation. The main assumption was that the submission stance sometimes taken by the Indians as a survival tactic was almost an innate form of behavior, and an immutable consequence of a passive personality. However, those same sources may be read so as to substantiate a very different interpretation of native behavior. It is clear that the Napo Runa responded to those Jesuit strategies with a clear assessment of their economic position, rebelling against the missionaries' paternalistic attempts to decide on their way of life, and resisting punishment by resorting to the law, by force, and even with considerable humor. This latter form of subtle resistance is particularly evident in the oral tradition about the Jesuits handed down to Rucuyaya Alonso by his parents and grandparents. It is also evident that the Napo Runa understood quite well the bureaucracy of the local white government, the psychology of the merchants, and the prime cause of their conflict with the missionaries. They did use the licencias to manipulate all three powers on their behalf, of course, within the constraints of the economic structure with which they had to cope. On the one hand, they bribed the white authorities with gold to extend their licencias for longer time periods—thus flouting the missionaries. On the other, they sought the protection of the Jesuits against the ill treatments inflicted on them by the authorities, while at the same time pleading with the missionaries not to report these complaints to those same authorities.

Strategies to Discipline the Labor Force

Just as the Spanish conquistadors in the preceding centuries, the only way the Jesuits could gain access to the native labor force was indirectly through the Indian leaders, either natural or imposed, constituting what was known as "Runa government." However, this native government did not act as an autonomous body, and was almost nothing more than a political and productive arm of the whites. These authorities, who in Tena-Archidona were known as *justicias* (justices) or *varas* (staff-holders), were elected among the dominant families within the muntun, and a son could inherit the position of his father as was true in Rucuyaya Alonso's case. Sometimes powerful shamans would be internally selected to the highest office. The white authorities and the missionaries used the justicias to marshal native labor for all kinds of jobs and services as well as for administering punishment to those who refused to comply. Owing to his authority within the kinship group, a particular Indian official could successfully play that role. That very same authority, however, allowed him to also use the labor force of his muntun to pan gold or to prepare pita for the white traders, or to simply organize his group for flight into the forest. Consequently, from the missionaries' point of view, the justicias were not entirely reliable and punishment inflicted on the other Indians was almost useless. As an alternative, some missionaries suggested instituting what they thought of as "incentives," such as installing blacksmith's or carpentry shops in an endeavor to govern the Indians by turning them into artisans. Efforts to make them settle down also required that they clear land for crops around the villages. The missionaries themselves introduced cattle with the idea of "preparing a solid basis for the formation of community property and providing an allurement for the Indians so that they might be reduced to village life." Another Jesuit report suggests that given the "indolent nature" of the Napo Runa, it was impossible to secure forced labor from them and that they should therefore be appropriately remunerated. The payment was usually made in cotton cloth although in Tena-Archidona the Indians had to pay the missionaries for the masses and other religious ceremonies with four gold pesos or their equivalent in pita, or in food. The Napo Runa could obtain all these goods only near their tambus, far from their villages. Despite this obvious contradiction between their economic and ideological demands, the Jesuits did not alter their tactics of trying to "reduce" the Napo Runa into villagers.

In summary, native resistance, plus the traders' hostility to the missionaries and the smallpox epidemics that broke out in Tena-Archidona—resulting from the very attempts to establish villages—compounded to hamper and finally to prevent the success of the Jesuits' socio-economic evangelizing strategies, which in themselves were ambiguous and contradictory.

Decadence of the Jesuit Missions

In the 1870s one of the most powerful traders opposed to Jesuit interests in the Napo was Faustino Rayo. He took undue advantage of his authority as governor to impose repartos on the Indians in exchange for gold and pita, until he provoked a widespread revolt in Puerto Napo. Soon after the Jesuits came into Tena-Archidona, a conflict arose between the Vicar of Napo, Father Guzmán, and Rayo, who had become the spokesman for the merchants' interests. Rayo refused to comply with the new trade legislation imposed by the missionaries. He used the discontent pervasive among the Indians caused by all the hardships they had to endure in building Archidona, to support an attempt against Father Guzmán's life, seemingly with the Tenas' active involvement. Jesuit sources themselves acknowledge that the main cause of the uprising and of Father Guzmán's leaving the Napo mission were the tasks and punishments to which the missionary had subjected the Indians.

On entering Archidona the new Vicar of Napo found it deserted; the natives had fled to the forest, taking with them "eight North-American machetes, a similar number of hoes, a little cotton cloth," and the dogs and other animals. To reestablish missionary authority, the new Vicar reimposed the custom of being carried on a litter by the Indians from town to town. He also punished those Indians allegedly guilty of the attempt against Father Guzmán's life who had sought refuge in Puerto Napo. Reversing previous Jesuit policy, the Vicar himself entered into an agreement with the white traders whereby they were allowed to operate on credit, provided they charged fair prices, and to reside in Archidona, under the condition of submitting to Jesuit authority.

Additional measures taken by the Vicar were an even more direct and profound violation of Napo Runa deeply held cultural values and principles of social organization. What they found particularly offensive was to be forced to bury their dead in the Christian cemetery instead of in their houses, and to suffer interference in their marriage alliances. In addition to other Jesuit imposed obligations, these new measures further fueled the restlessness and discontent among all the Indians of that area, consisting of about 1,000 in Archidona and some 500 in Tena at that time. A smallpox epidemic in 1875 triggered the usual flight of the Indians. The most reluctant in returning to the villages were the Tenas, then considered by the Jesuits as the most rebellious. López San Vicente noted that "either because they had longer enjoyed the free forest life, or because they were more obstinate by nature than the rest, [the Tenas] refuse to return, brazenly replying that they will do so once the soldiers have already ousted the fathers."

The conflict between the Jesuits and the traders worsened when the former used their influence with the President of the Republic to have Rayo removed from his official duties in Napo, and came to a head in 1875, when Rayo murdered President García Moreno in Quito. Other political interests were also involved in the president's assassination, but their explanation is not relevant here. Following the death of García Moreno, a free-trade decree allowed the whites to again operate in the Napo without any restrictions, but the Indians persistently rejected being governed by the missionaries. In 1876 they once again took the legal course of resistance, by sending a delegation of Indian officials to Quito to demand that the Jesuits be expelled "because they punish greatly," and that the Vicar be replaced by a single civil government for the entire province. The Indian official from Tena directly confronted the Vicar to have him resign his office as civil governor. These actions seem to have been successful, for shortly after, the new governor came to Napo accompanied by twelve soldiers and sixteen civilians. From that moment on, deprived of García Moreno's political and financial support and faced with the continued hostility of traders and Indians, the Jesuit mission's authority was weakened and its chances of expanding in the Oriente were seriously curtailed. According to the Jesuits, their personal circumstances became unbearable because even their most loyal Indians, such as the Ahuanos, turned against them. A still weak state could not govern the Oriente without the missionaries' intermediary role, however, and soon the civilian government that succeeded García Moreno cooperated with the Jesuits, especially in their educational efforts. In 1891, the Governor of Oriente declared: "Harmony now reigns among the missionary Fathers and the civil authority," and exhorted the whites living in town to obey the missionaries.

García Moreno's experiment in establishing a "theocracy" in the Napo under the paternalistic tutelage of the Jesuits lasted five years. Attempts at regularizing and moralizing the economy were thwarted by the makeup and composition of the merchant class: a combination of adventurers and former soldiers, many of them foreigners. These people never considered the Oriente as a permanent place to establish a well-organized civic society. This was not an instance of pioneer families opening up a frontier for colonization, which may account for the few references to white women or children in the historical sources of that period. The "rough" nature of its extractive economy, and the "hostility" of the forest environment, were two important factors prevalent in the Oriente's initial attraction of men prepared to use violence and cunning in order to prevail against the Indians' unwillingness to work for them, and desirous of easy wealth and a quick exit from the area. In this respect, these "republican pioneers" were not very different from the first conquistadors of the land of Gold and Cinnamon. For their part, the Napo Runa rejected the "theocracy," not so much for ideological reasons, but because they felt that it was contrary to their material and cultural survival as an autonomous ethnic entity. Rationally choosing between two "evils," they allied themselves with the traders against the Jesuits to resist a forced and ethnocidal acculturation.

Notes

For complete references and footnotes, consult the original version of this piece, in Blanca Muratorio, *The Life and Times of Grandfather Alonso: Culture and History in the Upper Amazon* (New Brunswick, N.J.: Rutgers University Press, 1991), chap. 5.

1. Gaetano Osculati, *Explorazione delle Regioni Equatoriali lungo il Napo ed il fiume delle Amazzoni: Frammento di un viaggio fatto nelle due Americhe negli anni 1846–47–48* (Milan: Fratelli Centenari e Comp, 1854), 102, 107.

2. William Jameson, "Excursion Made from Quito to the River Napo, January to May, 1857," *Journal of the Royal Geographical Society* 18 (1858): 337–49.

3. Rucuyaya Alonso was a Pano Runa, an indigenous person belonging to the group of Quichua speakers that originally settled on the banks of the Pano River in the Amazon.

Negri della valle del Chota.

"Blacks of Chota," Ecuador 1897. (Photo by E. Festa, courtesy of Taller Visual)

II

A New Nation

Ecuador likes to claim that the "first shout for independence" was screamed in Quito on 10 August 1809. But rebellion was in the air throughout the Andes, Latin America, and the world. In addition to uprisings throughout the Andes, there were the American and French Revolutions; the invasion of Spain by Napoleon; and the attraction of modern political, social, economic, and scientific thought. The northern part of South America united forces under Simón Bolívar, the Liberator, and Ecuador first achieved independence from Spain in 1822 as part of the Confederation of Gran Colombia. Gran Colombia—which included present-day Venezuela, Colombia, Panama, and Ecuador—was a vision of Bolívar, who believed that the new nations of America needed to be relatively large in order to remain economically and politically independent from European powers. The experiment, however, was doomed not only by internal political divisions, but by the fact that Gran Colombia was effectively bankrupt and still struggling with the costs of war. Venezuela first broke from the union; Ecuador then established itself as an independent country in 1830.

Despite great proclamations from Ecuador's political elite, independence brought few immediate changes to the social and political structure of the country. Elites squabbled over political control of the government and monopolized the country's wealth. It was Juan José Flores, a Venezuelan general who had been a commander under Bolívar, who would become Ecuador's first president (1830–34, and again during the period 1839–45) and dominate the political scene for the first fifteen years of Ecuador's history. A staunch Conservative, Flores helped consolidate the power of a new ruling class (that looked a lot like the old one) made up of the church, large landowners, and the military.[1] His departure brought little change, though the slightly more Liberal stance of governments during the 1850s led to the end of slavery (1852) and yet another expulsion of the Jesuits, who were among the country's largest landowners.

The next fifteen years, from 1860 to 1875, would be dominated by another conservative, Gabriel García Moreno (president from 1861 to 1865 and 1869 to 1875). In García Moreno, the Catholic Church found its ideal ally, one who saw church and state as inseparable. He gave the church control over education and extended all sorts of privileges to the clergy. He also concentrated power in his own hands while attempting to modernize the fiscal running of the government, build roads, create a modern banking system, and improve education. By the early 1870s, however, his conservative ideas seemed more and more out of place. When he attempted to run for the presidency a third time, he was assassinated.

García Moreno's relative success in creating a modern Ecuadorian state was directly related to the rise of export crops, particularly cacao (cocoa), during the latter half of the nineteenth century. The colonial state's principle source of public revenue—Indian tribute and tithe—was abolished during this period, forcing the government to rely almost exclusively on exports as a source of income. As Ecuador became a major exporter of cacao during the late 1800s, the capacity of the Ecuadorian government—to build infrastructure, establish schools, promote business, and so on—grew tremendously. García Moreno's governments saw some of this wealth, but the cacao "boom" itself really began around 1880 and lasted until 1920. During that period, cacao exports accounted for between 60 and 70 percent of the country's total exports. Coffee, "Panama" hats, and other products were also exported as the Ecuadorian economy became rapidly integrated into the world market, but cacao dominated the political and economic scene during the decades before and after the turn of the century.

The rise of cacao also helped bring about the end of the Conservatism represented by García Moreno and ushered in the "Liberal Revolution" led by his rival, Eloy Alfaro, in 1895. For the next couple of decades the Ecuadorian state would be a fairly coherent instrument of class rule dominated by a landowning export elite based on the country's coast. To be sure, Liberals would rely on electoral fraud to remain in power. Eloy Alfaro is rumored to have said, "what we won with bullets we will not lose by ballots." Coastal landowners would dominate the Liberal Party, the government, major banks, and significant sectors of the Ecuadorian economy during this period. The cacao boom would also open up the coastal region to colonization and lead to the rapid expansion of Guayaquil as the country's largest city and industrial center.

The collapse of cacao during the 1920s was transformative. Coastal elites quickly lost control of the national government, and in 1925 a group of low-ranking military officers instituted what is known as the Julian Revolution. The "revolution" ushered in a new period—covered in subsequent parts of *The Ecuador Reader*—characterized by two important features. First, from the end of Liberal rule in 1925 until the beginning of the banana boom in 1948, no single sector of the elites could maintain control over a central government that changed hands over twenty times. Second, from this moment on, popular classes had to be taken into account by those who ruled. The cacao boom had generated enough wealth and expanded the government sufficiently to create a growing middle class of professionals, bureaucrats, and intellectuals, as well as a small urban proletariat and an increasingly organized class of rural workers and peasants. Politics, once defined by the odd uprising or the palace intrigue of elites, took a definitively popular turn.

Note

1. Mark J. Van Aken, *King of the Night: Juan José Flores and Ecuador, 1824–1864* (Berkeley: University of California Press, 1989).

The Construction of a Ventriloquist's Image: Liberal Discourse and the "Miserable Indian Race" in the Late Nineteenth Century

Andrés Guerrero

Translated by Tristan Platt

Once Ecuador became an independent nation in 1830, elites faced a number of problems, but perhaps none more vexing than how to control the indigenous population. Prior to independence, the colonial state effectively administered indigenous communities through a system of tribute. With independence, a less centralized system emerged which effectively rendered the indigenous population invisible. Andrés Guerrero explores how this happened, paying particular attention to the images and discourses used by elites to represent and define indigenous peoples in certain ways—and how those efforts to dominate became a channel for Indian resistance.

In the image, the body loses its corporeal reality; in the rite, the non-corporeal becomes flesh.—*Octavio Paz (1969:120)*

At dawn on Wednesday July 6th 1990 the country was informed by radio and television that a great Indian uprising was blocking the roads in the Andean region, above all in the center and the North. In the provinces, various capitals were besieged by a population estimated at hundreds of thousands, women and men of all ages. That day, and the following, the urban markets remained empty. By force, but without violence, the Indian organizations took control of radio transmitters in the cities, so as to publicize their programs. They further requisitioned supplies and distributed them. Finally, they called the provincial authorities to the market places to listen to their demands: directly and in person.

That morning, confronted with a political situation of such magnitude, which would paralyze the country for several weeks, the President had to intervene. In a speech charged with indignation, Dr. Rodrigo Borja Cevallos gave his version of the facts by putting forward an image of the Indian:

> Agitators without patriotism or national feeling are trying to split the coun-
> try, *making malicious use* of the highland Indians. . . . I want to say to the
> peasants of my Fatherland, . . . that in five hundred years no government,
> whether colonial or Republican, has done more to solve the problems of
> the Indian communities than my government, seeking a solution to their
> problems and obliging everyone *to treat them as human beings*, as Ecuador-
> eans with the same rights and duties. (emphasis added)

In these words we can perceive a mental schema rehearsing the topics of an image preserved for over a century in the unchanging recesses of the white-mestizo politicians' historical memory. It consists of images inherited by children from their parents, by grandchildren from their grandparents, persisting through generations of families made up of politicians, senators, deputies, and ministers, until at last there emerges a President. Thus the great-grandfather of Dr. Rodrigo Borja Cevallos had already sketched a similar image of the Indian at a congress toward the end of the last century:

> My father[1] was indignant with the *false redeemers* of the Indian race, and
> exclaimed in one of the Congresses which he attended as Senator: "these
> Reforms are being carried out, not from love of the Indians but from ha-
> tred of the whites." And Dr. Borja (the President's great-grandfather), as
> is well known, was distinguished by his feelings of piety and compassion
> toward the Indian race. . . . And there have been, and are, other landown-
> ers like Dr. Borja, generally those who belong to the better social classes,
> who have treated the *Indian as a human being*. (emphasis added)

This discourse projects an image with two sides. On one side, the Indi-
ans appear as simple-minded beings, ingenuous creatures who have not yet reached adulthood, since they remain the object of "malicious" strategies and manipulations. On the other side, the image is that of the dominant classes, with a strategy of condescension: the magnanimity—noblesse oblige—of "treating the Indians as human beings."

Sustained by this image, both commonplaces exceed the limits of a merely individual ethic and mental perception; they describe a political imaginary frontier which differentiates the progressive landowners blessed with "piety and compassion," the "true redeemers," on the one hand, and those who are "soulless and compassionless," the reactionary "false redeemers of the Indian race," on the other. Pronounced in a congress—that is, in a site saturated with political resonances—such phrases suggest that, by the end of the nineteenth century, certain mental perceptions had managed to delimit—as political discourse—a new polygon of forces, or field of play for white-mestizo politicians. A symbolic division, the shadow of the image of the Indian, had separated the politicians in the last decades of the last century, marking out their ideological positions and their legitimate and legitimizing discourses. These matrices of thought indicated divisory thresholds between those who recognized them-selves—and were recognized by others—as Conservatives and Liberals; they established a crossing-point within the political coordinates.

How was this image of the Indian formed—the image manipulated by President R. Borja Cevallos to explain the uprising that had paralyzed the country? Or rather, what was the political game which allowed its emer-gence? And what was its function in the strategies of power? In the following pages I attempt to explain some of the historic processes and contexts which led to the formation of one image of the Indian (the political one) at the end of the nineteenth century, and its subsequent officialization by the State in the Liberal Revolution of 1895. Amidst forgetting, revivals and changes, certain aspects of this imaginary construction persisted till the present. Moreover, they managed to spread (and hence legitimize themselves) as a Liberal inheri-tance in socialist and communist political and literary circles during the first three decades of this century. The same discourse flowered on several hori-zons, in different moments and places of political conflict: it was a spearhead forged in the struggle against the Conservatives and the Church, condensed in confused discourses concerning the Indian, at once juridical, racist, and political.

To understand these processes I consider unavoidable a historical peri-odization and a theoretical detour which concern the conditions under which an image is formed. There are two periods: during the first stage (1830–57) the new Republican State administered the Indian population directly as a public entity, following—with minor variants—the model of its colonial predecessor. Then, in a second stage, once the condition of tributaries was eliminated in the mid-nineteenth century and the status of citizen extended in principle to all Ecuadoreans (with restrictions as regards the female gen-der, age-groups, wealth, and work-status) the relation of the State with the Indians changed.[2] By an act of omission rather than a policy of State, the administration of this population was delegated surreptitiously (avoiding all legal specification) to a varied, heterogeneous, and private organism: it was handed over to local, or rather regional, powers. Thus, during this second stage which lasted—in a state of deep disintegration—till the middle of the twentieth century, ethnic administration becomes a private rather than a public phenomenon: it corresponds to the configurations of power, at the level of a valley or a region, formed by the haciendas and the parish church, the municipal councils and the functionaries of State, the ethnic mediators and the personal links—economic and ritual—between "town whites" and Indian commoners (*comuneros*).

In the second half of the nineteenth century, with citizenship extended—potentially—toward the population previously recognized as Indian "tributaries," there emerged a strange and contradictory phenomenon. The Ecuadorean State hid the existence of an ethnic majority of non-Spanish speech. However, rather than simply ignoring this majority, what it did was remove from its codes and organizing principles the presence of populations marked by ethnic difference. The old "tributaries," who did not fit into the category of white-mestizo citizenship, were shifted into an implicit category: they were transformed into ethnic subjects of the Republican State; they remained enclosed in a silent category, never legislated upon, in the depths of the citizen body.

Now, this process of change in the form of ethnic administration from public to private, and its effect of concealment upon the Indians, should be associated, from a theoretical point of view, with the conditions of formation of an image considered as a mental representation. Indeed, "the image is an act which indicates, in its corporeality, an absent or nonexistent object, by means of a physical or psychic content which is only delivered, in fact, as the analogical representation of the object indicated." In other words, the image implies an omission, an *intuitive-absent* object (emphasis in original). The act of State alchemy which abolished the ethnic condition—that is to say, the omission of the Indian population beneath the cloak of citizenship—together with its relegation to the status of subjects, was undoubtedly the condition of possibility (in a transformation of the discourse-image concerning the Indian) for one of the political forces in conflict (Liberalism) to sculpt a figuration of the Indian to the measure of its interests: an effigy could then be designed, used as a strategy of power, and imposed like a threat which, at the dawn of the twentieth century, would defy the Conservatives and the Church.

The Political Concealment of the Indian (1857–95)

In 1857 the status of tributary was abolished and the apparatus of ethnic classifications eliminated by the State. A long historical period that had begun in the sixteenth century was over. The status of tributary originally referred to a condition linked to Spanish royal sovereignty, which included the "natives" of America as colonial subjects, members of the Crown on a lower level. For the State and in society their juridical, political, and social condition was marked by the obligation to pay an annual head tax: the Indian tribute. As we have seen, shortly after its inauguration the Republican State restored the category, an act which was denounced by many politicians of the period as incompatible with the notions of equality, citizenship, and the principle of popular sovereignty, the three cornerstones of the new State. But finally, with the abolition of tributary status there only remained a single modern category to express the relationship between national population and public powers: that of citizenship.

However, the de facto reality, both public and private, continued to be organized by means of ethnic segregation. Since they could not speak Spanish, much less read and write it, the population previously identified as indigenes remained, by definition, on the margins of full citizenship.[3] For the citizenry of the nineteenth century—that is, adult, male, literate, and wealthy white-mestizos—the unthought was practically unthinkable, namely, that the Indians, people whom they were accustomed to treat as their inferiors at home, on the land, in the streets and markets, could possibly be free and equal Ecuadorian citizens.

In State registers the decree of 1857 had an effect of political magic, for it simply obliterated the Indian population from the documents. They disappeared from all the central registers of the State: from the laws, population censuses, State budgets, reports of ministers and governors, and from the correspondence between the higher authorities. The men and women previously classified as indigenes belong to an implicit status which places them in an ambiguous and, above all, undefined condition in the symbolic corpus (the juridico-political) and State practices of identification. They are Indian subjects of the Republican State and, therefore, a population abandoned to its customary devices in the private sphere, with its institutions, practices, and norms. The notion involves an imprecise collection of social groups, ethnic authorities, and communal institutions which have no legal existence, but are governed by means of a quasi-legislation of rulings, circulars and reports, written norms, and verbal orders. They are people subject to a private and everyday administrative power which emerges with the disappearance of the tribute and the ensuing withdrawal of the central State from Indian administration. The State tacitly delegates its sovereignty to local forms of ethnic domination. Perhaps the basic characteristic of this private ethnic administration consists in the fact that conflicts of power occur in regional backstages, dispersed and segmented, ruled by their own gestural and oral codes which exclude all written normativity with its anonymous and general application.

With the concealment of the Indians, in this second half of the nineteenth century, there emerge the only two efforts—so far as I am aware—to construct a political image of the Indian. Early in 1870 the historian Pedro Fermín Cevallos,[4] a man of law and a politician with a long trajectory, dedicated the final volume of his *Summary of the History of Ecuador*—a work declared an "official text" in 1871—to the customs and—briefly—the composition of the

Ecuadorian population, with a table of ethnic, racial, and psychological classifications. A decade later, just as the Liberal Revolution was breaking out,
the writer and politician Abelardo Moncayo analyzed the work conditions
in the haciendas in a little book called *El concertaje de indios*, which describes
the labors, life, and—above all—the character of the Indians. Both writers,
each in his own way and from different party positions, consolidate the liberal
tendency of thought in the second half of the century: they maintain a critical
position toward the society and State of their day, and work for its transformation. Both were also celebrated public figures and reached high positions
in the State. I concentrate on Cevallos and Moncayo, not only because their
discourses converge and mesh together, but because they crystallize a long-
lasting vision of the Indian, which would later became official.

The Political Discourse concerning Concierto Indians

The idea of associating the general description of the Indian race in society
with the rejection of the work conditions in the hacienda is not exclusive
to Abelardo Moncayo. Another intellectual, Nicolás Martínez, published in
1887 various articles in the newspapers and unreservedly denounced the labor
laws of *concertaje* [concertaje and concierto are synonyms that refer to a labor system that tied Indians to a hacienda through indebtedness] which have
established, he explained, "a slavery harder . . . than that demanded of the
blacks." "The Indians are the true pariahs of Ecuador; they have no political
rights and the Constitution and the laws have not been written for them. . . .
With such elements, can there be a true Republic in Ecuador?"

His articles introduce themes that will become commonplaces amongst
those who rejected concertaje until its abolition in 1918. For example: the sale
of peons together with their farms; the impossibility of paying the debt and
leaving the haciendas, the town prison, the "imaginary debt" (words which
A. Moncayo will repeat without citing the source).

The exposition of Martínez is of interest here, not only because it works
against the discursive constructions of those years concerning the Indian, but
because the contrast reveals meanings concerning the conditions of production of a political image. How does he proceed to put together his exposition?
In spare prose he tells of situations of oppression. He emphasizes lived experiences or experiences known by him at first hand: that a certain *concierto* came
to him and told him . . . , that such or such a landowner was taken to court
and the judge . . . , that a few days ago an *hacendado* . . . , that the laws. . . . By
this I mean to indicate that, as far as content and form are concerned, his denunciation does not wallow in the topic of the feelings, the character, or the
morality of the Indian. He does not evaluate his degree of awareness, under-

standing, or intelligence; nor does he conclude that subjection has submerged him in a state of near animality. Although he declares himself by principle and conviction a "defender of the most unhappy class in our society," Martínez does not aim consciously or unconsciously to produce and impress an image on public opinion. He indicates and warns, describes and explains, but he does not compose a phantasmagoria of the Indian which might serve as the rallying point for a party. Nor, of course, did he perform as an outstanding ideologue in the ranks of Liberalism, or occupy high posts in government.

Abelardo Moncayo, on the other hand, who reached among other posts that of General E. Alfaro's Minister of the Interior (1898), did assume the task of linking Indian oppression and the contemporary political struggle to create a political image. His pamphlet (*The Concertaje of the Indians*) seeks an explicit objective; he tries to draw attention to the evils which afflict the Indian in terms appropriate to the concierto of the hacienda, in order thus to identify the causal agents and propose a programme and a task: "the overwhelming accusation that can be leveled against Conservatism is the present state of the Indian."

Who are the accused? From the second page Moncayo focuses his lens on a whole spectrum of social agents, from the hacendado and parish priest, to the police, passing through the military and the State authorities in the towns. What are the accusations? Nothing less than that they produce the Indian: "The condensation of all possible shadows and miseries, a walking degradation, ignorance . . . servility . . . behold the Indian, behold the masterpiece of the Christian, eternal domination of Conservatism!" What is the history of this situation? "Four centuries of near national existence (*sic*) . . . and the injustices of the Conquistador still in full bloom!" And the social consequences for the whole nation? They contaminate the "character and spirit" of the Ecuadoreans; a "cancer" (*sic*) is growing: servility is the matrix of a collective psychology tinged with passivity, the evil which afflicts the Indians. And the remedy or task? "Suppress the atrocities of concertaje, suppress the preponderance of the priesthood in our society, and the Republic will cease to be an absurdity here."

In this x-ray of his social situation, the silhouette of the Indian appears in negative. The discursive strategy adopted follows a logic based on the denunciation of the oppression of the concierto, and therefore of the hacienda, and also of the Church as landholder and educator. The arrogance of the dominator and the obsequiousness of the dominated: "servility" from both perspectives produces a historic process of cultural, mental, and physical degeneration, which is the cause of the brutishness of the Indian population. However, Cevallos' racist conception is split with Moncayo, who even seems anxious to avoid the use of the notion of race. In some paragraphs he seems to take his inspiration from Montalvo's thought: freedom is a factor which ennobles people, enlivens the intelligence, and molds a "lofty" character (for Moncayo, an antonym of the concierto Indian's servile and passive character) which is impelled toward progress. A proof: it is enough to confront the concierto with the free Indian in mentality, physiognomy, and bearing. Both share misfortune and oppression. The free Indian can also be perceived as suspicious, timid, and distrustful, qualities which our author declares to be "instinctive, inbred." But he sees differences, for "in the face of the free Indian what he feels is almost evident, you divine in him a life of his own, you feel the presence of a soul, if only in embryo. The mere idea of freedom has been enough for a little of our halo, dignity, to appear on his forehead . . . Intelligence already sparkles, you notice in him a will and therefore an awareness of his own being." Further on, when he specifies a program of social reforms, Moncayo will explain what he understands by Indian freedom.

In the ten sections dedicated to him, the denunciation of concertaje touches aspects already dealt with by Cevallos and Martínez, such as the initial, unpayable debt, the distribution of kind (*socorros*) which inflate that debt, the hard labor to which they are subjected. Moncayo's originality lies more in the form than in the content. The pamphlet seeks to produce rhetorical effects, a symbolic incitement to emotion: it tries to move the reading public. The text appears destined to oratorical delivery before a heated party assembly. The linking of the paragraphs does not follow strictly the order and coherence required by a sociological or historical exposition; the theme of each section seems deliberately diffuse. It obeys a different logic that advances by leaps, by association, and the oratorical exaltation of one phrase summons up others, combined and put together with words that are related in sound, content, and emotive resonance. The composition, syntax, words, punctuation, the flow of the phrase, the reiteration of themes: the whole texture of the writing communicates a meaning in itself. No question but that through the form the author indicates that we are hearing a political communication which seeks to echo in the senses and secure the acquiescence—emotive rather than rational— of readers in his proposals. The text carries the impress of the purpose and the hand that writes it.

The Protector-State and the Ventriloquist's Representation

Undoubtedly, there were several arenas where images and discourse emerged at the end of the century and in the heat of the conflict between Liberals and Conservatives, such as, for example, public services, the control and registration of births, marriages and deaths, the administration of cemeteries, civil marriage and divorce, or the properties of the "dead hands." However, among all these figurations, the effigy of the Indian occupied a dominant position. It sustained a power-strategy that implied a redefinition of State functions in Ecuadorian society, in particular as regards the Indian population.

With the Revolution, this imaginary sleight-of-hand obtained pragmatic results. Public authorities reassumed the task of protecting the Indians, not, as in the first half of the century, in order to protect Indian tributaries but rather to convert them into citizens. Besides, with the discourse of protection the Liberals also responded to a need engendered by the very functioning of a Republican State: it was necessary to establish a link with that part of the population which did not fit into the category of "citizen"; that is to say, the State needed a code and a channel of communication that would connect Indian subjects with the central public powers and establish a form of political representation, even if only de facto.

Thus it was that, still beneath the smell of gunpowder left by the Revolution, the provisional government in Guayaquil emitted a decree that suppresses "subsidiary labor," an ancient labor obligation (several days per year) on the public roads which, obviously, fell above all on the community Indians. Of interest here are the introductory clauses, which explain the protective mission entrusted to the State:

1895
Considering:

1) that the unfortunate condition of the Indian race must be relieved by the public authorities;
2) that the Liberal government inaugurated in the country by Sr. General don Eloy Alfaro, Supreme Chief of the Republic, is duty-bound to protect the descendants of the first inhabitants of Ecuadorian territory; and
3) that in the campaign for national honor the Indians have been of great assistance to the Liberating Army, demonstrating thereby that they are ready to adopt the practices of modern civilization.

A few years later the protective and civilizing role toward the Indians became an organic obligation of the State, fixed in various articles of the two Liberal constitutions dictated in 1897 and 1906.[5] A review of the parliamentary debate on these articles tells us nothing new. The arguments presented by the constituents recover and reiterate unchanged a vision of the Indian which by then Liberal ideology had fully absorbed. However, it is interesting to pause over the debate because it offers one new detail concerning the act itself of speaking the discourse concerning the Indian, and in the way it is spoken. The words shift from ideology to denunciation in a linguistic code adapted to the redefinition that the Revolution had imposed on the functions of the State.

This was noted by the Vice-President of the National Convention of 1896 in the preamble to the opening of the debate: "since the political transformation is liberal," it is necessary that the Constitution should include the words: "the protection which is imperiously required for its improvement by the most defenseless race of our species." For his part José Peralta, perhaps the most lucid Liberal theorist and, in any case, another historian who became a minister, justified the protective function with a baroque litany that combined again well-worn topics about the image of the Indian. His intervention signifies, by the place, the tone, and the words employed, that we are present at a process of ritualization. The ceremony as such is what matters in this parliamentary session, as a gestural whole. By reciting the list of evils which afflict the Indian and enumerating the causal agents in the sacramental site of representation, in the laboratory of Republican political alchemy, where reality is forged with invocations which, when converted into Law, acquire performative power, José Peralta and the other parliamentarians fulfill a ritual that institutionalizes the Liberal image of the Indian, and in doing so they install the protective function of the State. The liberators achieve, then, the culminating moment of their political recognition and legitimacy. They exhibit their power to invent reality and they fulfill the illusion of every politician: they remodel the State in their own semblance and image with a profile taken from the Liberators, just as they appeared reflected (it will be remembered) in the third level of the Indian considered as symbolic analogy and reflexive structure. The parliamentary debate on the articles of the Constitution must be read in this context of ritual discourse:

> Debate in the National Convention (1896) on an article of protection of the Indian race in the Constitution of the Republic:
>
> Sr. José Peralta:[6]
>
> . . . because I am persuaded that one of the most efficient means of regenerating the Republic is the emancipation of the Indian race; that unhappy race, once prosperous and today maltreated, insulted, degraded, placed on a lower level than pariahs and helots. Yes, gentlemen, the grimmest slavery in which we keep the Indian in our Republic is an affront to civilization . . . For myself, I confess it, the clamor of my conscience humiliates me, even though I have never ceased to cry out for the freedom of the Indian in the press and the courts! There goes the pariah; see him! : covered with rags, led by hunger, with his degradation weighing on his shoulders like a sepulchral slab . . . There is the Ecuadorian pariah—see him, fathers of the Fatherland!

The mental figurations in 1896 do not emerge as in 1855 in discourses which at the end of the day are ingenuous, nor are they exercises in the ephemeral transposition, in an improvised rhetoric, of the material and symbolic interests of the participants. They belong to a different type of discourse, to a reworked ideological construction which demarcates a symbolic field. The difference is qualitative, and does not depend only on the transformation of unconscious mental schemata into conscious ones, or on the passage from gesture to words, nor even on the transmutation of volatile oral expressions to the permanence of writing. In the debate the important thing was to institute Liberalism as a form of the State. This is the reason why the triumphant power legitimizes and legalizes its political victory by inscribing it in the Constitutions. It expropriates, displaces and subordinates the Church, the central bulwark of Conservative power, an institution homologous with, but opposed to the State. It changed the function of the images in play, and even the rules of the game: it composed a complete redefinition of the political field.

The second pragmatic effect of this discourse on the "poor oppressed race" (the image of the Indian) was its definition and utilization. The language of protection was not circumscribed to the walls of offices and other central sites of public power. The image trembles with a halo of enlightenment. It indicates the type of meanings that can be transmitted, and surrounds the Indian with a semantic field; that is, it opens a specific channel of communication from the State to the Indian population, a conduit which will be exploited for multiple maneuvers of ethnic domination and resistance. Indeed, the construction of the image and its incorporation into the State, as one in need of protection, initiated a new method of representation: it established a political ventriloquy. Through the ethnic mediators, both private and public, of the progressive block (from the political lieutenant to the petty lawyer, passing through compadres in the town or capital), a set of white-mestizo social agents talk and write in the name of the Indian in terms of his oppression, degradation, and civilization. There seems to come a voice from the Indian subject.

The population excluded (de facto) from citizen rights takes advantage of the Liberal Revolution and presents "petitions" to the higher authorities. It makes use of, and recuperates the new channel of communication to make itself understood by the newly appointed authorities, who are sensitized to its sad destiny. What do they say? How do they say it? Who says it? I extract a document from the many piled up in the series "Correspondence" of the archive of the Minister of the Interior corresponding to the second government of General E. Alfaro. Seventeen commoners from Cotacachi canton beg the "Citizen President" to "suppress quickly, energetically and effectively the institution of the Indian mayor (*alcalde de indios*)." They present three accusations: the mayors are abusive, they are manipulated by the local authorities and whites of the town, and finally, they claim to recruit workers for opening a supposed road to the coast. The charges themselves need not detain us here, still less the counterattack presented by the political chief (*jefe político*) of the Canton, but rather the form of the document's production and transmission. As for the text, it takes its inspiration explicitly from A. Moncayo's pamphlet *El concertaje*, whose author was at that moment Minister of the Interior, and its author employs an obvious strategy since he claims to make his text more effective by capitalizing on available forms of legitimacy:

> Citizen President . . . it would be enough for us to have received the news of the specific purpose of your administrative programme, that of looking after the most disinherited race in America . . . If we tell you that Indians are speaking to you, your heart will already be moved . . . (. . .) There you have before all the distinguished writer who has pleaded our case so well in his articles on Concertaje. . . .

> The Indian mayor is the immediate agent of all legal, civil ecclesiastic and military authorities . . . (. . .) Add to this the Indian's natural submissiveness, never prepared to discuss any obligation . . . , and it is not surprising the omnipotence of a mayor over his peers and all those who receive orders from him, for bread or a blow in the face, which inspire in him equal thanks from the hand of the white. . . .

It is obvious that this petition derives from the expositions elaborated by Liberal ideologues. It raises the flag of the disinherited Indian, submissive and passive, who must be freed; it uncovers the link with the agents responsible for oppression, and uses a symbolic emblem of oppression to refer to local authorities. The words of the document follow the norm of the communicative code which the State demands be evoked to establish a connection with the central instances of power from the ethnic periphery. Yes, "Indians are speaking," but the pen, the ink, the words, and above all the logic are provided by an unknown ethnic mediator who is nevertheless known to all. He is a social agent who serves as intermediary and sets in action the political mechanism of representation which transforms the verbal complaint (in Quichua?) of the Indians into a strategy of sign-words that are intelligible to the Liberal State, an ideologized code. The reply of the political chief of the Canton tells how the document was produced. The petitioners, warns the official, "went to Quito to deliver their contribution (i.e., payment) to *the author of the text* . . . a detail which figures in the declarations of the Indians themselves" (emphasis in original). A clue in the document backs up this assertion. At the foot of the page we read the phrase: "because they do not know how to read or write, and as witness"—and there appears the signature of the representative of the seventeen commoners who "speak," the witness himself a literate and Spanish-speaking citizen. It becomes evident that the words of the document are the work of a ventriloquist, a social intermediary who knows the semantic field that has to be put into the mouth of the Indians, who knows the content, the range, and the tone of what the Liberal State is willing and able to understand. The "ventriloquist" knows the circuits of power in the bureaucracy, and manipulates the "game-meaning" (Bourdieu) of the political field, as much in the regional backstage as in the central arena of power. He does not only translate nor transcribe. The ventriloquist performs a *trans-scriptural act*: he draws a strategy of representation.

Moreover, a decree of 1896 of General E. Alfaro established the rules of ventriloquy in the relations of the Indians with the apparatus of justice. To protect them he declared them Ecuadoreans covered by "the benefit of the protection of poverty," a variant on their old condition of "miserable." The statute made clear that the demands of those illiterate Indians (almost the whole population) should "be signed by their respective attorney or defender, without whom their petitions cannot be admitted" (emphasis added).

Of course, the figuration of the Indian presents the opportunity for various interwoven, even contradictory, maneuvers of power on the part of the ethnic mediators, the politicians, and the Liberal State. This is characteristic of a symbolic artifact. Besides, the Indian subjects of the Nation themselves manage to subvert it, since it offers them a terrain from which they can claim rights and protests, "make themselves heard." The previous document illustrates one case among others that the researcher finds in the circuit of administrative archives that go from the parishes, with their villages and communities, to the Ministries in the capital city. Indian participation in these micro-games of power by means of a ventriloquist, besides the absence thereby implied, endowed with political effectiveness the channel of communication with the Liberal State.

Notes and Abbreviations

For complete references and citations, see the article by the same name in the *Journal of Latin American Studies* 29, no. 3 (October 1997): 555–90.

AB/FL: Archivo y Biblioteca de la Función Legislativa.

ANH/Q: Archivo Nacional de Historia, Quito.

BE/AEP: Biblioteca de Autores Ecuatorianos Aurelio Espinoza Páez.

1. The reference is to Dr. Luis F. Borja, that is, the great-grandfather of President Borja Cevallos, who was one of the founders of Ecuadorean liberalism, a well-known jurist, several times senator, and Minister-Judge of the Supreme Court at the end of the nineteenth century.

2. There was a first attempt at suppressing the condition of "Indian tributaries" in 1821. The tribute was reinstated in 1828 by Bolívar himself. After the formation of the Republic of Ecuador in 1830, it continued until 1857.

3. The Indians continue till 1873 beneath the statute of "protection of poverty," which was an intermediary condition for recognizing citizens incapable of exercising their rights because they were "miserable." Serie Indígenas 1873, ANH/Q.

4. P. F. Cevallos' career is impressive. Between 1843 and 1883 he occupied seven high positions, was Deputy, Minister Judge, and Minister of State.

5. Article 138 of the 1897 Constitution orders: "The public powers owe protection to the Indian race, considering its national improvement." That of 1907 repeats the same text, but adds the detail that the public powers "will take the most effective measures that will lead to prevent the abuses of concertaje." F. Trabuco, *Constituciones de la República*, 317, 345.

6. José Peralta was a conspicuous ideologue of radical Liberalism and author of the Constitution of 1906.

Four Years among the Ecuadorians

Friedrich Hassaurek

A native of Austria, Friedrich Hassaurek participated in the European uprisings of 1848 before coming to the United States, where he settled in Cincinnati and became a journalist. He was also President Abraham Lincoln's minister to Ecuador. Hassaurek's book, Four Years Among the Spanish-Americans, *is based on his experiences in Ecuador, where he traveled widely during his stay. At the time of publication (1868), the book was one of the few, and certainly among the most detailed, English accounts of Ecuador. Most studies had focused on Ecuador's mountains, volcanoes, and jungles. Hassaurek did not ignore the country's natural beauty, but ultimately focused on Ecuadorians— their domestic and political arrangements, their daily difficulties, their cities and villages, and so forth. Today, his work is perhaps most valuable in terms of what it says about how Americans and Europeans understood and saw Latin America and Latin Americans during the nineteenth century.*

Imbabura Province—Last Looks

We stopped at a shed under which the Negroes were engaged at a sugar mill. These mills are set in motion by a large wheel, propelled either by hydraulic or horse power. The workmen employed are all Negroes. The Indians have entirely disappeared from the valley. The Negroes, who have taken their places, are *concertados*, like the Indian farm laborers. They are slaves in fact, although not slaves in name. Their services are secured by a purchase of the debts which they owe. As long as they remain in debt, which state, thanks to the skillful management of their masters, almost always lasts till they discharge the great debt of nature, they must either work or go to prison. Like the Indians, they are ignorant of their legal rights. They are hardly ever able to pay their debts, which, on the contrary, continually increase, as their wages of one-half *real* to one *real* are insufficient to satisfy their wants. When slavery was abolished in Ecuador, the owners of the Negroes in the sugar districts immediately employed them to work for wages, and managing to get them into debt, secured their services as debtors. Thus it may almost be said that they profited, instead of losing, by the abolition of slavery. They pocketed the compensation which the law provided for the slave owners, and at the same time retained their slaves. It is true the blacks do not work so much now as when they were bondmen, nor can their masters beat them as unmercifully as they did before; but, on the other hand, it must be considered that it is much cheaper now to purchase a Negro than it was then. Now, by paying a debt of fifty or seventy dollars which the poor fellow owes to somebody, his services may be secured, while formerly it took, perhaps, ten times that amount to purchase a slave.

Almost all the haciendas in Chota Baja formerly belonged to the Jesuits, until 1767, when they were confiscated and sold by the Spanish government. Sugar and rum are the principal productions of the valley. The rum is filled into hides. Two hides form a *botija*, which contains one hundred and sixty bottles, and just makes up a mule load. The coffee which grows in the valley is excellent, but it is not planted in sufficient quantities.

While I was at Chamanal, the hospitable owner of the hacienda gave me the spectacle of a Negro dance, which is called *bundi*, and is exceedingly interesting. The Negroes of the hacienda, men, women, and children, assembled in the hall, bringing with them two characteristic musical instruments—the *bomba* and the *alfandoque*. The former is intended for a drum. It is a sort of barrel, over which a hide is spanned, and to beat which no drumsticks but the fingers or fists are used to make the singers keep time. The alfandoque is a hollow cane or reed, into which a quantity of buckshot, peas, or pebbles is put, whereupon the openings are closed with cotton or a bundle of rags. By shaking this queer instrument a noise is produced similar to that made in theaters to imitate the sound of falling rain. It is, however, shaken to the time of the songs, and chimes in not at all unpleasantly. But the main part of the orchestra consists of the voices of the women and children, accompanied by the voice of the player of the alfandoque. Clapping their hands continually they sing a great variety of songs, to which the bomba and alfandoque keep time. In musical talent and taste, these Negroes are infinitely superior to the Indians. Their melodies are neither so monotonous nor so lifeless as those of the aborigines. On the contrary, they are varied and fiery and full of exciting vigor. Their dance is not the slow, measured step of the Indians, but is characterized by that wild sweeping and dashing, and the extravagant gesticulation peculiar to the Ethiopian. They dance various dances, some of which are irresistibly comic. In this they are of a higher inventive genius than the white and cholo rabble, who cannot advance beyond the slow and monotonous *alza que te han visto*. There was one figure which was particularly funny. It was a pantomimic representation of *toros* (bullfights). The step was that of the *alza que te han visto*, although much quicker. The woman dancing attacks her male partner, whom she tries to butt, as if she were a bull. He, without falling out of time or losing the step, dodges her. This is continued for several minutes, when the parts are changed and the man attacks the woman, who in her turn dodges him. Woe to the partner who is not quick enough to avoid the butt; its force may fell him to the ground. The dance is generally accompanied by the vehement and comic gestures peculiar to the Negro race. The partners keep on dancing without interruption, one pair at a time, until somebody else steps in to relieve them; but the change of performers does not interrupt the performance for a single moment, nor is there an intermission of the song. Even the fellow who beats the bomba never stops. When he is treated to a cup of rum, some one of the company presents it to his lips, and he swallows it while his hands continue to beat the drum. Perspiration pours down his face, but he has no time to wipe it up. With the agility of a monkey, he keeps on beating his bomba as long as there is a pair not too exhausted to keep up the dance. The male partner in a dance must keep on as long as the lady does, or until somebody steps in to relieve him. At Esmeraldas and other places on the coast, it would be considered an insult to withdraw from the dance without being relieved. The friends of the lady thus injured would be but too apt to resent the offense on the spot. Rum, as a matter of course, is not spared on such occasions, and the excitement and enthusiasm increase from hour to hour. The din caused by the shrill voices of the women and children, the drumming, and clapping of hands, and the noise of the alfandoque, together with the occasional exclamations of the dancers and bystanders, completely drowned the words of their song. I was unable to make out any of the verses, but my companions told me that the songs were composed by the Negroes themselves, and in their own dialect. Like the Negroes of the United States, the Negroes of Spanish America have a dialect and pronunciation of their own. The same guttural voices, and almost unintelligible pronunciation, the same queer gesticulation and shaking of the body, the same shrewd simplicity and good humor, the same love of fun and merrymaking that characterize the Negro in the rice swamps and cotton fields of Georgia and South Carolina, distinguish his race on the banks of the Chota, at Guajara, and La Concepción.

The wages paid to workmen in *trapiches* (sugar establishments), are one *real* a day; but the laborers are not entitled to the suit of clothes which is given to Indian farm laborers once a year. In other respects their situation and treatment are the same.

Insects such as beetles, cockroaches, mosquitoes, etc., abound in the valley. Snakes, too, are found, but not many, and it is generally believed that they are not poisonous. Chills and fevers are frequent, although I believe the valley is healthy, and that diseases are contracted only by exposure. The sterility and barrenness of the mountains continue as far as the eye can reach.

It is not until you travel two or three days in the direction of Pailón that the forests commence. In the rear of the mountain range of Chamanal is the Cordillera del Chiltazón, in which mines were formerly worked, of which vestiges are still to be found. But at present, mining seems to be abandoned all over Ecuador. Both capital and energy are wanting to carry it on.

Note

This is an excerpt from Friedrich Hassaurek's, *Four Years among Spanish-Americans* (New York: Hurd and Houghton, 1868). Excerpt is drawn from pages 327–47.

Selection from Juan Montalvo (1832–1889)

Juan Montalvo

Translated by Frank MacDonald Spindler

and Nancy Cook Brooks

Born in Ambato in 1832, Juan Montalvo is one of Latin America's greatest writers, and one of Ecuador's strongest advocates of liberalism during the nineteenth century. He played important roles in bringing down three of Ecuador's most important political figures, including President Gabriel García Moreno. His consistent opposition to dictatorship in any form got him exiled on three separate occasions. He died in Paris in 1889, six years before one of his collaborators, future president Eloy Alfaro, ushered in the Liberal Revolution of 1895. The following selection, published in 1868, articulates the right of freedom of association.

Of the Spirit of Association

Enlightened peoples, whose political institutions do not shelter slavery, are extremely sociable. The ruler who does not fear the assembly of citizens trusts in the law, leans on the benevolence of the people, and, surrounded by friends, walks secure and majestic toward the goal of association. The good ruler has a clear conscience and does not lift his head in fear when he hears that a certain number of people have gathered together. In despotic realms, where tyranny is the method of ruling, this brief notice sounds terrible to the ears of him who rules: a secret society exists. And why secret? It is secret because it could not be open; because the timorous tyrant disperses by force those who assemble, fearing the meeting of wills and abhorring the sonorous voice of free men. For if these seek anonymity, it is his fault. And take heed, for the dagger is often sharpened in darkness. In broad daylight, assassination has never been discussed, nor is there anyone who, having light for an audience, will propose an illicit action. Persecute societies and soon you will have carbonarism (practiced by members of the Carbonari).

Why take from men the right to deal with what is advantageous? If they do not usurp sovereignty; if they respect the laws; if with good intentions and for a good purpose they assemble, leave them alone. And not only leave them alone, but protect them, encourage them. That is good government. However, always to consider wrong communication among the inhabitants of a city and to consider dangerous the sharing of thoughts and purposes are to tend toward tyranny and to be unenlightened. Thereupon the government must have a hundred eyes: a vigilant Argus, it sees all, it inquires into everything secretly, and there for its own advantage; it is notified of everything that is going on in the Republic. It lives in the middle of an acoustic vault; the slightest sounds reach its ears—not all of them like thunder because its eardrum is in perfect health. Its touch is delicate; its hand of the most sensitive feeing. It passes it over the society it rules. On society's forms that hand moves, discovering the rough and the smooth, the sick and the healthy. Good government, wise government, is a wise man; philosophic government is a philosopher; paternal government is a father. In political science there are marvelous secrets, miraculous essences, and magic elixirs that favorably change ever desperate illnesses. Thus one can infer that to govern it is necessary to be governed by a luminous, flexible, and elevated inner agent: that is to say that the soul of the ruler must be found on the top of a mountain. Is it not rational, is it not just that the best should rule? Where the worst are sought out for such a great task as is the governing of peoples let us say that dark clouds rule and amongst them only fearful things can occur, because darkness is the absence of light, which is the source of wisdom.

The government that sees only danger in whatever occurs in the Republic is a Polyphemus, having only one eye: a cruel and villainous giant, he seizes his guests and devours them; a formidable son of the earth, he makes all tremble. But no one lets pass the opportunity to throw a stone at him and, when the moment comes, to deprive him of his sight. In such a manner the bad government is in a continuous anguish. It suspects everything, everything threatens it. It is like that wicked man who lived enclosed in a crystal lamp to protect himself from the light. The tyrant (and) bad government, live enclosed in a small vault. They are like dead men, they have little space, and in that miserable sphere, a terrible drama takes place; the worms actively crawl over their body, biting into the heart. Misgivings, founded or unfounded, anxiety, suspicions, fears, uncertainties, compunctions—are they not hungry insects that gnaw away at the heart? If we fear our brothers because we are in command, it would be wiser to descend to their level and to walk in peace: it is truly a terrible thing to have been raised up to do good and to become a perpetrator of injustice! Oppression is taken for politics in certain unenlightened nations and the president, very convinced that he is not a tyrant, trifles with the laws with the greatest innocence; he annuls the social contract in a thousand ways. He controls his associates and thinks that he is governing, for ignorance is the art of governing in some unfortunate nations. Let them kill, exile, impose taxes (for such outrages they have a pretext); but let them respect the right to write, the faculty to speak, and the citizens' need to assemble. For God's sake, let the governors respect these rights!

What is that multitude over there which begins to appear, shouting in the shadow of a hundred unfurled banners? Order reigns in it, it approaches inoffensively, and in good order it enters that grandiose garden with firm step. It is a free people which gathers to proclaim a right, to cry out against an abuse, to discuss a legislative plan. Look at that person over there who is raised aloft on the shoulders of the people! A great silence falls on the crowd; they all wait, all listen: he is an orator, a tribune who is going to speak and in eloquent discourse move a thousand hearts. He spoke: liberty in the form of an angel comes from his lips and sears above the people, fluttering in the manner of a celestial emissary much as flames issued from the mouths of some ancient prophets. The crowd applauds, a thousand votes authorize the law that is going to be proposed to the Parliament, and, satisfied with themselves and with their sovereign, the people scatter through the innumerable streets of the immense city. The monarch meanwhile had remained calmly in her palace; the popular outcry did not upset her, nor did the police of the kingdom lend a suspicious ear. Each one was within his rights; each one discharged his duty. In free England the people and the government are brothers: neither one of the two distrusts nor is wary of the other. The people assemble, the government does not pay attention; the people shout, the government hears but pays no heed. At times the people become excited, they raise a sullen appearance, they raise their voice suddenly. It is allowable, being an effervescence which will subside of its own accord; neither are active efforts necessary to quench that frothy bellicosity. The Queen does not interrupt her speech, the Ministers do not move from their chairs, the Lord Mayor carries out his normal duties, and the people are filling the metropolis of the empire with noise. A legal outcry, a golden clamor, the Sound of a free and enlightened people.

It would not occur spontaneously to anyone to diminish the right to assemble in the United States: Mr. Johnson could shoot Jefferson Davis in the square in Richmond; but woe to Mr. Johnson should he try to restrict the societies of the Americans. Gatherings are a law of nature: free peoples are very prone to assemble; the members of a family are gathered together; those citizens of the State gather together in societies; states gather in confederations. The enlightened are very prone to gatherings: the wise and the patriots assemble; the wise to propagate learning, the patriots to nurture and disseminate love of country. The ignorant assemble to study; beneficent men to practice charity—everything is done in assemblies. There are historical, philosophical, and literary societies. There are agricultural societies, welfare societies, and societies of noble games. Even here is heard the clamor of the American citizens who repair to a meeting place to find out carefully about their rights: freedom is their field, freedom is their guide, and freedom their object. The sovereignty of the people takes concrete forms in those grandiose meetings in which the silent speak through the mouth of the tribune, in which the humble man rises up and touches with his hand the fruit of the Republic, forbidden in other parts. Those popular commotions are very peaceful; the government is at ease with them. Some are factious, others authorized. All under the shadow of the law advance with enormous strides toward their aggrandizement. What a people! There, indeed, liberty dwells in all houses; it walks along the streets; it travels through all the roads. This is not a corrupt nor perverse liberty, but an honest and well-intentioned liberty, a holy liberty. Where liberty and wisdom go hand in hand, man is not inferior to an angel.

In division the seneschal has a powerful element of tyranny. When he sees men separated and ignorant he says to himself, "These men I can easily enchain; if they do not join forces, each one of them is inferior to me. I can rule them in my own way. Stupid is he who being able to have slaves contents himself with brothers. No one lives grandly if he does not have subordinates who offer him veneration." And with the speech converted into deed, he is master of the people. These people who did not understand one another as men now groan in the chain gang like brutes.

In less-experienced and less-advanced nations, men are indifferent to societies. They assemble, of course, but for a petty purpose. I often *hear—Dance Society, Recreation Society, Society of* . . . Ah! How can gambling be mentioned here? If those dancing citizens had sheltered in their breasts the flame of freedom, they would not have been servants for so many years of every miserable tyrant. Well-dressed, perfumed lackeys, they follow along behind their master through those dark bays and bends of the river which tyranny is wont to know. They are Apollos without divinity, painted fetishes which the savage makes dance with his wand. If he is not pleased with them he shaves their heads with blows or he whips them mercilessly. Those who are content to dance while the despot breathes easy do not have a fatherland, nor are they worthy to have it. Leaves tossed by the south wind dance in the air without aim or balance. When they fall there is no animal that does not trample them. I should like to ask those showy youths: if amid their absurd rejoicing, their hearts are not moved by the cadenced blows of the fatherland; if in their breasts does not swing that resplendent star which lights and vivifies the free man; if they do not experience the delicious emotions that learning causes in the breasts of her sons. The Negro is by his very nature mischievous, happy, and very given to clamor; the Negro dances, sings, and moves actively at every opportunity; the Negro lives for the moment; he is content with current pleasures. The Negro is a slave! What does this matter since he dances?

Young men, you who focus your five senses on trifles, lift up your eyes and look, for through the firmament a dazzling globe passes over. It is the sun, my friends. Do you realize it? Of a student we may make a wise man; of an artist, a good citizen; of a soldier, a hero. Of a dandy, of an affected coxcomb, nothing can be made but a rag, unless a tenth of them are culled for executioners. The youth are the hope of the fatherland and among those nations of noble customs and advanced thinking the young are the principal part of the nation. That is why virtuous Sparta, conquered by her enemy, abode by an agreement to give as hostages fifty mature man and not ten adolescents. Uncorrupted youth is an element of wisdom, nobility, and greatness. The youth are the future and in the future we have the right to look forward to happiness. When we sigh under the yoke and the oppressed breast expands in a moment of inspiration, we look to the future and an indescribable alleviation lightens our hearts. The young are the future; the future walks full of hope; hope is a happiness. Does good by chance consist of physical satisfaction? You all already realize that in the material substance we are animals and that the spirit is our noble part. Cultivate it and you will be worthy of your Creator. The spirit of man polished in that sublime apparatus of study, tempered in the forge of love, and measured by philosophy is the great work of the universe, and the Almighty smiles benignly when He contemplates such a perfect thing. Through contemplation we raise ourselves to our origin; sparks loosed from the great globe of eternal light, we return there, and we are like seraphim. Through study we cross rapidly the immensity of the ages and, recently arrived at respectability, we now can contemplate the events of thousands of years. Through study we become acquainted with the great man, honor of the human race, and glory of all time. Through study we are sane, learned, and experienced. Having before our eyes examples of virtue and greatness, we ourselves are in a position to be great and virtuous. Ignorant liberty is an inferior divinity; it is a hybrid between divine and human; it inspires scant veneration. Enlightened liberty, wise liberty, is the pure; the chaste: the great divinity. Let us adore her. And in order to adore her, let us assemble. The adoration of an entire nation more readily reaches God.

Railway and Nation in Liberal Ecuador

A. Kim Clark

During the late 1800s and early 1900s, the railroad came to symbolize modernity and progress throughout Latin America. As a result, when the modernizing Liberal elite based in Ecuador's coast finally took power in 1895, one of its principal projects was the construction of a railroad between the coastal port of Guayaquil and the highland capital of Quito. The anthropologist Kim Clark suggests that the national debates surrounding the railroad provide a particularly interesting window for understanding Ecuador at this crucial moment, including the regional conflicts between elites, the role of the church in society, and the place of indigenous people in a "modern" nation.

In 1908 the Guayaquil-Quito Railway was inaugurated in Quito, linking by rail four of Ecuador's five largest cities (Guayaquil, Riobamba, Ambato, and Quito; Cuenca was excluded). Ecuador's principal railway thus provided an unusual degree of national integration, compared to many other Latin American railways, since it was built to link up important population centers rather than to move export products from their zones of origin to a port. By some measures, the railway project could be seen as a failure: for instance, the railway only generated a profit for a few short years, and indeed, in 1925 the U.S. company that owned the line decided to sell its majority shares to the Ecuadorian government rather than undertake the expense of repairing the rail line when it was heavily damaged in landslides and flooding. However, the railway did inaugurate profound changes in Ecuador, as it was instrumental in facilitating labor migrations and generating an internal market in agricultural products. It was also the cornerstone of a broad-ranging project of national reform in the liberal period, that was capable of mobilizing a certain degree of consensus among many social groups about projects of national modernization. The railway project was immersed in and illuminates social relations in Ecuador at the end of the nineteenth century, and illustrates how some of these social relations were transformed in the first decades of the twentieth century.

In Ecuador in the late nineteenth century there were two strong, regionally based dominant classes: one in the highlands, associated with *haciendas* (large estates) producing for local markets, and the other on the coast, producing cocoa for the world market on plantations. The coastal elite tended to be liberal, while the highland elite tended to be conservative. Throughout the nineteenth century political power in Ecuador had been concentrated in the highlands, in the hands of large landowners closely linked to the Catholic Church. In 1895, coastal liberals, whose economic power had been growing for some time, based on the expansion of coastal cocoa exports and the declining importance of highland textile production in the late colonial period and the nineteenth century, finally seized political power in the Liberal Revolution. In some sense, different political ideologies were "naturally" rooted in the distinct economic and social terrain of the coast and the highlands. Liberal coastal elites were involved in the import-export trade and production for the world market; thus they sought fewer barriers to trade. In addition, the coast was much less influenced by the conservative ideology of the Catholic Church: not only did the church own few rural properties on the coast (reducing its economic and political power in the region), but the coast had relatively few churches and even fewer convents or monasteries. Anticlericalism on the coast was also due to the increasing proportion of coastal contributions to church revenues during the nineteenth century, through the payment of tithes that amounted to ten percent of gross production, which was seen as reducing the competitiveness of Ecuadorian cocoa in international markets (not to mention, the profits of coastal planters). In contrast, the highlands tended to favor more protectionist policies, given that the textile industry, long the center of the area's economy, was undermined by British imports after Independence. In addition, the Catholic Church was overwhelmingly concentrated in the highlands, where it was one of the largest landowners, where the majority of convents were located, and where members of the clergy were often elected to congress or the senate. The majority of the Ecuadorian population lived in the highlands, a center of dense indigenous population since pre-Columbian times.

While the 1895 Liberal Revolution represented the rise of the coastal elite, as they achieved political power to match their increasing economic dominance, nonetheless this group was unable to impose a project that was exclusively in its own interests during the liberal period. This was due in part to the fact that, while the liberals were able to control elections of the executive (among other things, through well-documented electoral fraud), it proved much more difficult to engineer elections to the legislative branch, where the much more populous and conservative region of the highlands tended to dominate. As a result, an uneasy working relationship developed between the two dominant classes, creating an atmosphere of competition and tension that had implications for the possibilities open to subordinate groups as well.

One of the central projects of the liberal government after 1895 was the construction of a railway between the coastal port of Guayaquil and the highland capital of Quito (the other main project was the separation of church and state). The Guayaquil-Quito Railway held a key position in public debates about the country's modernization. In discussions about the railway, a widely shared rhetoric emerged centering on the need to transform the nation through movement and connection. While this was developed principally in regard to the importance of a railway to stimulate the economy out of its "stagnation," it was increasingly applied to other issues: the need to eliminate "routine" (such as rote memorization) in education, the need to stimulate immigration and the free flow of modern ideas, the need to break down the rigid hierarchies of society (as supported by the Catholic Church), and the need to teach criminals and vagrants the value of work and school-children the value of exercise. The positive values attached to movement and connection were contrasted with stagnation, routine, and backwardness in public debate about a wide range of social and political issues. The fact that the railway in particular was of interest to groups in the highlands and coast allowed for the constitution of a general consensus about national renewal among elites from these two regions, and among liberals and conservatives, at the turn of the century. Indeed in general, the rhetoric of movement, connection, work, and energy as developed around the railway was ambiguous enough to appeal to a broad audience, various components of which could see in this project something of interest to them.

In general terms, the valorization of movement and connection developed around the railway was perfectly appropriate for a nation whose economic prosperity was linked to the movement of a primary product out to the world market. Nonetheless, this product, cocoa, was not moved by the railway: it was produced on the coast and moved to the port of Guayaquil by a system of steamboats on coastal rivers. While railway construction was one of the definitive liberal projects in Ecuador, coastal liberals in fact had some reservations about it: for instance, they objected to the fact that export earnings generated in their region (which were used to guarantee debt payments associated with the railway) were being used for a project that did not benefit their production directly. On the other hand, the agro-export elite of the coast was closely integrated with import interests, and the construction of a railway between the port and the capital did suggest the possibility of selling imported products in the country's interior, which had been very difficult to reach previously (travel between the regions was suspended for several months each year due to landslides, and at other moments was a treacherous two-week journey by mule, which greatly limited inter-regional trade and transport). While the liberal state carried out a series of controversial policies to separate church and state between 1895 and 1910, the value of movement was also cited by coastal liberals to criticize the Catholic Church's control over education, to promote the free circulation of published works and freedom of expression in general, as well as to condemn the church's resistance to immigration of non-Catholics and its role in reducing the competitive advantage of Ecuadorian cocoa on the international market. However, perhaps most importantly from the perspective of coastal elites, it was hoped that movement and connection would break down the insularity of the highlands and thus stimulate a flow of workers from the highlands toward the coast, and in general the formation of a labor market in order to expand coastal export production. The movement of people, in the form of indigenous workers from the highlands (who made up half or more of the national population in this era), was very much in the interest of coastal plantation owners, since the relatively scarce population of the coastal zone meant that wages there were much higher than in the highlands. The emphasis on movement and connection and the construction of the railway in particular were part of the broader project of coastal elites to transform the highlands to free indigenous labor from the control of highland landowners and to undermine church power, as well as to attain modernity and progress in general.

The movement of indigenous workers toward the coast was not in the interests of the highland landowning elite, whose agricultural estates had always relied on large numbers of Indian laborers, working for very low wages or a subsistence plot and bound to the estates through debt peonage and strong ties of paternalism. However, another kind of movement, also to be stimulated by the railway, was very much in the interests of highland landowners. They were especially attracted to the possibility of forging an internal market, moving highland agricultural and livestock products to the coast by train. With the rise of the coastal cocoa economy and the rapid urban growth of Guayaquil in the late 19th and early 20th centuries, an important market for food staples was created. However, due to the difficulties and high cost of transport from the highlands, the coast was provisioned through imports of food: for instance, it was cheaper to bring grains by steamer from Chile or the United States to Guayaquil than to transport them from the Ecuadorian highlands, only a few hundred kilometers away. Indeed, the lack of easy access to markets discouraged the expansion of agricultural production in the highlands, since it was difficult even to move products between neighboring highland provinces divided by transverse mountain ridges, much less up and over the Andes and down to the tropical coast. A railway would facilitate the transport of highland products, especially bulky, heavy, or perishable goods which were difficult and expensive to move by mule. While some highland landowners were engaged in incipient attempts to expand and modernize their production at the end of the nineteenth century, these efforts were necessarily limited by the lack of efficient transport routes.

Thus in the railway project, and the broader emphasis on movement associated with it, elites from both the coast and highlands could identify some—although not all—of their own interests. However, underlying what appeared to be a shared project were two rather different projects of movement and connection. While the railway would promote both the formation of a labor market and the strengthening of the internal market, at times these two projects were in fact in contradiction with one another. For instance, the intensification of highland agricultural production for the internal market usually depended precisely on increased control over labor, since mechanization was carried out only to a limited extent (for instance, in dairy production). The appearance of consensus that the railway made possible masks the fact that in some ways these two projects could not be pursued simultaneously.

As suggested, for coastal agro-export elites, the emphasis on movement and connection was most closely related to the project of generating labor migrations to the coast, to lower labor costs and extend the agricultural frontier. Coastal agro-export elites looked to the new liberal administration after 1895 to stimulate labor migrations, through a loosening of labor ties in the highlands. Coastal planters saw highland landowners as "artificially" maintaining a monopoly over labor, using various non-economic means to immobilize and control the indigenous population: paternalism, debt peonage, and the legal institutionalization of various "traditional" labor services provided to highland landowners and other local power holders. In so doing, highland elites were seen as sabotaging the prospects for national development through export production. In this context, the liberal state attempted to gain the moral upper hand over highland landowners precisely by insisting on its own role as protector of highland Indians from the abuses of both "traditional" highland landowners and the Catholic Church (which was also a large landowner). The liberal goal of generating a labor market thus involved the development of a rhetoric emphasizing liberty of contracts, and political measures to undermine highland landowners' control over labor (in the form of specific laws and government pronouncements), rather than the use of force to generate flows of labor or to dispossess indigenous peasants of their lands (policies established by liberal governments in some other Latin American countries). The "freeing" of indigenous peasant labor for its employment in export production thus did not occur through a violent transformation of this sector into a class of landless laborers, but rather through a series of legal regulations that gradually undermined the power of highland landowners as well as the church. These included the elimination of the subsidiary labor tax and of various special labor services due to clergy, as well as the establishment of measures to modify the institution of debt peonage on highland estates. The latter included the requirement that indigenous laborers enter freely into their work contracts and that state officials oversee these contractual relations, and a prohibition on the heritability of debt. There were also limitations placed on local political authorities' ability to recruit indigenous labor for local public works. Together these legal provisions contributed to the transformation of local labor relations into contractual relations agreed to by ostensibly free and equal individuals, and they indeed had the effect of stimulating labor migrations to the coast. (Railway construction itself also stimulated labor migrations, given the relatively high wages paid during construction, and the increased ease of travel to the coast following construction.)

How were these legal measures operationalized in highland areas, once they were passed as laws or executive decrees? Once the central state passed legal measures, they took effect principally due to the actions of subordinate groups, who called on the central state to limit local abuses (whether by clergy, landowners, or the local authorities closely allied with them). Indeed, in addition to national laws, many of the legal resources used by Indians to resist various claims on their labor by local political authorities, landowners, or the church were specific orders and decrees passed at the national or provincial level in response to Indians' complaints about abuses of their individual rights. These complaints typically took the form of citing a specific instance in which, for example, local political authorities used the pretext of the labor recruitment system for municipal public works to illegally force Indians to work on their own agricultural properties or those of their friends and allies. Indians would cite the constitutional article that prohibited forced labor, and ask the supralocal authority to protect them from these local abuses. The superior authority would then send a specific order to local officials detailing fines that would be levied (or other consequences) for abusing Indians' rights. In these processes, Indians were able to call on the authority of the central state to limit abuses of local officials. In the particular case of labor abuses in local public works in the Alausí area of Chimborazo province, through a judicious combination of work evasions and well-placed petitions, local Indians managed to dismantle the existing system of labor recruitment for public works by the end of the 1910s.

If this is how local Indians responded to the coastal elite's project to generate a labor market, how did they respond to the highland elite's project to forge an internal market? The latter involved the intensification of agricultural production in highland areas in order to maximize the products available for transport to the coast. This project gained momentum during the First World War, when the paralysis of international trade led to a crisis in cocoa exports, and hence the impossibility to continue importing basic food products for coastal consumption. Highland elites took advantage of this con-juncture to argue for the importance of increasing agricultural production in the highlands through a series of government incentives, which they argued was in the national interest. A group of modernizing highland agriculturalists successfully organized themselves into the Sociedad Nacional de Agricultura and became a consultative body for the national government on agricul-tural policy. One of their greatest achievements came when they designed a new law called the Law of Agricultural Development. This law, passed by the Ecuadorian Congress in 1918, represented the first attempt to administer highland agricultural policy at the national level, and to expand and mod-ernize the production of food staples. The law mandated the distribution of information about modern agricultural techniques, allowed the importation of farm machinery, seeds, and livestock free of customs duties, and through various measures facilitated the movement of products from field to national markets, drawing again on the emphasis on the importance of movement.

At the local level in the highlands, a series of conflicts between haciendas and indigenous communities arose in the late 1910s and early 1920s precisely due to the efforts to expand and modernize agricultural and livestock produc-tion to provision coastal markets (again, transport depended on the railway). In the area of Alausí in the central highlands, strategically located as the first highland county on the railway's route inland from the coast, strong indig-enous resistance to the intensification of labor demands in agriculture led those large landowners with access to high-altitude pasture lands to respond to new marketing opportunities by expanding labor-extensive livestock pas-turing rather than labor-intensive grain production. This was accompanied by efforts both to enclose indigenous lands, and to limit indigenous peasant access to hacienda pastures for their own herds. The latter took the form of closing down paths that crossed haciendas, a strategy that became widespread in the Alausí region in the late 1910s and early 1920s. These conflicts were re-corded in government archives precisely because the closure of customary paths through haciendas became the motive for repeated peasant complaints to the county agricultural development committee. Since the increased cir-culation of agricultural products was a central goal of the Law of Agricultural Development, road closure had been made subject to fine under this law. Of course, the particular paths being closed by estate owners were those leading through their haciendas, rather than between hacienda and market. This dis-tinction was not noted in the law itself, allowing local Indians to engage this legislation in their struggles with hacendados, but it made a great deal of differ-ence to landowners striving to modernize and expand their production: closing down internal paths allowed them to protect their investments in improved livestock breeds and pasture, precisely to take full advantage of improved external paths leading to markets. These events were also significant because indigenous peasants raised petitions to various high-level political authorities (including the nation's president) in their conflicts with landowners. This led to an investigation which took the local police chief onto an hacienda, and into an indigenous community, in order to mediate labor disputes between the two. This was unprecedented in that era, and occurred at the instigation of indigenous peasants who argued that their freedom of movement was violated by local landowners through the closure of customary paths.

Another set of conflicts also arose at the local level in association with the efforts to move highland agricultural products to the coast by train, in the form of marketing disputes. These took place when merchants bought up large quantities of staple foods in local markets in the highlands, knowing that they would fetch higher prices in coastal towns and in Guayaquil. Interestingly, these disputes produced a series of conflicting statements and claims about the operation of monopoly and of the law of supply and demand, which precisely focused on the importance of the circulation of products. That is, local townspeople claimed that large merchants were "monopolizing" goods when they paid prices that were beyond the reach of local consumers. Townspeople also drew on precedents set during the First World War, when price-fixing had been undertaken by the national government to combat speculation in food products. Merchants, however, countered with the argument that they were simply facilitating the operation of the "natural" law of supply and demand; in contrast, they argued that when municipal authorities attempted to control the flow of goods, they were the ones promoting monopoly. In these conflicts, local townspeople attempted to use public rhetoric in ways that redefined what freedom of movement should mean: they stretched liberal rhetoric by arguing that the draining of food products from the region was "monopoly," penalized by law. However, of the various ways that the language of movement was engaged during the liberal period, this particular argument was the least successful, possibly because it was associated with purely local interests rather than involving an alliance of local and regional or national elite interests.

Thus during the liberal period in Ecuador, a rhetoric emphasizing the importance of freedom of movement was engaged in many different ways. At the national level, it facilitated a tenuous consensus between two regionally based elites, who could each identify some of their own interests in the railway project. While they debated what the content of this project should include, they did not debate the importance of movement as a source of progress, modernity, and economic stimulus for the country.

At the local level, the project to promote the free movement of laborers was incorporated strategically into indigenous resistance to local power holders.

That is, Indians adopted the rhetoric and laws of the central state to claim their rights before those who abused them. The particular kind of rights they were able to claim were defined for them: most importantly, these were the rights to form and dissolve individual labor contracts and to resist forced labor recruitment of various kinds. In contrast, they were quite pointedly not able to claim collective rights through this language. The project to promote greater production and circulation of staple foods, in turn, was resisted at the local level by various social groups, given that this provoked both agrarian conflicts and marketing conflicts. However, the form that resistance took was precisely to engage elements of the language of movement. In the agrarian conflicts peasants called on central government authorities to deal with landowner abuses, and claimed their rights as citizens to move freely and to enjoy constitutional guarantees. Interestingly, one of the legal resources that peasants drew on in resisting hacienda expansion was precisely part of the Law of Agricultural Development, the same law that facilitated the expansion of production in the first place. This law was passed due to lobbying by large landowners, but some of its articles could also be used against them. Law and rhetoric from national sources were also appropriated in struggles over the marketing of food products: for instance, when local authorities attempted to control commerce in situations of local scarcity, drawing (unsuccessfully) on regulations that had been used to deal with national scarcity during the First World War. In all of these cases, local social groups adopted the language of the liberal project precisely to resist some of its effects at the local level.

Not only did local Indians use the idiom of citizenship and claims to freedom of movement in their petitions to higher authorities, but in the 1920s they actually invited state officials into their communities to mediate labor disputes with haciendas, something that was unprecedented in previous years. In addition, during the 1920s, Indians increasingly sent delegations to provincial capitals and Quito, taking advantage of their ability to mobilize themselves by train, to complain to higher authorities about the abuses of local officials and landowners. This indicates the success of the central state in positioning itself as the protector of indigenous rights against abuses by local power holders in the highlands.

While the expression of subordinate groups' interests through the language of movement in liberal Ecuador indicates the strength of this process of national incorporation, it should be noted that this "dialogue" was broken at both the subordinate and dominant levels toward the end of the liberal period. In the early 1920s a series of indigenous uprisings occurred that did not limit themselves to complaints and petitions to the state. And in 1922 a workers' strike ended in a government massacre of workers in Guayaquil that continues to hold a central place in the historical memory of the Left and workers' movements in Ecuador. In 1925, the liberal government was overthrown in the Revolución Juliana by a group of progressive military officers allied with the middle classes. The 1930s in turn saw economic crisis and profound political upheaval, with 15 governments in that decade alone, the emergence of new political parties and urban populism, and the establishment of new forms of organization among peasants and workers. One of the results of economic and political crisis was the establishment of social policy, which represented a real achievement for the lower classes, but also provided a new legal framework within which struggles could be carried out. In this sense, new public debates emerged in the 1930s which gave the struggles of that era a quite different tone from those of the liberal period.

Note

This is an abridged version of an article published as "The Language of Contention in Liberal Ecuador," in *Culture, Economy, Power: Anthropology as Critique, Anthropology as Praxis*, ed. Winnie Lem and Belinda Leach (Albany: SUNY Press), 150–62. For additional information and complete references, please see that article and A. Kim Clark, *The Redemptive Work: Railway and Nation in Ecuador, 1895–1930* (Wilmington, Del.: Scholarly Resources, 1998).

Guayaquil and Coastal Ecuador during the Cacao Era

Ronn Pineo

Referring to Guayaquil, Theodore Wolf commented at the turn of the last century: "The change and improvement . . . is so considerable that anyone seeing the city 25 years ago, on his return today would scarcely know it." In 1880, Guayaquil was a city of roughly 170 blocks, thirty major public buildings, and a population of 25,000. By 1920, it had grown to some 700 blocks, ninety major public buildings, and more than 100,000 people. Nor was it alone. For most Latin American cities the late nineteenth century and early twentieth proved a time of rapid and dramatic change; significant expansion of exports gave rise to a process of swift urbanization across the continent. Guayaquil and its cacao (or chocolate bean) producing hinterland shared fully in the rush of change. The city and region enjoyed an economic boom, becoming more tightly linked to international markets as the world's leading producer of cacao. Large planters and merchants built great fortunes, impoverished Indians flooded down to the coast from the highlands, and Guayaquil grew to become the largest and richest city in Ecuador. In this essay, the historian Ronn Pineo offers a sketch of these years, examining the structure of the coastal economy and related patterns of social and political change.

Guayaquil and its hinterland, blessed with a superb natural harbor and fertile conditions for growing cacao, responded strongly to the pull of the new commercial opportunities in the world market during the late nineteenth and early twentieth centuries. The city stands at the conclusion of the 25,000 square mile Guayas River Valley, a region crisscrossed with navigable rivers. This fluvial network served as a liquid highway, funneling cacao down into Guayaquil.

Cacao greatly influenced the economic life of Ecuador, and it dominated that of Guayaquil. The value of Ecuador's cacao sales rose over 700 percent from the 1870s to the 1920s. Cacao typically accounted for about three quarters of Ecuador's total exports in these years, nearly all of it shipped from Guayaquil. Port traffic rose considerably in this period, rising from 149 oceangoing vessels

Figure 1. Guayaquil waterfront, ca. 1890. (Julio Estrada Ycaza Collection)

calling in port in 1869 to over 400 by 1922. Cacao filled Guayaquil. "Everywhere along the river front," wrote one visitor, "the pleasant aroma of cocoa" perfumed the streets.

Guayaquil relied heavily upon imports to feed and sustain its growing population, for the city and the coastal hinterland proved incapable of providing for their own needs. One possible solution, bringing in food grown in the highland provinces, was not viable. The towering Andes effectively blocked the development of affordable transport from the highlands. Asses provided the chief means of transport from the *sierra* (Ecuador's mountainous interior), but even in good weather and in the best of circumstances the journey from Quito could take two weeks, with few hotels or boarding houses along the way. Ecuador had built a road in the highlands in the 1870s, but already by 1885 it was of little use. Wrote one weary traveler, "long neglect . . . [left] no other road than a meandering, never worked mule path" for much of the way. After the completion of a national railway in 1909 (a stunning engineering feat, if an excessively expensive one) transportation costs still remained prohibitive. Limited rolling stock, the need for frequent repairs, and high operating costs plagued the railway from its inception. The railroad company almost never operated at a profit. Accordingly, in Guayaquil, goods shipped down from the sierra could not compete in price against cheaper foreign imports. Highland Ecuador sold few products to outsiders

Figure 2. Aerial view of Guayaquil, 1922. (Julio Estrada Ycaza Collection)

and bought few items from without, while the prosperous economy of the coast bounded ahead.

The coastal provinces, especially Los Ríos, Guayas, El Oro, Manabí, and Esmeraldas, all boasted important levels of cacao production. Inevitably, the larger and more successful cacao growers began to displace the small- and medium-sized landholders; by the 1880s vast estates controlled much of the land. The best of these nestled in along the shores of the many navigable rivers above Guayaquil, giving them the advantage of access to cheap water transport as well as the prized farmland of the heavily silted banks.

The great estates developed via several methods, employing both economic strength and their control over local government. Large landowners could appeal to authorities for the right to occupy vacant lands. Of course, sometimes the land already had occupants, whom they uprooted and kicked out. After 1896 such "vacant" land was no longer free, although it could be still purchased from the government for four sucres a hectare. Few found payment actually necessary. Vaguely drawn estate boundaries made it easy to illegally enlarge one's holdings by encroaching on those of the neighbors. Some of the larger growers lent money to lesser planters, thereby acquiring more land when the borrowers failed to repay. In sum, in cacao country during the boom years great estates dominated. A few large planters monopolized the best land and access to transportation, and controlled key sources of credit and the critical marketing links.

People

As the cacao frontier rapidly pushed up into the hill country of the coast (especially after the 1880s introduction of the heartier Venezuelan variety of cacao) growers continually complained of labor shortages, especially during the peak harvest periods in December and from April through June. Great estates owners turned for workers to the vast pool of internal migrants who were fleeing the overcrowded and impoverished sierra.

For ordinary people, the highlands offered very little to recommend staying: low pay, an appallingly heavy tax burden, and all too frequent abuse at the hands of hacienda owners and public officials. U.S. travelers to the region often drew the obvious parallel to the conditions of ante-bellum Southern slaves that they had seen. "Poorly fed, ill clad, . . . ignorant . . . , superstitious," living in "squalor and poverty," the "servility [of Ecuador's highland residents was] . . . positively painful to behold," reported one. In the sierra land was scarce and labor relatively plentiful. People left for the coast.

On the coast the great cacao estate owners tried several strategies for assuring a sufficient labor force for the critical harvest periods. Some growers experimented with paying off the debts of sierra workers, also providing free transportation to the coast. Some other large estate owners sought to tie workers to their haciendas via a system of debt peonage, granting cash advances, and allowing purchases on credit—at a stiff markup—at the hacienda store. The debts workers acquired had to be paid off before one could leave the hacienda, with existing debts passed on to one's heirs. The growers also secured anti-vagrancy laws and other legal measures to restrict the freedom of coastal workers. For example, in the 1860s the Province of Los Ríos passed a law requiring all farm hands to purchase a pass from the government to certify that they did not owe debts to any hacienda owner.

Yet for all of these efforts, a system of purely coerced labor did not emerge. In the end the owners found that the only sure way to assure access to an adequate workforce at harvest was to offer higher wages. As a consequence, workers could earn enough money in two days to get along for a week. Each family also typically received a small plot to raise their own food. Planter efforts to ensnare their employees in a web of debt may have actually proved to be a benefit to many workers. Rival growers, desperate for field hands, constantly pilfered workers from other estates, paying off workers' debts, or more typically, enticing them to skip out on their existing obligations with offers of fresh and yet more generous advances. If one did happen to fall into the clutches of an overly demanding *hacendado* (or great estate owner), it was easy to flee. Owners complained endlessly about runaways who left a string of debts trailing behind.

So migrants streamed down from the sierra at an ever quickening pace, coming to take advantage of the higher wages and relative freedom of the coast. Coastal mestizos and Indians did not have to pay the onerous tribute burdens as did highland Indians. Best of all, coastal hacienda owners also had obtained laws exempting their employees from impressment into road gangs or the army.

Most of the employees on the cacao estates labored as *jornaleros*, or day workers. While the haciendas harvested some cacao all year, most jornaleros and their families worked for the landowner only during the two principal cacao fruitage seasons, spending most of their time tending their own small food plots. Typically, the entire family labored together in getting out the cacao harvest. After the harvest, a smaller group of workers would be asked to stay on as workers at the great estate, helping maintain the cacao orchards or tending to the other crops, such as tobacco, rice, or sugar, or looking after the livestock.

Most migrants from the sierra first took jobs as jornaleros, but some soon improved their situation. If one had learned enough about cacao, was older and responsible enough, he might after a few seasons obtain a position as a *sembrador*, or cacao sewer. To get a contract, a man typically had to be married and have a family, for the entire family would be expected to work. *Sembradores* received a plot of virgin land from the landowner, which, after clearing and burning the tropical growth, they planted with seedlings supplied by the hacendado. Next to the young cacao plants they placed faster growing banana trees, whose leaves would protect the cacao seedlings from scorching tropical rays. In between the rows they planted subsistence food crops like yucca, corn, and beans. After four or five years, when the cacao trees reached maturity and began to offer their first harvest, the sembrador family turned the land back over to the owner, the sembrador receiving a fee (twenty to thirty cents) for each healthy tree. After completion of a contract the sembrador generally sought a new one, or if he had acquired no debts, might move on to another hacienda.

Overall, the population of the coastal provinces increased seven times over from 1873 to 1926, from 165,280 to 1,115,264. Likewise, Guayaquil's population rose rapidly after 1870, when it had numbered but 20,000 to 25,000 people. By 1890 its population reached about 45,000; by 1900, 60,000; by 1910, 80,000; reaching over 120,000 in 1925.

The city's record of population growth is rather remarkable given that deaths almost always exceeded the number births in Guayaquil each year. Of course, Guayaquil was hardly alone in this regard; most nineteenth-century cities, especially port and tropical ones, exhibited the same grim pattern of disease and death, the increased human proximity and poor sanitary conditions of urban centers combining to spawn a wide array of lethal afflictions. Cities of this era, in Ecuador and elsewhere in the world, could maintain their numbers only with a steady stream of fresh recruits from the healthier countryside.

But Guayaquil was a special case, and the city was arguably the unhealthiest place in Ecuador. If in this period in Ecuador as a whole births typically outnumbered deaths, in Guayaquil this situation almost never obtained. While Ecuador was always growing in population from natural increase, Guayaquil almost never did. Natural increase did not account for the swift growth of the population of Guayaquil.

Neither too did immigration. Guayaquil carried a reputation as one of the most disease infested cities of the world; if city boosters proclaimed Guayaquil the glistening "pearl of the Pacific," more knew of the city as the "pest-hole of the Pacific." Sadly, this was a reputation that the city all too richly deserved. Guayaquil's well-known and continuing problems with yellow fever, bubonic plague, and many other dreaded diseases killed enthusiasm for immigration. In Guayaquil, immigrants totaled probably no more than ten to fifteen percent of the population during this era, with most coming from neighboring Colombia and Peru.

Lowland hacienda cacao workers, shifting easily from estate to estate, drifted about in all directions, especially when demand for labor went slack after harvest times. Many followed the natural currents of the fluvial network, floating downstream to where all the rivers met: Guayaquil. In 1899 about one third of the people who lived in Guayaquil had moved from elsewhere in Ecuador and slightly more than half of these migrants had traveled down from the sierra. Internal migration from the sierra fed the growth of Guayaquil and its hinterland.

Arriving in Guayaquil on makeshift rafts (*balsas*), bringing loads of charcoal, fruit, or straw hats to market, these migrants might spend a few days peddling their wares and taking in the city. Many evidently decided that they liked Guayaquil well enough to stay, or perhaps they lacked funds for the trip back up river on steam powered *lanchas*. Some never really settled, wandering back and forth from hacienda to city, scouting about for the best work opportunities.

Guayaquil, like most cities, could be at once beautiful and ugly, exciting and exasperating: the movement and commotion of the crowd, the arrival of a ship, a fight, an accident, a thief; the quiet of the morning, the sounds of the birds, the colors of the sunset, the cool breezes and the beauty of the river and Santay Island in the evening. It was elegant: with its immaculately groomed parks, somber bronze statues peering out over the gently flowing Guayas River, or the lovely colonial style homes with their characteristic second story overhang and wooden slat windows that opened from the bottom to catch cool updrafts; it was squalid: with its hideous slums, legions of roaches, swarms of mosquitoes, and the intense heat and humidity of the Equator. The city smelled wonderful: of cacao drying in the streets, of plantains frying, or of bread baking; the city reeked: from the slaughterhouse, from men urinating by the riverbank, or from the ubiquitous garbage, manure, chickens, pigs, and raw sewerage. But mostly Guayaquil teemed with life. Iguanas ate leaves and small birds in the trees in the parks, the river swam with an abundance of fish, and bats sped about among the buildings at dusk. People walked, ate, sat, and filled the city with the sounds of their talking, laughing, and music.

For the crush of newcomers to the city, however, Guayaquil could offer but few steady jobs. There were only a few positions to be found in the limited manufacturing sector, for Guayaquil developed almost no industry. Entrepreneurs avoided such investments—wisely too, given the city's relatively modest size, a most unpromising consumer base of impoverished workers, a still thinly populated hinterland, and awesome geographic barriers to potential highland markets or distant foreign ones. Instead, the Ecuadorian and foreign entrepreneurs who profited from the cacao trade—especially importers, exporters, and the owners of great cacao estates—found in real estate speculation, retail sales, opulent living, and extended foreign travel sufficient outlets for their money. A few workers took employment at the rice processing plant north of town or as hands in some of the small manufacturing shops scattered through the city, but such opportunities were rare. In 1883, when the city population was about 36,000, there were but sixteen small "factories" each employing but a few workers. In 1909, with the city now numbering about 80,000 people, there were still but forty such manufacturing enterprises, these producing beer, ice, cigarettes, cigars, biscuits, candy, noodles, brooms, bags, and electrical power. As a rule, local industry did not challenge imports: if an item could be imported, it was.

Some more fortunate workers might secure steady employment as unskilled service workers, such as restaurant help, trolley conductors, or bellhops. Some others found positions as skilled service workers, such as teachers, reporters, or cashiers. But most people in Guayaquil found only sporadic employment as unskilled service sector workers. Indeed, the percentage of workers in such types of jobs steadily increased. Most men settled for employment as day laborers, especially as cacao handlers (*cacahueros*)—sorting, drying, and bagging cacao—or as dockworkers—hauling the bags aboard and unloading the vessels returning with food and consumer items from western Europe and the United States. Women typically took jobs as seamstresses, cooks, laundresses, maids, or prostitutes. Many people worked in itinerant retail sales, roaming the streets shouting the names of their products. Some turned to begging, and others to crime.

Guayaquil's active commerce had a mixed affect on artisan and middle class jobs, at the same time creating and eliminating some of these scarce, better paying, positions. Guayaquil supported a variety of artisan crafts. There were masons, carpenters, butchers, leather workers, teamsters, blacksmiths, coppers, mechanics, painters, bakers, barbers, typesetters, shoemakers, printers, hat makers, glass makers, tailors, plumbers, silversmiths, marble workers, and others.

But if the number of people working in these trades probably increased as Guayaquil grew, their percentage of the total workforce steadily dropped. In 1890 there were 353 artisan shops in the city; by 1912, after twenty-two years of rapid population growth, there were 8 fewer. The city's nearly 400 retail outlets by 1909 imported many foreign made consumer products: shoes, hats, ready made and pre-dyed clothing, and so forth. This steady stream of cheap, modern consumer imports was obviating the need for old-style artisans.

The ranks of white collar professionals who counted, sorted, and kept track of the profits, also grew somewhat. There was an increased need for white collar professionals; people of some education who could staff the private offices of banks and commission houses or run the government bureaucracy. The number of physicians and lawyers also increased with the rising numbers of those who could afford their services. Still, there were but a handful of white collar jobs in Guayaquil, in these years.

For the unskilled service workers who made up the bulk of the city's adult population, wages were relatively low when compared to what others in the city received. The men who worked irregularly as day laborers earned about seventy-five cents per day in the 1880s and one to two sucres per day after the turn of the century. Women earned less. Seamstresses or cooks earned from four to twelve sucres a month. This money did not go far. A pound of lard and a pound of corn together cost more than a seamstress could earn in a day. A pair of shoes cost a male day worker a quarter of his monthly earnings. Even death was expensive. At twenty-seven sucres even a simple send-off cost half a month's wages. The forty to fifty sucres a month that steadily employed laboring men earned must have seemed quite small when compared to the 150 sucres per month a university teacher earned or a 350 sucres per month judge's salary.

The number of wealthy people in Guayaquil grew rapidly from 1870 to 1925, as too did the size of their fortunes. Economic growth in Guayaquil paid handsome profits to some. But even though raising cacao was important to Ecuador, it was not the only way men enriched themselves in Guayaquil during this period. Indeed, a minority of Guayaquil's elites owned cacao producing estates. Some made money in exporting cacao, but the greatest wealth came from the import business. The merchants arranged the overseas sales

of growers' cacao and then imported European and U.S. consumer items ped-
dled in the shops and streets of Guayaquil. As the city expanded, merchants
became wealthier and wisely protected their fortunes by engaging in other
economic activities. All of the city's elite spread out their business risks by
investing in various enterprises. Some landowners became involved in banking, cacao export, and the city's commerce. Many exporters reinvested their
profits in the domestic economy. In sum, Guayaquil was an entrepôt, with
its merchants having diversified their holdings. Guayaquil developed an export and service related economy, its elites, generally importers, exporters,
retailers, and planters. The fortunes of these men rose with cacao shipments
aboard.

Socially, the relatively small size of Guayaquil afforded its elite the chance
to become well acquainted with one another. As their economic interests intertwined, so too did their social interests; they attended the theater together,
escaped Guayaquil for the seashore during the hot rainy Ecuadorian winters
together, and they married one another. Significantly, however, the coastal
elite did *not* mix with the sierra aristocracy.

Politics and the Failure of Urban Reform

Commensurate with its expanded economic role, coastal Ecuador gained a
larger share in the distribution of national political power during the cacao
boom period. Nevertheless, Guayaquil and the coast faced a variety of continuing political frustrations in these years. Central to Guayaquil's political
dilemmas was the intense regionalism of Ecuador, "the political expression
of the division and isolation imposed by geography." Ecuador has historically lacked a strong sense of national consciousness. This is a country cut in
half by some of the world's tallest mountains, the towering Andes, and profound local differences—in ethnicity, language, religiosity, and culture—have
developed naturally. The people of the coast and the sierra too often have
regarded one another with a mutual sense of heartfelt contempt and dark
suspicion. Most Ecuadorians never traveled outside of their native provinces
and so tended to define their interests by household, extended family, village,
or region. To these people "nationalism" had little meaning.

The sierra, and especially the capital in Quito, had been home to the colonial
elite, people who had early on fixed their efforts on exploiting the large population of Indians. Religion, education, and the arts soon came to be centered in
Quito, "reenforc[ing] . . . [an] attitude . . . of cultural superiority [there, and a
certain] . . . cultural defensiveness in Guayaquil." Meanwhile, the port harbored
a special sense of separateness and a spirit of independence. The municipal government of Guayaquil asserted this sentiment of autonomy repeatedly.

Cultural differences divided Ecuador. To racist whites of the sierra, the swarthy *montuvios* of the coast were a bastard race—part European, Indian, and Negro—and living proof of the evils of miscegenation. *Serranos* (people from the sierra) referred to *costeños* (people of the coastal region) as "monos" (monkeys), belittled what they considered to be the port city's crass intensity for making money, and sternly objected to Guayaquil's relatively lax religious attitudes. Costeños replied that serranos were "longos," a term otherwise reserved for obsequious Indian houseboys, saw *Quiteños* as prideful and sanctimonious, and claimed that the ostentatious piety of the sierra was wrought with hypocrisy.

"Less a nation than a series of loosely articulated regions," to the extent that any Ecuadorians showed an interest in national politics, they focused their energies on the spoils of office or on obtaining pork barrel legislation to benefit their home districts. Ecuadorians generally behaved as motivated by local needs and interests; as a result, the national interest suffered.

Such then was the national context for coastal politics. For Guayaquil the principal political difficulty was that its cacao exports were the only important cash producing activity in Ecuador; the import and export taxes on this trade provided almost all government revenue. Ecuador had abolished the Indian tribute and the tithe on farm production by 1889 and there remained no significant sierra tax. Customs taxes collected generated from fifty-three to eighty-one percent of ordinary national tax revenues from 1895 to 1925. Still, this money had to be used to pay the mounting bills of the national government in distant Quito and the sierra before the needs of Guayaquil might be considered. In some years Guayaquil received nothing from the national government to pay for the desperately needed public works for the growing city. For that which it did receive Guayaquil hardly felt thankful. After all, most of these revenues had come from the Guayaquil customs house in the first place.

Interregional battles resulted. Political elites in each zone—the traditional, autarkic, landed oligarchy of various districts in the sierra and the non-immigrant merchants and great estate owners of the coast—worked assiduously to defend their own interests and, if possible, to seize control over the national government and use its power and resources to further advance these interests.

Unity might have come to the country if a strong single power block from any region had been sufficiently ascendant to impose its vision of national policy. But such was not the case in Ecuador; the regions remained fairly evenly balanced. Despite the economic growth of the coast, Quito and the sierra always proved powerful enough to insist upon a large share of the revenues collected in Guayaquil. Quito, the seat of government since the beginning of colonial times, had the advantage of history on its side. Moreover, for all the demographic expansion of the coast, the sierra continued to have a much larger population. Led by a sturdy old elite with considerable social and economic resources, when challenged the sierra could quickly conscript Indians and field sizeable and menacing armies. For Guayaquil, this meant that the efforts of the local elite to oversee the city's progress were importantly restricted by the fiscal and political realities imposed by Ecuador's regionalism.

City expenditures rose as a crush of migrants to Guayaquil generated new urban needs. Unable to raise enough revenues through taxes to pay the heavy start-up costs for necessary new public works projects, the city turned to loans, especially in the 1880s. As the debt ballooned, the city slowed further borrowing, and struggled just to keep up interest payments on its previously incurred debt. But as the city's population continued to grow, and Guayaquil could not afford to borrow more, existing city services became swamped.

The urban reform problem of Guayaquil was thus. The sierra consumed, but did not produce government revenues. The cacao economy of the coast had to pay for all of the heavy national expenses *and* provide tax revenue for the urgent social needs of the city of Guayaquil. This double burden it could not bear.

Guayaquil officials felt that the national government got in the way, told Guayaquil what it needed and where, and generally tried to usurp local authority. Moreover, white serranos tended to monopolize the coveted positions in the national bureaucracy in Quito. That Quiteños largely controlled this critical source of white collar employment deeply angered middle class *Guayaquileños*. That politics were the biggest business in Quito was all the more galling since Guayaquil's busy commerce filled the national treasury.

Finally, and in the largest sense, the nature of the coastal monoculture export economy and the resulting social and political patterns that emerged played the most powerful role in shaping politics for Guayaquil. This was a city and region where the economy, society, and polity, were effectively dominated by a small group of privileged elite. Upriver from Guayaquil the great estate owners monopolized the cacao trade. In the city a handful of merchants, growers, and their families tightly controlled the rising cacao riches.

Conditions favoring the development of a broad middle class of relatively well-off, educated urban professionals and small businessmen did not exist. Guayaquil's pattern of concentrated wealth brought little "trickle down." The dearth of industry meant there was also little economic "spin off" and hence relatively few managerial positions or opportunities for small entrepreneurs. The fact that the nation's capital remained in Quito also severely limited the size of Guayaquil's middle class; coveted white collar jobs in the government bureaucracy were in the sierra, not in Guayaquil. What was absent in Guayaquil was a middle class of growing resources, one that could have become a driving force for progressive change, starting voluntary organizations, agitating for legislation, lobbying, voting, and successfully demanding that its needs be taken seriously. At the same time, powerful worker organizations—aggressive, defending the interests of their constituents—could scarcely be expected to develop in Guayaquil's unpromising socio-economic context: unemployed *jornaleros* and women who take in laundry, cook, or serve as maids make unlikely union members. Thus, it fell to the small group of wealthy elite to tend to Guayaquil's progress, and while they cared about their city, their notions of the correct order of priorities were not effectively challenged and tempered by large, organized, and powerful competing groups or classes. Because of this, in Guayaquil the call for social reform was faint. Accordingly, the governing elite knew that they could safely ignore worker interests—and usually did. A popular saying summed up this sentiment: "the public interest is nobody's interest." For the ordinary women, men, and their families who came to the city during the cacao age, Guayaquil offered only the hope for a better life, not the reality of it.

Note

This essay is drawn from my book-length study on Guayaquil, *Social and Economic Reform in Ecuador: Life and Work in Guayaquil* (Gainesville: University Press of Florida, 1996). For a comprehensive listing of the sources used for this essay, please consult the notes and bibliography sections in *Social and Economic Reform in Ecuador*. (Portions of this essay are reprinted from *Social and Economic Reform in Ecuador* with the permission of the University Press of Florida.)

Mountaineering on the Equator: A Historical Perspective

Rob Rachowiecki

Ecuador's highest peaks—among the most spectacular in the world—have been attract-ing explorers, scientists, and hikers for centuries. In fact, Ecuador's highest mountain—Chimborazo—was once considered the highest peak in the world. The travel writer and mountaineer Rob Rachowiecki sketches a brief history of our fascination with the north-ern Andes.

Tropical Ecuador boasts ten permanently snowcapped mountains which ex-ceed 5,000 m in height. All are of volcanic origin, and some remain active to-day. Unlike their Andean counterparts to the south (Peru, Bolivia, Argentina, Chile), there is no evidence that local indigenous people ascended any major mountains prior to the arrival of the Spanish conquistadors. The Spaniards contented themselves with noting major volcanic activity in their journals, recording the eruptions of Cotopaxi (5,897 m) and Tungurahua (5,029 m) in 1534. The earliest recorded ascent is that of the Ecuadorian José Toribio Or-tiguera, who reached the crater of Pichincha (4,675 m) in 1582. After many years, this was followed by a disputed record of an ascent of Pichincha by Pa-dre Juan Romero in 1660, the same year that a major eruption buried Quito in forty centimeters of volcanic ash. Generally, though, there was little interest in exploring the mountain summits during the first two centuries of Spanish occupation.

This changed during the eighteenth century. By then it had been estab-lished that the world was round, though controversy still raged over the concept of polar flattening. In an attempt to settle the issue, the French Aca-démie des Sciences organized expeditions to the Arctic and the equator. At this time Africa was still the "dark continent," Indonesia was little known, and the Amazon Basin was virtually unexplored. Consequently Ecuador, with its capital, Quito, just twenty-five km south of the equator, was the obvi-ous venue for such an expedition. This took place from 1736 to 1744 and was led by the Frenchman Charles-Marie de la Condamine, accompanied by two countrymen, two Spaniards, and the Ecuadorian Pedro Vicente Maldonado. Surveying was undertaken, and their calculations of the distance from the equator to the North Pole became the basis of today's metric system (a meter was originally defined as one ten-millionth of the distance between the North Pole and the equator). During the course of their investigations, the explorers concluded that Ecuador's highest mountain, Chimborazo (6,310 m), was the highest peak in the world, a belief generally accepted in the Americas and Europe until the 1820s. They made the first serious attempt to scale this mountain, reaching an altitude of about 4,750 m. The less important peaks of Pichincha and Corazón (4,788 m) were successfully climbed, and most of Ecuador's major peaks were surveyed.

La Condamine's expedition's surveys and measurements started a series of disputes which have not been resolved to this day. For example, they measured Cotopaxi, Ecuador's second-highest peak, at 5,751 m. Successive expeditions turned in considerably higher measurements: 5,753 m by the German scientist and explorer Baron Alexander von Humboldt in 1802, 5,978 m by the British mountaineer Edward Whymper in 1880, 5,940 m by Ecuadorian climber Nicolás Martínez in 1906, and the highest of all, 6,005 m, was published by Arthur Eichler in his book *Ecuador: Snow Peaks and Jungles* in 1955. The height most generally accepted today is 5,897 m, as surveyed by Ecuador's Instituto Geográfico Militar in 1972. Nevertheless recent sources are still unable to agree on the correct elevation. Similar perplexing situations exist with other peaks.

After La Condamine's departure, there was little exploration of Ecuador's mountains until 1802, when an expedition led by Alexander von Humboldt reawakened interest in the Ecuadorian highlands. Humboldt noted how Quito and Ecuador's main highland cities lay between two volcanic Andean ranges and dubbed this inhabited area "the Valley of the Volcanoes," a name still used today. He visited and studied various peaks including Cotopaxi, Pichincha, Antisana (5,752 m) and El Altar (5,319 m), but it is for his research on and attempted ascent of Chimborazo that his expedition is particularly remembered by mountaineers.

Accompanied by the Frenchman Aimé Bonpland and the Ecuadorian Carlos Montúfar, he identified many plants (including some new species) as well as noting barometric data during his attempted ascent of the southern flanks of the mountain. He made a sectional sketch map of Chimborazo, which shows the plant species, various geographical landmarks, the expedition's penetration beyond the snowline, and finally, high above the surrounding paramo the comment includes a note regarding a crevasse which prevented the travelers from reaching the summit. This indicates the point at about

5,875 m, where Humboldt and his companions, suffering from altitude sickness, with cracked and bleeding lips and badly sunburned faces, were forced to turn back. This attempt is particularly noteworthy since despite their failure to gain the summit, they did reach the highest point thus far attained by Europeans.

Since Chimborazo was still considered the highest mountain in the world, other attempts on its summit soon followed. The Venezuelan liberator of the Andean countries, Simón Bolívar, climbed to the snowline in 1822 and nine years later Bolívar's colonel, the French agronomist Joseph Boussingault, managed to reach about 6,000 m on Chimborazo's southern slopes, again increasing the altitude thus far attained by European explorers.

President Gabriel García Moreno, though a much criticized and despotic ruler, was the first Ecuadorian leader to take an active interest in the environment. He enacted several conservationist laws, and in 1844 climbed to the crater of Pichincha. In succeeding years several European expeditions arrived. In 1847, the Italian traveler Gaetano Osculati spent a year in Ecuador, and although he made no attempts to climb any of its peaks he left us with some interesting paintings and drawings of Ecuadorian mountains. The year 1849 saw the first recorded expedition to the highly active volcano Sangay (5,230 m) where the Frenchman Sebastian Wisse counted 267 strong explosions in one hour. During the 1850s and 1860s several expeditions from various nations visited Ecuador but achieved little, and it was not until 1872 that the next major breakthrough in Ecuadorian mountaineering occurred.

In this year the German Wilhelm Reiss, accompanied by the Colombian Angel Escobar, succeeded in reaching the summit of Cotopaxi by climbing the southeastern flank, rather than the northern route which has since become accepted as the normal route. The following year another German, Alfonso Stübel, accompanied by four Ecuadorians—Eusebio Rodríguez, Melchor Páez, Vicente Ramón, and Rafael Jantui—reached the summit via the same route: it was the first major peak to have been climbed by Ecuadorians. The two Germans then joined forces and in 1873 made the first ascent of the active volcano Tungurahua as well as attempts on other summits.

A disastrous volcanic eruption on 26 June 1877 temporarily left the slopes of Cotopaxi almost bare of ice and snow, and several climbers took advantage of this situation and climbed the volcano by the northeast side. Then a remarkable expedition in 1880, led by the renowned English climber Edward Whymper, succeeded in spending a night by Cotopaxi's crater, still considered to be the highest active crater in the world.

Whymper had already established his reputation as a climber by making the first ascent of the Matterhorn, at one time reputed to be impossible. His Ecuadorian expedition must surely rate as one of the most successful mountaineering expeditions ever undertaken: with the Italian cousins Louis and Jean-Antoine Carrel, Whymper proceeded to climb not only Cotopaxi but also made the first ascent of Chimborazo, a climb which raised a storm of disbelief and protest. To quell his critics Whymper repeated the climb later in 1880 accompanied by two Ecuadorians, David Beltrán and Francisco Campaña. Ecuador's third-highest peak, Cayambe (5,790 m), and Antisana, the fourth highest, also fell to the ice axes of Whymper and the Carrel as did Iliniza Sur (5,248 m), Carihuairazo (5,020 m), Sincholagua (4,898 m), Cotacachi (4,944 m), and Sara Urco (4,676 m). In addition to these eight first ascents, several other climbs were made by this expedition, including ascents of Corazón and Pichincha and an unsuccessful attempt on El Altar, which is Ecuador's most technical snow peak and which was not climbed until 1963. Edward Whymper is well remembered in Ecuador. There is a street named after him in Quito and other cities; and the country's highest mountaineers' refuge, the new and well-equipped hut at 5,000 m on Chimborazo's eastern slopes, has been named Refugio Whymper.

After Whymper's memorable exploits no important expeditions occurred until the twentieth century, a period which saw an awakening of interest in mountaineering by national climbers. The father of Ecuadorian mountaineering is Nicolás Martínez, who in the first decades of that century succeeded in making many notable ascents. In 1900 Martínez climbed Tungurahua, and in succeeding years climbed this peak several more times. His interest in mountaineering awakened, Martínez made first Ecuadorian ascents of many major peaks: Antisana in 1904, a failed attempt on Cayambe in 1905, and successful climbs of Cotopaxi and Chimborazo in 1906. Succeeding years saw various successes and failures in Martínez's climbing career. A particularly noteworthy ascent was that of Iliniza Norte (5,126 m) in 1912; this peak is the only one of Ecuador's ten 5,000 m peaks which was first climbed by an Ecuadorian.

World War I and its aftermath left little time or money for new foreign expeditions to Ecuador; it was not until 1929 that a U.S. expedition, led by Robert T. Moore, achieved the first ascent of Sangay. This, the most continuously active volcano in Latin America, was then experiencing a rare period of tranquility. Moore's expedition also made various other notable climbs, including the first ascent on the part of an American of Chimborazo.

By 1929 all but one of Ecuador's ten 5,000 m peaks had been conquered. The exception was El Altar, Ecuador's fifth-highest peak, which was not climbed until 1963, when an Italian Alpine Club expedition led by Marino Tremonti succeeded in reaching the summit. In the intervening years many repeat ascents of the major peaks were made by climbers of various nationalities, and several minor peaks were conquered for the first time. These included Cerro

Hermoso (4,571 m) by four Germans in 1941 and Quilindaña (4,877 m) by a large party of Ecuadorians, Colombians, Frenchmen, and Italians in 1952.

In the 1940s two Ecuadorian mountaineering clubs (Quito Nuevos Horizontes and Ascencionismo del Colegio San Gabriel) were established, which ushered in the modern era of climbing for Ecuadorians. The founders of San Gabriel were Hernán Rodríguez Castelo, Luis Andrade Reimers, and Padre Salvador Cevallos. Largely through the efforts of these clubs, Ecuadorians began to take a strong interest in mountaineering. Padre José Rivas was instrumental in supporting the young climbers of the San Gabriel climbing club for over fifty years. He is famous for giving a mass on the summit of Cotopaxi in 1979. He also raised funds for the construction of the Cotopaxi and Cayambe refuges and continued climbing through his seventies!

The 1960s and 1970s saw a new approach to mountaineering in Ecuador. With Tremonti's first ascent of El Altar in 1963, all the major peaks had been climbed and emphasis was laid on climbing new routes and lower summits of the more important mountains. El Altar's eight unclimbed lower peaks provided great impetus and excitement to Ecuadorian mountaineering as, one by one, they were climbed between 1965 and 1979 by climbers of various nationalities, including three first ascents by Ecuadorian climbers. During these decades Ecuadorian mountaineers were consistently in the forefront of finding new climbs, such as the second and third summits of Antisana; new routes on Cayambe and Iliniza Sur, the Central Summit on Chimborazo; the first ascents of the minor peaks of Achipungo and Ayapungo; and many others. In connection with these new climbs the names of the Ecuadorians Bernardo Beate, Marco Cruz, Milton Moreno, Ramiro Navarrete, Rómulo Pazmiño, Hernán and Mauricio Reinoso, Santiago Rivadeneira, Hugo Torres, Iván Rojas; the American James Desrossiers; and the Frenchman Joseph Bergé will long be remembered. Many Ecuadorian climbers also made notable ascents in different parts of the world. Particular mention should go to Fabián Zurita, who, perhaps more than any other Ecuadorian, has brought the mountains of Ecuador closer to its people through his frequent and nontechnical articles in the Ecuadorian press and his summer mountaineering camps.

This generation of climbers formed the provincial association of mountaineering clubs and founded the provincial mountaineering school, Escuela Provincial de Alta Montaña, in 1974. This school helped bring new standards to climbing in Ecuador. Several university climbing clubs founded in these days still remain active.

The leaders of the next generation of climbers who emerged in the 1980s–1990s were more focused on new technical routes. This highly ambitious and well-trained group of Ecuadorians also ventured to other ranges in Peru,

Bolivia, and the Himalayas. Some of their accomplishments in Ecuador are listed below:

> The north face of El Altar was summited from inside the crater by Oswaldo Morales and Gilles de Lataillade on 10 December 1984.
>
> The south face of Canónigo of Altar was summited from inside the crater by Luis Naranjo and Mauricio Reinoso on 30 December 1984.
>
> The west face of Tabernáculo of El Altar was summited by Luis Naranjo, Mauricio Reinoso, Fabián Cáceres, and Peter Ayarza on 28 December 1987.
>
> The east face of the south peak of Rumiñahui was summited by Pablo Fernández, Galo Bustos, and Pablo Cruz on 15 October 1993.
>
> The very challenging southeast ridge of the south peak of Antisana was summited by Oswaldo Freire, Gabriel Llanos, and Oswaldo Alcocer on 28 December 1993.
>
> All twelve of El Altar's peaks were summited during a single expedition in December 1995 by Oswaldo Freire and Gabriel Llanos, assisted by Edison Oña and Oswaldo Alcocer.
>
> The northeast face of Cotopaxi was summited by Jurg Arnet, Gabriel Llanos, and Gaspar Navarrete in May 1997.
>
> The first ascent of the Yanasacha rock face on Cotopaxi was completed by Eduardo Agama, Edison Salgado, Jorge Peñafiel, and Danilo Mayorga on 1 May 1989.
>
> The first solo ascent of the Yanasacha rock face on Cotopaxi was accomplished by Santiago Quintero in 2002.

Extremely difficult routes—such as Arista del Sol Canónigo of El Altar, Arista Helena of Cayambe, and a second ascent of the north face of El Obispo—have been unsuccessful to date, despite attempts by many Ecuadorian climbers.

Since the 1960s mountaineering in Ecuador has become an economically important tourist asset, and refuges have been constructed to accommodate climbers. The first of these was the now destroyed Fabian Zurita refuge built in 1964 at 4,900 m on the northwest slopes of Chimborazo. Since then several more mountain huts have been built and upgraded on Chimborazo, Iliniza, Cotopaxi, Cayambe, Tungurahua, Sangay, Cerro Hermosa, and Pichincha. Some are of the basic "roof over your head" variety, while others provide food, cooking facilities, rest areas, lockers, and sleeping bunks.

With its network of climbing huts and their easy accessibility, Ecuador is an important mountaineering center attracting thousands of climbers a year. For experts it provides the opportunity for good new routes, but Ecuador is of particular interest to intermediate climbers who wish to experience the excitement of high-altitude ascents on mountains that aren't necessarily technically demanding. It is also very useful as a training ground for climbers wishing to test and improve their high-altitude skills before attempting ascents in the difficult mountains of the more southern Andes.

Exactly how long mountaineering in Ecuador will be able to continue is a worrying question. According to Ecuador's Meteorology Institute and various international organizations, global warming has resulted in alarming reductions of Ecuador's glaciers. Cotopaxi has lost over a third of its ice since 1976, and lower mountains could lose all of their glaciers within the next couple of decades. Many highland cities depend on snowmelt for their water supply, and this also is threatened by global warming.

The Ministry of Tourism states that foreign visitation is Ecuador's fourth most important source of income after oil and other exports. Mountaineers provide a substantial portion of this influx of tourist dollars. With the glaciers disappearing, the future of this sport could be quite bleak a generation from now. Nevertheless, mountaineering is currently one of the most attractive adventures that Ecuador has to offer to international visitors.

III

The Rise of the Popular

Ecuador was rapidly integrated into the world market during the second half of the 1800s. Global demand for minerals and "tropical" products from Latin America—such as sugar, rubber, bananas, coffee, cacao, and other commodities—expanded rapidly during this period of industrial growth in Europe and the United States. This globalization transformed the Americas. Latin American governments built hospitals, schools, highways, railroads, and ports while elites positioned themselves as the harbingers of "modernity," "progress," "civilization," and even "democracy." Despite such vocal proclamations, however, oligarchic power remained entrenched. Familiar divides between rich and poor; town and country; white, mestizo, indigenous, and Afro-descendants continued to define the socioeconomic landscape.

Nevertheless, by the first decades of the twentieth century, kinks in the oligarchic armor were apparent. The impact of the cacao boom was felt throughout Ecuador, from the growth in government coffers and the colonization of the coastal region to the development of related industries, the expansion of towns, and the visible presence of urban proletariats and middle classes. The collapse of cacao would bring much of this growth to a screeching halt, but popular classes—who were becoming real players in the nation's political system—did not simply disappear when their jobs or businesses evaporated.

The most visible, early, expression of this crisis was the now infamous November 1922 General Strike in Guayaquil in which workers brought the country's most politically charged city to a complete standstill. They were quickly massacred by police, but the massive presence of working people in the streets of Guayaquil signaled the slow and uneven symbolic breakup of the old order.

The contradictory rise of popular power was subsequently confirmed in the form of José María Velasco Ibarra, Ecuador's famous populist demagogue, who was elected president for the first of five times in 1934. His election both signaled and stimulated the dramatic growth in popular organizing, political activity, and cultural expression during the 1930s and 1940s. A simple statistic tells part of the story: prior to 1929 there were four unions in all of Ecuador;

AGRICULTURA. CACAOTALES. LA ROSA.

Cacao plantations, Santa Rosa, Ecuador, 1890. (Photo by Julio Vascones, courtesy of Taller Visual)

during the next decade that number climbed to seventy. Strikes in Guayaquil (now a city of 250,000), Quito, and other urban centers became a feature of Ecuadorian life, a process that only intensified after the "May Revolution" of 1944 and Velasco's return to power. The major national unions, including the Communist Party's own trade union—along with women's, students', and literally hundreds of peasant organizations—all formed during this exciting period.

The sustained and conspicuous presence of popular sectors on the political scene did not mean that the social structure was suddenly overturned. The collapse of the cacao economy and the onset of the Great Depression in the 1930s weakened the bargaining power of working people, most of whom were simply struggling to survive during the 1920s and 1930s. Most indigenous peoples remained under the thumb of landed elites, and Afro-Ecuadorians in the northern coast were marginalized in every sense of the word. But by the 1930s it was clear that a relatively modern, if imperfect and highly undemocratic, political system was emerging in which the country's traditional elite could no longer rule by fiat. Working and middle classes were making their voices heard, and elites were forced to listen.

This period was also characterized by acute political instability. Between 1924 and 1947 Ecuador had twenty-seven chiefs of state, six different constitutions, and a number of minirevolutions. Perhaps the phrase that best summarized this sense of political chaos was Velasco Ibarra's own: "Ecuador is a very difficult country to govern."

Ecuador also experienced a literary and artistic florescence during this period. In 1930, Demetrio Aguilera, Enrique Gil Gilbert, and Joaquín Gallegos Lara published a collection of short stories, *Los que se van*, which inaugurated the heyday of social realism and Indigenism (a diverse body of work aimed at defending and vindicating the continent's indigenous peoples. Some of it was romantic, but much of it addressed the social plight of indigenous peoples) in Ecuadorian fiction. The movement would last for two decades, even as Indigenist painting and fiction became incorporated into the state's nationalist mythology in the mid-1940s with the creation of the Casa de la Cultura Ecuatoriana. The Indigenist impulse would subsequently be charged with paternalism, even racism, with respect to the indigenous peoples that the movement sought to liberate. Nonetheless, social realism and Indigenismo were important artistic and literary routes that helped delegitimize hierarchical, racist, and semifeudal social relations. The most remarkable and best-known novel within this genre was Jorge Icaza's *Huasipungo*, first published in 1934. For their part, Ecuadorian painters—inspired in part by Mexican muralists— put behind folklorist themes and focused on the exploitation of common people, in particular indigenous peasants. The most well-known works of social realism are those of Eduardo Kingman and Oswaldo Guayasamín.

This renaissance of artistic expression was made possible by the transformations that the Liberal Revolution had ushered in. The secularization and expansion of education, combined with the general modernization of the country, allowed for the emergence of middle-class intellectuals who did not belong by birthright or ethnicity to the country's white elite. Many of these intellectuals would becomes key political figures within the Socialist and Communist Parties; others, such as Icaza, joined forces with the populist Concentración de Fuerzas Populares (Concentration of Popular Forces) and challenged the social order by denouncing the exploitation of the poor.

In the years immediately following World War II, Ecuador pulled itself out of this period of economic and political crisis (and creativity) by turning to another export product. In 1947, the country exported few bananas. During the next decade it would become the largest producer in the world, a transformation that would further stimulate the popular expressions that had cracked open the old order during the 1920s and 1930s.

Portrait of a People

Albert B. Franklin

Part anthropology, part history, part travel log, Ecuador: Portrait of a People, *was published in 1944 at a time when, according to its author, Ecuador was emerging from "hundreds of changeless years in which she has almost lost the sense of change" (v) and was now standing on the cusp of "modern life, of action, of change, and of progress." Indeed, Franklin was not the only (or last) observer to suggest that Ecuador was struggling to shake off its past—a past that supposedly had not changed since the Spanish Conquest. Limitations aside,* Portrait of a People *is a wonderfully readable and at times incredibly insightful account of Ecuadorian society during the tumultuous years between the collapse of the cacao economy in 1920 and the beginning of the banana boom in the late 1940s.*

When the sun rises on the Day of the Dead, in Otavalo, the Indians are all at the cemetery. The cemetery lies down the road toward Quiroga beyond the church. The Indians, with their great mushroom-shaped stiff felt hats, have been there since before dawn. They sit in little groups among the graves, cooking, and eating, and drinking. The bright pepper red of their ponchos and shawls and the white and russet of their hats form a colorful background for the black and white of the parish priest as he goes among them blessing the dead and sprinkling his holy water upon the graves. The priest is through with their graves early, to pass along to the Creole cemetery farther up the road, where the townspeople gather in decent black to await him.

The Otavalo Indian is the great tourist attraction of Ecuador. Clean, handsome, strong, and happy, he is very different from the Indian of the central provinces. Many, if not most, of the Otavalo Indians own their own property. Aside from their subsistence, which they draw from their parcels of soil, they are famous weavers, and the sale of their woolen cloths brings them that extra income which enables them to buy their harps, to indulge in imported cloths as well as their own brilliant weaves, and to strengthen their resistance to political and social absorption by the rest of the country. The Otavalo Indians' chief contribution to the welfare of Ecuador is the money which flows into Quito from Otavalo through the national tax on alcohol.

As yet, the Otavalo Indians are "unspoiled." They treat the frequent tourists with indifference or scorn. Their customs have changed not at all since Hassaurek visited them eighty years ago. Then as now the custom that caught the attention of the foreign traveler was that of traveling always in pairs, man and wife, to and from fiestas. The wife never gets more than just a little intoxicated. This leaves the man free to drink his fill, and after the fiesta the wives walk slowly along the roads, forcibly holding their violently drunken husbands from dashing into the path of automobiles, or squat patiently by the roadside, pillowing their husbands' heads. They have always been quite musical and fond of dancing. Their musical instruments are the harp, the *rondador*, or pipes of Pan, and the rustic flute. The Catholic Church offers them the ritual, the imagery, and the fiestas that their spirits need, and they are all, or almost all, devout and munificent supporters of the local parish.

Though the town of Otavalo has only thirteen telephones, it is one of the most wealthy and best cared for of minor Ecuadorian municipalities. It has unexcelled sidewalks, though the Indians prefer the wide stones built into the cobbled streets. It has also a municipal swimming pool, extremely modern and hygienic, which is never used by Indians.

Tourists come to Otavalo to "see" the Indians. What they "see" depends upon what they bring with them. Many come, as Rousseau would have done, and see a tribe of happy humans, untouched by the ills and diseases of civilization, happy, clean, carefree, peaceful. Some see a society so perfectly organized before the Spaniards came that its organization has not been broken down, except superficially. The Otavalos remain an undigested and perhaps undigestible nucleus within the Spanish colonial empire and within the Republic. Whoever comes to Otavalo knows, as he stands among the Indians in their cemetery, or at their market, that he is a ghost. He, the tourist, is like the Yankee in King Arthur's Court. He is there, and yet he is not there. He could show these people the wonders of which he has learned in school and college, and they would laugh with him at his brilliance, and when he was gone, they would return to the ways they never really left.

Surely the cholos of Otavalo are members of a feudal society, but you can enter with them into their cockfights, bet with them, talk with them. But whatever conversation in Spanish or Quichua you may pry out of an Otavalo, you are not allowed to forget that you are not talking with him, but making him talk to you. He won't let you forget. To him you are something unknown and untrusted. He doesn't believe in you. You probably don't exist. The priest, the *teniente*, the *mayordomos*, the hacendados, these exist. The man from the city is a ghost.

From the market, on Sundays, the Indians go to their churches, some in Otavalo, some in Quiroga, some in Cotacachi. After the market the crowds of

Indians begin gathering outside of the churches, waiting for the bell to ring. In Quiroga the priest, on a fine, imported horse, rides up the steps and onto the stone terrace before the church, and disappears around the side.

In Otavalo proper there are not so many Indians. The majority of the parishioners are townsfolk. In Cotacachi, a heavy-tolling church bell calls Indians and townsfolk inside.

After the bright sunlight, Rosa, the *patrona*, the artist who had joined us, and I could not for a moment get accustomed to the darkness. The church was filled. We moved forward through the crowd, halfway down the side aisle. All the seats were full. Near us, toward the center of the building, a group of twenty girls from the convent school, children of the townspeople, were in attendance in their blue and white uniforms. Their voices rose and fell in unison before the beginning of the Mass as their Sisters led them in a responsive reading of their own, which they knew so well that they had no need of books. As they crossed themselves at the end of their particular devotions, the Indians nearby looked up, murmured, and crossed themselves too. Sitting cross-legged on the floor at my feet was a massive Indian woman with a child in her lap. As the soothing voices stopped, the infant began to cry. The woman looked down, made clucking noises, and with a movement of her shoulder released a well-filled breast from her shift and pressed her child's face to the nipple. The whole church was filled with the murmur of hundreds of rosaries.

After the service there was a fiesta down the street in a tavern. The artist stood for a moment on the church steps making a few sketches from memory of what he had seen, and then brought us to the tavern. The patio was filled with Indians, but the tavern keeper insisted on our drinking our *chicha* [corn-based fermented alcoholic beverage] in a private room on the side. Upon the *patrona*'s protest that she enjoyed Indian music and had not heard enough of it, the musicians were brought in from the patio, where they had been entertaining some sixty of their own kind, and performed for us alone.

They were a flautist and a guitarist. Their music was pathetically simple and repetitive. Three simple phrases for the flute, and three simple changes for the guitar, repeated over and over. First the two Indians, fine handsome boys they were, sat on a bench, playing together, until they felt they were doing well together. Then they got up and stood in the middle of the room. Gradually their feet began to move. They held their eyes on each other's faces and stomped, without raising their feet more than a few inches from the floor. As they played and danced they looked like two fighting cocks warily moving around each other looking for an opening. This is their manner of dancing also when they are dancing with their women. Their concentration helps give the dance the appearance of a complicated ritual.

There is a movie in Otavalo. White people and cholos sit on the ground floor. The very poor and the Indians go upstairs. It is the Indians who really support the movie house. Frequently the ground floor is almost empty. The reaction from the gallery is never predictable. The movies are in English, and the people represented move in a world which to them is less than fiction. Their ideas of family relations among these strange, flickering beings must be strange. The gallery in the Otavalo theater may suddenly burst out laughing as one man at a point where nothing in particular seems to be happening. At the most exciting times they may be sitting, talking in Quichua to one another, entirely unconcerned with the movie. One thing is clear. They like color better than black and white and cartoons better than photographs. Animal cartoons they understand and follow, and an animal cartoon, if properly advertised, will bring the Indians on foot from miles around. When movies are accompanied by a musical score, they apparently listen to the music and forget the movie.

Their reaction to music is surprising. On another visit to Otavalo, in the evening, sitting in a café over steaming mulberry *canelazos* [an alcoholic drink made from sugar cane] with some friends, I took the guitar down from its peg on the wall, where it hangs in all Ecuadorian cafés, and intoned a Western cowboy song, not too well, but with the abandon of one who knows that the great artists of the microphone are thousands of miles away. When I was through, I followed my friends' glance to the door. Around the doorjambs, wide-eyed, peered delighted Indian faces. In a panic of stage fright I hung the guitar back on its peg. The Indians did not leave. They stayed there patiently for over an hour, on the off-chance that the foreigner would again be seized with the desire to sing the songs of his country. Their patience wore out my resistance. I tried another. No. That wasn't what they wanted. They wanted the first one again. After I was through, they were more expectant than ever. Why? They thought, since I'd sung it twice, I might do it again any time. I gave them a last rendition and resolved never to touch a guitar again except in private. Much later, when we went out, to go home, three Indians were sleeping on the sidewalk, their backs against the wall, waiting.

You Are Not My President

José María Velasco Ibarra

The following letter was written by the former president of Ecuador, Velasco Ibarra, from Chile in 1941 to then current president Carlos Arroyo del Río. It is vintage Velasco Ibarra. He impugns Arroyo for just about everything, including Arroyo's undemocratic usurpation of power, his disastrous defeat in a border war with Peru, and his mishandling of the economy. Velasco would return to the Presidency in 1944.

Santiago, Chile, 2 August 1941.
Doctor Carlos Arroyo del Río,
Quito. (Ecuador)

Sir,

It is not possible to call you President of the Republic of Ecuador. Political Constitutions are given for a purpose in free countries. The President of the Republic of Ecuador is a magistrate, Chief of the Executive branch of the government, and elected by direct suffrage by a sovereign people. You were not appointed by a free suffrage. In certain regions, as in Quito, the inscription of electors was hindered by unworthy and despicable means. In other regions, as in Guayaquil, where I spent the second day of elections, the police kept the air ringing with their shooting; killed, wounded, and made everybody run. You did not arrive to the government through frauds usual in some Spanish American countries. No. The crowds of Ibarra, Ambato, Riobamba, Guayaquil, and all of Ecuador expressed in formidable masses their hatred of you. You grabbed power through the action of challenging material forces. You are not, therefore, the President of Ecuador, if any seriousness is to be given to words. You are a dictator, as Federico Páez, as Colonel Enríquez; a dictator, a very intelligent one, with a large and profitable experience, always at the service of foreign interests, in the handling of low methods that disguise everything in order to squirm through the greatest plights.

In view of the civic consciousness to which Ecuador has arrived in the last years, an usurpation of power as yours condemned you to a government of violence and craft, as no popular support could you possibly find in these serious moments that distress all nations. You were menaced by economic chaos and general discontent days before an international tragedy, without a parallel in our history, which was to come and darken the face of our country with the deepest sorrow. A whole province occupied by the enemy and you yourself forced to withdraw a decree in the way that was imposed on your administration and of your foreign policy.

What is inconceivable is that you still remain in government. All governments responsible for national disasters have invariably left power, in order to give place to the free trial of the men responsible, for reparation and for reconstruction. You have recently and solemnly made declarations of facts and dates and Peru has recently given you the lie, making use of your own words as expressed in a public document. It is not possible for you to continue in the rank of chiefs of State. You damage the international respectability of our country.

Our country is in need of a return to its international personality, of rebuilding its moral, economic and military foundations, and of becoming once again what it was in the American world in the days of Montalvo and Luis Felipe Borja, Julio Andrade and Gonzales Suárez, Alfaro and Plaza. Your permanency in the government will only be an inducement for continuous revolutions, an inevitable divorce in the Ecuadorian people, and, possibly, a near disaggregation of our country.

Ecuadorian history, that will not record a single great act or directing principle of yours, will with justice accuse you of a violent usurpation of government, of the most unmerited and unhappy international defeat. Let us hope it will not also accuse you of having been the grave digger of the country.

Many people abroad think that you encouraged the attacks of Peru in order to divert problems of internal politics. It is because of this that the voice of Ecuador has not been listened to either with respect or attention. You said that the ideal of American unity it is not as yet a real conquest. You perhaps refer to the fact that solidarity amongst American nations is not as yet effective. But in order to encourage juridical cooperation among American countries, should it not have appeared to you and to your Minister of Foreign Affaires that it was an elementary duty to have rudimentary international courtesy with Chile, that is one of the main powers in Spanish America and also a traditional friend of ours? It is now for more than a year that the Legation of Ecuador in Santiago is without a Minister Plenipotentiary. Peru boasts an Ambassador who is intelligent, active, and cultured. . . . Your government insists on keeping the Ecuadorian Legation in Santiago without a head and this in the most difficult international times and all too near 10 August (Ecuador's national holiday). You and your Minister do not realize how complex and delicate international sentiments are. I will be left for another occasion to tell you how important your mistakes toward Chile have been. Diplomacy should not find its inspiration in silly jealousies. Diplomacy is the wise handling of great interests between nations. You cannot have posts vacant because others occupy them. You have no right to feel discouraged; you should tactfully insist. You may not forget vital points; you should double your efforts and means in order to obtain victory. Ecuador fights Peru with a Colombia that is indifferent and a Chile that is hurt; this shows lack of elemental foresight on the part of the Government. In 1910 General Alfaro came out victorious because he knew how to win diplomatic and popular sympathies from Chile and Colombia; at a cost of heavy sacrifices, it is true. The life of Ecuador is well worth many a sacrifice.

The very mediation of Brazil, Argentina, and the United States should not have been encouraged except with wise consideration in order to accept it fully, tactfully, so as to avoid the displeasure of Chile and of Colombia.

The nation that wishes to exist should primarily count on its own diplomatic and military resources; and, without trusting on quixotic sentiments from any, make use of the interests of all. Only the strong have allies.

The Ecuadorian Army is not responsible for our defeat. It is unjust to hold it so. Responsibility solely lies on you, your Minister of Foreign Affairs, your Minister of Defense, who investigated nothing, nor foresaw or avoided anything. Ever since November, I learned with horror in Piura that Peru, angry, it was said, by the policy of border clashes started by Dictator Enríquez, had began to accumulate stores against Ecuador. Your Minister of Foreign Affairs was duly informed. He ought to have been informed, in any case. What did he do in order to weather the storm? When are the resources of diplomacy to be used? Was it not possible to give the alarm to friendly nations? Your Minister should have addressed them with dignity, with high-mindedness, without exposing us to the shame of being called to order in points of courtesy for the language employed. It was the time to weather the storm as it has ever been done even by great powers until our defensive resources were strengthened. The flag of a country, its military traditions, the sovereignty of a State are not things with which one can gamble. If the army had been criminally weakened, everything should have been done to make it invincible for the defense of the dignity of Ecuador and its territory.

When, around 1934, I asked that Peru be treated as from a nation to another nation, as an equal to an equal, with no bluff but with dignity, I was accused by you and your followers of compromising the dignity of the Republic. With deep sorrow before the reality of a horrible prevision, I wrote as follows in my book *Consciousness or Barbarity*: "If Ecuador continues to be insolated it will be crushed by Peru. Ecuador is in need of developing its international relations and friendships. It is in need of avoiding two extremes: the one is believing in the quixotism of nations and [the other] that of eternally blaming them at the moment when no effort is made to develop the means for its own strength and responsibility."

And now, solely in order to flatter your vanity with the empty applause of a people who love their country, you rush or let yourself be blindly rushed to a military enterprise with no other help than that given you by the most senseless of diplomatic moves.

At the hour of dismal sorrow, at the moment when the most cherished treasures of a country were ravished in your hands (its autonomy, its right to dictate its own laws and decrees), we, Ecuadorians, turned our ayes to the glorious and traditional horizons of Ecuador, in both its civil activities and its military prestige; Rocafuerte was a diplomatic agent of Mexico; Olmedo lent the greatest services to the independence of Peru. Blood of Ecuadorians was shed in the fields of Ayacucho; and in the public square of "2 de Mayo" in Lima a monument bears witness to the fact that Ecuador effectively cooperated with Peru and Chile in order to refuse an attack on American sovereignty.

Your mistakes will be absorbed by so much splendor; and the effort of our youth, of our people, and of our army will see to it that the sun of the Ecuadorian nation will never set.

J. M. Velasco Ibarra

The Wonderland

Raphael V. Lasso

Raphael Lasso was the founder of the Ecuadorian American Chamber of Commerce of the United States and the editor of the magazine Ecuador. *Written in 1944,* The Wonderland *provides a fairly detailed description of Ecuador's political, economic, and territorial status during that decade. Today, it is valued less as a historical portrait of Ecuador than as a window into American perceptions of Latin America during this period.*

"Yale" and "Harvard" Hats

Like the color and design of the ponchos, the type of headdress also denotes the tribe to which an Ecuadorean Indian belongs. This fact is also true of Peru and other Andean countries.

In the Ambato region, to the South of Quito, both the men and women wear small white felts hats amazingly similar to those worn by "Varsity men" at Yale and other American Colleges. In fact, the Indians in Ambato give the brim exactly the same twist as that of "Eli's," front part down and the back up, and in order to make the resemblance more marked, they even wear these hats at an exaggerated angle on the back of their heads. All that they require to pass unnoticed in the "Harkness Squad" is a crew haircut and a Camel's hair coat.

In Quito proper, those Indians who have adopted the European customs, have a penchant for narrow-brimmed brown felt hats. Like their cousins from Ambato, they turn the front part of the brim down, the back up, and slide the hat back over their napes. The result, a "Harvard man." But it is pushed back and as far down as the poncho, which fortunately no Ecuadorean Indian will discard, no matter how near he may approach the adoption of the European customs.

At Otavalo, to the North, most women wear a white cotton turban loosely fitted atop their heads. Other women as well as all the men wear large hats with wide, up-turned brims. These hats are made of wool which is dipped into a substance similar to mucilage, through which it secures an iron-like consistency. The women, generally, when wearing these hats instead of turbans, drape a folded shawl over the crown. Both men and women braid their hair into long pigtails, so that young males might often be mistaken for girls, were it not for the fact that their bare legs are exposed below their poncho.

From the old women of the tribes, who sit calmly spinning yarn, to the bright-eyed children, there is not even the slightest commotion or the least excitement, when the buyer or traveler moves along from one group to another for the purpose of examining the quality of the wares or even for comparing the prices.

Should the visitor make a purchase, the Indian will accept his money, give him a shy smile, and thereupon hand over the merchandise. If otherwise, the Indian simply arranges his wares in their proper place and silently resumes his traditional crouching position. The impassiveness of these peaceful, kindly people is well-nigh amazing.

Among Ecuadoreans, the Otavalo Indians are considered the cleanest and best dressed of all the other tribes. In other Andean regions most of the Indians have a tendency to be ragged and untidy; but among the Otavalo Indians this condition is completely reversed. Water being plentiful in this region, they pride themselves in their cleanliness.

Their costumes are the most colorful and authentic in all of the Northern Andes. The men as a rule wear short white cotton trousers reaching only as far as the knees and a white shirt of the same material with a turned-up collar similar to that on a Russian shirt. These collars are beautifully embroidered with red, blue, and green designs. The trousers and shirt are held together by a long, finely embroidered belt which the Indians wind around themselves in spiral fashion, so that it resembles a belt of extraordinary width, although actually it is only an inch and a half wide. Whether it is cold or warm, the Indian wears over this, his traditional poncho. That denotes the tribe to which he belongs. This is a heavy woolen blanket partially opened at a seam in order to permit the head to pass through. The colors of these ponchos are gorgeously delicate, yet remarkably vivid: various shades of red, ranging from maroon to magenta, while dark blue and tan predominate. The ponchos, in most instances, are further embellished with multicolored stripes at each end.

Patrón and Peon on an Andean Hacienda

Jorge Icaza

Translated by Bernard M. Dulsey

The burden placed on haciendas by the smallness and unreliability of regional markets was not borne completely by their owners, since part of it could be passed on to the workers by holding their wages below market level. This shifting of the burden depended in part on the use of coercive mechanisms such as debt peonage to hold workers on the estate, but it also reflected the fact that the conditions of life in independent landowning communities were often such as to make it possible for the hacienda to attract laborers by providing a degree of economic security. Though he might effectively pay them nothing, a patrón was expected to take ultimate responsibility for the welfare of his peons. The novel Huasipungo *(1934), from which the following excerpt is taken, shows us how ingrained these expectations were and suggests that a hacendado who failed to live up to them was likely to drive his peons into revolt. Like the Peruvian writer Ciro Alegría, the Ecuadorian writer Jorge Icaza gained an international reputation during the 1930s for his novels of social protest, of which* Huasipungo *was the first and best known.*

After speaking to his neighbors on the slope of the big hill, where hunger and the necessities of life had become more and more urgent—in that area where families of the *huasipungueros* [a resident laborer who received a small plot of land (huasipungo) in return for labor on a hacienda; a very onerous system] displaced from the banks of the river were clustered in caves or in impro-vised huts—the crippled Andrés Chiliquinga climbed down by the shortcut. It should be added here that the Indians who had lost their *huasipungos* and all the peons of the hacienda, some bitterly and some with naive illusions, were expecting the *socorros* [a yearly handout by the patron]—the annual help—that the administrator, the owner, or the tenant on the land had always been accustomed to sharing after the crops had been harvested. "Will it be on the patron saint's day? Will it take place on Sunday? Maybe for the feast of the Holy Mother? Perhaps on . . . ? When will it be, pes [then]?" the Indians asked one another as the days kept going by.

In truth, the socorros—one and one-half bushels of *corn* or barley—with the huasipungo loaned to them and ten cents a day wages (money which the Indians never even got a whiff of because it went to pay for, with no possibility of amortization, the hereditary debt of all living huasipungueros for the advances on the saints' or Virgins' feast days of the *taita cura* [parish priest] for the sake of the dead huasipungueros) made up the annual payment that the landowner granted to each Indian family for its work. Someone from the valley or from the mountain asserted that the *patrón* must have forgotten the traditional custom, but the gossip that ran through the village was different:

"No. . . . He won't give any socorros this year. The Indians have been screwed," "They're screwed. . . ." "He's buying up grain to fill his granaries." "He's buying like crazy. . . ." He's buying so he can fix his own price later when we'll be screwed also, ~~cholitos~~. "He won't give a single grain to anyone. Nooo."

When the waiting period could no longer be endured and hunger was an animal barking in their bellies, a goodly number of the Indians, old and young, on Don Alfonso's property swarmed up to the patio of the hacienda in a dark, noisy, and unrestrainable group. Since it was very early, and drizzling besides, each one sought some shelter in the corners until the patrón should awaken and decide he was ready to listen to them. After a long hour of waiting they again solicited the help of the *cholo* [person of mixed Indian and white blood] Policarpio, who was going in and out of the house constantly:

"Be kind to us, pes, master *mayordomo*. Socorritus. . . . We have come to ask for socorritus."

"For socorritus."

"The master mayordomo already knows."

The cholo, become more sly and proud because of the Indians' entreaties, spread news of vague hopes:

"Now . . . the patrón is up now, goddamit."

"We only hope so, pes."

"He's drinking his coffee. Don't bother him now."

"Taitiquitu."

"He's angry . . . angry . . ."

"Ave Maria. God help us."

With a big frown and a whip in his right hand, Don Alfonso showed himself on the porch that faced the patio.

"What's the matter? What do you want?" he cried in a grating voice.

Suddenly the Indians, both men and women, with a magical briskness and in an apparently humble silence, gathered at a prudent distance from the porch. In those first few seconds—as they urged one another forward with little pushes and elbowings—not one of them dared to compromise himself by stating their urgent case to the patrón. Impatiently, tapping his boots with the whip. Don Alfonso again shouted:

"What do you want? Are you going to stand there like a bunch of idiots?

Somewhat unhappily, and with the attitude of a dog fawning on its master, the mayordomo, who also would profit by several bushels from the socorros, spoke up:

"Well, it's like this, patrón. They've come to request a little charity from your worship."

"Eh?"

"A little charity, pes."

"More? More charity than I already give them, goddamit?" interrupted Don Alfonso icily, hoping to eliminate once and for all the daring attitude of the Indians.

He knew . . .

"The socorritos, pes! The poor Indian is dying of hunger. He has nothing. They've always given socorros, *su mercé*," dared to request in chorus the Indians who were of the group displaced from the banks of the river. And then as if someone had opened the floodgate of the physical needs of that sullen, dark mass, all suddenly found their tongues to tell of the hunger of their babies, the sickness of their old people, the increasing boldness of the Indian girls, the tragedy of the devastated huasipungos, of the endurable misery of past years, and of the unendurable misery of the present one. It quickly became a threatening clamor, chaotic and rebellious, in which diverse cries would rise and fall:

"Socorrus, taiticu!"

"We've always received them!"

"All-1 -1-ways!"

"The baby, too . . ."

"The wife, too . . ."

"Socorrus, a little corn to roast."

"Socorrus, a little barley for porridge."

"Socorrus, a few potatoes for a fiesta."

"Socorruuus!"

Like surging waves the supplications rolled on to the hacienda porch enveloping the increasingly nervous patrón, increasingly bathed in that fetid bitterness of the peons' outcries. But Don Alfonso, shaking his head, was able to shout:

"That's enough, damn it, that's enough."

"Taiticu."

"I've told you over and over that I'm giving you nothing this year. Do you understand me? It's nothing but a barbaric custom!"

"What do you mean, patroncitu?

"That's what I pay you for. . . . That's why I give you the huasipungos. . . ."

"We need the socorritus, too, pes."

"You're still complaining, goddamit? Get out of here! Get out!"

The complaints stopped all at once, but the throng stayed on, motion-less, petrified, grim. Meanwhile some miserly calculations went through the landowner's mind: "I must not give in. Four or five tons just to give away to these barbarians. No! They can fetch a good price in Quito. It would bring enough to pay the priest for the use of his trucks. Enough to . . . If I give in to them I won't have enough to do business with the gringos. Oh, they've met their match in me. They'll learn I'm a real man!" Mechanically Pereira took a step, two steps forward until he came to the edge of the first stone step of the porch. Then he arched the flexible whip handle with both hands and, break-ing the silence, shouted:

"You're still here? You didn't hear me, goddamit?

Solid as a wall, the Indian throng didn't budge. Confronted with such resis-tance Don Alfonso for a few long seconds didn't know what to say. Perhaps for an instant he felt beaten, swallowed up by what he believed to be an unheard-of rebellion. What could he do with them? What could he do with his pent-up rage? Almost crazed with wrath he went down the three stone steps and, approaching the nearest group, he grabbed a young Indian and shook him like a filthy rag, all the while uttering half-choked oaths. Finally the victim was rolling on the ground. The mayordomo, fearful of what might occur, for he could see how icy was the fury in the eyes of the Indians, helped the fallen Indian to his feet and reproached the crowd in a loud voice so that all of them could hear:

"Don't be so ill-mannered. You shouldn't get the poor patrón so angry. He'll die of rage. He'll just die. What'll happen to you then? Don't you under-stand or don't you have any hearts?"

Hearing the cholo's words Don Alfonso felt himself to be a martyr to his duty, to his obligation. In a voice hoarse with fatigue he managed to shout:

"These . . . These Indians are driving me to an early grave.

I'm the one to blame, goddamit . . . for having spoiled them as though they were my own children."

"Poor patrón," said the mayordomo, and instinctively, in defense against any possible attack from the outraged Indians, mounted his mule.

The landowner, on the other hand, inspired by the example set by the priest, lifted his eyes and hands to heaven and in a voice that demanded an infernal punishment for his cruel enemies, screeched:

"Oh, my God! My God! You watch us from above . . . You who have often told me to be harsher with these Indian savages."

"Protect me now. Defend me! Don't you hear me? Send a punishment for a warning to them . . . Or a voice."

Don Alfonso's attitude and his request stunned the Indian throng. It was dangerous for them when the priest or the patrón began a dialogue with Taita Dios. Yes, it was. It was something superior to the weak efforts of Indians caught in the trap of the huasipungo, to the feebleness of men dirty, meek, and forsaken. They forgot the socorros, forgot why they were there, forgot everything. A desire to flee overpowered them and, immediately, some covertly, others openly, they began to dissolve.

"Goddamit! Turn the dogs loose on them. The fierce dogs!" the mayordomo then shouted, his kindness and fears abruptly transformed, with a devilish cynicism, into the cries and actions of an executioner.

The angry dogs and the whips of the mayordomo and the Indian servants of the patrón's house angrier still, swept the patio clean in a few minutes. When Policarpio returned to the patrón he said to him with slavering deviousness:

"You'll see, su mercé. Just now when I was chasing the Indians I overheard them swearing to return in the night to take the socorros by hook or crook."

"What's that?"

"They're starving. They could even kill us."

"That they may be able to do with some fool coward, but not with me. Here I am the power and the law."

"You're right, of course, pes," murmured the cholo, just to be saying something.

"Go at once to the sheriff and tell him to send me the two peasants who are his deputies. Armed . . ."

"O.K. patrón."

"Oh, and tell him to telephone Quito and ask the Police Inspector in my name to send us a squad to crush any possible criminal uprising among the Indians. Don't forget: in my name. He knows what to. . . ."

"Sí, certainly, pes."

The mayordomo went off like a shot from a cannon, and Don Alfonso, feeling himself all alone—for the *huasicamas* were, after all, Indians and could betray him, the cook and the female servants were Indians and would not inform him—was stricken with a strange fear, an infantile, stupid fear. He ran to his room and took the pistol from his night table and, with terror-crazed violence, aimed at the door as he shouted:

"Now, goddamit! Come on, now, you filthy Indians."

When the echo of his threat was his only answer he became somewhat mollified. Nevertheless he advanced a few steps and looked suspiciously in all the corners. "Nobody's here . . . I'm just like a woman. . . ." he said to himself, and he laid the pistol down. Then, exhausted from the nervous fright brought on by the impertinences of the Indians, he flung himself headlong on his bed like a betrayed woman. Of course, he didn't cry: but instead sadistically evoked macabre scenes which proved to him the savagery of the Indians. How did they kill Don Victor Lemus, the owner of Tumbamishqui? By making him walk on a gravel path after first flaying the skin of his hands and feet. And they disposed of Don Jorge Mendieta by tossing him into a caldron of boiling cane syrup at the sugar mill. And Don Ricardo Salas Jijón by abandoning him on the mountain in a pit dug to trap beasts. "All . . . All because of stupidity . . . Because one doesn't give them what they want. . . . Because one gets their lands or water through some court action. . . . Because the brazen young Indian girls have been violated at a tender age. . . . Because . . . All little insignificant things . . . Stupid things . . ." Don Alfonso thought. That night, the presence of the two armed peasants and Policarpio restored his peace of mind. Nevertheless, when he went to be, he said to himself: "These criminals will rebel one of these days. And when that happens we won't be able to choke it off as we did today. . . . Today . . . Then I'll . . ." A charitable voice vibrated hopefully in the great señor of the region: "The hell with those who come after me; I'll be gone by then."

"Yes. To hell with them," Don Alfonso muttered in the darkness, with a smile of diabolic selfishness.

The Man Who Was Kicked to Death

Pablo Palacio

Translated by Wilfrido H. Corral

Pablo Palacio (1906–47) is widely considered the founder of the avant-garde novel in South America. This is a late recognition, as literary historians insisted in portraying the artist as a troubled man because of the metafictional and "odd" themes he displayed. He started publishing short stories as an adolescent, and the quality of his work never diminished. His first and most important collection, Un hombre muerto a puntapiés (cuentos) *(A Man Kicked to Death [Stories]), appeared in 1927, the same year in which he published his first novel,* Débora, novela *(Deborah, Novel). Both works were vastly different from the social realism that was the norm for his contemporaries. Palacio's best-known novel,* Vida del ahorcado: Novela subjetiva *(Life of the Hanged: Subjective Novel) is from 1932. A critical edition of his complete works, which includes philosophical essays, was published in 2000 by* UNESCO's *Collection Archives.*

"How can we dispose of sensational Street events? Clarifying truth is a moral act."
—El Comercio, Quito

"Last night, around 12:30 AM, Police Officer No. 451, assigned to that precinct, found a man named Ramírez lying completely flat between Escobedo and García Streets. The unfortunate man's nose was bleeding profusely, and when questioned by the officer he said he had been the victim of an assault by unknown individuals just because he had asked them for a cigarette. The officer asked the victim to accompany him to the police station to provide a statement that could shed some light on the matter, but Ramírez flatly refused to do so. The officer, following orders, then asked one of the drivers at the nearest taxi stand for help, and they drove the injured party to the police station, where he died within a few hours, in spite of Dr. Ciro Benavídez's medical attention."

"By this morning, the Captain of the 6th Precinct had followed all the usual formalities, but he was unable to discover anything about the murderers or about Ramírez's identity. The only information known, by chance, was that the deceased had vices."

"We'll try to keep our readers up to date on what is found out about this mysterious event."

The *Diario de la Tarde*'s police page said no more about the bloody event.

I don't know how I felt then, but the fact is I laughed my head off. A man kicked to death! As far as I was concerned that was the funniest, the most hilarious thing that could possibly happen.

I waited until the next day and eagerly leafed through the paper, but there wasn't a line about my man. Nothing the next day either. I think after ten days nobody remembered what happened between Escobedo and García Streets.

But that began to obsess me. Everywhere I went the hilarious phrase "A man kicked to death!" followed me. All the letters danced before my eyes so joyfully that I resolved to reconstruct that Street scene or at least fathom the mystery of *why* a man was killed in such a ridiculous way.

Damn!, how I would have wanted to do an experimental study, but I've read that such studies only investigate the *how* of things. Between my first idea, which was that of reconstruction, and that of finding out why *certain individuals* would attack and kick another, the second seemed to me more original and beneficial for humanity. Well, it is said that the why of things is within the domain of philosophy, and I actually never imagined that my investigation would contain anything philosophical, and besides anything that even sounds like that word annoys me. So, half-fearful and half-discouraged, I lit my pipe. It is essential to do that, very essential.

The first question that comes up before all those who muck up these investigations is that of method. All University students, Teachers' colleges and High School students, and in general all people who want to better themselves, have this information at their fingertips. There are two methods: deduction and induction (see Aristotle and Bacon).

The first, deduction, didn't interest me. I've been told that deduction is a mode of investigation that goes from the best known to the least known. A good method: I confess. But I knew very little about the event and so I had to skip that page.

Now, induction is something marvelous. It goes from the least known to the best known . . . (How does it work? I don't remember . . . Well, who knows about these things anyway?) If I am right, this is the method par excellence. When you know a little, you have to induce. So induce, young man.

Thus resolved, I lit my pipe and with that formidable weapon of induction in hand, I was still irresolute, not knowing what to do.

Fine, and how do I apply this marvelous method? I asked myself.

If only I had studied logic! I was going to remain ignorant of the famous events of Escobedo and García Streets all because of the damn laziness of my early years.

Discouraged, I picked up the 13 January *Diario de la Tarde*—the unlucky paper had never left my desk—and taking vigorous puffs on my fired-up, big-assed pipe, I reread the bit of yellow journalism reproduced above. I had to wrinkle my brow like all studious men—a deep line between the eyebrows is the unequivocal sign of attention!

I read and I read, until I was struck by something that left me almost dazzled.

The next-to-last paragraph, especially the one that said, "By this morn-ing, the Captain of the 6th Precinct . . ." was the one that really startled me. The last sentence made my eyes sparkle: "The only information known, by chance, was that the deceased had a couple of vices." And I, by means of a secret power that you wouldn't understand, read it like this: A COUPLE OF VICES, in huge letters.

I believe it was a revelation from the goddess Ishtar. From then on the only point that interested me was to verify what kind of *vice* the dead Ramírez had. Intuitively I discovered that he was . . . No, I won't say it so as not to ruin the memory women have of him . . .

What I knew intuitively I had to verify through reasoning, and if possible, with proof.

For that, I went down to see the Captain of the 6th Precinct, who would be able to give me the revealing data. The police hadn't cleared up anything. He even had trouble figuring out what I wanted. After lengthy explanations, scratching his forehead, he said:

"Oh! Yes . . . That Ramírez business . . . You see how we've already given up . . . It was all kind of strange! But, sit down; why don't you sit down sir . . . As you might know already, they brought him in around one o'clock and he died a couple of hours later . . . Poor guy. We took two photos, just in case . . . some relative . . . Are you related to Mr. Ramírez? You have my sympathy . . . my most sincere . . ."

"No, sir," I said indignantly, "I didn't even know him. I'm a man who is interested in justice, nothing else."

I smiled deep down inside. What a well-chosen phrase! Huh? "I'm a man who is interested in justice, nothing else." How it tormented the Captain! So as not to embarrass him further I quickly added:

"You said you have two pictures. If I could I see them . . ."

The dignified civil servant pulled open one of his desk drawers and turned over some papers. He then opened another and turned over some other pa-pers. In a third, already getting angry, he finally found the pictures.

And he was very proper about it:

"You are interested in this matter. Just take them sir . . . That is, as long as you return them, he said, nodding his head up and down as he said these last words, taking pleasure in showing me his yellowed teeth . . ."

I thanked him profusely, and kept the pictures.

"And tell me, Captain sir, you wouldn't be able to remember some distinguishing marks about the deceased, some piece of information that might reveal something?"

"Something special . . . some information . . . No, no. Well, he was a completely ordinary man. More or less my height"—The Captain was a bit on the tall side—thick, with flabby flesh. "But a distinguishing mark . . . no . . . not that I remember . . ."

Since the Precinct Captain couldn't tell me any more I left, thanking him again.

I hurried home; shut myself in my study; lit my pipe and took out the pictures, which along with the newspaper article were precious documents.

Sure that I could not get others, I resolved to work with what fate had placed within my grasp.

The first thing to do is to study the man, I told myself. And I went to work.

I looked and looked at the pictures, one by one, studying them completely. I would bring them close to my eyes; separate them, stretching out my arm; trying to discover their secrets.

Until finally, after having them in front of me for so long, I managed to memorize every hidden feature.

That bulge sticking from his forehead; that large and strange nose—that looks so much like the crystal stopper in the water bottle of my cheap little restaurant!—that large and limp mustache, that pointed goatee; that straight, messy hair.

I took a piece of paper, and traced the lines that make up the dead Ramírez's face. Later, when the drawing was finished, I noticed that something was missing; that what I was looking at wasn't him; that some finishing indispensable detail had escaped me . . . Yes! I picked up the pen and finished his chest, a magnificent chest which, had it been made of plaster, would have fit right in in some art academy. A chest whose breasts have something womanly about them.

Then . . . then I was merciless and put a halo on him! A halo that you put on the skull with a little nail, just like they put them on the statues of saints in churches.

The dead Ramírez made a wonderful figure!

But, Why do I mention this? I was trying . . . trying to learn why they killed him; yes, *why* they killed him . . .

Then I concocted the following logical conclusions:

The late Ramírez was called Octavio Ramírez (anyone with a nose like the deceased's couldn't have had another name);

Octavio Ramírez was forty-two years old.

Octavio Ramírez was short of money.

Octavio Ramírez was poorly dressed; and, finally, our deceased was a foreigner.

With these precious data, his personality was totally reconstructed.

The only thing that was missing, then, was the motive, which for me gradually began to take on the quality of hard evidence. Intuition revealed everything to me. The only thing I had to do, as a small matter of honesty, was to eliminate all the other *possibilities*. The first, his own declaration, the issue of the cigarette, wasn't even worth considering. It's absolutely absurd to victimize someone in such a vile way for such a trivial matter. He had lied, hidden the truth; worse yet, he had murdered the truth, and he had done so because he didn't want to, he couldn't say *the other thing*.

Was the late Ramírez drunk? No, that couldn't be, because the police would have noticed that immediately and the newspaper story would have confirmed it, without a doubt, or, if it wasn't on record because of the reporter's carelessness, the Police Captain would have revealed it to me without any hesitation.

What other vice could our wretched victim have? He certainly had a vice—nobody can convince me otherwise. The proof of that was his stubborn refusal to state the reasons for the assault. Any other reason could be explained without embarrassment. For example, how embarrassing would be the following confessions:

"Some guy tricked my daughter; I found him tonight in the Street; I went blind with rage, called him a bastard; grabbed him by the throat, and he, helped by his friends, did this to me" or

"My wife cheated on me with a man I tried to kill, but he was stronger than I, and started to kick me furiously" or

"I had an affair with a woman, and her husband took revenge by cowardly attacking me with *his friends*"?

If he had said something like that no one would have thought it strange.

It also would have been very easy to say:

"We had a fight."

But I'm wasting time, these hypotheses are untenable: In the first two cases, the family of the unfortunate man would have said something; in the third his confession would have been inevitable, because the first two would have still been honorable deaths; and the fourth we would already know because, wanting vengeance, surely he would even have provided the names of his *assailants*.

Nothing that had stuck in my mind was obvious. There is no more room in my head for more reasoning. So, gathering up all my conclusions, I reconstructed, in brief, the tragic events that occurred between Escobedo and García Streets, in the following way:

Octavio Ramírez, an individual of unknown nationality, forty-two years old and of mediocre appearance, lived in a modest ghetto hotel until the 12th of January of this year.

It seems that this Ramírez had some income, certainly very little; he did not allow himself excessive expenses, much less extravagant ones, especially with women. Ever since childhood he had a small misdirection of his instincts, which soon degenerated to the point that, by a fatal impulse, they had to end with the tragic results that concern us.

For clarity's sake, let it be on record that the individual had arrived only a few days before to the city that was to be the theater of these events.

The night of January 12th, while he ate in a cheap restaurant, he felt a familiar urge that bothered him more and more. At 8:00, when he left the restaurant, he was agitated by all the torments of desire. In a strange city, the difficulty of satisfying it because of his unfamiliarity with the area urged him on powerfully. He wandered almost desperately, for two hours, through the downtown, anxiously fixing his sparkling eyes on the backs of the men he encountered; he followed them closely, hoping to take advantage of any opportunity, but afraid of being turned down.

Around eleven o'clock the desire became an immense torture. His body trembled and he felt a painful emptiness in his eyes.

Considering it pointless to walk around busy Streets, he turned toward the slums, always looking twice at the passers-by, saying hello with a trembling voice, stopping now and then, not knowing what to do, like a beggar.

When he got to Escobedo Street he couldn't take it any more. He wanted to throw himself at the first man who passed by. He wanted to sob, to tearfully tell him about his tortures . . .

Far off, he heard quiet, measured footsteps; his heart beat violently. He leaned against the wall of a house and waited. In a few moments the hard body of a laborer filled the sidewalk. Ramírez turned white; when the guy came close, he reached out and touched his elbow. The laborer quickly turned and looked at him. Ramírez tried a sweet smile—that of a hungry pimp left in the gutter. The laborer let out a guffaw and a dirty word and kept walking, slowly, making the heels of his shoes ring out loudly against the stones. After a half-hour another man showed up. Our unfortunate man, shaking all over, dared make a flirtatious comment that the passer-by answered with a vigorous shove. Ramírez got scared and left quickly.

Then, after walking two blocks, he found himself in García Street. Ready to collapse, his mouth dry, he looked from one side of the Street to the other. A short distance away a fourteen-year-old boy was hurrying along. He followed him.

—Psst! Psst!

The boy stopped.

—Hey, cutie, What are you doing out this late?

—I'm going home. What do you want?

—Nothing, nothing . . . but don't go so soon, honey . . .

And he grabbed the boy's arm.

The boy tried to pull away.

—Let go! I already told you I'm going home.

He wanted to run. But Ramírez jumped and hugged him. Then the frightened boy started screaming:

—Dad! Dad!

Almost immediately, a few feet away, a door opened, suddenly throwing some light into the Street. A tall man appeared. It was the laborer who had passed by before on Escobedo Street.

Seeing Ramírez he threw himself on him. Our poor man stood there staring back at him, with eyes as big and fixed as a plate, trembling and silent.

—What do you want, you dirty bastard?

And he kicked him furiously in the stomach. Octavio Ramírez collapsed, with a long painful gasp.

Epaminondas, that must be the laborer's name, seeing the bastard on the ground, considered that one kick was too little punishment, and gave him two more, splendid and marvelous ones, on that large nose that provoked him like a sausage.

How those marvelous kicks must have sounded!

Like the splattering of an orange, vigorously thrown against a wall; like the collapse of an umbrella whose ribs smack and shiver; like a nut cracked between two fingers; or better yet, like the firm sole of a shoe running into another nose!

Like this:

Whack!

with a delicious space between

Whack!

And then: How Epaminondas must have been driven by the perverse instinct that makes murderers riddle their victims with stab wounds! That same instinct that pushes some innocent fingers, just for fun, to squeeze friends' throats harder and harder until they turn purple and their eyes blaze!

How Epaminondas's shoe sole must have slammed against Octavio Ramírez's nose!

Whack!

Whack! Dizzily,

Whack!

while a thousand points of light sewed the darkness like needles.

The Indian's Cabin

Henri Michaux

Translated by Robin Magowan

A Belgian-born French painter, journalist, poet, and mystic, Henri Michaux explored the human experience through Eastern meditation, fantasy, and experimentation with drugs. Both his painting and writing are very difficult to classify, but continually explore man's internal world and the threat posed to that world by external forces. Ecuador: A Travel Journal by Henri Michaux, from which the following is excerpted, was originally published in 1929 and is something of a poetic antitravel travel journal. It is a challenging and seductive read.

The Indian's Cabin in the Cordillera of the Andes

The Indian's cabin is not any modest chalet. No, it is something absolutely revolting. But its intimacy is such that after a few months in one you cannot imagine yourself living anywhere else.

To the white man the Indian's cabin is just one more proof of his idiocy. And it is true of course that it does not have a chimney. And quite a number of other items are also lacking. But *not having* one thing of necessity means *having* something else. Which is why the Indian's cabin yields such a definite plus. It is crammed full. You enter, threading your way through all kinds of thickness. It exudes darkness, a well-padded, smoke-crammed darkness . . . No chimney, just smoke. The white man's habitations have no center. They have windows.

The Indian's cabin is just that—nothing, nothing from without, all from within. That smoke is from the corn they are roasting for dinner. The smoke both chokes and caresses you, then goes slowly out the door to make room for more smoke, warmer, more recently left the wood.

Crammed full of anesthesia, of smells, of filth, of people.

Just full.

The Salvation Army apparently is considering dispatching over there some dedicated idiots, who will teach the Indians how to pierce their chimneys. But then what will the Indian have left? He needs his wealth.

One more thing is to know the earth from the bottom up, to hold it respectfully by the feet and know it in its whole stretched-out length. And you have to know it stretched out.

His cabin is also a place marvelously suited for playing music. They pipe into a kind of Pan's flute, delighting in a much reiterated phrase which tells more about themselves than any one other thing they do or work at, their pot-making included. Here is how it goes. At the beginning a three-note group, the first of which is not very high (the Arabs start much higher, carried away), the second higher, and the third down again—and exactly as much down as the previous one has been up (interval of ten of a third). Then another three-note group, for which the first is again the pivot, the second up, and the last down; then other groups of three with here and there an occasional, insignificant trill. And the whole, after several attempts to attain an elevation (which constitutes the range of the phrase), falls back, settling to that bottom note which is its end, or rather its suicide, or even better its mortal exhaustion. That open water where it had to founder.

Alcohol

The Indian enjoys getting drunk like nobody else, and the smoke in his cabin is but the necessary small change. He has the reputation of being a brute. Possibly. But when it comes to drinking he knows what he is up to.

First, they don't get drunk one evening or two. No, they get drunk for three weeks straight—beginning, say, with the feast of San Juan—not letting up for an instant and their wives pouring it into their mouths once they are no longer completely blacked out. They are not looking for separate little emotions, like getting high, or more coordinated, none of that jumble of bits and pieces which the White Man likes. No. He concentrates himself and from this center assaults the drink—eyeing it, pushing it, jostling it, mauling it—with a courage, a coolness, an impassivity, and, most of all, a singleness of purpose that takes your breath away.

He has made up his mind to have alcohol. O.K., so he really gives himself the works. For days you will not see him even stumble, then toward the sixth or seventh he will all of a sudden fall down, arms crossed. I have seen a whole settlement like this—out with their arms crossed—they got my horse frightened. There were some people still reeling about in their ponchos, but this was rarer. There were also some corpses.

Of any drug they ask the same thing, and since they know how to wait it all ends by giving them the same thing. They don't give a damn about the preliminaries; they want the intoxication to engulf them and knock them out; they want to be defeated.

Tattoo Marks

The jungle Indians do not, in the strict sense, tattoo themselves. That is, they do not make deep incisions in their skins.

They may make a design on their faces to go have lunch at a friend's, then rub it out on the way home. Everyone has mentioned how attractive this is. There are certain colors, however, that smudge badly. For us they would be an inconvenience. The Turks were quite right to have pointed out how unseemly a face is. There it is on top of your clothing, sticking out, with glances escaping from it like madmen. Everything unhealthy and bestial that your skin has about it vanishes with the application of a line, a spot of rouge. Your face becomes not so much intelligent as intellectual, it becomes *witty*. That calms. It was always my feeling when my Indians had tattooed themselves that now we would be able to talk (the exception being the case where the design confines itself to a stupid exaggeration of the facial contours and their one or two basic elements).

It does not take much of a prophet to predict that before long the white race will on its own take up tattooing. I am told that current opinion is flatly opposed to this—and much else. Prophets say, "You'll see"; that suffices for both them and me.

I only add that tattooing, like all ornamentation, can both bring out a surface and even more readily make the same surface disappear, just as a tapestry makes the whole length of a wall disappear. Well, now is the time to have the face disappear. It is truly impossible with a face to have a modest look—provided that it has not been specially arranged for that.

"Heroic Pueblo of Guayaquil"

José María Velasco Ibarra

Translated by Carlos de la Torre

On 28 May 1944 an insurrection of junior army officers and common citizens proclaimed José María Velasco Ibarra president of Ecuador. This insurrection deposed Carlos Arroyo del Río, who was accused of losing a major war with Peru in 1941, when Ecuador lost half of its national territory, and of preparing electoral fraud against Velasco for the incoming election. Velasco Ibarra had inaugurated Ecuadorian populism. He became president on five occasions: 1934–35, 1944–47, 1952–56, 1960–61, and 1968–72. On 4 June 1944 Guayaquil appeared to be in a day of fiesta to receive Velasco, who was proclaimed the Great Absentee. Eighty thousand people in a city of around 200,000 inhabitants gathered to receive President Velasco, who arrived by plane from Quito at 2:15 PM. A parade took him to El Palacio de la Zona. Velasco started his oration by referring to the audience as "heroic, heroic pueblo of Guayaquil." In what follows, he elaborates a moral and political definition of pueblo.

You all, in this solemn moment of the nation's history, are showing the world that the material is only a transitory aspect of the life of man; that what is eternal is the striving for moral greatness, for progress, and for liberty; that what is eternal in men is the hatred for hypocrisy and tyranny, and you, Guayaquileños, who have written another glorious episode in your history, by the emotion through which you distinguish yourselves among all of the peoples of Ecuador, have broken forever the most ignoble of tyrannies, and have implanted forever in our homeland the great principles of liberation, of democracy, and of integral justice for all men.

Heroic pueblo whom I love and with whom I feel connected, after bearing four years of the most ignoble of tyrannies, confusion, and fright in the national soul, you destroyed the secret police, which allows us to speak now; you conquered power for all citizens wresting from the police the absolute power that they maintained through the person of a despot who promoted the arbitrary disposition of the national territory and of her revenues, the squandering of public funds, the corruption of local government, of the Judicial Power, and of all the Nation.

Oh soldiers of Villamil [regiment]! You showed the *carabineros* and the tyrants of the homeland (*applause*) that the force of ideals is greater than the force of imbeciles; and that savage force, for however large it seems, is incapable and must be imprisoned and burned and destroyed when it meets the fire of the Guayaquileño bullets and the army that was affected by the Guayaquileños' emotion (*Loud applause and "vivas" to the army*).

Now that you have suffered and waited so long and are now gathered here, allow me. . . .

Guayaquileños, this is a complete revolution; but it is a transcendental revolution, a profound revolution, it is a true and purposeful revolution because it is a total revolution; you have here a magnificent synthesis of the political parties; the Communists . . . the Conservatives. . . and the Liberals. . . and all of the parties are congregated here today. And why? Precisely because the current revolution is synthesized in something which is like the whole of honorable people and that can only be rejected by slaves and the vile: the regime of popular autonomy, of suffrage of the people, of the Government of the people by their own collective will. (*Applause, "Viva el Ecuador," "Viva el doctor Velasco Ibarra."*)

Will we be indulgent and tolerant? No! No! the perverse will be punished. (*Applause.*) They will punish [*se castigará a*] "the thieves and exploiters." (*Thunderous applause.*) It pains my soul to respect them. I wish we could crush the traitor, who threw away half of the national territory. (*Loud applause and "Death to Arroyo" and "Viva Velasco Ibarra."*)

Believe señores, believe in me. I do not belong to the school of men who make politics a question of cleverness. For me politics is part of morality. I want to be a statesman who cultivates in his people national pride, collective prestige: the pride of the individual to belong to a great nation and here on the Ecuadorian soil to serve each other by redeeming the weak from misery, from injustice before the power of capital.

To this modest citizen you have entrusted Executive Power. Believe me friends, believe me; this responsibility fills me with terror, fills me with fear. Perhaps I will not pass. If I fail I will not be able to hold up my head. The country will remain in diapers before progress and all the Americas, perhaps my life itself will be rightly in danger. Would I betray this revolution? Believe me. I am a man of conscience. I am terrified by the position that I occupy. But I am also aware that Ecuador trusts me because I have never stolen, because I have never led you astray. (*Great applause and "viva Ecuador" and "viva Velasco Ibarra."*) Because I have never attempted to use National Power as a pedestal to elevate my own self-importance . . . No citizens, what I have always tried to do is to serve you, to express to you some modest idea of mine that might serve in your collective orientation, and I prefer a single minute of command, if that minute of command is translated in a sense of direction, to twenty days of command, to twenty years of command, if those twenty years produce rejection by the pueblo, the tyranny of individuals, and the international discredit of the country. (*Applause and "vivas."*)

Do not oblige me to develop a Socialist, Communist, Liberal, or Conservative program. Don't force it on me; I am not for that.

The current moment is a difficult moment. It is an essentially vital moment. It is a moment in which the Communist stands side by side with the Catholic. It is a moment in which the basis of the homeland must be demonstrated. I will not serve any specific ideology. I will not serve any specific party, I will be the Leader of all the Nation, I will be the servant of the pueblo, I will be the servant of Ecuador in search of its nationality, of morality, of a tolerant government, of liberalism, of national concentration, of hygiene, of social reform so that others, younger, stronger, with fewer gray hairs than I, who have suffered less, can develop to the maximum their respective programs of social reform, liberal or conservative or whatever. . . .

Demand from me then that I govern in accordance with the moment. Demand sincerity from me. Recognize that the falseness of the government of Arroyo del Río is the most repugnant thing on earth.

Note

The text of Velasco's speech is taken from *Obras completas*, vol. 12a (Quito: Ed. Lexigama, 1974), 32–40.

Textile mill, one of the original facilities of a colonial mill near Quito, ca. 1870.
(Anonymous photo, courtesy of Taller Visual)

IV

Global Currents

In contrast to the acute political turmoil of the 1930s and 1940s, the long decade between 1948 and 1961 was characterized by relative stability. Three presidents of different ideological backgrounds managed to finish their terms; even populist Velasco Ibarra managed to finish a full four years. Such political stability was sustained, in part, by the banana boom. Within less than a decade after the end of World War II, Ecuador had become the largest producer in the world, a process that literally transformed the country's political economy. Although foreign banana companies, such as the United Fruit Company, played key roles, banana production itself remained largely in the hands of Ecuadorians (who contracted with the multinationals). As a result, wealth from the industry, although concentrated, nonetheless filtered into many sectors of the economy. Large numbers of Ecuadorians left the highlands for the coast as banana production expanded, regional urban centers emerged throughout the coastal region, and the state grew dramatically from revenue generated by banana exports.

Strong caudillos retained their mass appeal, but the period was also characterized by political innovation and the uneven surge of popular political power. New political organizations, such as the Concentración de Fuerzas Populares, not only promoted populist leaders, but developed an entire clientelist machinery through which candidates exchanged votes for services and political loyalties. Insidious as clientelism can be, it provided an avenue through which working people could engage the political process—or at the very least exchange their votes for services, favors, and even jobs.

The banana boom also stimulated the broader growth and political emergence of the middle class—particularly a professional class broadly connected to the growing state bureaucracy. Workers, peasants, teachers, truck drivers, and other groups organized and pressed the state for certain privileges and resources. Even neighborhoods used their political leverage to force politicians to deliver goods and services.

Stability, alas, did not last for long. In 1961, Velasco Ibarra was replaced by his vice-president, Carlos Julio Arosemena, who was then forced from office by a military dictatorship in 1963. Democracy was on shifting ground. Politicians did not respect the democratic rules of the game and were constantly inviting the military to remove the president, end corruption, and restore order. Indeed, the banana boom generated wealth, but it is also exacerbated social conflicts, highlighting the growing divide between urban and rural regions as well as the "backward" semifeudal nature of social relations in much of the countryside. Traditional haciendas remained bastions of economic exploitation, political marginalization, and racial oppression. As late as the 1950s, highland elites owned three-quarters of the total agricultural area and virtually all of the best land. Indigenous people, peasants, Afro-Ecuadorians, and the poor were often excluded from the vote by literacy requirements (and elites worked to keep marginalized people illiterate and uneducated).

Once the democratic door was pushed open, however, it was difficult to close again, and efforts by the military governments of the 1960s and 1970s to repress popular political expressions were met with stiff resistance. Peasant demographic growth, popular organizing, calls for agrarian reform, and populist rhetoric against elite privileges generated an intense cycle of protest. Peasants took over haciendas, and even got rid of the United Fruit Company in Tenguel. After Cuba, "Revolution" was in the air, and not limited to calls for agrarian reform and rural justice. Velasco Ibarra spoke of "a revolution of the soul and of the spirit." As in all of Latin America, a new generation of Ecuadorian intellectuals and artists became revolutionaries and advocates of radical transformation in their artistic works.

This back and forth between, on the one hand, repression led by economic and military elites and, on the other, popular political mobilization, characterized the 1960s and 1970s. As mentioned earlier, Velasco was ousted in the early 1960s and military rule installed. By 1968, Velasco was back for his fifth and last term and then forced into exile in 1972, once again replaced by the military. This time, however, the new military government—inspired in part by a reformist military regime in Peru—not only embodied some of the progressive impulses of the period but found itself awash in money generated by Ecuador's third major boom: oil.

With oil, and the right (military) leadership, Ecuador would enter the modern era. Or so was the theory. Unlike the previous export booms, profits from oil went directly into state coffers, thus expanding the government's capacity to implement reforms. The military regime of the 1970s pushed for an agrarian reform that took land away from the most inefficient landowners while bolstering the peasantry and (particularly) a class of capitalist farmers producing for the export market. At the same time, the government also implemented import substitution policies in an effort to stimulate industry.

The oil bonanza accelerated processes that were already under way: rapid urbanization, the expansion of the middle class, and better wages and working conditions for unionized workers. It also led to the deforestation of the Amazon, and resulted in oil spills and other ecological disasters caused by both multinationals such as Texaco as well as the Ecuadorian state's own oil company. Such disasters, in turn, led indigenous people to defend their land with even greater tenacity.

When the military finally relinquished power to civilians in the late 1970s, many technocrats, intellectuals, and politicians saw it as an opportunity to "modernize" the political system by finally getting rid of populism, caudillism, and clientelism. In this context, modernism was conceived as a rational struggle over ideologies and the transcendence of Velasco's populism. Coincidentally, the elder statesman himself conveniently died in 1979, right at the beginning of the transition to democracy.

Two Experiments in Education for Democracy

Galo Plaza Lasso

Galo Plaza Lasso was president of Ecuador (1948–52) during the early stages of the
banana boom. The son of a former president, Leónidas Plaza Gutiérrez, Galo Plaza
was born in New York in 1906 and studied agriculture and economics at the University
of California, Berkeley, and the University of Maryland. He was known as a modern-
izer and innovator, both on his farm (where he experimented with modern techniques
and imported Holstein cattle) and as a politician. The following is his account of an
educational/civic experiment that he implemented and viewed as a model for up-
lifting Indians living throughout the Andean highlands. Although his rhetoric was
drenched in paternalism—with "a helping hand, offered with kindness . . . a more
attractive, colorful and happy group [of Indians] could hardly be found anywhere"—
Galo Plaza, it is worth noting, was on the progressive end of the spectrum in terms of
elite perceptions of Ecuador's indigenous peoples. At the very least, he recognized that
their current situation was the product of centuries-long exploitation. This account
gives a good sense of state-Indian relations, the condition of indigenous communities
in the 1950s, and the growing importance of internal migration among Indians, who
increasingly lacked enough land for subsequent generations.

An experiment in rural education in the Andes is of greater importance to
Latin America than might appear at first sight. At least three countries, Bolivia, Ecuador, and Peru, should be deeply interested, because it might shed
some light on the solution of a major problem that concerns a large sector of
their populations.

Elementary Education in the Andes

From Ecuador in the north, to Bolivia in the south, there lies a high plateau, at
an altitude that varies from 6,000 to 14,000 feet above sea level, bounded on the
east and west by the great Andes and crossed by minor ranges which run between the major Cordilleras forming many isolated valleys. The region is about
2,000 miles long and with an average width of one hundred miles in Ecuador

to four hundred miles in southern Peru, and covers an area of roughly 300,000 square miles. In this region there live ten million people, about six million of whom are Indians, mostly descendants of the proud Incas, while some come from more ancient stock. Their ancestors built a great civilization in this land, where they have lived for centuries, and there they remain today, sidetracked by civilization, stolid, indifferent, and isolated, since the Spanish conquistador defeated their nation and subjugated its people.

In the high altitudes above 14,000 feet, beyond the timber line, where frost will kill off the most rugged of crops, the Indians graze their sheep and llamas; the cold wind blows fiercely and life is at best a cruel struggle with nature. In the lower protected valleys the climate is mild and an incredible variety of crops can be grown, but the land has been subdivided from generation to generation, among a constantly growing population and the soil has been overworked for centuries, so the Indian is forced to supplement his income by working on large estates, in the mines, or in public works. At the foot of the Andes, toward the west on the Pacific Coast and eastward in the Amazon valley, there are large areas covered with rich volcanic soil, untouched by man; but the climate is hot and humid and the people from the highlands fear the dangers that await them in the tropics.

Over-population in the high plateaus is slowly but surely forcing the Indians to migrate to the fertile unused land at lower altitudes. Such a movement of population, although at most a matter of a few hundred miles, is a far greater ordeal than the migration of Europeans from central Europe to the Great Plains in the United States. The European immigrant moved within his own temperate zone, and although his new home was over 3,000 miles away from the old country, he did not have to face major problems of readjustment to a new environment. It is true that medicine has made great strides in safeguarding human life in the tropics, but to be able to take advantage of these advancements in science, some training in health and sanitation, and at least a rudimentary education is necessary; even so, moving from the cool highland valleys to the tropical lowlands, a new and different world, constitutes a major ordeal that presents many severe problems in readjustment.

The Indian, with a few exceptions, does not participate in the social, cultural, and political life of his country. Economically speaking, he is a factor in that he is a farm worker and road builder or a miner, but his life is so primitive, his needs are so meager, that he is self-sufficient to a remarkable degree. He scarcely sells or buys anything. In his primitive society he is firmly rooted to his community, but his sense of nationality is very weak; he takes no part in civic activities and is practically a foreigner in his own country. In spite of all these negative characteristics the Indian is an intelligent, hardy, and persevering human being. He has been the victim of centuries of abuse and exploitation, and he has every reason in the world to distrust the white man. Yet it is incredible how he can react to a little help, offered to him with kindness and understanding, and promptly pull himself out of the state of degradation that centuries of iniquity have made part of his being. If the Indian is to become a free human being, a full citizen of his country, and if his country is to become a true democracy by incorporating into political and civic activities a large sector of its population, the only effective course of action is to give the Indian an education along practical and sensible lines.

If it is a fact that the highland valleys are becoming the most densely populated regions in the world and that a mass migration to newer and more spacious land is inevitable, the Indian will have to be taught to live in a new environment; his living habits will have to be changed so that he will not fall prey to the dangers to his health and even his life that await him in the tropics, and which are practically nonexistent in his highland home. Again only a rational program of education can help solve this major economic and social problem.

The governments of the three countries mentioned have lately shown increased interest in these vital problems and several steps in the right direction have been taken. Probably the most significant, because of their far-reaching possibilities, are the new land reform laws in Bolivia. In 1953 a joint mission of the United Nations, with the cooperation of several of its organisms, and the Organization of American States, visited the three countries and submitted to the respective governments a basic plan for action that, if carried out, should be a great contribution toward incorporating the Andean Indian into civilization.

The experiment on which I wish to report is being carried out on a small scale by a private concern in a remote little valley in the Andes of Ecuador, inhabited mostly by Indians who are representative of those who inhabit the region referred to above. The experiment seeks to demonstrate that a well-planned program of practical education, coupled with a basic program in health and sanitation, can raise the standard of living of a rural community to a remarkable degree in a relatively short time, in relation to other communities in the surrounding region that are not being benefited by such a plan. The experiment is being carried out in Zuleta. Zuleta is a farm devoted to dairying and the growing of wheat, barley, corn, and potatoes. It is located in a small valley at a mean altitude of about 9,000 feet, sixty miles north of Quito, in the Ecuadorian province of Imbabura. It covers an area of 2,400 acres. On 640 acres of this land there are 140 farm workers and their families, 1,025 persons in all (1950 census). Each family cultivates for its own benefit an average of 4.5 acres of land and grazes its cattle and sheep freely on land set aside for this purpose.

They work for the hacienda five days a week and part of their wages goes to cover the use of the land they farm. This system is common throughout the region, although in some cases the plots of land are much smaller, seldom larger, and in some cases, particularly in Peru and Bolivia, no cash payment is made for work. These Indians are probably better off than many who farm their own incredibly small landholdings, but their case is fairly representative.

When the project started, there was a rural school with four grades and one teacher to serve this community. The government paid the teacher's salary and the farm provided the school house. A special tax is collected by the government from landowners to finance its program of rural education. Although in 1935 the first rural normal school was founded, and today there are eight such schools in Ecuador, little has been done to differentiate programs of study adequate for the rural environment from those in effect in the urban communities. Texts are the same and directives from the Ministry of Education vary little. The result is that the child in the country learns about a world different from his own; his reader describes things which do not fit into his environment; hence his interest is limited. When he leaves school he will probably forget what he has learned or, at best, such schooling will contribute toward migration from the farms to the city, which is a major problem in most of Latin America.

A more practical program was urgently needed, one that would help the Indian child grow up in his own community, that would help him better understand the world about him and teach him how to make better use of it, so that he could become a good farmer and obtain more for his work. Parallel to schooling, an effort to teach the Indian better living habits is indispensable in order that his greater earning power may be channeled into improving his home, his diet, and his clothing, and that of his family, instead of being spent on alcoholic beverages.

One of the major drawbacks to putting into effect such a program was the lack of properly trained personnel. We were conscious of this fact, and although we had been toying with the idea of setting up a pilot project as an experiment in rural education for some time, we were only able to get started in 1952, when we found in Colombia an order of Catholic nuns, the Sisters of Mary Immaculate, whose mission is religious indoctrination among the Indians. They are trained as nurses and school teachers and speak the Quechua language. After exhaustive interviews, two nurses and two teachers were selected for our mission and work started in June, 1953. The rural four-grade school with one teacher, provided by the government, was reduced to three grades and an assistant teacher added. We have made every effort to improve the curriculum, but the main drawback has been the lack of appropriate textbooks. Thanks to some splendid readers prepared by the Pan American Union in collaboration with UNESCO we will remedy this situation next year. We made available a plot of land for small agricultural practices. The nuns were put in charge of the fourth, fifth, and sixth grades and here we have been able to introduce a few subjects that are of practical interest to the students, such as weaving and truck farming for the boys and dressmaking and needlework for the girls. Whatever they produce in the field or make in the shop is given to them to take home. Vegetables are scarcely consumed among the Indians, but by giving to them those that they cultivate themselves, we are developing in them a taste for a new and valuable food that will serve to improve their diet greatly. All the handiwork done in the shops has a practical value in the homes, such as clothes in general, dresses, blouses, bedspreads, pillowcases. The students are also taught bookbinding in order that all their school notes can be saved and kept in proper form for future reference. The children receive books and all school supplies free of charge. They also get a free lunch made up of a generous amount of hot chocolate milk and a banana every school day; this is supplemented with what they bring along with them from their own homes. It is not only Indian children who go to the school, for the children of white farm employees, from those of the manager down, also study and play with their little Indian friends.

Besides the regular course of study for children, we run a literacy school for adults during the summer months and two manual training projects, one for men and another for women, that are already very successful. The Indians in our valley have been weavers for centuries; they own flocks of sheep and were taught to process their wool and weave it into cloth for their own use by the Jesuits, who received the land in the sixteenth century from the King of Spain. The techniques and equipment have hardly changed since then and the final product is coarse and defective. In 1950 the Ecuadorian government, in a joint enterprise with the United States government, through the Institute of Inter-American Affairs, set up a weaving improvement project among the Indians in the nearby valley of Otavalo. New techniques are being taught in the washing and dyeing of the wool and all the different steps until the yarn is ready for weaving. New looms are being introduced that are capable of producing as much as five times the amount of cloth as the ancient methods produced with the same human effort. We sent three of our boys to Otavalo for a three months' course and one of our nuns has already learned to weave with the new looms; so we have been able to set up our own weaving school, open to newcomers, young and old. As soon as a pupil is thoroughly familiar with a new loom and is convinced it is a great improvement over his old one, we assist him in financing the purchase of one to set up in his own home. The cloth produced is of a far better quality as to fastness of color, uniformity, and tightness of weave, than anything produced before, and the variety of materials is much greater, both in cotton and wool. This is indeed a dramatic example of what technical assistance can do by changing, in a relatively short time, techniques and types of equipment that have been in use for centuries.

Milking on the farm is done by hand by Indian girls. They milk the cows in the early morning and again in the evening, and to give them a useful as well as profitable occupation during the day, they were taught needlework so that they themselves could make their beautifully embroidered blouses, which are a part of their native costumes. They have become so proficient that five months after the shop was set up, these thirty-four young Indian girls, under expert direction, are making most of the lovely embroidered blouses that the best folklore shop in Quito sells to tourists from all over the world. They select their own design and color combinations and more often than not, the final product is a handsome as well as an unusual and colorful garment. By using up their idle time profitably, they have now been able to double their income. A more attractive, colorful, and happy group could hardly be found anywhere.

This program is being developed parallel to another in health and sanitation. Indians in general are very reluctant to take advantage of whatever medical facilities are offered them; they dread hospitals and are horrified at the prospect of being vaccinated or inoculated by hypodermic needles. They have confidence in witch doctors, who can still be found anywhere throughout Indian country. Tearing them away from these harmful and sometimes deadly practices is a major problem, quite hopeless in the case of most members of the older generations.

Our health and sanitation department is headed by a doctor who, although living in the city, visits the farm periodically. Two trained resident nurses work under his supervision. We have a well-stocked dispensary and an infirmary with four beds and an operating room for minor surgery. We also maintain permanent facilities in the hospital of the nearby city of Ibarra in case of serious illness.

An incredible amount of skill as well as kindness was necessary to gain the confidence of and win over the first cases from the witch doctor. A few cases that had been given up as lost by the witch doctor were dramatically saved by the use of antibiotics, winning the day for modern medicine; and today we no longer have to round up children by force for vaccination. Whenever an epidemic of whooping cough or a case of smallpox appears, for instance, all we have to do is notify the parents of the day on which the children will be vaccinated and mothers can be counted on to come punctually, followed by their offspring. A glance at one of the monthly reports prepared by the nuns gives a good idea as to the scope of their work. Their report for June, 1954, reads thus:

Total visits to the dispensary 230
Injections 83

Treatments 71
DDT house disinfections 13
Hygiene instructions 9
Medical control 3
Emergency treatments 3
Mother and child attentions 15
Treatment of children 43
Dental extractions 5
Lectures on hygiene in school 3
Vaccinations for smallpox 81
Night visits
Infirmary cases 2

This project has been in full operation one year, and the results are already evident. There are fewer absences from work because of illness; labor and management relations are excellent; the consumption of intoxicating beverages has declined; and the Indians show that they fully appreciate the benefits offered to them.

There are more children coming to school, particularly girls, for whom schooling was not thought necessary if their activities were to be confined to the home. We are particularly interested in women, because if any major change of living conditions is to be hoped for, the mother of the family should be won over to the cause. In the Andean Indian community, while the head of the family works out in the field, his wife manages the home and is responsible for the upbringing of the children, hence she is the key to any possible improvement in her domain.

New improved farming practices and more extensive use of farm machinery are no longer a problem to this younger generation of Indians who can read and write and have been exposed to new teachings that have a direct and favorable influence on their way of life. They are alert, confident, and, above all, anxious for improvement both for themselves and their families.

This is a case history of a small experiment, in a small community, but living in such communities are six million Indians who inhabit Bolivia, Ecuador, and Peru. We hope that we are proving that this forgotten man, the Andean Indian, is not a total loss. A helping hand, offered with kindness, understanding, and respect for his dignity can convert him into a useful citizen. Government action at the national level can put into effect an overall program that should permeate down to the rural community in terms of a simple and practical program, like the one I have just described, if our countries are to convert these serfs into free men, and only then can we hope to become true working democracies.

The Origins of the Ecuadorian Left

Adrián Bonilla

Translated and summarized by Carlos de la Torre

Ecuador is not Cuba or Nicaragua, or even Chile. The Left never carried out a social-ist revolution. But leftists have played an important role in mobilizing popular sectors, challenging elite power, and otherwise shaping Ecuador's political scene. The following, by one of Ecuador's foremost scholars, provides a brief, coherent, description of a very complicated history. As this contribution makes clear, what stands out about the history of the Left in Ecuador—and here it shares a lot with much of Latin America—is how vibrant and fragmented "it" has been. Even in a country the size of Ecuador, leftist unity has often been elusive.

Socialist ideas were introduced to Ecuador by immigrants, sailors, and well-to-do intellectuals who had studied in Europe or who were oriented toward the Old Continent. By 1926, this political and intellectual expression coalesced in the form of the Socialist Party. Early members were radicalized liberals; others were anarchists with influence among artisans in Guayaquil; and still others were influenced by the Bolshevik Revolution. In 1931, the latter group split from the Socialist Party to form the Communist Party, an organization that would maintain the political line of the Third International [Comiterm] and the Soviet Union.

Between the 1930s and 1960s, however, the split between Socialists and Communists was relatively minor. They worked in different spaces and had few open confrontations. Communists focused their efforts on those social classes who, according to Marxist theory, were central to the revolutionary project: workers, peasants, and artisans. They founded the Central Federation of Ecuadorian Workers (CTE) in 1944 and the Ecuadorian Federation of Indians (FEI) in 1945. By contrast, the Socialist Party fought the good fight on all fronts. They presented candidates, struggled to control local governments, and got involved in conspiracies and revolts. Socialists, in this sense, were more op-portunistic and less rigid in terms of strategy and tactics. Communists, in turn, stuck more narrowly to the revolutionary path, assured that they knew the road to the promised land.

By the 1960s, however, the Marxist left underwent an acute process of differentiation. Relative harmony gave way to factionalism as the number of leftist groups proliferated and intense debates emerged over the nature and timing of revolution. Such tensions were caused, paradoxically, by the growth and success of the left on an international scale. External factors such as the Cuban Revolution (1959), the growing struggle between the Soviets and the Chinese, and the proliferation of guerrilla movements throughout Latin America were all felt (and played out) within the Ecuadorian left during the 1960s and 1970s. Was Ecuador capitalist or feudal in nature? Was the time ripe for revolution, or was Ecuador not yet ready? Who would carry out the revolution: peasants, workers, intellectuals? Was violence a necessary part of the process?

Ultimately, three ideological currents emerged during this period: the Communists, who tended to follow orders from Moscow (and were eternally waiting for the right revolutionary moment); the Maoists, who were inspired by the Chinese break from Moscow (and the possibility of *rural* revolution); and the Radical Socialists. The latter groups supported the Cuban Revolution, and rejected Moscow's insistence that socialist transformation could only be achieved by passing through a series of stages. They were not willing to wait for capitalism, or even revolution, but believed that revolution must be made, and made now.

Even within these tendencies there existed considerable division. In order to create a broad youth movement, for example, the Communist Party created the Unión Revolucionaria de Juventudes Ecuatorianas (Revolutionary Union of the Ecuadorian Youth), or URJE. Once created, however, this youth organization was not easily controlled by party leaders. In fact, the URJE became a critical space where Communist militants and other leftists questioned the tactics and strategy of the party. Members of URJE became involved with Latin American revolutionaries who were organizing guerrilla movements—despite mandates from the party that insisted the time was not ripe for revolution. They also violated party discipline by organizing activities outside the purview of the party such as military training.

The event perhaps most revealing of divisions within the Communist Party was the attempt to create a guerrilla front in Toachi, 200 kilometers from Quito, led by the Communist leader Jorge Rivadeneira. The guerrilla movement itself had little lasting impact on Ecuadorian history; the insurrectionists were apprehended almost immediately. But the failed revolt did lead to a serious housecleaning within the party. The party expelled or sanctioned midlevel cadre involved in the revolt, and ended its association with the URJE.

In August 1964, the Maoist-oriented Marxist Leninist Ecuadorian Communist Party (PCMLE) was formed. For Maoists, Ecuador of the 1960s was a semifeudal and semicolonial nation that needed an anti-imperialist and anti-feudal revolution (not unlike China). The time for revolution was now and depended largely on the will of party militants.

Another important group during this period was the Revolutionary Leftist Movement (MIR). It was a dissident group of the Communist Party that split over the handling of the Toachi guerrilla affair. The MIR proclaimed the need for socialist revolution based on the guerrilla strategy of Régis Debray, a French intellectual and revolutionary closely aligned with Che Guevara. As a result, the MIR organized rural guerrilla movements that failed for the same reason as many Guevara-inspired revolts: the urban middle-class leaders had little organic connection to the peasants they were trying to turn into revolutionaries.

Socialists were hardly of one mind during this period, but were much more likely to work within the existing political system than were their Communist/Maoist counterparts. In the 1960 presidential election, the Socialist Party was divided between a faction that supported ex-President Plaza, a group that supported the ticket of Antonio Parra and Benjamín Carrión, and a sector who rejected all pacts with the bourgeoisie. The radical section of the Socialist Party, later renamed the Ecuadorian Revolutionary Socialist Party (PSRE), under the influence of the most important Ecuadorian Marxist ideologist, Manuel Agustín Aguirre, developed the thesis that Ecuador was a backward and dependent capitalist country that needed a socialist revolution. Its theses differed from the insurrectionist line proposed by other radical organizations, but it shared the call for an immediate socialist transformation.

The most important issue for the Marxist left during the 1960s was revolution—when, how, under what circumstances, and who [would lead it]. Beyond that, there was little agreement. In this, Ecuador was on par with many of its Latin American neighbors.

The Progressive Catholic Church and the Indigenous Movement in Ecuador

Carmen Martínez Novo

Beginning in the 1960s, missionaries of the Salesian Society (a Roman Catholic Order) helped indigenous peoples in Cotopaxi create one of the most active branches within the broader indigenous movement in Ecuador. As the anthropologist Carmen Martínez shows, this effort was not without tension or mistakes, but the overall process was empowering for indigenous peoples as it strengthened their educational systems, ability to access resources, and capacity to mobilize in order to be recognized by the Ecuadorian state.

From the sixteenth until the beginning of the twentieth century, Zumbahua—a small town in the province of Cotopaxi in the central highlands of Ecuador—was a large hacienda property of the Augustinians, a Catholic order. Due to the high altitude of most of its lands, the hacienda consisted largely of pastures used for sheep-raising, an activity that provided wool for a textile factory that the order owned close to the provincial capital, Latacunga. In 1908, with a law that nationalized Church properties, Zumbahua became property of the Social Assistance, a public institution that rented lands to finance hospitals, orphanages, and other charities for the urban poor. Paradoxically, labor conditions were often harsher on public haciendas. The Zumbahua hacienda subjected its workers to the systems of *concertaje* and later *huasipungo*, contracts based on a custom through which the worker exchanged his and his family's labor for the usufruct of a small plot of land (*huasipungo*), a nominal salary that most of the time was not paid, and some other benefits. In 1964, with the first agrarian reform law, Zumbahua, like other public haciendas, was distributed among the peasants. Social differences that originated in the hacienda period were reproduced in the land distribution process, causing inequalities and tensions. The Salesians had to confront these tensions in their search for a more egalitarian peasant society.

The Salesians sought to combine peasant evangelization with human development. They understood human development as helping and advising peasants in their struggle for access to the land and for a better exploitation of this resource. In order to struggle to make the agrarian reform law effective, or to get government credit, or to have access to development funds and technical advice, peasants needed to organize. Therefore, the Salesians promoted social and political organization through intercultural bilingual education or by directly creating and strengthening peasant organizations.

From the point of view of rural development, the Salesians had goals that may seem contradictory to us: They sought both to promote a self-sufficient peasant community based on the Quichua tradition *and* to modernize agriculture in the style of the green revolution. Among the first goals of the mission were the improvement of roads, the introduction of enhanced seeds and new agrarian techniques, the selection of animal species, and so on. These noble goals and intentions, however, confronted important limitations due to the low quality of eroded land, the difficulty of cultivating steep slopes, and the smallness of land plots. Given these limitations, peasants in the Cotopaxi highlands have not been able to live solely on agriculture. They typically combine several economic activities that include trade, smuggling, temporary construction work in cities, crafts in the case of Tigua, and incipient tourism. Despite this reality, the Salesian priests perceived the inhabitants of this area as peasants and criticized migration as a source of social disorganization, violence, and destruction of traditional culture. This "peasantist" focus is reflected in the kind of education promoted by the mission, which focused on rural needs. The Salesians educated rural teachers and experts in agrarian and animal husbandry techniques. This rural-oriented curriculum has been questioned by young highlanders who prefer a professional urban-like education based on the use of computers and knowledge of English and other modern languages. In their own words, peasants want to be ready for what they perceive as the "modern" world. However, they seek this kind of education without detriment to the study of the Quichua language and culture, as well as radical politics that are useful for young peoples' insertion into the indigenous movement, an important source of social mobility in the last two decades. It is important to note, to the Salesians' credit, that mission education has adapted to the desires of the youth, offering classes in computers and modern languages. Again, the Salesians have not perceived a contradiction between the reinforcement of ethnic traditions and the education of youth in those aspects related to modernity.

Nevertheless, the Salesians still think in terms of a peasant-oriented project. To confront the agrarian crisis of the Zumbahua area they propose reforestation and the migration of highland peasants organized in cooperatives to subtropical lands. The Salesians do not perceive craft making, tourism, or migration to cities as valid alternatives. This enduring representation of indigenous people as subsistence peasants is also reproduced by scholars and indigenous organizations and has important political consequences as more complex economic realities and identities are not taken into account in the movement's political strategies. Even educated leaders whose culture is urban and who live in the city and return to the countryside only on weekends and vacation periods pretend to be peasants in order to be perceived as "authentic" Indians.

Education

Since the 1970s, the Salesians sponsored intercultural bilingual education in an area where 70 percent of men and 95 percent of women had been illiterate. The Salesians started with informal literacy programs in Quichua in 1976, and continued with a network of elementary schools. Later, Jatari Unancha, a high school to graduate rural teachers, was created in 1989. Finally, the Salesians opened in Zumbahua the Cotopaxi Academic Program, a branch of the Polytechnic Salesian University, to educate rural teachers and agrarian engineers. It is important to note that the Salesians were pioneers in intercultural bilingual literacy and education programs both in Cotopaxi and among the Shuar of the Ecuadorian Amazon much before these programs became official in the rest of the country in 1988.

The Salesians perceived organization under an ethnic banner as an appropriate way for indigenous peasants to articulate themselves into the nation. The Salesian Zumbahua project (1971) noted: "It is important to create a new rural school that preserves and develops the culture that exists in the indigenous world and that achieves in this way integration to the national culture." The peasants of the area agreed with the Salesians on this point because they too perceived intercultural bilingual education and ethnic political organization as ways to be recognized by the Ecuadorian state. Indigenous teachers not only wish to be officially recognized, but would like to become part of the state. This is understandable since official recognition carries economic benefits: the state starts to pay bilingual educators the salaries and benefits that other mestizo teachers already enjoy.

Although the Salesians' motivations for integrating highland peasants into the nation while reinforcing their indigenous culture may have been largely idealistic in the beginning, peasants kept projects and programs grounded. As Salesian Father Javier Herrán notes:

> We did well because before the start of the [national] literacy program we had already gotten economic help for the literacy teachers through

the Provincial Directorate. There was a lot of interest on the part of the people. That is why they learned. But we could not give them their official elementary school titles. Then, the Provincial Directorate in Cotopaxi gave us a hand because the Provincial Director was a good guy, because I did not find opposition or difficulty but support. He allowed us to give a special examination . . . and the supervisors were thrilled. They felt that the kids knew a lot, even more than those graduating from regular schools. And then, they gave them their elementary education titles. That provided a lot of strength to the people. Then the indigenous schools started to gain prestige for the community. Because the teachers were not *cholos*, mestizos, or white, they were *runa* [how Quicha speakers refer to themselves as indigenous peoples; literally, human]. And they said, "That *runa* does not know anything because he is *runa*." But when they started to find official certificates . . . Then, their attitude changed.

What's interesting here is bilingual education and ethnic political organization are seen not as ways of becoming separate from the state (i.e., some form of ethnic separatism), but as a way of becoming included into the national arena.

What, then, did the Salesians understand by promoting indigenous identity, and what impact did these ideas have on the political culture of the indigenous movement? The Salesians thought that one important reason to promote cultural identity was to reinforce the self-esteem of peasants. The Salesians taught the Quichua language and philosophy, but they did not extract this knowledge from the indigenous peasants. On the contrary, they believed that peasant Quichua was corrupted with profuse influences from Spanish and sought to teach a purified, more classic version of the language, one used by university-based linguists and by priests. Quichua culture should also be preserved while purifying it from those aspects considered by the Salesians contrary to ethics or development such as the oppression of women. A Salesian priest added that the well-known trait of Andean reciprocity should also be transformed into the Christian value of gratuity: in other words, when a person does something for another person, she should not necessarily expect something in return. In short, the Salesians sought to change those cultural aspects that collided with their modernizing and ethic utopia.

This reinforcement of indigenous culture, which the Salesians appropriately connected with improving self-esteem, confronted resistance by indigenous peasants. Communities did not always trust indigenous teachers, and many peasants thought that teaching in Quichua was a waste of time. Wasn't the whole point of going to school learning Spanish in order to become stronger, less vulnerable, in relation to the dominant culture? For instance, Rodrigo Martínez, a white-mestizo teacher who collaborated for decades with the Salesian project, states:

> Why did we emphasize the philosophy of bilingual education? Because indigenous people themselves were not convinced of the value of indigenous education. They always thought that it was a second-class situation. They were not convinced that an education that is relevant to the cultural reality could also be an education with possibilities to achieve quality. Then, we spent our time convincing them that the Indian is a person with value, that indigenous people are valuable as a people, that their culture includes valuable things. And so we spent our time, until they were able to consolidate their collective identity.

Ethnic Political Organization

The struggle for land, rural development, and intercultural bilingual education had an impact on indigenous political organization: to get land and credit peasants needed an organization that could become an interlocutor with the state and nongovernmental organizations. Intercultural education created a political consciousness based on ethnic pride and formed a new generation of leaders. The Salesians also promoted political organization in direct ways. The Zumbahua Project (1971: 20) gave priority to this aspect:

> In order to solve the indigenous problem, indigenous peoples themselves have to become agents in liberating actions . . . through a consciousness raising process that leads them to transform every unfair socio-economic structure. Therefore, the main goal of all our action should be to lead the indigenous community to a true self-management. Our work as agents of change is just temporary, transient, and subsidiary.

The Salesians did not aim to preserve indigenous social and political organization, but to transform it in ways that made it more just and efficient. For instance, the Salesians had to struggle against forms of exploitation and inequality among peasants that came from hacienda times. Because of their fight against local caciques, the Salesians were close to being lynched and expelled from the area. Father Javier Herrán highlights the outstanding role of the Salesians in the creation of the Indigenous and Peasant Movement of Cotopaxi (Movimiento Indígena y Campesino de Cotopaxi, MICC):

> We held a first meeting. It was in Chugchilán if I remember correctly. We [the Salesians] did everything. We called the people through the radio. We hired buses so people could come. After three and a half years, our

role continued to be central. We animated the meetings and were able to congregate the peasants. In that period, support for the struggle to acquire the land was central. In general, what we wanted was to create something that helped people to be able to make their own decisions. We did not see it appropriate to continue with the traditional organization systems of our area.

Through thirty years of sustained work, the Salesians have had a progressive influence in Cotopaxi. Although the process has not been without tensions and contradictions, the Salesians have successfully promoted indigenous organization and identity by tackling a series of quite concrete problems, including bilingual education, outdated agricultural techniques, and the development of infrastructure. Nonetheless, indigenous groups continue to struggle with a problem faced by many marginalized groups within Ecuador. On the one hand, they struggle to develop organizations and identities that are autonomous from the state; on the other, they desperately want and need to be included within the Ecuadorian nation as full citizens.

Note

A preliminary and longer version of this chapter was published as "Los misioneros salesianos y el movimiento indígena de Cotopaxi, 1970–2004," in *Ecuador Debate* 63:235–68. Please see this version for full citations.

Man of Ashes

Salomon Isacovici and Juan Manuel Rodríguez

Translated by Dick Gerdes

Salomon Isacovici was born to a farming family in western Romania, growing up among the scents of alfalfa, hay, and clover. One day in 1940 his family woke as Hungarians, altered overnight by the changing borders of the Second World War. But to other Hungarians they were Jews, and week by week their world grew worse. First came indifference, then bullying, then beatings. In 1944 the Germans arrived and Isacovici, his family, and every Jew from his town were pushed into cattle cars and taken ever closer to the soot and smoke of Auschwitz. He became a man of ashes.

At the war's end, Isacovici returned to his home only to find another family living there. In his quest for a new life, he moved from one European country to another, eventually emigrating to Ecuador with the family of a woman with whom he was romantically involved. Once in Ecuador (he becomes nationalized there in 1958), Isacovici struggles to survive while noting the connections between his experiences in Nazi concentration camps and the treatment of indigenous people in his new home. Man of Ashes is his autobiography.

Just before descending into Quito, the plane had throttled back and seemed to glide over the city. We had to skirt around gargantuan mountains that seemingly had risen out of the ground only yesterday and were now covered with intensely green vegetation. We started our landing by circling the city. I could even see the Spanish roof tiles on the houses and, looking down from above, the separations between the houses looked like trenches. I thought that the city must have been under siege, startled to think that I had just left Europe looking for peace and here I was about to land in a city at war. But I calmed down once I was on the bus with Frida and her brother and discovered that those divisions were simply adobe walls between the lots.

Reunited with Frida, I was able to forget some of my problems, among them my lost suitcase. When we got to her parents' apartment, I had expected to get the cold shoulder but it didn't turn out that way at all. Her family was hospitable and courteous. I imagined that by then they had given some serious thought to our relationship. Such a long trip and having come from so far away was proof enough that our love for each other had grown much more than they had imagined since the first time I had asked for their daughter's hand in marriage.

That same day I found a cheap place to live on the corner of Tarqui and 12 de Octubre streets. I knew practically no Spanish; what I did know I had learned from the bullfighters who crossed the Atlantic with me on the *Yagielo*. I could sing a few lines of "Se va el caimán, se va el caimán, se va para Barranquilla," but despite those few words, which wouldn't even get me a job singing in a bar, I hardly understood anything.

From the very beginning, I was taken by the accent of the people of Quito: they seemed to whistle as they talked, as if they were mumbling some prayer between their teeth. And people would always say hello and shake hands. Humble people would tip their hats to me on the street and courtesy murmur "patruncito"—master—upon which I would nod and smile because I had no idea what they were saying to me. The lack of communication was going to be a serious problem.

But the most serious problem was my dire economic situation. My suitcase had been lost in Panama and, without exaggerating, I had little more than the shirt on my back. I had four dollars and two cartons of American cigarettes on me. The Romanian sailor had given me the cigarettes. By selling them I could pay my first month's rent, but I still had to eat and buy some clothes, razor blades, soap, and shoes. Basically, I could make it for two months, so I had to find work immediately. Not knowing the language was a big disadvantage. By communicating with gestures and practically wearing out my only pair of shoes, I finally landed my first job in Ecuador. I began as a welder for the Ecuadoran Iron and Steel Company. I also taught soldering and chroming classes to young apprentices. While learning the language, all I could do was utter monosyllables and make mistakes. After a month on the job I received a small raise.

The Ecuadorans were very friendly and hospitable. Practically no one knew about what had happened in Europe, so no one asked me about my past. Since I was obsessed with trying to forget about what I had left behind, I turned myself entirely over to my work. I had decided to spend two extra hours a day at work, meaning that along with the raise I had received, my weekly salary was going up.

In order to learn a new language, I had to start speaking it; I began to talk as much as I could with those fine people. Since I would mix French and Romanian with Spanish, my co-workers would laugh and enjoyed listening to me talk. After four months I could speak with some fluency, but I still had a foreign accent by then I was able to understand what the phrase "se va el caimán" meant.

It wasn't long before the Goldstein brothers, German immigrants who owned a soap factory, hired me as a salesman. I figured that by leaving the steel company and doing sales work, I could earn more through commissions and eventually save enough to start my own business. The soap factory was nothing more than two halves of a metal barrel with handles welded to the sides that hung from a tripod and under which a wood fire would heat the basic ingredients inside—coconut oil and caustic soda.

Within two weeks the number of orders I had secured from neighborhood stores had far outstripped the factory's ability to meet them. That same week, I demanded that the Goldstein brothers put their books in order and pay me the commissions that had come due. They gave me a pittance of what they owed me, rebuked me, and then fired me.

Stimulated by the apparent success of their soap factory, I decided to start one of my own. So, I hired a guy who was working for the Goldsteins, but I offered him a better salary and a share in the sales. Of course, he came to work for me immediately. I rented a space and called my business venture the "Universal Soap Company."

I bought a barrel and cut it in half. One half was for preparing the first-class soap and the second barrel was for the speckled second-grade soap, to which we would add the dregs of the first-grade soap. I constructed a collapsible box that I lined with galvanized zinc to prevent corrosion from the caustic soda. That box was used to prepare the soap mixture. Then I built a tool to cut the soap into bars and also molds to give them an attractive shape. I copied the image of a small fish from a glass ashtray that would be molded into one side of the bar and on the other side would appear the name of my company. I made the molds out of scrap aluminum. I poured the cast metal into clay molds I made with my own hands. They came out looking perfect.

Once everything was ready to go, my employee and I began to mass-produce bars of soap. We would let the soap mixture cool in the collapsible box, where the paste would begin to solidify. Then we would cut the soap into pieces, press them into the individual molds, and out would come the bars of soap that looked to me like bars of gold. We would let them harden in the sun.

The next morning I was out on the streets of Quito plying the wares I had made with my own hands. Very few store owners would pay me cash on the barrelhead; just about all of them offered only a small advance up front and then agreed to a long-term payment if they were to accept the merchandise.

Within the month I went broke because I had no working capital to buy the raw materials. Once again I was back on the street without a job or a cent to my name. I managed to earn a little here and there doing part-time soldering jobs for different welding shops.

Nevertheless, Frida's parents finally agreed to set a date for our marriage, I saved every cent I could in order to have enough money to rent a house and purchase furniture and utensils. Frida had been working as a seamstress. When we would take walks through the main park, La Alameda, near the center of town, we never discussed Europe; it was as if it had never existed.

Finally, the big day had arrived: 23 January 1949. The wedding took place in a restaurant and about eighty people attended. Except for Frida's family, I didn't know anyone there. Someone had loaned me a suit and a pair of shoes, the latter of which didn't fit me at all. I think other than the immense happiness I felt when Frida became my wife, the most imposing impression I have of my wedding was the intense pain of sore feet that made me remember the "Death March."

Our honeymoon lasted one day, less time than it look for the aches and pain in my feet to go away. I escorted my wife to Tarqui and 12 de Octubre streets as if to the most luxurious hotel in the world. The next morning I was already at my new job. As it turns out, I had met a veterinarian at the wedding, and after talking with him for a while we became friends. When I told him I was unemployed, he said I could work for him on his farm in Conocoto. And so it was that on the second day after getting married I became a farmer. I could have earned good money but it only lasted six weeks, and once again I found myself without work. Frida was making only little money as a seamstress. I felt guilty that I was unable to support her and even more ashamed that I had to hit the streets again in search of part-time work as a welder. I was best at utilizing the mechanics I had learned in Sighets [Romania] and later in Paris; but industry was scarce and even a skilled worker's chances were almost nil.

After four months of marriage, I found a stable job as a tractor driver and administrator of a hacienda way up on a mountain called Pasochoa. The salary was great and we got all the milk we wanted. Working in the countryside fortified my spirits. The beauty of the landscape was breathtaking. The snowcapped mountain peaks reminded me of my homeland near the Carpathians.

My job consisted of overseeing the hacienda staff, including a foreman and twenty-two Indian peons and their families who worked on the land in exchange for small parcels of land. Basically, they worked for nothing and they were required to do menial tasks for the foreman, Segundo, who acted as the head of their families. Work was assigned to every family member regardless of their age or sex.

Up there on those high, barren plateaus, where the wind would sweep fiercely down the rocky gorges and craggy terrain, the spectacular vistas seemed to be in harmony with nature—except for the poverty-stricken condition of the unfortunate Indians. Their faces, like scorched adobe cracked by the harsh sun, their unabated hunger, their innumerable diseases, and their servility to the boss—all filled me with the same anxiety that I felt in the concentration camps. These were human beings living out their death. The twenty-two families were scattered about the bleak, cold wilderness where only a little straw would grow. They lived in mud huts covered with straw roots and no ventilation. They would enter through a minuscule doorway, seeking warmth; there, they lived in squalor among lice and pestilence. Their wretchedness was only comparable to those who had been dispossessed of everything, namely, the inhabitants of the Nazi concentration camps. Like those prisoners, no peons rebelled, no one would dare to look a white person in the eye. They were always staring at the ground and seemed resigned to endure any kind of insult and to carry out the orders of the heartless foreman.

Segundo, a fierce mestizo, was the absolute authority among the Indian peons on the hacienda. He assigned the work not only the way he saw fit but also according to the relationships he had established with each one of them. The treatment they received depended upon the sympathy or disdain he held for them, which, in turn, depended on the gifts and contributions they would make to him. The gifts ranged from chickens, eggs, and guinea pigs, to a daughter of one of the peons.

The children of the peons were required to work as servants in the house of the hacienda owner. Just as I had been unable to fathom how some of the most advanced civilizations in Europe could inflict cruelty on my people, I simply couldn't believe that such deplorable conditions—anonymity, poverty, and slavery—could still exist in contemporary times.

The local medicine man—Juancho Quispe—was the only person who demonstrated any concern for the Indians' well-being. He would prescribe liquor and herbs, taken from the barren plateaus, to the sick and agonizing people. He'd grind up the ingredients to make tonics or rub them on their ailing bodies.

That world was really disheartening, even though one learns to become indifferent, to look the other way, or simply cease to see that he has to face misery up close. Wanting to help in some way, I would buy them medicines—powdered sulfate, iodine, pills—in order to cure their illness. But the foreman reprimanded me saying I couldn't heal Indians with white man's medicine because they only believed in Quispe's ways of healing.

The suffering I had experienced in death camps was no different from what they were living, except that they didn't know any better, nor did they strive to improve their situation. But they had to know life could be better; they were aware of how the foreman lived and they had seen the owner's house, yet their state of peonage made all that seem no more than an impossible dream. You never saw them smiling. When they drank they would fall into a drunken stupor and lose consciousness; cheap booze didn't make them happy either.

Their faces, seemingly sculpted by fire, were as expressionless as rocks. Never once did they tell me about their suffering or misfortunes. They never dared to question the foreman's orders. Despite the harsh treatment and the constant abuse, they still trusted Segundo more than they did me because I was a white man. To be white created a barrier between two worlds, and there was nothing I could do to win them over.

On the weekends they would walk down to the nearby town of Amaguaña in order to buy salt, animal fat that they called *mapalmira*, and unrefined sugar. While in town, they would sit on the ground bundled together in their frayed ponchos around a barrel of *chicha*, a fermented corn drink. Groups of Indians would line up to buy it by the bucketful and drink the alcohol from a wooden cup that they passed along from one to the other until they became stupefied. Chicha, which was prepared in a wooden barrel, required corn, cane-sugar, and ammonium, making it a highly toxic drink. By nightfall they were stumbling all over the place; the women, reeling and tottering like sacks of grain with their babies strapped to their backs, would stagger back to their huts into which they would tumble and fall asleep on the dirt floor. On Mondays they were useless because they were still unable to get up and go to work.

Suffering from the lack of nutrition since birth and having to start working at an early age, both men and women were worn out and ancient by the time they reached thirty years of age. Those who looked old were simply early to middle-aged men and women who had been consumed by the endless suffering, abuse, poor food, and endemic sickness.

Typically, a peon would earn barely pennies a day, women even less. That miserable salary was complemented by what they managed to raise on their plot of barren land—where hardly anything would grow—their guinea pigs, a few chickens, and perhaps a sheep or two. The land was as destitute as they were and, in order to fertilize it, they would pilfer manure from the cattle stalls. Then they would plant a little barley, potatoes, and corn. Their principal food was toasted corn and broad beans. When I tilled the land on the hacienda, their children would follow behind and compete with the buzzards for the fat white grub worms that they would take home, fry, and eat. That "delicacy" was called *cucaito*.

Happiness did not figure in anyone's life on those high, bleak, barren plateaus. Even though I had always enjoyed working on the land, there wasn't much that could induce me to smile. But one of the most enduring memories I have of that era was learning that Frida was pregnant. Amid the joy of knowing that we were going to have a child, I pondered my situation and worried about the lack of medical assistance for Frida in that godforsaken place. But I couldn't just quit my job; there was nothing else that paid so well. While I spent a lot of time worrying, Frida's abdomen began to expand. The abundant rainfall that year gave new impetus and hope to the hacienda.

Meanwhile, Segundo was doing everything possible to get my administrative position on the hacienda. To him it meant the power to pillage the hacienda brazenly and unscrupulously; naturally, the peon had no part to play in that power struggle.

Finally, it came time for Frida to leave the hacienda and go back to live with her parents in Quito, in the event there were any emergencies during the pregnancy. I stayed on, and Segundo's harassment didn't let up. One night I thought an earthquake had occurred. All around the house the ground was shaking as horses stampeded. Every night Segundo and a group of peons would run the horses around the house to frighten me and to thwart my sleep. A light sleeper because of the nightmares of the past, I would wake up at the drop of a pin. Images of the Nazi destruction would pop into my mind as if they had been fired by catapults. One day I ordered a shotgun from Quito. The day it arrived, I loaded it and waited for the onslaught of the horses that same night. Then I walked out onto the brick patio and fired two shots into the air, for that's all it look to rid myself of the Riders of the Apocalypse. Nevertheless, Segundo's harassment didn't let up: he really wanted my job.

One day I had to inspect a corn field and I left the mule I used for getting around the hacienda tied to some bushes. Nearby, there was grass for him to graze on. Once I had finished surveying the area, I went back to my mule and climbed on. Nervous to begin with, the animal was spooked by a bird and began to buck. The saddle slipped and suddenly I was holding onto the animal's stomach for dear life as he galloped like a bat out of hell. My right foot was caught in the stirrup. The mule headed full speed for the hacienda. I fell to the ground and the animal just kept on dragging me across the tilled soil until he reached a fence. As the mule jumped it, I grabbed a fence post and held on. The saddle came off the mule.

My entire body was battered and bruised. The peons had loosened the cinch in order to make me fall. In great pain, I slung the saddle over my shoulder and walked back to the hacienda. I told one of the servants to catch the mule and tie it to a post. I was so angry that I found a strap and gave the animal a good thrashing. Suddenly a sharp pain pierced my hip. The servant helped me get into bed, where I remained for several days unable to move.

During my third day of immobility, Quispe came around to see me and for the next two days he gave me massages. Then he said, "Get up, *patrón*." As if by magic I stood up and within days I was completely well.

During my convalescence I received a message to return to Quito immediately because Frida was about to give birth. I went down to Amaguaña and took a bus to the capital. On the way, I was able to observe all the haciendas in the Los Chillos Valley, one of the most beautiful areas of the entire world. It reminded me so much of my homeland! Then I thought about my family and that soon I was going to be a father and start my own. I looked up at the sky. Clouds were floating by. "They see me," I said to myself, "and while they wouldn't be happy with my present situation, this is what life is all about and I'm ready to do what ever it takes for my new family."

When I arrived, Frida was already in the delivery room. I stood vigil in a waiting room with white walls and haggard people. After two hours of waiting, I received the news that my son Roberto had been born. I took care of everything at the hospital and went back up to the hacienda. As I traveled back to those desolate, barren mountains, I thought about how my son's birth was going to change my life.

Frida was unable to join me for a while. Loneliness was like a nostalgic cloak that enveloped me. Even though I didn't like it, I had to immerse myself in my work to make time pass quickly. Six weeks later, Frida and Roberto were able to join me at the hacienda. The adobe walls and the frosty plateaus were not the best of environments for them, but Frida never complained. She had told me once that she would follow me to the end of the world, and even though that line sounded like something out of a movie she meant it.

One day I ordered the peons to plow a particular stretch of land on a hill for planting barley. One of them wouldn't obey and said something nasty to me in Quechua, upon which I popped him so hard that he went rolling down the side of a ditch. I was afraid that I had killed him. As I ran down to help him, I prayed that he wasn't dead.

I reached the bottom. The Indian, Nieves, looked up at me and began to scurry away on all fours. I was relieved when I saw that he was still alive. But that incident made me think about the type of life I was leading on the hacienda. I was a long way from what we call civilization, the salary wasn't anything to brag about, and I lived in a hostile environment. I climbed up a hill and looked out over the fields where the peons were working. They were plowing with teams of oxen, gripping the handles of the plows as the steel blades attempted to penetrate the hard clay. The earth didn't want to yield.

The rays of the sun bounced off their stolid faces and apathy was the only expression that could be discerned.

I rode my bay horse back to the hacienda. Frida was surprised to see me return so early. I told her what had happened and about my decision to leave. Frida, who hadn't complained once for over a year and a half, jumped for joy. We immediately began packing the few things we owned and then spent a peaceful last night on the hacienda.

By six o'clock in the morning we were already heading down to Amaguaña. Avelino Gualachico, the only peon who ever trusted me, carried our belongings on his back. Two other peons brought along a dozen chickens. By the time we reached Amaguaña, however, only a few were still alive. The peons had broken their necks so that I would have to give them away, which is what I did.

On Monday, I went to the office of the hacienda owner, who lived in Quito, I asked for my salary for the last twenty days that I had worked on the hacienda. While he was courteous to me, he sent me away without paying me, saying that I had abandoned my job and broken our contract. That was in March 1951.

The tormented peons and the foreman who was always exploiting them had made me see reality. I had sought refuge at the end of the world and I had wanted to forget the past, but I had come to understand that the past is never completely swept away and forgotten. It is with us always, for better or for worse. Suffering and misery were as much a part of those barren plateaus as the past in my soul. The past can never be forgotten or erased permanently; it only allows for certain distractions. Simply put, I had seen up close another facet of humanity, just as terrible as the concentration camps, even though the situation was relatively unknown by most people and of little concern to others. In much the same way that no one wanted to recognize the existence of the concentration camps in Europe, Ecuadorans were denying the fact that some of their fellow citizens were being tortured by the stinging whip of exploitation.

Was God aware of how those forgotten people were subjected to annihilation? Or was it like the concentration camps, where everyone just looked out for themselves? I didn't have an answer. At that moment when the setting sun had painted a yellowish tinge on the hills around Pasochoa, it suggested the majestic presence of a superior being whose hand touched every one of us. But for what purpose?

Men of the Rails and of the Sea

Pablo Cuvi

Sociologist, journalist, photographer, storyteller. Pablo Cuvi has a unique knack for capturing much of life in a few words and images. In addressing many of the themes that have defined twentieth-century Ecuador, from migration and markets to regional integration and urbanization, "Men of the Rails and of the Sea" translates the tensions, sensibility, and beauty that is modern Ecuador.

I was about two years old, just learning to talk, when my dad left the railroad and took us to Manta, where he hoped to make his fortune in the risky export game that made and unmade empires in a matter of months. From then on, his best stories always began with the simple, ritual phrase: "When I worked on the railroad . . ." So, without ever having ridden in a wagon, I grew up longing for the rails and the great whiskey and card sessions at the Railway Club in Riobamba, an obligatory stop coming and going.

Years later, when I finally took the train to Durán, I had the feeling that I was making a sacred journey, a pilgrimage to my origins. Then, the impetuous Chanchan River took the rails, and in waiting for it to be rebuilt, I understood that it had also taken this report's chance to appear in my first book of travels through Ecuador.

But that doesn't matter, because in June it will be eighty years ago that the train came to Quito for the first time, and we're traveling through Chimborazo's wild plains of straw with my friend Palomeque who's taking me as far as Alausí to catch the Sunday railway car that switch-backs along the legendary Nariz del Diablo.

("Oh, this is a devil's nose!" engineer John Harman had exclaimed when that promontory of live rock rose up before his eyes. So, to get through it, they brought four thousand black Jamaicans, experts in handling dynamite and in making little mulattos with the white women of the area, before malaria or the blind blast of the powder took them.)

We go past the outskirts of Riobamba and the Colta Lagoon and, at sunset, cross the desolate, sad Palmira. "It was just a pothole," says Palomeque, on his first trip down to Alausí, while eleven months of drought punish the sterile hillsides. Night falls over the benches along the avenue, where old men sit in ponchos and hats because of the cold. A noisy voice invites residents to play the lottery, the only nighttime diversion. Suddenly, as in a theater, all the lights in town go out and only then do we discover the fabulous star-filled sky. Following the general's recipe, we decide to drown our fear of the unknown with three mugs of steaming *canela* (water boiled with cinnamon).

("And now, general, what do we do?" Archer Harman asked when a landslide destroyed the railbed under construction. "First we have a whiskey to keep the devil at bay," Alfaro responded. "Then we'll see what's to be done.")

Along the Nariz del Diablo

"Seven hundred a sack!" the potato seller offers from his small pickup parked alongside the cheap market kiosks. Indigenous residents of distant communities have come down the mountains to the Sunday market. In the animal plaza, the lambs blend in with the chaps of their owners carrying the handle of their whips across their backs. Everything is stone and dust and women out of time, static, curled up under their colorful shawls.

We stroll through the steep cobblestone streets of this town, which has preserved its traditional Sierra architecture, with some tropical touches on doors and zinc roofs. Palomeque, who has to continue south, says goodbye at the railroad platform. "Write," he jokes. Letters or articles? "It's all the same." Two black pigs are tied to a railway car so small it's not clear which is doing the restraining. And up to the rack they're hoisting a set of chairs, some sacks of food, and seven goats bleating like genuine prisoners sentenced to death.

Inside, there's no room for another passenger. The whistle sounds and the foreman runs to change the direction of the rails. Sitting on a sack of potatoes next to the gearshift, I make small talk with Don Carlos, the engineer. "If you're going to take photos just let me know and I'll stop and you can send me one to remember you." The fat matrons in the first row tease him about being a ladies' man. "Me, where, when?"

And so, with laughs and spicy comments, we negotiate the first switchback and descend in reverse, flirting with the abyss of the oft-mentioned nose. Don Carlos stops in Sibambe. "Hey, we're going to get stuck here! Keep going, keep going, to the manager's office." The gentlemanly engineer steers his railroad car up and we leave each matron off at her door, the only train in the world that makes home deliveries.

Now I ride on the metal roof with the boys on their way to see the bullfights in Huigra, breathing in the warm, sweet wind that comes licking the sugar cane fields. The minuscule chapel and those lovely agaves, like white-flowered palms, stand out on the hill. A peasant crosses the bridge to the highway and makes gestures of anguish. What's the matter? He's forgotten a basket of eggs. Damn, that was a scare! We go riding along, content, to the canvas tube where they still get water from the falls and the sun cools down on the rivers edge.

"Careful, the tuuuuunnel!" the boys shout as we dive into the dark emptiness of the mountain, three times before getting to Huigra, which has been partying, the lucky mother, since 8 December, the day of the Immaculate Virgin of the Grotto, señor.

("When I was a girl," the smiling Dona Isabel reminisces, "English, Americans, the families of railroad employees lived in Huigra. Everything was owned by an Englishman, Edward Morley. He brought a little Belgian nun and they built a school where a lot of the rich little girls went to study. People from Guayaquil came, too, to spend the winter: it was the season of the *monas* [nuns], we used to say."

"Before they built the Sibambe-Cuenca railroad, we did a lot of business with Azuay. There were two great warehouses, my fathers and Señor Medina's, and they brought wagons from Durán filled with sugar, rice, that sort of thing. Then the muleteers from the south came with teams of mules and the town filled with animals. It was lovely."

"There were two headquarters in Huigra," adds Don Rómulo Barragán, her husband, who came to keep the records. "The railroad was a unique organization in the country: all the trains arrived on time. When they opened the Club Ferroviario and dedicated the statue of Eloy Alfaro, Mr. White organized a magnificent party, making two trains available for guests and asking the poet Remigio Romero y Cordero to write an elegy."

Don Rómulo, who studied by correspondence to be an engineer, will never forget the first stanzas, nor the day when he drove an express train for dictator Páez, who was going to embark in Guayaquil.)

Small Town Matadors

I take a shabby room at the old Hotel Huigra, which also belonged to Morley. Is it safe? I ask the silent woman who is changing the sheets. "There are no thieves in this town," she says. Maybe because old Alfaro is still keeping watch from the little central park, says I. A pile of ties rests in front of the club. An old woman trots by alongside her mare, a grandchild on its back. And at the corner store, a group of indigenous men have gathered. They're acculturated: the usual pigtail is absent, and they are wearing brilliant nylon shirts and carrying huge boomboxes.

After lunch, the music of Toro Barroso announces the arrival of the band. Dressed as a Cordoban, the town queen comes out to dance with her keen subjects, including yours truly, to whom they offer, out of curiosity, a few shots of aguardiente. And so we walk in procession on the long dirt street, presided over by one of Manolete's fragile apprentices who offers drunken passes with his cape at the balconies until reaching the bull ring.

Manolete is soon knocked down by a paramo cow with the complicity of fans in the stands. The game continues with dodges and sprints, but nobody manages anything even approaching a respectable pass. The real passes are taking place at the large pans overflowing with pork and blood sausages, until a young bull gets out of the ring and causes a ruckus of screams and broken glass at the surrounding tables. Above, the pretenders to the royal court continue dancing, and the stand also looks like it's going to come crashing down. Finally, the last bull sends the drunk, who is now fighting with a handkerchief, into the air and when his friends come to the rescue, the offended matador starts throwing punches left and right and the bullfight ends in a phenomenal brawl, olé!

"They're a bunch of brutes," a man wearing shades and a railroad jacket comments later. "I'm from Chunchi, but since I was a baby I've lived in Naranjapata and here." The man guides me among the quiet wagons of red wood to the edge of the ravine that the Chanchan River devours every winter. Then he points at the hills. "They raise everything here, beans, tomatoes, cabbage, lettuce. All this used to belong to the gringo Morley. He's buried at the Virgin's grotto. You knew that the gringo married the mother superior at the school? . . . Sure did! And when he died, the nun sold everything, even the hotel, and was never seen in these parts again. How about that?"

Little town, big hell, I comment in Christian fashion.

Around midnight, the festival music flows among the wood and adobe houses along Azuay Street. Crabs, blood sausages, and hot alcoholic drinks boil, as does a firecracker that hits the eaves of a house on its way to the heavens and explodes at the feet of the intrepid dancers. But in the dawn mist, the men who return to their farm chores look like a line of ghosts in the headlights of the bus, like lost porters and muleteers and stumbling coastal farmers disappearing in the dust of the road.

Playas de Villamil

At the beginning of the century, when the peninsula was still covered with trees and mangroves, Playas was the beach preferred by Guayaquileños. In those days of horses and long rivers, the distance between that town and Salinas was measured in days.

But today I travel by bus, surrounded by a group of cholos going back to their fishing chores in Posorja. Short, square, and strong, as though pulled from the pages of Aguilera Malta, the young men chatter at the top of their lungs. "Me, when I want a woman, I take her," says one with hair bleached by the sun. "What do you say, Handsome?" But Handsome, toothless and ugly as sin, confesses that he left a woman a week ago and just saw her with someone else. "You mean she's been cheating on you the whole time," jokes a third, a big curly-haired mulatto. "I'd beat them both to a pulp!"

We go along the thirsty plain, from which an immobile flame of acacias in flower and *ceibos* (ceiba trees) in anthropomorphic shapes stand out. In Progreso, the soft drink and fried banana vendors get on board, and the aroma stays with us all the way to General Villamil.

On the beach, the implacable midday sun burns pebbles and snails, while the wind from the sea is about to blow away the little fabric shelters rented to bathers. At the far end, impassive, the old Hotel Humboldt awaits its reopening. I pass the sultry hour comforted by an ice cold beer and delicious lobster at El Bucanero. Then I walk along the wet sand to the loading dock at the bend.

Because the residents of Las Playas make a living by fishing, there is a lot of activity around the boats, where they're cleaning and preparing their nets before going out for the catch. "To catch sea bass," a boy called Pedro tells me, but he doesn't fish anymore because his uncle is old and he doesn't have a motor. Beyond, a very talented cholo repairs one of those pre-Columbian rafts used for fishing with a hook. And those with nothing to do play ball in front of the concrete skeleton of the first apartment building.

The sun sets. A dog chases sea gulls along the resplendent beach at low tide. In the taverns, the fishermen, shirtless, drink and play cards, while Julio Jaramillo still sings "Fatalidad" and night descends to sleep in the amusement park.

But everything begins again on the beach the following morning. The thieving frigate birds nose-dive into the sea to steal fish, and the middle-men steal with their scales. I spend a long time diving into waves, until a raft made of four logs throws out a net and two rows of tanned men start to pull it in. Then I recognize the fisherman from yesterday and go out to help. And when I feel the rough, wet cord in my hands, I close my eyes for a moment and understand that it is impossible to leave the sea.

"It's a pain to travel with other photographers," Pepe.

Here Come the Girls from Bucay!

Avilés complains five years later, when we get to Pallatanga.

"Take it easy," I say, "I'm going to shoot a couple of photos and then I'm out of here."

Pepe is working on a photo essay about circuses and whorehouses, which he calls coastal-style *chongos* (slang for whorehouse), and he wants to get to Bucay before nightfall. I, on the other hand, remain faithful to my custom of chatting with residents and digging for signs of the train.

"They raise a lot of beans and tomatoes here," says a cabinetmaker who came fleeing urban madness. "The city is terrible. Here everything's close, time seems to stand still, while in the city you can't make it, everything is far away. Here we pay in cash, you don't see many checks. And you make money. A lot of folks have gotten rich on tomatoes. The people of Pimampiro came to work the land here because it's exhausted back there. And the locals learned."

Just a few, because the majority go to work in the shrimp pools and banana plantations. Next to the new cement dwellings on the village plaza there's a tall wood house with scenes of war painted on the walls, where they sell everything from vHSS to vegetables.

"Those paintings are at least seventy years old. He was an old drunk, he had a drink and kept on painting," the sheriff remembers. "From here on it's coast. The mountain you see used to be pure jungle. Listen, here they used to get what they called the chills, malaria. Here you find potatoes alongside cassava, mangos next to peaches. It's unbelievable."

We leave Pallatanga in the Budget Trooper, driving past vacation farms belonging to Guayaquileños who come for holidays. Flat, green bean fields reach as far as the Sal-Si-Puedes ravine, the canyon through which the Chimbo River flows and whose bridge was inaugurated by Dr. Velasco Ibarra himself, naturally. It functions as a time tunnel as well because a '37 Renault with Manabi plates crosses the bridge, alive and kicking. Looking for fresher history, we drive against the hot tropical air to the birthplace of Lorena Gallo Coronel de Bobbitt, the lady of the impulsive slash that set the world to trembling, introducing the term *penis* into the daily news and opening the way for a mended John Wayne to play in a porno flick.

"I felt bad for her, for her whole family," remembers Doña Leonila, who lives in the house next door to the blue two-story dwelling where little Lorena lived until she was ten, when she moved to Venezuela. "There were demonstrations supporting her; the entire town saw the trial on television, and we celebrated when she was freed. There was a mass, and Silvana even came because she grew up here, too, and when she was a little girl she sang for fiestas."

So the most desirable Ecuadorian woman of '89 and the most feared of '93 did their basic training in Bucay, who would have thought it? Ximena, Doña Leo's daughter, jokes,

"When we walk along the beach and the boys realize who we are, they say, "Ohhh, put it back in your pants, here come the girls from Bucay!"

But now no one talks about it much except when a stranger shows up. The town has returned to the routine of the train that travels up to Huigra and down to Durán, day after day. The streets look neglected, the men play Ecua-volley (similar to volleyball) at the side of the tracks, and the Hotel Cumanda, on the other side of the river, isn't anything to lose your head over. And to top it off, there's no chongo or circus for Pepe to shoot. Without Lorena or Silvana, the town of Bucay has sunk into anonymity.

Ten Drugstores for One Cabaret

A kiddie train and a poor circus truck travel at sunset along the road to Naran-jito, paved in spots, running between trees and pastures, until the pineapple plantations appear, looking somewhat bedraggled because new varieties or other crops haven't been planted. The setting sun casts a pink glow over the sugar cane fields as we leave the comical wanderers behind and enter Naran-jito, a city that, from one end to the other, sports the train lines that gave it life during the golden years, as the traditional homes on the main street testify. Sitting around a small table near the door of a cafe, men talk about soccer and bananas; nearby, nubile girls play on the tracks.

After downing a beer, we go on to Milagro, whose name is a reminder of the miraculous cure of a colonial judge's wife who was given quinine infu-sions. Today, the city, sugared by the neighboring Valdez refinery, has more than 100,000 inhabitants and a good share of pharmacies, as though every-body were sick.

"I've never seen so many drugstores in one place," Pepe comments.

"I would give ten drugstores for a good hotel," I say.

"Or for a photogenic cabaret," Pepe adds.

"They're not mutually exclusive, are they?"

For now, the taxi drivers recommend the Hotel Nacional, right on the cor-ner where hundreds of swallows sleep, shit, and shriek. And at the hotel, they send us to dine at an acceptable restaurant while the entire town watches soccer on television: Barcelona is winning; the celebration is winning. Later, by way of a long, dark dirt road, we show up at the red light district. But it's still early for this sort of thing, and the chongos have the look of ordinary discotheques, with lights and strident sounds. As if that weren't bad enough, the other circus, next to the stadium, has just folded its tent. No way to sleep, to bed with the swallows and the noise of Barcelona fans.

Better, to wake up with the swallows long before the French locomotive makes its triumphal entry into town. A locomotive made to pull a hundred wagons through Siberia, attached to five half-empty coaches. Someone made a lot of money on the locomotive deal, they comment at the station, because this is going to end. It's a traveling market on rails, with fresh fish for sale on the flatbed wagon and foreign tourists on the metal roofs. Three stevedores load battered easy chairs destined for Alausí and Riobamba: pure nostalgia for an oddity whose days are numbered . . . by the neoliberals.

Creolization and African Diaspora Cultures:
The Case of the Afro-Esmeraldian *Décimas*

Jean Muteba Rahier

The northern coast of Ecuador—particularly the province of Esmeraldas—is home to Ecuadorians of African descent. Part of the broader African diaspora in the Americas, the Afro-Ecuadorian culture that has emerged in this part of the coast is the product of cultural fragments of various origins as well as original creations. The anthropologist Jean Muteba Rahier explores one of these interesting mixtures, the Afro-Esmeraldian Décima, a traditional oral poetry recited by (often illiterate) Afro-Esmeraldian men. The formal origin of this cultural expression is written poetry that was quite popular during the Renaissance in Spain and in Europe in general: the gloss (la glosa).

The word *décima* signifies in Spanish a stanza of ten verses. The Afro-Esmer-aldians use the term *Décima* to refer to an oral poetry composed of forty-four verses.[1] These forty-four verses are mostly octosyllabic; however, verses sometimes have seven, ten, or even eleven syllables. There is no conscious nor rigid rule that regulates the verses' meter. The *decimeros*—the male poets who recite the Décimas—are very proud of the complexity of the formal structure of the poems. The forty-four verses are divided into five stanzas in this order: one of four verses (a quartet), then four of ten (actual décimas).[2] Each verse of the initial quartet is repeated at the end of each ten-line stanza that numerically corresponds. In other words, the first verse of the quartet is also the last line of the first ten-line stanza, the second verse of the quartet finishes the second ten-line stanza, the third verse finishes the third ten-line stanza, and so on ($1 = 14$, $2 = 24$, $3 = 34$, $4 = 44$). Sometimes, the verse from the quartet is slightly transformed when repeated at the end of the ten-line stanza, but maintains the same meaning. This is due to the particularity of the Afro-Esmeraldian oral tradition, which permits one to finish a ten-line stanza with some liberty. On rare occasions, the verse completely changes when repeated at the end of the ten-line stanza. Here is an example of Afro-Esmeraldian Décima:

¿QUIÉN ES ÉSTA QUE ESTÁ AQUÍ?

1. ¿Quién es ésta que está aquí?
2. ¿Quién es esta hermosa rosa?
3. ¿Pregunto: quién es tu madre?
4. ¿Que te parió tan hermosa?

5. ¿Quién es ésta que está aquí?
6. ¿Quién es esta bella rosa?
7. ¿Pregunto: cuál es tu madre?

8. ¿Que te ha parido tan hermosa?

9. ¿Quién es ésta tan bonita?

10. que ha venido a dar aquí,

11. que a penas la distinguí,
12. ¿para contar su atención?

13. Y pregunto con atención:
14. ¿quién es ésta que está aquí?

15. Tu risa me ha cautivado,   a
16. tu mirar mucho mejor,   b
17. y tu talle con primor,   b

18. sin sentido me ha dejao'.   a
19. Me hallo tan apensionado   a
20. de verte tan buena moza,   c

21. tan afable y cariñosa   c
22. para ser tan bella dama.   d
23. Y se puede correr tu fama,   d
24. ¿quién es esta bella rosa?   c

25. Cómo te llamas no sé,   a
26. ni tampoco te conozco,   b
27. pero te diré que estoy loco   b

28. al tiempo que te miré.   a
29. Y a todos preguntaré   a
30. si tienes marido o padre,   c

31. o si está aquí tu madre: c

WHO IS THIS ONE WHO IS HERE?

1. Who is this one who is here?
2. Who is this beautiful rose?
3. I ask: "who is your mother
4. who gave birth to you so fair?"

5. Who is this one who is here?
6. Who is this beautiful rose?
7. I ask: "which one is your mother

8. who gave birth to you so pretty?"

9. Who is this good looking woman

10. who came to establish herself here?

11. who as soon as I saw her,
12. I wanted to draw her attention?

13. And I ask with great attention:
14. who is this one who is here?

15. Your laughter captivated me,
16. your glance even more,
17. and your incredible silhouette

18. left me numb.
19. Passion overwhelms me
20. to see you as attractive as you

21. so affable and loving,
22. such a beautiful woman.
23. May your fame travel,
24. who is this beautiful rose?

25. I don't know your name,
26. nor do I know you,
27. but I'll tell you that I'm crazy

28. since the first time I saw you.
29. And I will ask everybody
30. if you have a husband or a father,

31. or if your mother is around:

32. tengo que hacerle un secreto.	d	32. I have to tell her a secret.
33. Y así con mucho respeto	d	33. And that's with great respect
34. ¿pregunto: quién es tu madre?	c	34. that I ask who is your mother?

35. Tu madre debe de ser	35. Your mother must be
36. una estrella reluciente.	36. a shining star.
37. Tu padre por consiguiente,	37. Your father consequently
38. es un hermoso clavel!	38. is handsome carnation!
39. Que naciste de ella y d'él	39. You were born from her and him
40. blanca, amable y buena moza,	40. white, lovable and good looking,
41. alumbras más que una estrella.	41. you shine more than a star.
42. Ay, dime a'ónde estará	42. *Ay*, tell me where will
43. esta madre tuya, m'hijita	43. your mother be, my dear
44. ¿que te parió tan hermosa?	44. who gave birth to you so fair?

An anonymous couplet known by all the decimeros summarizes some of these aspects of the Décimas' formal structure using "popular terminology," that is, formal or technical terms with a new and very different meaning:

1. Cuarenta y cuatro palabras	1. Forty-four verses
2. tiene la décima entera;	2. make the entire *Décima*;
3. diez palabras cada pie,	3. ten verses each ten-line stanza,
4. cuatro la glosa primera	4. four the first quartet.

The decimeros use *palabras*, which literally means "word" in Spanish, for "verse"; *décima entera* for "the entire poem" (the Décima); *pie*, which means "foot" (rhythmic unit), for a ten-line stanza; and *glosa primera*, "the first gloss," for "the first quartet." This illustrates how the decimeros have transformed even the formal vocabulary of poetry. These structural rules of the Décimas make the initial quartet the synthesis of the central ideas of the poem, which are more fully developed in the four ten-line stanzas.

The declamation of the Décimas is similar with each poet, and emphasizes rhythm. The poems are delivered in nine parts separated by short pauses. First comes the initial quartet, and then the four first verses of the first ten-line stanza, then the six following verses of the same ten-line stanza, etc. (4/4.6/4.6/4.6/4.6). The decimeros' pitch usually rises in the last two syllables of the next to the last verse of each ten-line stanza, and then falls in the last two syllables of the last verse. The goal is to emphasize the last verse, the conclusion of the stanza, which is the repetition of the last line of the initial quartet, thereby marking the rhythm of the declamation. Sometimes, older decimeros make pauses that the others do not make. Instead of saying the forty-four verses according to the model previously indicated, their declamation follows this pattern—(4/4.4.2/4.4.2/4.4.2/4.4.2)—the pauses that separate the stanzas being slightly longer than the pauses which separate the verses of a same stanza. Logically, the described declamation is intimately related to the organization of the content, the story of the Décima, into groups of verses that correspond to grammatical sentences. When transcribing the oral texts, one can always finish the fourth verse of each ten-line stanza with a period [or exclamation point] or a semicolon. There is no overlapping between the fourth and the fifth verse. They are always clearly separated.

The decimeros distinguish between two categories of Décimas: the *Décimas a lo humano* (about human matters or profane) and the *Décimas a lo divino* (about divine matters). These two categories of Décimas are not recited in the same contexts. The previously cited Décima is a poem a lo humano.

We can see in the Décima "¿Quién es ésta?" (Who Is This One?) that the majority of verses are octosyllabic, that there are forty-four verses divided into an initial quartet and four ten-line stanzas, that the verses of the quartet are repeated at the end of their respective ten-line stanza (with the exception of verse 2, *¿Quién es esta hermosa rosa?*, which becomes in verse 24 *¿Quién es esta bella rosa?*), and that each ten-line stanza constitutes the explanation, the gloss, of a verse of the quartet. This poem is also representative of the kind of rhymes one can find in the Décimas: They seem to be arbitrary rather than subject to strict rules.

The Spanish Glosa (Gloss)

The gloss or *glosa* is a poetic form that was very popular among European writers from the fifteenth century through the eighteenth. What historians of Spanish literature call "the normal type of the gloss" was a poem composed of forty-four verses, divided in two parts: the "text," and the actual "gloss" or *glosa*. The text—in Spanish *texto*, *cabeza*, or *retruécano*—was a short poem which had been composed by a previous poet. Its extension could vary from one to twelve verses, and sometimes more. Nevertheless, the "most common form of the gloss"[3] presented a text of four verses.

The second part of this form of Spanish poetry, the actual gloss written by the *glosador* (glosser), was a commentary of the "text." It was used—as its name indicates—to gloss an already existing poetry in a certain number of stanzas, by means of interpretation, paraphrase, and extension in general, of each initial verse. The number of stanzas of the gloss (second part of the poem) was determined by the number of verses included in the "text." Each stanza of the gloss interpreted and paraphrased one verse of the "text." The glossed verse was then found sometimes at the middle, but more often at the end of the stanza.

The "most common type" of the Spanish gloss (entire poem) had for "text" a *ronda*, a four-line stanza, with *rimas envueltas*, "enveloped rhymes" (a.b.b.a.), or *rimas cruzadas*, "crossed rhymes" (a.b.a.b.a.), which was commented upon in four ten-line stanzas, with the verse from the "text" repeated at the end of each stanza. The disposition of the rhymes followed the formal characteristics of the type of ten-line stanza chosen by the poet who composed the glosa.

Here is an example of Spanish gloss, composed by Lope de Vega to celebrate the wedding of Philip III and Princess Marguerite of Austria:[4]

NACE EN EL NÁCAR LA PERLA

1. Nace en el nácar la perla,
2. En Austria una Margarita,
3. Y un joyel hay de infinita
4. Estima donde ponerla.

5. Cuando el cielo que el sol dora,
6. Para formar perlas llueve
7. Las que en el norte atesora
8. Abrese el nácar y bebe
9. Las lágrimas del aurora.
10. Desta suerte, para hacerla
11. A Margarita preciosa
12. Quiso el cielo componerla
13. De la manera que hermosa
14. Nace en el nácar la perla.
    (14 = 1)

15. Para un joyel rico y solo
16. Buscaba perlas España,
17. Y piedras de polo a polo
18. O en nácares que el mar baña
19. O en minas que engendra Apolo.
20. La fama, que en todo habita,

21. Le dijo, viendo el joyel,

22. Que al sol en belleza unita,

THE PEARL IS BORN IN THE NACRE

1. The Pearl is born in the Nacre,
2. In Austria a Marguerite
3. And a very special jewel
4. Ponders where to place her.

5. When the sky gilded by the sun,
6. Forms pearls of rain
7. Which are stored in the north
8. The nacre opens and drinks
9. The tears of dawn.
10. In this way she is made
11. A Precious Marguerite
12. The sky wanted to compose her
13. In such a way so lovely
14. Is the Pearl born in the nacre.
    (14 = 1)

15. For a rich and solitary jewel
16. Spain was looking for pearls
17. And stones from pole to pole
18. Or in nacres bathed by the sea
19. Or in mines engendered by Apollo.
20. Fame, that lives inside everything,

21. Told her as he examined the jewel,

22. That the sun with beauty unites,

23. Que hallaría para él	23. So would find for him
24. En Austria una Margarita.	24. In Austria a Marguerite.
(24 = 2)	(24 = 2)
25. Austria también pretendía,	25. Austria was also courting,
26. Dudosa, informarse della,	26. Doubtful, obtaining informa- tion for her,
27. Y certificóle un día	27. And one day guaranteed her
28. Que Margarita tan bella	28. That such a beautiful Marguerite
29. Sólo en Felipe cabía.	29. Could not be but for Philip.
30. Luego España solicita	30. Later Spain requested
31. Con tal tercero⁵ a tal dama.	31. Such a man to such a lady,
32. Y con su pecho la incita,	32. Be invited with all her heart,
33. Donde hay oro de gran fama,	33. Where there is gold of great renown
34. Y un joyel hay de infinita.	34. And a very special jewel. .
(34 = 3)	(34 = 3)
35. Este joyel español	35. This Spanish jewel
36. Se hizo a todo distinto	36. was very unique
37. Y tan sólo como el sol	37. He was like the shining
38. Del oro de Carlos Quinto,	38. Gold of Charles V,
39. Siendo Felipe el crisol.	39. Philip being the crucible.
40. Deste, para engrandecerla,	40. With it, to exalt her,
41. Se engosta, adorna y esmalta,	41. He adorns and embellishes himself,
42. Este pudo merecerla,	42. He does merit her,
43. Que ninguna hay de tan alta	43. No women is as exalted
44. Estima donde ponerla. (44 = 4)	44. Ponders where to place her. (44 = 4)

The "normal type" of Spanish gloss had different components: octosyllabic verses and four- and ten-line stanzas. The octosyllabic verse, also called by the philologists *verso de arte real*, *verso de ronda mayor*, or *verso de arte menor*, is the most commonly used verse form in Spanish literature. In Spain, it is considered national verse form. It can be found in both aristocratic and popular poetry from the 11th century on. It has retained its vigor in the popular poetry of Spain as well as in the popular poetry of Latin America.

There are two types of four-line stanzas utilized as "text" in the "normal" or "classic" Spanish gloss: the *ronda* or quartet with "enveloped rhymes" (a.b.b.a.), which prevailed almost exclusively since the Siglo de Oro; and the quartet with "crossed rhymes" (a.b.a.b.), which is the oldest type of four-line stanza in Spanish literature. In Afro-Esmeraldian Décimas, despite the repetition of certain syllables at the end of each line, marking the rhythm of declamation, the rhymes are more arbitrary than the glosses' rhymes. However, some Décimas can be found with either an "enveloped rhymes" quartet or a "crossed rhymes" quartet. Here are two examples from the *Décima San Lorenzo*, and the *Décima El Cangrejo* (The Crab), respectively:

Con justiciera razón,	a	With a justified reason,
San Lorenzo está pidiendo,	b	(the town of) San Lorenzo is asking,
diré mejor insistiendo,	b	better said insisting,
ser elevado a cantón.	a	to become a county.
Un cangrejo con su espada,	a	A crab with its sword
me quiso poner un cacho.	b	wanted to stab me.
Yo le di una patada	a	I kicked him
y le quebré el carapacho.	b	and I broke his shell.

The ten-line stanza has been popular in Spanish poetry since the end of the Middle Ages. To comment upon the four-line "text," the "classic or normal type" of the Spanish gloss used both the *copla real* (royal couplet), and the *Espinela*.

The royal couplet is comprised of two stanzas of five verses, that can have identical rhymes, or the first one some rhymes, and the second one others (a.b.a.b.a.c.d.c.d.c.), which was usually evaluated as being better. Because the royal couplet is the combination of two five-line stanzas, it is also called the *falsa décima* (the false ten-line stanza) or also the *doble quintil* (the double five-line stanza). This distribution of the royal couplet into two five-line stanzas is also marked by the punctuation, which always divides the ten-line stanza in two parts of five verses (see the previously cited gloss composed by Lope de Vega).

The *Espinela*, from the name of its promoter, Vicente Espinel (1550–1624), is, in his classic form, a stanza of ten octosyllabic verses with four rhymes which are invariably (a.b.b.a.a./c.c.d.d.c.). It is actually composed of two quartets of enveloped rhymes which have an identical rhyme scheme (a.b.b.a. and c.d.d.c.), plus two connecting verses at the middle: the first one repeats the last rhyme of the first quartet, while the second anticipates the first rhyme of the following quartet: (a.b.b.a./a.c./c.c.d.d.c.). The rhyme scheme is not the only peculiarity of the Espinela. A ten-line stanza is considered Espinela if, in addition to the indicated rhyme scheme, it shows a clear break in the content and delivery of the poem after the fourth verse. This pause gives the fifth verse a special status: according to the rhyme scheme it belongs to the first part of the ten-line stanza, but the content pertains to the second part. Juan Millé y Giménez summarized the role of the Espinela's fifth verse:

> This fifth verse is the axis, the key of the entire *Espinela*. If by the sound we have to consider it as united to the first part of five verses, in terms of meaning it belongs to the second. In this way, the composition is left symmetrical as far as the sounds are concerned, but presents a kind of overlapping by the meaning that unites one five line stanza to the other, giving birth to a new unit of versification.

Rudolf Baehr also wrote about this break in meaning:

> Until the break in the meaning after the fourth verse, the argument has to dispose itself into the progression of its development, and in this way present the theme. The following six verses may not introduce a new idea; they have to amplify what has already been presented in the first part of four verses. Because of its rigorous presentation, form and development, the *Espinela* can be placed with dignity beside the sonnet.

Here is an example of *Espinela* (composed by Vicente Espinel in 1592):

1. Suele decirme la gente	a	1. The people use to tell me
2. que en parte sabe mi mal,	b	2. that in part they know my pain
3. que la causa principal	b	3. that its principal cause
4. se me ve inscrita en la frente;	a	4. is written on my forehead;
5. y aún me hago valiente	a	5. and even if I pretend
6. luego mi lengua desliza	c	6. my tongue always reveals it
7. por lo que dora y matiza;	c	7. with embellishment and nuances
8. que lo que el pecho no gosta	d	8. what one cannot swallow
9. ningún disímulo basta	d	9. no dissimulation suffices
10. a cubrirlo con ceniza.	c	10. even covering it with ashes.

This description of the formal components of the "classic model" of the Spanish gloss demonstrates quite well that the Afro-Esmeraldian Décimas originated in the "normal type" of gloss using the Espinela. All of the more than sixty Afro-Esmeraldian Décimas I worked on show this grammatical pause characteristic of the Espinela's fourth verse. The first four verses serve to present the theme that is developed in the six following verses, until reaching the conclusion in the tenth verse. The periods and semicolons which separate the fourth and the fifth verse of the Décimas' ten-line stanzas are placed, in the written version of the Décimas, by the ethnographer who recorded them.

The decimeros, who most of the time are illiterate, and who have a purely oral relationship with the poems, do not place them at the end of a verse. The ethnographer does. It is significant that when transcribing Décimas, one always has to separate the fourth verse of a ten-line stanza from the fifth with a period or a semicolon. The content of the stanza as well as the recitation of the poem asks the transcriber to do so. The pauses made by the decimero between the fourth and the fifth verse of a ten-line stanza are in accordance with the characteristic specialization of the verses of the Espinela; they do not interrupt the presentation of the argumentation. Furthermore, despite the fact that no strict rule systematizes the Décimas' rhymes, sometimes one can find in particular Décimas the same characteristic Espinela rhyme scheme—or vestiges of that scheme. That is the case of the Décima "¿Quién es ésta?" for instance, which has its second and third ten-line stanzas (verses 15–24 and verses 25–34) reproducing the Espinela rhyme scheme, while the first and the fourth do not.

Obviously, the formal structure of the Afro-Esmeraldian Décima is derived from the Spanish gloss format. However, the Décimas are not simply copies or bad imitations of the latter. Décimas and glosses constitute very distinct poetic genres (texts and contexts). At the formal level (meter and rhyme) the gloss is much more strictly defined than the Décima.

The Afro-Esmeraldian Poets, or Decimeros

In the small villages in the northern sector of the Province of Esmeraldas, the tradition of reciting Décimas is reserved for men, who are for the most part older and illiterate. They are respected for their knowledge and memory. Usually, Décimas have unknown composers, despite the fact that many of the decimeros will claim to have composed the Décimas they recite. It is quite common to find decimeros who live a hundred kilometers apart claiming to have written the same poem. During my various journeys in the Province of Esmeraldas, I met only one decimero (he was then in his mid-forties) who actually wrote his Décimas. He was very proud that one of his compositions had been published by an organization that has as its objective the preservation of Afro-Ecuadorian cultures.

The decimeros, and with them the Afro-Esmeraldian population in general, divide the Décimas into two categories: the *Décimas a lo divino* (about divine matters) and the *Décimas a lo humano* (profane poems). The Décimas about divine matters are declaimed in different contexts than the profane Décimas. While the Décimas a lo humano are declaimed in informal gatherings, the Décimas about divine matters are recited in four different contexts:

funerals for adults (*alabados*), the funerals for children (*chigualos*), saints day celebrations (*arrullos*), and as a mean of protection against forest spirits. Here is an example of *Décima a lo divino*, which is recited during the *arrullo al Niño Dios*, the celebration performed on Christmas Eve:

YO VIDE A MI DIOS CHIQUITO	I SAW MY GOD AS A BABY
1. Yo vide a mi Dios chiquito	1. I saw my God as a baby,
2. dándole el pecho su madre	2. his mother was breast-feeding him
3. y San José como padre	3. and his father Saint Joseph
4. le decía: "calla, Niñito".	4. was telling him: "Be quiet my son."
5. En un dichoso portal	5. In a happy porch
6. vi a San José y a María	6. I saw Saint Joseph and Mary
7. que en los brazos lo tenía	7. who was holding him in her arms
8. dándole al Niño mamar.	8. while suckling him.
9. Con tanta amorosidad	9. With so much love
10. le da sus pechos bendito,	10. she gives him her sacred breasts,
11. le dice: "Mama, Niñito,	11. telling him: "Suck, my little one,
12. este manjar oloroso".	12. this perfumed sustenance."
13. Tomando el sustento hermoso,	13. He was drinking,
14. yo vide a mi Dios chiquito.	14. I saw my God as a baby.
15. Los tres Reyes del Oriente	15. The three Kings of the Orient
16. se pusieron en camino	16. began their journey
17. en busca del Rey divino	17. looking for the divine King
18. donde lo hallaron presente.	18. until they found him.
19. Herodes bajó en persona	19. Herod welcomed them himself
20. tan solo por degollarle.	20. because he wanted to kill Him.
21. El ángel les vino a hablar	21. The angel came to speak to them
22. y para Egipto salieron.	22. and they left for Egypt.
23. Estaba el Niño en sus brazos	23. The Baby was in her arms,
24. dándole el pecho su madre.	24. his mother was breast-feeding him.
25. Cuando fueron a adorarlo	25. When they went to worship him
26. bajaron por el Oriente,	26. they left towards the Orient,
27. sólo de guía pusieron	27. and their only guides

28. las estrellas al poniente.
29. Era tan resplandeciente,
30. no había con quién compararlo.
31. Cuando fueron a adorarlo

32. sólo tres santos habían:

33. la Magdalena y María,
34. y San José como padre.
35. Cuando nació el Sumo Bien

36. dijo el gallo: "¡Nació Cristo!"
37. Respondió Diego Laurito:
38. "'Onde nació jue en Belén."
39. Iban los Reyes también
40. con sus rosarios benditos.
41. Pastores iban contritos

42. hincaditos de rodilla.
43. Y el Cordero sin mancilla
44. le decía: "Calla Niñito."

28. were the stars in the sky.
29. It was shining so much,
30. there was nothing to compare it with.
31. When they went to worship him

32. Only three saints were already present:

33. Magdalena and Mary,
34. and his father Saint Joseph.
35. When the Supreme Good was born

36. the cock sung: "Christ is born!"
37. Diego Laurito responded:
38. "He was born in Bethlehem."
39. The Kings were going too
40. with their blessed rosaries
41. Shepherds were going repentantly

42. kneeling down.
43. And the Lamb without stain
44. was telling him: "Be quiet my son."

Notes

For a longer version of this piece and for complete references, please consult Jean Muteba Rahier, "Blackness as a Process of Creolization: The Afro-Esmeraldian *Décimas* (Ecuador)," in The *African Diaspora: African Origins and New World Identities*, ed. Isidore Okpewho, Carole Boyce-Davies, and Ali Mazrui (Bloomington: Indiana University Press, 1999), 290–314.

1. I differentiate *décima* (a ten-line stanza) from *Décima* (the Afro-Esmeraldian poem of forty-four lines).

2. Ten-line stanza.

3. I mean here the entire poem.

4. In Spanish, *Margarita* is a synonym of "pearl."

5. *Tercero* is a reference to Philip III.

Julio Jaramillo and Music as Identity

Hernán Ibarra

Translated by Mayté Chiriboga

Julio Jaramillo Laurido was born in Guayaquil on 1 October 1935 to a working-class family. He began singing with his brother José, and they were known in the popular music field by the deprecatory name of "lagarteros" (the sly ones). Jaramillo then moved to radio and public appearances before recording duets with Fresia Saavedra, a renowned national music singer. Hernán Ibarra briefly introduces us to a popular icon seen by some as representing the soul of Ecuadorian national music.

By the middle of the twentieth century, a modern mass culture was established in Ecuador based in large part around popular music. It was structured by the phonographic industry, radio, jukeboxes (*rocola*), and a public presentation system. Radio stations had auditoriums for musical appearances and cinemas offered live music together with movie presentations.

The introduction and propagation of jukeboxes in the 1950s, together with the advent of "singles" (45s), served to popularize not only national music but Latin American popular music more broadly. Toward the 1960s, jukeboxes were artifacts disseminated in restaurants, brothels, ice-cream parlors, and canteens. They played local and international music, but did not yet include what came to be known as *rocolera* music.

Popular music tended to have a strong local and urban character during this period, and although Ecuadorian music was mainly represented by the *pasillo*, it encompassed musical traditions from other Latin American countries. Julio Jaramillo emerged within this dynamic music scene and was able to move amidst a repertoire that included *pasillos, yaravíes, and pasacalles,* together with *valses* and *boleros*. His music was broadcast mainly through jukeboxes and radio. His most popular songs are of a romantic nature, and others refer to the Guayaquileño identity.

His success was ultimately rooted in his international appeal. His long stays in Venezuela and Mexico enabled him to assemble a larger audience, one that ultimately included Central America, the Caribbean, and even the Southern cone. He recorded duets with Olimpo Cárdenas, Alci Acosta, and Daniel Santos. He developed a special friendship with Santos and together in 1974 they recorded *En la cantina*, an LP that re-creates an experience in a canteen.

His presence in Ecuadorian popular imagination was nurtured by his periodic returns to the country. His early demise at the age of forty-two (Guayaquil, 8 February 1978) also served to place him as a cultural referent of national identity. When he died, he was reported to have fathered some twenty-seven children and have made more than 300 LPS. Even during the 1970s, when a nationalist mood rejected popular-folk roots, Ecuadorian mestizo nationalism discovered in JJ an icon from a popular origin that enabled a sense of belonging. And he has lived on in death. In 1981, the movie *Nuestro juramento* (Our Oath) premiered, a Mexican-Ecuadorian coproduction which chronicles his life (a version of this film in DVD is *El señor de las cantinas* [The Lord of the Canteens]). Later on, during the 1990s, an Ecuadorian television series tried the same (with much less success).

The rocolera music that surfaced in the late 1970s after JJ's demise is a medley of Ecuadorian musical rhythms (pasillos, valses, and boleros). At a time when jukeboxes were disappearing, the *rocolera* song had as great a following among urban popular sectors as it did among indigenous migrants, thus generating a new development cycle within popular music.

It is difficult to say whether JJ is, or will remain, an image that represents the spirit of national music. New popular vocalists from the middle classes shape the spaces and senses of music. National music is not what it used to be. Globalization alienates large audiences from vernacular music. Nevertheless, popular groups are oriented by rocolera music and *tecno-cumbia*.

To be sure, JJ is not absent from national imagery even today. Biographic chronicles are centered on his agitated love life, his taste for alcohol, his generosity that led to squandering of a fortune, and anecdotes from the artistic scenario. Dates are scarce in these accounts. Little is known, either, of the social and cultural atmospheres of the time and his prolonged visits abroad.

At least two statues, one in the western suburb of Guayaquil and another in Santo Domingo de los Colorados, perpetuate his memory. Nevertheless, more important than the monuments are the annual commemorations of the date of his death and radio programs that broadcast his music daily. Certainly, Julio Jaramillo will continue to nourish memories, nostalgia, and national pride. He was a vocalist who attained a presence on the international scene that few Ecuadorians have since reached.

The United Fruit
Company's Legacy in Ecuador

Steve Striffler

*After the collapse of cacao (chocolate bean) exports in the 1920s, Ecuador's political econ-
omy went into a decades-long crisis that ended with the emergence of banana production
throughout Ecuador's coast after the Second World War. By the 1950s, Ecuador was the
largest banana producer in the world, a process that transformed the entire country. In
this essay, the anthropologist Steve Striffler explores this process from the ground up by
tracing the history and inner workings of what was arguably Ecuador's most important
banana plantation: the United Fruit Company's Hacienda Tenguel.*

Hacienda Tenguel, located approximately 100 miles south of Guayaquil, in the
long strip of fertile coastal plain that runs along Ecuador's southern coast,
began producing bananas after global markets opened up at the end of World
War II. Confronted with growing problems in Central America and Colombia, United Fruit purchased Tenguel in 1934 and moved into Ecuador. In the
early 1950s, as demand for bananas exploded and Ecuador became the world's
major supplier, Hacienda Tenguel was the centerpiece of United Fruit's Ecuadorian operations, employing several thousand workers and producing more
than five percent of the country's total banana exports.

During its first years in Tenguel, United Fruit was unable to secure a stable,
disciplined, and trained labor force. The Ecuadorian state had barely established a physical presence in the region and could not be counted on to construct roads or systems of communication, much less deliver, discipline, and
control the movement of labor. Nevertheless, once United Fruit installed basic
infrastructure in the late 1940s, the area became an attractive source of employment. Inducements to stay in the zone ranged from high pay, excellent housing, and cheap food to company-sponsored sports teams and social clubs.

From the outset, United Fruit equated a stable labor force with a married
one. The company not only wanted to attract men, but young men, generally between 20 and 25, who would bring their families and reside in the zone

permanently. By the early 1950s, Hacienda Tenguel was well established and approximately two thousand married workers were living in company-owned housing. One former administrator explained the company's policy as follows:

> Married men were always preferred. Some men would come by themselves and be put in single quarters. But this was with the idea that their family would quickly follow and they would move into houses for families. [After the hacienda was established] the only single men we hired were sons of workers. It was felt that the community would be easier to manage if there were families instead of single men.

The plantation labor force was exclusively male; even company stores and food halls were run by male workers. Women, however, did not seem to regret the lack of employment opportunities. As one explains:

> There were no jobs for women. But we had plenty of money and a good home. There was no need for women to work. My husband was making more money than ever and the work was consistent. And we had children. I had to go to the company store and keep the house clean. And we [women] were involved with the schools, churches, and community.

For most, the middle-class ideal of a family model based on a male bread-winner and female housewife was unattainable prior to arriving in Tenguel. Regardless of their origin, migrant families were poor, and women were accustomed to working outside the home. Once in Tenguel, however, women no longer "needed" to work (in fact, could not work) and their economic dependence on men grew.

At the same time, women clearly benefited from the higher wages and benefits received by their male relatives. They ate better, lived in well-maintained houses, and paid less for basic goods. In addition, because the company saw the nuclear family as a key to its productive enterprise—as a way to secure *and* reproduce a permanent labor force—women's claims on their husband's wages, homes, and benefits were strengthened. The relatively high salaries obtained by male plantation workers were predicated on women's exclusion from the labor market and the assumption that men would maintain their families. It was a family wage in every sense of the term. Men could not obtain a house without a wife and family. Due to prevailing understandings of "women's work" and masculinity/femininity, men "needed" a wife to acquire food from the company store, care for children, and wash laundry. They also "needed" women to maintain the home at a level of cleanliness required by the company's almost fascist standards. Because women, as housewives and providers, were essential to the jobs, high wages, and benefits received by their husbands, and because the company actively supported the nuclear family, women could make serious demands on their partner's wages and benefits. If a male worker did not maintain his family, he faced the possibility of losing his job or home; if he abused his wife or children, he was visited by the company police, company priest, or administration.

Although some of the company's methods of control, such as the police force, limitations placed on the movement of single women, and the regulation of fiestas, were clearly repressive, most were of a more paternalistic nature and actively created the image of the company as a benevolent father. As part of the broader effort to create an enduring community, United Fruit supported a wide range of services and benefits, including schools, theaters, clubs, and sports teams. As one worker recalls:

> The company sponsored all the soccer teams. They provided us with uniforms, balls, and the necessary equipment. The company also financed the social clubs. The field bosses had their buildings and furnishings. But different groups of workers had social clubs as well. The clubs would help the community or schools. And of course they had fiestas.

With practices such as sports teams and social clubs, the company moved well beyond work and subsistence-related areas and into the more culturally delineated and community-forming occasions during which male workers, and to a lesser extent their families, exercised, drank, and socialized. Introduced in the early 1950s, the social clubs were an attempt to control the timing, scale, and nature of fiestas and other social occasions at a time when the community was rapidly expanding. By providing the material basis through which these customary occasions took place (the uniforms, fields, etc.), the company was sending a subtle, but nonetheless clear, message: We not only control your source of labor, your basic subsistence, but directly provide you with the means through which you are able to interact during special events such as fiestas and sporting events. We are the source of everything.

In what appears to have been a rather blatant attempt to keep its labor force politically divided, United Fruit created separate clubs for railworkers, administrators, field bosses, and different groups of field workers. Members of particular clubs not only worked, partied, and exercised together, but established long-lasting familial ties. Few workers failed to note the importance of the social clubs in everyday life. As one recalls:

> Everything was done through the clubs. Parties, elections of queens, events to help the community, even classes, were all done through the clubs. The clubs got money from the company. And people from the clubs generally played on the same soccer team. This is because we worked in the same

jobs. Carpenters had their own clubs. Administrators . . . It was like a small community. People from the same club married each other.

Such practices, sponsored as they were by United Fruit, seemed to have served two rather contradictory purposes. On the one hand, they allowed United Fruit to create and maintain a hierarchy. Even as they improved the workers' lives, the social clubs and other services sustained divisions, undermined more political forms of organization, stabilized the workforce, and enabled the company to extend its sphere of control into the daily life of the workers. They were creative forms of labor control in a situation where—in the absence of a sustained state presence—the company had to induce (not coerce) workers into remaining on the hacienda.

On the other hand, the social clubs also provided the setting through which recently arrived migrants were able to meet and develop bonds of friendship and dependence. As socio-cultural creations, the clubs, like the nuclear family, were *simultaneously* a source of company control and worker autonomy. The clubs, regardless of their form—as company creations, workers' organizations, or (later) state cooperatives—were simultaneously a source of worker resistance and the framework through which workers were incorporated and controlled by state and capital. That the organizations endured and proved effective both as sources of resistance and oppression is due in no small part to the fact that the social clubs were the sites where workers forged cultural, political, and economic ties in the realm of daily life.

The most insidious form of labor control, however, was the pro-management workers' union created by United Fruit during the mid-1940s. This practice, common to United Fruit's plantations in Central America, was a preemptive effort on the part of the company to weaken attempts by workers or outside groups to form independent, anti-management, labor unions. As company documents demonstrate, United Fruit administrators were concerned with the spread of communism, popular organizations, and the unpredictability of Ecuadorian governments during this period. Consequently, they not only organized a labor union at Tenguel during Velasco's second administration (1944–47), but created two factions of workers who competed for its control. As one ex-worker put it: "There were two groups of workers struggling for control of the union. They appeared antagonistic to each other, but *both* were really pro-company. The competition was a fiction. Both were run by the company. It was really Macini who was in control of the union. He led both groups."

Whether or not Juan Macini, the union leader, was in the company's pocket from the beginning, or was only later seduced, is somewhat immaterial. Macini himself, and the aura of confrontation he created, gave the union its credibility, but also made it impossible to create a more authentic workers' organization. According to one former worker,

> Macini would start ranting and raving against the company. Others would get up and join him, really agitating the workers. They would denounce abuses or make demands. Then a day or so later he would announce that the company had agreed to our demands. The company never agreed to all of them. This made it seem more genuine. It was only later that we began to realize that Macini was a traitor. Imagine, he was working for the company.

Once Macini's illicit relationship with United Fruit was exposed, it was only a matter of time before the workers realized that the union itself was a company-sponsored tool. This realization, and the subsequent transformation of the union into an authentic workers' organization, were intimately tied to the spread of the Panama Disease and the deterioration of the hacienda in late 1950s. The Panama Disease destroyed most of Hacienda Tenguel's banana trees by 1960, and conflicts with neighboring peasants made it impossible for United Fruit to expand production into new areas. Consequently, services were cut and regulations that had never been enforced were suddenly cause for dismissal. It was in this context of growing insecurity that the company-sponsored union began to look ridiculous. According to one worker, "hundreds were getting fired and the company was cutting back everything. Yet, Macini and the union would ask for a small wage increase or for better care of the soccer field. This was absurd. We were losing everything and he asked for small things."

The loss of jobs, reduction in wages, cuts in electricity, and disappearance of the company store were threats to a way of life that sustained work, family, and community, and in which both men and women had much at stake. This sense of loss quickly turned political. The set of shared experiences that surrounded plantation life had forged a certain solidarity among the workers. However, once the economic benefits and privileges that sustained not only those experiences, but the particularities of men's domination over women and notions of masculinity, were withdrawn, forms of solidarity, community, and even family took on a much more politicized form. One worker conveys this politicizing sense of loss and his own movement from the social clubs to the worker's union:

> I did not know what to do when I was fired. How was I going to feed my family? They closed the store, then the hospital, then the building where

our club met. They said we had to leave our houses. Where would we go? This is when I left the social club and began participating in the union. I had never been political. I didn't even know what communism or Cuba was! But when the company tried to force us from our homes! They were attacking my family. They would not let us use the land. How could we survive?

The withdrawal of services undermined the nuclear family supported by United Fruit, including both the male provider and the female housewife; in so doing, it united men and women, leading women to join the men in strikes and talk at rallies. As conditions worsened, women organized a support committee that eventually evolved into one of the first women's political organizations on the coast.

The basis for women's increased political activity and presence in the public sphere was rooted in, and legitimized by, their role as housewives—a social form whose particularities had been shaped by United Fruit and the hacienda's production regime. The type of family and community that had been supported by the company created a unity of interests among men and women that was based on a broadly similar sense of emotional and material loss and entitlement. As Hacienda Tenguel declined, the struggle for wages, food, health services, schools, and other benefits became, more than ever, a class struggle rooted in the family and plantation community. Once their stability was undermined, both the household and social clubs—forms of social organization directly supported by the company itself—became critical sources of labor militancy and union solidarity. Integral forms of labor control became crucial sources of resistance, and the company's paternalistic utopia collapsed.

According to Tenguelenos, two factors finally forced them to invade Hacienda Tenguel in March of 1962. First, they were literally starving and it became clear that the state was not going to intervene on its own. Recognizing that there was little hope for future employment, the workers disbanded the labor union and formed a cooperative, a productive form of organization designed to acquire land from the state. The formation of the cooperative, and the invasion itself, were attempts by the workers to demonstrate that agrarian reform was necessary and that they were worthy beneficiaries—to encourage the state to act on their behalf. Second, and of more immediate concern, local capitalists were not only trying to buy the hacienda, but had begun to train a private police squad on Tenguel's soccer field; they announced that the workers would be physically evicted on March 30, 1962. The workers invaded on March 27th, an event that pushed United Fruit out of the zone, forced the state to intervene, and initiated a long process of agrarian reform in both Tenguel and Ecuador as a whole.

The Banana Industry Today

In an effort to establish and maintain a reliable workforce, United Fruit spent years supporting a stable family and community. The irony, of course, was that although the family and community supported the company's capitalist enterprise, once that stability was undermined, both the nuclear family and the plantation community became important sources of labor militancy and resistance. In contrast, contemporary plantation owners work to create a labor force that is *temporary* and *unstable* in several senses. Most simply, plantation workers are not permanent; they receive no benefits, move from one hacienda to the next, and are not organized into unions. A large portion work full-time, but they rarely work on the same hacienda for over a year. Workers are also temporary in the sense that they have no future as workers. Several factors, including low pay, the intensity of the work, and management policies, cause workers to abandon plantation labor after no more than five years; few workers are over the age of thirty. Plantation labor, therefore, underwrites a way of life that cannot possibly reproduce itself over the lifetime of a single worker. Finally, the work is temporary in that it has been devalued by both workers and plantation management. It has little of the status once associated with plantation labor.

The tangible rewards of employment vary little from one plantation to the next. Low wages and no benefits are now the rule. Patricio, an agricultural laborer on the 100-hectare Hacienda Claudia María, earns about six dollars a day, has no security, and receives no formal benefits. Ironically, the lands that make up Hacienda Claudia María used to belong to those such as Patricio's father, Julio, a former United Fruit worker who participated in the invasion of Hacienda Tenguel and was subsequently incorporated into a state-controlled cooperative. After years of struggling with both debt and local landowners, Julio, along with most of the other cooperative members, sold his land to outsiders like Antonio Sánchez, the current owner of Hacienda Claudia María. Patricio, then, is working on the same land that his father once worked for United Fruit and later owned as a cooperative member. As Patricio astutely noted: "My father worked this land for a company called United Fruit. A foreign company. There was a union, they provided good houses, and the pay was excellent. Today, I work for an Ecuadorian who pays me shit. But he controls nothing. He contracts with Dole. It is also a foreign company."

Like hundreds of other domestic planters, Patricio's boss, Antonio Sánchez, has a contract to produce bananas for Dole Fruit. Hacienda Claudia María is the largest of Sánchez's three plantations and one of the most modern in the zone; every hectare is filled with banana trees, primary and secondary canals, an underground system of irrigation and drainage, as well as an overhead rail system that moves the bananas from tree to processing facility. Dole, the exporter, provided all of the initial financing, sends a technical expert several times a week, and continues to supply Sánchez with nearly everything, from protector bags and insecticides to the familiar cardboard boxes and little Dole stickers that are attached to every cluster of bananas. Dole even holds educational classes for administrators, agronomists, and workers. Dole does not, of course, do all of this for free. The costs of the protector bags, boxes, and advice are all deducted from production every time Hacienda Claudia María places a box of bananas on a Dole truck.

It should be noted that this system of contract farming does little to mask the unequal power relations that sustain the entire industry. As Patricio succinctly explained: "The workers produce the bananas. Antonio Sánchez does nothing. How could he? He is never here. Dole does not produce the bananas. How could they? The Dole technical expert comes twice a week for ten minutes to laugh with the administrator. We produce the bananas but Dole has control and Sánchez makes millions." Although it fools no one, the system of contracting nonetheless provides export companies like Dole, and domestic capitalists such as Antonio Sánchez, with a number of political advantages. Dole Fruit, whose signs and advertisements are found in some of the most remote corners of the southern coast, is extremely difficult to physically locate. The foreign company, a major player in the global banana industry, maintains a minimal presence in Machala, the banana capital of the world and a major city-port in Ecuador's southern coast. In rural zones such as Tenguel, the Dole agronomist who travels from hacienda to hacienda is Dole Fruit. Dole owns no land, directly employs few workers, and has almost no fixed capital in the zone. For his part, Antonio Sánchez, confident that his administrator, in conjunction with the Dole agronomist, will keep the profits flowing, spends little time on Hacienda Claudia María. To workers, he is known by his fancy truck. "To tell you the truth," one worker noted, "I don't think I have ever seen him; he is always in his big truck and the windows are darkened." Another worker explained the broader implications of such a system as follows:

> Who would we organize against? The owner never comes to the hacienda. The exporter is at the port, but controls everything. The exporter is not my employer. It is illegal to organize a big union and if you do you get fired. We make appeals to the state. But the state is controlled by the same people.

It is difficult to organize against a form of class power that is hard to confront or even locate. Exporters and landowners remain ephemeral figures that spend little time in zones where bananas are actually produced. At the same time, despite the elaborate system of contract farming, bananas must be produced in particular spaces. It is to this labor process, its implications for labor organizing, and the state's role in its reproduction, that we now turn. All banana plantations have two types of work days: normal days and days of *embarque*. On normal days, field workers are paid by task. A worker must complete a certain job, such as spraying chemicals over a particular area. On days of embarque, when the fruit is cut, cleaned, inspected, and boxed, field workers are paid by the number of boxes processed and earn slightly more than the six dollars they earn on normal days. Depending on the number of boxes needed by Dole, the field crew, numbering about forty, arrives at Hacienda Claudia Maria at 5:30 AM on days of embarque. They are immediately split into groups and sent to different sections of the plantation, where they begin removing the banana stems from the trees. The stem is quickly cut, attached to the rail system, and prepared for its trip to the processing facility by women members of the field crew. By the time the field crew has brought several groups of bananas to the processing facility, the *cuadrilla* has arrived. The cuadrilla, or processing crew, is typically comprised of between ten and fifteen men and women. They come to the hacienda only on days of embarque when the fruit is taken from the trees and boxed. They are responsible for cutting bunches of bananas from the stems, cleaning and inspecting them, and then packaging the fruit in Dole boxes.

Members of the cuadrilla are paid by the number of boxes processed. Unlike the field crew, however, they are not employees of the hacienda. The administrator of Hacienda Claudia María contracts with the head of the cuadrilla who is responsible for bringing *his* crew to the plantation on days of embarque. The head of the cuadrilla is told how many boxes of fruit Dole wants and is promised a certain amount of money per box. He then pays *his* workers. A typical Dole-contracted hacienda such as Claudia María will generally have two to three embarques every week all year round. However, Claudia María is not Antonio Sánchez's only plantation; the same processing crew is contracted for his other two haciendas. More importantly, although members of the processing crew work on one of his landholdings six days a week, they are not, according to Ecuadorian law, "employed" by Sánchez and therefore cannot organize as employees of one of his plantations.

But what of the field workers such as Patricio who account for about three quarters of the labor force on Sánchez's three plantations? Most workers on Claudia María have worked on the hacienda for more than three months and should be classified as permanent workers. Some, in fact, have worked on the plantation for years. A number of factors, however, make organizing difficult. In the absence of state enforcement, it is plantation owners and administrators who decide which workers are considered "permanent." In the past, administrators would simply fire and then rehire the same workers every three months. This formality is no longer necessary. As one plantation administrator frankly noted: "I have temporary workers who have worked on this plantation for thirty years. If they try to organize we kick them off." To make matters worse, an industry-wide labor union is simply illegal. Workers from Sánchez's plantations cannot form a union with similarly situated workers from plantations throughout Ecuador's coast. In fact, the law is even more restricting. Although Sánchez has three plantations within several kilometers of each other, each is technically owned by a different company. As a result, workers from Sánchez's legally distinct business enterprises cannot organize together. According to the law, it makes little difference that the three plantations have a single administrator, or that the workers are routinely moved from plantation to plantation. Workers from Haciendas Claudia María, Santa Clara, and Florentina, all plantations owned by Antonio Sánchez, may not form a collective labor organization. They work at "distinct" businesses.

The current system of contract farming and associated forms of state regulation not only make labor organizing difficult; they make it hard to identify as a worker in any subjective sense. In comparison to former workers of United Fruit, most of whom recount with pride the difficulty and intensity involved in their work, it is remarkable how little contemporary workers have invested in their labor. Most, such as Patricio, insist that they are not even workers.

> I am not an agricultural laborer. This is just temporary. I am saving money to start a business. Well, yes, I have been working here for almost a year. Before that I worked on another hacienda. We all have to do wage labor sometimes in order to survive. But I am not a wage laborer. It is not my life.

Workers invariably explain their presence on plantations as part of a momentary effort to earn cash. Full-time workers, even those that have been working on plantations for over five years, rarely identify themselves *as* workers. This is in part explained by (and helps explain) the lack of value that both men and women ascribe to their own labor. As an older male worker explains:

> The [labor] process is now different. Before things were simpler but more difficult. It required more strength. The work today is more delicate because the fruit is more delicate. There are jobs that women can do. Cleaning, inspecting the fruit, and putting the stickers [on the bunches] are all thing women can do. Many women can do it more quickly. Their hands are better for peeling the stickers.

A familiar story indeed.

Few male workers have such a detailed and historical explanation for women's presence on banana plantations. Most welcome women, noting that they work hard and are capable of doing virtually all of the work found on plantations. Many also point out that the constant banter between the sexes makes the day go by faster. Moreover, despite the presence of women, banana plantations remain a very masculine domain. Women make up less than twenty-five percent of the workforce and only one minor task is done exclusively by women. Men are found in every aspect of the production process while women are thoroughly excluded from a number of tasks. It should also be stressed that women's presence in agriculture came after plantation labor was economically devalued through the process of capitalist change outlined above. A temporary, non-unionized, and poorly paid labor force was created by decades of struggle and repression—at which point women were allowed access to plantation labor.

The Panama Hat Trail

Tom Miller

The Panama hat has been made in Ecuador for centuries, with its origins dating back to the sixteenth century, when the Incas began weaving the hats from the toquilla plant. The hat only became known as the "Panama" hat when workers on the Panama canal began to wear the hat for protection against the sun. The author Tom Miller recounts some of this intriguing history in his modern travel classic The Panama Hat Trail.

The hats to be made from Domingo's harvest, not yet even woven, had already been ordered by a company in the United States. Unknown to the *pajeros* in Febres Cordero, six months earlier, while the straw was in its final months of growth, a hat manufacturer in Texas had placed its annual purchase orders with several New York–based representatives of Cuenca exporters. The orders called for a variety of sizes and quality grades to meet the United States demand for dress, casual, and western hats made of straw. That year the Resistol Hat Company needed 60,000 straw-hat bodies. The company based its requisitions on projections in United States fashions, sales during recent years, availability from Ecuador, and its own capacity to prepare the hats for shipment to stores around the country.

Resistol started supplying haberdashers with hats in 1927, when it was known as Byer-Rolnick after its two founders: E. R. Byer, a Michigan jeweler who bankrolled Harry Rolnick, a hat maker. One of the company's brand names was Resistol. In the early 1960s Byer-Rolnick bought the Ecuadoran Panama Hat Company in New York, finishers of straw-hat bodies from Ecuador. With it came its supervisor, Irving Marin, the premier Panama hat craftsman in the United States. "He had such a keen eye for straw hats and how to treat them in the plant," a co-worker said of him. "We'd had seventy-two thousand straw-hat bodies in the warehouse for years. Everyone wanted to throw them out, but Irving turned them from junk into dollars. He could make chicken soup out of garbage."

Byer-Rolnick was eventually swallowed by Koret, a California clothing manufacturer, but retained its own identity and headquarters in Garland, a suburb of Dallas. In 1979 it assumed the name of its best-known brand, Resistol. Among the California forty-niners, the dreamers who first popularized Ecuadoran straw hats in the United States, was a young immigrant from Bavaria named Levi Strauss. In 1980, the San Francisco–based jeanswear company bearing his name took over Koracorp Industries, the new name for Resistol's owners. The straw that Domingo cut near Febres Cordero and shipped to Víctor González's warehouse in Guayaquil was now entering the pipeline to be handled by the largest apparel manufacturing firm in the world.

No one knows who first developed the idea of processing shoots from the toquilla plant to weave into natural fiber hats, or in which century this triumphant marriage of form and function took place. A primitive but inexorable process simply occurred, much as in evolution: There was a need for lightweight protection from the sun, and toquilla was a handy plant to use. Where did they learn to open up the toquilla shoot, to boil it, to strip it into thin strands, and to style the weave so that the hat would fit the head? Trial and error. Natural selection. Other plants, no doubt, were used and rejected until the right fiber and the right process went hand in hand.

From *Straw Hats—Their History and Manufacture*, by Harry Inwards, London, 1922: "Claims are made that in the Province of Manabi, a native named Francisco Delgado first made a Panama hat about 300 years ago. The very Spanish name for a native evokes a suspicion that the date given was the first Spanish record . . . for it is most probably that the making of grass fibre hats in the Western Hemisphere was . . . of the most remote antiquity."

Inwards was probably right. When the conquistadors first wandered through Manabí, they saw people wearing a strange headdress shaped like vampire wings. Perhaps to test the Spaniard's gullibility, the natives said that the hats were woven from actual vampire skin. With these hats the Spaniards protected themselves from the sun, and because the hats were woven so tightly, they would carry water in them as well. Later the Spanish learned they had been fooled. The headdress was made from a locally grown light fiber.

The most delicate of the woven headdresses were worn by women like a linen handkerchief on their heads or around their necks. Men wore them with feathers sticking out or with bands around them. They were called toquillas, from the Spanish *toca*, or headdress. In the seventeenth and eighteenth centuries the hats made in Manabí gained wider distribution. Craftsmen were sent south from Manabí to Guayaquil and Peru to teach hat making. The hats and toquilla straw were sold as far inland as Cuenca. A small number were shipped to the United States, where, according to one account, "it was believed that they were fruit from the paja toquilla tree, and that these hats hung from its branches. One had only to pick them when they had turned white in color, a sign that they were ripe."

In 1834 rival officers vied for power within the new republic. One faction, attempting to control Manabí, ordered that all the Panama hats in the towns of Montecristi and Jipijapa be collected to raise money. The hats were hidden from the plunderers and smuggled out to Peru and Colombia. Montecristi, Manabí's main straw-weaving town, shipped its hats through Guayaquil, 120 miles south, and Manta, 12 miles north. In 1849, at the height of the California gold rush, Ecuador exported more than 220,000 straw hats.

Manta today is a lively port town busy with sailors and fishermen. Extensive beaches, an archaeological museum, and boating attract visitors. Playing on the beach one day were new recruits from California for the Summer Institute of Linguistics, the missionaries known in the United States as the Wycliffe Translators. The young group was staying at a nearby retreat. They acted like they had just gotten off the boat. "We're the ones who translate the Bible into native tongues," one said. "A couple of our people got killed in, where was it, Peru? Colombia? Anyway, we figured we'd fatten up and get a good tan before we got it too." "Yeah," his sidekick added, "so the pictures of our corpses will look good."

At Manta's museum schoolchildren marveled at a display illuminating life in the Valdivian period, more than 1500 years BC. At the yacht club, a bedraggled boat captain walked up to the table where I drank Pilsener with a few members. The captain, from Los Angeles, said he was on his way down the Pacific Coast to the southern tip of South America. "Mind if I dock at your club for a couple of days?" The yachtsmen looked at him, then at his schooner, then at each other. "Sure," they replied. "Everyone else does."

Everybody in town advised me to visit Fernando Zevallos Marzumillaga. He knows more about the history of Manabí than anyone. Just walk up to his door.

Don Fernando received me cordially. In his eighties, he was frail of body but keen of mind. Unfortunately, I couldn't understand his Spanish. Like many *costeños*, he eliminated most *s*'s and swallowed the last syllable of most words. I prayed for s-less endings and three-syllable words, and yearned for the clear Castilian of the sierra. Don Fernando's son Alejandro, fifty years old, repeated his father's words in more accessible Spanish. "I have some things you might like to see," Don Fernando said. "First, so you will know who I am, this is my card."

FERNANDO ZEVALLOS MARZUMILLAGA

Titulado y Condecorado Benemérito de Montecristi, Miembro de la Casa de la Cultura del Ecuador, de Unión Nacional de Periodistas del Ecuador, del Centro Cultural "Manta", del Patronato Histórico "Guayaquil", Asesor Histórico del Concejo de Manta, Emérito del Instituto Ecuatoriano del Seguro Social, Miembro de Honor de la Sociedad Jurídico-Literaria de Manabí y Miembro Asesor de la Comisión de Límites del Consejo Provincial de Manabí, Colaborador del Mercurio de Manta, La Provincia y Diario Ecuador de Portoviejo.

Titled and Decorated Meritorious Benefactor of Montecristi, Member of the Ecuadoran House of Culture, of the Ecuadoran National Union of Journalists, of the Manta Cultural Center, of the Guayaquil Historical Foundation, Historical Adviser to the Manta Council, Emeritus Member of the Ecuadoran Social Security Institute, Honorary Member of the Legal-Literary Society of Manabí and Advisory Member of the Boundary Commission of the Provincial Council of Manabí, Contributor to the Manta Mercurio, La Provincia, and the Diario Ecuador of Portoviejo.

"I have here some old clippings. Take a look." From his files he had retrieved fifty-year-old brochures about Montecristi, articles about the heyday of Panama hats, and mementos of General Eloy Alfaro, Manabí's favorite son. Alfaro, born in Montecristi in 1842, led the Liberal Revolution, which brought a measure of enlightenment to the country when he became its ruler in 1895. Costeños have traditionally had more progressive ideas than people from the interior, since ships docking in port towns unload news and ideas as well as goods from the outside world. Prior to Alfaro's regimes—he held office twice—a Roman Catholic theocracy ruled. Only Roman Catholics could vote, hold office, or teach. The Liberal Revolution restricted the influence of the Church, brought about separation of Church and State, instituted secular public education, and allowed for civil marriage and divorce. Church land became state land. For this Alfaro is a national hero, revered in the tradition of Washington and Lincoln.

Alfaro's father, Manuel, and later Eloy himself, made a good living exporting Ecuadoran products to Panama, especially toquilla straw hats. Manuel, in fact, is often heralded as the first of the major hat exporters. In the Zevallos house hangs a color drawing of Eloy Alfaro, with mountains in the background. Don Fernando showed me a postcard of Alfaro brandishing his sword aboard a steamer at the 1884 battle of Jaramijó, near Manta. Sixty-year-old sheet music sang the praises of the Liberal Party, whose beginnings the Alfaro family helped finance. A bust of John F. Kennedy sat next to the lamp. A 1909 German typewriter rested on a table. Its keys were to the left and right side of the carriage rather than in front of it. It had no keys for punctuation. Don Fernando had used it until recently.

He recited local history with the passion of a historian credentialed by devotion to his subject and love of its people. "Toquilla straw hats have covered the heads of Napoleon of France, Edward VII and George V of England, and Hoover and Roosevelt of the United States." I told him that every United States president since Grover Cleveland has been given a Panama by the government of Ecuador. He arched his eyebrows, inserting that fact into his history of the region.

Reading up on the country's history, I had developed a theory I wanted to try out. "Oiga, Don Fernando," listen. "If the Alfaro family supported Eloy's political activities"—Zevallos nodded slowly—"and its money was made, in part, from exporting toquilla straw hats"—he nodded again—"then Panama hats are at least partially responsible for Ecuador's great Liberal Revolution. Isn't that so?" Zevallos smiled benignly.

His son was anxious to continue the discussion. He delighted in speaking with a foreigner in his house, teaching about his homeland and talking about travel. He poured me some weak instant coffee. I asked if he knew of the missionary retreat I'd been told about earlier. "Well, I've heard of it," he replied. "But tell me—why do they come?" He ticked them off on his fingers. "There are Mormons, Seventh Day Adventists, Jehovah's Witnesses—and Catholics! This country is ninety-eight percent Catholic and still they send missionaries." His face took on an air of incredulity. "Are they trying to capture the other two percent? And these hippies we see, why do they come? Why do they act the way they do?" Perplexity now colored his face. "Their dirty long hair! Is it really true they're from the families of the rich?"

Alejandro pulled out a picture album from a 1973 visit to the United States. "I had a wonderful time in your country. I went to the Macy's Thanksgiving Day parade. Here I am with the other members of the Dinosaur Club—that's an international group I belong to. I was their guest. Here I am with Snoopy." He showed off photographs of parade floats, marchers, and of himself with smiling New York City policemen. Picture postcards of Chinatown, the Rockefeller Center skating rink, and the San Francisco Bay bridge filled the next few pages. "I've never been to San Francisco," he admitted. "I just like the picture. I sent a Montecristi fino to the head of the Dinosaur Club in New York when I got home."

Together we walked downhill to the center of town. I had expressed some interest in going to Jaramijó, the town where the legendary Alfaro had fought. "It's a primitive fishing village, but you'll like it. Over there." He pointed to a main street. "That's where you catch the bus. It goes by the park with a statue of John F. Kennedy."

A half-hour later I was ordering lunch at the Bar Picantería Embajador in Jaramijó, an open-air restaurant on the beach looking out at the Pacific Ocean.

The Embajador was covered with a tin roof from which hung a bare light bulb. To reach the bathroom I passed through the town's schoolroom, which was behind the kitchen. Fishermen who were coming in from the Pacific with the morning's catch, rolled their old wooden boats up the beach at low tide over short bamboo logs. Children scrambled around each boat helping unload the fish into rubber buckets and plastic bags. Some carried fish away in their hands. A World Cup soccer match between Germany and France blared out over the radio. Among the boats on the beach a scrawny woman sat cross-legged, waving her arms wildly at the incoming fleet as if conducting a symphony at the finale of the last movement. "She's crazy," a teenager said, "but we're used to her. She's here every day."

Naval officers from Manta dined a few tables away with their girlfriends. An elderly lady walked up offering seashells for twenty sucres each, about thirty cents. Barefoot, she stood a few inches shy of five feet tall. "Twenty sucres? Why, I could walk out there and find some for free," I countered. "Yes, but not like these." Her shells possessed no special qualities, but her face wore a mask of urgent desperation. "OK," I said. "Ten apiece. I'll buy a couple." She beamed. Pelicans, dogs, and seagulls came by in groups of two. The seashell lady hovered around my table throughout lunch. Steamed fresh lobster cost three dollars.

Three buses leave Manta for Montecristi every hour, passing coffee-processing factories and dry scrub brush along the way. In Montecristi I hoped to find some weavers who saw that their precious heritage was bought for a few sucres and sold for lots of dollars; that they were at the poor end of an increasingly profitable chain in which each person made more and more money off their original labor. I couldn't explain the *Wealth of Nations* to them, or theories of productivity and profit, but I longed to see awareness beyond a shoulder shrug. Don Fernando nodded when I mentioned this to him earlier at his home in Manta. "I've got just the thing for you." He rummaged through his files and came up with a 1974 booklet promoting Montecristi. He turned to a page with a poem whose author is identified as Lupi.

EL SOMBRERO DE MONTECRISTI

A wondrous fiber, known
To the world under an assumed name;
Artful propaganda
Of poorly paid, silent labor.
The peacocking of pampered people;
A well-spring, fertile and enduring,
Of misfortune to the poor
And extravagance of the wealthy.

A fine warp, a painstaking marvel
That transforms the straw
Into exquisite high fashion.
The holocaust of a people who naïvely
Sponsor a pitiful way of life,
Bound into sheaves of trampled misery.

Note

Excerpt is from Tom Miller, *The Panama Hat Trail* (Washington, D.C.: National Geographic Society, 1986), chap. 7. The mayor and metropolitan council of Quito officially proclaimed Miller an Illustrious Guest of the city on 30 May 2008.

Deforestation in Ecuador

Diane C. Bates

Ecuador is known throughout the world for its natural beauty. The Galápagos Islands, the Andean mountains, and the Amazon Basin are widely recognized as ecological marvels worthy of protection. As the sociologist Diane C. Bates argues, the loss of forest within Ecuador is a serious problem, but not isolated to the Amazon. In fact, the most fragile forests are in the Andes and coastal region, places where higher population densities destroy forests at an even greater rate.

Responding to dramatic images of the Brazilian Amazon afire in the mid-1980s, worldwide concern over the fate of the tropical rainforests emerged as a global problem, emblematic of the unsustainable environmental course of this "Spaceship Earth." As Ecuador is one of the nine nations that include part of the Amazonian Basin, its forests also came under international scrutiny. Since this time, a plethora of national and international nongovernmental organizations, as well as governmental bodies, have become engaged in the study, protection, and restoration of Ecuador's Amazonian forests. Tourists come from all over the world to experience these forests before they disappear. Many internationals do not realize—although it is not news to Ecuadorians—that there are three major forested regions in Ecuador, and all of them have declined in size in the past fifty years. The first and perhaps most threatened of these regions is the Pacific coast, which contains significant mangrove forests as well as tropical rainforests. The second region includes the alpine forests of the temperate zones in the Andes, which originally contained substantial hardwood and coniferous forests but now also contains expansive tracts of eucalyptus. The third region is the Oriente, the eastern third of Ecuador that drains into the Amazon Basin. Identified as a biodiversity "hotspot," the Ecuadorian Amazon contains the largest forests in Ecuador.

While this essay will address deforestation in the Oriente in the most depth, the Amazonian forest is not the most threatened forest in Ecuador. Large tracts of rainforest remain in the Oriente, while the Andean and Pacific forests have been removed, converted, and replaced at much higher rates. Like the endangered Atlantic rainforest of Brazil, the Andean and Pacific forests have experienced a gradual and nearly complete removal of old-growth trees and other vegetation from all but the most inaccessible remnants, leaving these forests fragmented and with a reduced capacity to support the native fauna (especially large animals). Their very fragmented and endangered nature means that they receive little attention from international scientists, environmentalists, or ecotourists.

Andean indigenous people began converting forests in the mountains and intermontane valleys long before Europeans arrived in the Americas. Most Andean cultures were agricultural and exploited the microclimates of the mountains to produce temperate and tropical crops. With the arrival of Europeans in the sixteenth century, much of the rich valley land was taken for hacienda production. Indigenous people moved their agricultural activities onto steeper slopes, removing forest to plant their fields. Because of population growth and further concentration of valley land among Europeans (and later, wealthy Ecuadorians), small agricultural plots crept farther and farther up mountain slopes. The removal of alpine forests led to erosion and landslides, so in the 1960s the Ecuadorian government began reforestation programs. These reforestation programs favored fast-growing trees, notably the exotic Australian eucalyptus. As a consequence, today alpine forests may include eucalyptus groves.

[margin handwritten note: not surprised, population has a lot to do with it]

Today, the expansion of small farms up the mountains continues to endanger alpine forests, but deforestation is linked to urban, not agricultural, expansion. Due to the stagnation of the rural economy since the 1960s, more and more rural Ecuadorians have relocated to urban centers in the Andes, such as Quito, Cuenca, and Ambato. Poorer migrants inflate peripheral rings of spontaneous (largely squatter) settlements. However, because of the geographic location of Andean cities in valleys, this expansion often leads poor settlers to establish homes on the mountainsides. While not as dramatic an environmental problem in Ecuador as in Colombia and Venezuela, the removal of native (and sometimes exotic) vegetation on the slopes that surround cities has contributed to greater problems with landslides. In addition, the growth of middle-class and upper-middle-class suburbs, such as Cumbayá, near Quito, also contribute to the deforestation problem due to their more land-extensive design, but to date (at least) this is a much less important contributor to temperate forest loss in Ecuador.

Unlike the Andes forests, most of the Pacific forests were intact at the time of European contact. This was true for both the rainforests and the mangrove forests that lined much of the coast. Due to insects, heat, and transportation problems, the sparse indigenous people who lived in the Pacific region did not practice permanent, intensive agriculture. However, as Europeans developed commercial tropical plantations in the region, the forests rapidly disappeared. Ecuador remains a major banana producer, but most of the initial deforestation in the Pacific lowland plain was caused by the expansion of cacao production. Cacao, from which chocolate is derived, was an extremely valuable crop in the nineteenth century. Grown on plantations owned by wealthy Ecuadorians and foreigners, the high world price for the "golden seed" provided an incentive to convert large tracts of rainforest to cacao fields. With port facilities in Guayaquil and Esmeraldas and the opening of the Panama Canal in 1903, cacao was Ecuador's main export crop and, thus, source of wealth. High prices eventually gave way to overproduction, which, coupled with declining productivity, caused the price of cacao to bottom out and plantations to go bankrupt. Rising international demand for bananas, however, left little chance that abandoned cacao plantations would return to forest. Instead, the growth of banana plantations increased deforestation in the coastal plain. As Ecuador continues to depend heavily on banana exports, it is unlikely that any of this land will revert to forest in the foreseeable future.

Small-scale agriculture has had less impact on forests in the coastal plain, but does contribute to deforestation in the Pacific highlands rainforest. Workers on the plantations often live and have subsistence plots in nearby hillsides. During the 1950s and 1960s, the Ecuadorian government (with international funding) also promoted the colonization of the Pacific tropical rainforest, particularly in the region west of Santiago de los Colorados and east of Esmeraldas. In these programs, poor Andeans relocated to the rainforest and were given financial assistance and incentives to produce food and cattle. By the end of the 1960s, most of the available land in the Pacific had been claimed, either by colonists, small farms, or commercial plantations. Today, smallholders in the Pacific region continue to convert remaining forested land to agricultural uses and engage in some small-scale forestry, but neither of these activities compares to the massive deforestation associated with export agriculture along the coastal plains.

Perhaps the most threatened forests in the Pacific region are the coastal mangroves. There are two principal threats to these forests: urban expansion and shrimp aquaculture. Mangrove forests are part of the coastal wetland system, surviving in both brackish and salt water. Mangrove forests in Ecuador are major contributors to the biotic health of the coastal waters, as many fish and shellfish depend on mangrove swamps for their early development. Urban expansion has had the greatest impact in Guayas Province, where poor migrants to Guayaquil have removed natural vegetation, including mangroves, to develop squatter communities. Unfortunately, Guayaquil is surrounded by coastal wetlands rather than terra firma, so poor migrants must build their homes literally over the swamps. Many of Guayaquil's poor live in houses set upon platforms over wetlands where mangroves once grew. These homes are extremely vulnerable to flooding and other natural hazards, but there is nowhere else for these people to live. Thus, poverty and housing shortages in Guayaquil and similar coastal cities contribute to deforestation in much the same way as described in the Andes above.

Mangroves face another major threat, from the development of commercial shrimp ponds. As Ecuador seeks to diversify its exports in order to reduce its dependence on oil and bananas for foreign exchange, the government and international actors have encouraged the development of nontraditional exports, such as shrimp. In the past fifteen years, Ecuador has become a major exporter of shrimp; most of the shrimp is produced in small ponds carved out of the mangrove forests along Ecuador's coast. While shrimp are naturally found among Ecuador's mangroves, commercial production involves providing food from outside sources to shrimp in these ponds. Since shrimp production is no longer tied to the availability of food in the mangrove ecosystem, there is no natural limit to the number of ponds that can exist within these forests, and no need to protect the forest itself in order to continue producing shrimp.

In sum, the Pacific and Andean forests in Ecuador are currently smaller and arguably more endangered than the Amazonian forests. Historic economic activities, housing shortages in expanding cities, and the development of new economic activities have all contributed to deforestation. Most remaining forests can be categorized as remnants; there are few large blocks of forest in either the Andes or the Pacific. Reforestation efforts in these regions are mainly designed to prevent erosion and provide flood control, rather than replace the forest itself. Some sustainable forestry projects have been developed along the coast, especially in the north, and a few ecotourism destinations exist in the coastal rainforest in Esmeraldas. Private reserves and national parks exist throughout the Pacific and Andean regions, but these are essentially biological islands, surrounded by converted land. The future for unprotected forests in these regions remains grim, due to mounting housing pressure in cities and the economic reliance on commercial agriculture and aquaculture.

The situation is somewhat different in Ecuador's Oriente. The Amazon is the largest watershed in South America; the basin is roughly the size of the continental United States. The lion's share of the Amazon Basin is in Brazil, where rapid deforestation in the 1980s stimulated international concern about the fate of the world's largest contiguous rainforest. Satellite images that displayed thousands of fires burning in the Brazilian Amazon, photographs of eroded soils creating "deserts" in the heart of the rainforest, and celebrity attention turned the world's interest to this part of the world in a manner that is often discussed as the "internationalization of the Amazon." International environmental groups, financial and development institutions, and foreign governments began to make demands on Amazonian countries to stop deforestation. These demands centered around three interrelated concerns: biodiversity loss, the threat of global warming, and the protection of indigenous cultures. The widespread appeal of these three concerns has increased the visibility of the Amazon worldwide and spurred notable increases in rainforest-centered tourism.

Because of the Galápagos Islands, Ecuador offered a destination for nature tourists and hobby naturalists long before widespread concern developed about the Amazonian rainforest. As interest in Amazonian tourism increased, companies in Ecuador could offer tours featuring an Amazonian experience coupled with a trip to the Galápagos. Ecuador's Amazonian region, known as the Oriente, has now become a tourist destination in itself for several reasons. The Amazon is easily accessible from the international gateway at Quito: by bus or jeep, tourists can cross into the watershed in less than three hours; and by flight, they can be deep into the Amazon in an hour. Another appeal is that the Ecuadorian Amazon is visually dynamic: unlike the monotonous plains deeper in the basin, the Oriente contains both the eastern front of the Andes themselves and ranges of foothills. This topography is beautiful and exotic, full of cascading waterfalls, fast-flowing rivers, and deep valleys. In parts of the Oriente, one can look up from a lush tropical rainforest to see active, snow-capped volcanoes. In part due to this topography, Ecuador boasts an extremely high level of biodiversity—tourist literature boasts that there are more bird species in Ecuador than in all of North America. Ecuador's Amazonian indigenous people have been strategic and open to receiving tourists: indigenous people often act as naturalist guides; others offer instruction in shamanism; some indigenous groups even offer home stays in traditional villages. Perhaps most important, Ecuador offers a rainforest experience that is relatively free of violence, guerrillas, kidnappers, and drug lords—a stark contrast to the Amazonian regions in Colombia, Peru, Bolivia, and Brazil. While human dangers in the Oriente have increased in recent years (especially near the Colombian border), international tourists generally feel and are quite safe. As internationals developed more sustained interest in the Amazonian rainforest and the Ecuadorian Oriente in particular, deforestation in this region has piqued worldwide concern.

Before addressing the real causes of deforestation in the Oriente, it is important to dispel three common myths about this topic. First, there is no "hamburger connection" in Ecuador's Amazon. North American fast-food chains in the 1980s and 1990s purchased beef from Central America to lower the cost of their hamburger meat, and in so doing, encouraged the expansion of ranching into the Central American rainforests. However, hoof-and-mouth disease (also known as foot-and-mouth disease) and bovine rabies are endemic to Amazonian South America; as a consequence, beef and cattle from this region are banned in North America. Many residents of Ecuador's Amazon do raise cattle herds, but they raise them to meet demands in the national market. As in the rest of Latin America, domestic consumption of beef has increased substantially in the past few decades. Moreover, the production of beef cattle in Ecuador's Amazon usually takes place on family farms, not large commercial ranches. Cattle ranching is less a capitalist enterprise than a means through which families can store wealth. Given Ecuador's wobbly economic history (particularly before dollarization), farmers were reluctant to put savings in the bank, where the value of their accounts declined with inflation. Instead, they invest savings in cattle, whose value changes with inflation and which can be "cashed in" whenever the farmer has a need for money. They do not sell to multinational fast-food chains, but to local cattle merchants who supply urban Ecuadorian butchers, tanneries, and food manufacturers.

Contrary to the second widespread myth, there is very little large-scale commercial forestry in the Oriente. In fact, the biodiversity in the Amazon Basin overall has hampered the ability of large-scale timber firms to cost-effectively exploit wood resources. Unlike the teak forests of Southeast Asia or the coniferous forests of the Pacific Northwest, Amazonian forests do not contain many stands of single-species trees, much less high-value single-species trees. The Ecuadorian Amazon does naturally contain mahogany, cedar, laurel, and other commercially valuable trees, but these grow as single trees often at large distances from one another. An acre of Amazonian forest can be incredibly diverse in terms of tree species—in the case of many species, individual specimens grow acres apart. This is possible because many Amazonian tree species reproduce with the help of insects, bats, birds, and animals instead of the wind. Such distances reduce the likelihood of transmitting species-specific diseases or other pestilence. As a consequence of the tree diversity, the extraction of high-value woods cannot be done through heavily mechanized, cost-effective clear-cutting methods. Of course, this does not mean that valuable trees are not removed from Ecuador's forests—outside of protected areas, most accessible forests in the Oriente have already been selectively harvested for valuable hardwoods. Local landowners, using chainsaws and horses, harvest much of this wood, again mainly for local markets. Poaching of valuable trees in Ecuador's national parks also occurs—due in part to the inability of the resource-strapped park service to effectively patrol extensive and inaccessible park boundaries. For example, the Sangay National Park contains vast amounts of Amazonian rainforest, but is managed from its more accessible Andean side. Not surprisingly, poachers remove valuable wood resources from access points in the Oriente.

Contrary to a third commonly held myth, the farmers in Ecuador's Amazonian region know what they are doing. However, they see their activities quite differently and have different concerns than people who live outside the region. While it is true that many farmers in the Oriente do not have formal training in ecological sciences, they are acutely aware of the environmental degradation caused by deforestation because it directly affects their lives. Farmers know that intensive agriculture depletes the soil; they know that deforestation reduces animal populations; they know that deforestation has created local water shortages. They know this because they depend directly on the environment to provide for their families, improve their standards of living, and prepare a nest egg for their old age. Amazonian residents generally belong to what are known as "resource-dependent communities"—communities where livelihoods depend on agriculture, ranching, or the extraction of raw materials from the environment. If they were unable to do these things, they would have no work. It is thus unreasonable—and from their perspective, irrational—to stop doing what they are doing. Unless viable economic alternatives exist for farmers, ranchers, and tree harvesters, they will continue to farm, ranch, and extract trees. Regretfully, few such alternatives currently exist.

If not hamburgers, timber companies, and ignorance, what are the causes of deforestation in the Ecuadorian Amazon? There are four interrelated processes that are key to understanding the loss of forests in the Oriente: oil development, road construction, colonization, and urban expansion. Oil was discovered near the Colombian border in 1967, after many years of exploration (the community of Shell, just outside of Puyo, still bears the name of one oil company engaged in exploration). In partnership with state-owned Petroecuador, oil development intensified in the provinces of Sucumbios and Napo (including what is now the province of Amazonas). Although oil extraction in itself does not require widespread deforestation, the economic activity generated around meeting the needs of the oil workers does lead to forest conversion, particularly for their food and housing needs.

To facilitate the extraction of oil, Texaco completed the first major road to the oil fields in 1971. The Ecuadorian state continued to build roads that led into the oil fields, as well as develop a more comprehensive transportation network in the Oriente. When the Macas-Puyo Road was completed in 1987, all of the capitals of the Amazonian provinces were linked to one another, and had multiple road connections up into the Andes. All of the early roads in the Oriente could be classified as "penetration roads," because they generally cut through rainforest. These road corridors were widened initially by the wood needs of the road builders (such as for cooking fuel and construction), and later by people who moved onto this land to plant crops or use it as pasture—often for sale to the newly accessible urban centers. Attracted by the success of these farms, later arrivals established farms behind the road-side ones, and later behind those, creating an expanding corridor of deforestation along these roads.

Although road building in the Northern Oriente is closely associated with this type of "spontaneous colonization," Ecuador also had programs of planned colonization in the Amazon, as it had earlier in the Pacific coastal forests. Most state-supported colonization programs targeted the Southern Oriente, particularly the provinces of Pastaza, Morona Santiago, and Zamorra Chinchipe, where the absence of large economic activities (such as oil extraction) had failed to compel spontaneous migration. Designed to alleviate land scarcity in the Southern Sierra (especially the provinces of Azuay and Cañar), these programs received financial and technical assistance from the Inter-American Development Bank and the U.S. Peace Corps. Colonization schemes emphasized the development of small cattle herds and cash-crop production, while allowing colonists to secure title to their lands. Colonists generally were promised title to between thirty and fifty hectares (74 to 124 acres) of land, assuming that they occupied that land and demonstrated that they used it productively. As an indication of this use (as well as to secure their land from completing claims), colonists rapidly deforested their land upon arrival in the Oriente. In fact, to secure title, colonists were *required* to clear at least 50 percent of their land. Ironically, few colonists actually needed to clear this much land for their productive purposes: few had enough labor available to tend fifteen to twenty-five acres of any commercial crop or owned enough cattle to stock pastures at one head per hectare (or per 2.5 acres), locally considered as a sustainable stocking rate. To protect their own claims, nearby indigenous groups (most notably the Shuar) also began to convert their land to pasture. As road connections improved in the Oriente throughout the 1970s and 1980s, access to distant markets improved, and colonists (and to a lesser extent, indigenous people) expanded production of food crops and cattle. By the late 1980s, colonization zones in the Southern Oriente had been largely deforested except in remote or inaccessible regions, and even these forests had been selectively harvested of valuable trees.

The expansion of colonist agriculture reflects the growth in urban areas, both physically and in terms of consumption, that have reinforced deforestation in the Oriente. The discovery of oil, the development of road networks, and the increase in agricultural production all facilitated the growth of Amazonian cities by providing work, food, and trade opportunities. Lago Agrio and Coca, both in the Northern Oriente, are comparable in size to many long-settled Andean and coastal cities, and many smaller cities have emerged from former outposts along the base of the Andes. As in other regions of Ecuador, the expansion of these cities has resulted directly in deforestation, as people look for new places to live. More fundamentally, the growth of these cities (as well as Andean cities now linked by roads) increased the demand for products produced in the Oriente.

Given these four interconnected causes of deforestation—oil, roads, agriculture, and cities—in the Ecuadorian Amazon, will these trends continue indefinitely? The good news is that rates of deforestation have slowed in the Oriente, especially since the 1980s. This has resulted partly from the "closing" of the colonization frontier, when lowland indigenous groups were granted rights to most of the unclaimed land in Amazonia. Another contributing pattern involves the economic downturn known in Ecuador simply as "The Crisis," which has reduced all types of urban consumption and thus eased demand for Amazonian products. An additional change involves the reduced productivity in both cattle ranching and agriculture, caused largely by declining environmental conditions, an impulse for out-migration from this region. As colonists leave the area in search of opportunities in Ecuador's cities or in international destinations (mainly the United States, Italy, and Spain), land is allowed to reforest. Colonists who have remained now often engage in reforestation, both for economic and environmental reasons. In addition, mobilization—indigenous, national, and international—has protected some large blocks of forest in parks and reserves, such as Cuyabeno National Park and the privately held Jatun Sacha reserve near Misahuallí. Even oil companies have changed strategies in terms of opening new wells—in 1998, a French company used helicopters to develop an oil field east of Puyo instead of building a permanent penetration road. Finally, the growth of ecotourism, especially in the species-rich Northern Oriente, has provided an alternative form of economic opportunity for locals—one that requires the deliberate protection of forest resources.

Ecuador's Amazonian rainforests remain threatened, but they are less threatened than they were twenty years ago. In contrast, the forests of the Andes and coastal region of Ecuador may reach depletion within a foreseeable future. Forests do not cut themselves down. The underlying threats to all forests in the country are rooted in Ecuador's troubled economic situation, and will thus not be solved by simply promoting environmental education or creating new parks. So what can be done? Solving Ecuador's economic crisis is certainly beyond the capacity of any individual, but there are things that individuals inside and outside of the country can do to help slow deforestation. For a start, all interested parties should learn more about the complex processes that drive deforestation so that we do not rely on myths. We can also contribute time or money to local and international organizations that promote economic alternatives to intensive agriculture, ranching, and wood extraction. We should support policies, both international and domestic, that are sensitive to the social causes of deforestation and promote social development instead of narrowly focusing on increasing exports. This will involve some level of debt forgiveness or at least renegotiation, as Ecuador is currently compelled to export shrimp, bananas, and oil to meet its debt obligations. People lucky enough to visit Ecuador should make use of ecotourism facilities owned by Ecuadorians and linked directly to the local economy. While international tours may be easier to book from "home" and chain restaurants and hotels seem more familiar, locally owned businesses are more likely to create sustainable economic alternatives to forest destruction. Finally, internationals have to face up to their own contributions to deforestation through our participation in global commodity chains—not to spread guilt around the globe, but to promote a sense of common responsibility for the stewardship of these natural treasures.

Civilization and Barbarism

Carlos de la Torre

Ecuador's return to civilian rule and representative government in 1979 signified a real turn toward democracy. Political parties flourished, popular movements were reinvigorated, and the military has not taken formal, sustained control of the government since the 1970s. Yet, as the sociologist Carlos de la Torre shows, it is a fragile, incomplete, and contradictory form of democracy that remains clientelistic, prone to populist impulses, highly unstable, and ultimately corrupt.

Ecuador's "transition to democracy" (1976–79) was envisioned not simply as a return to elected civilian governments, but rather as the political complement of the economic and social modernization achieved by Ecuador during the military regimes of the 1970s. Ecuador was transformed from a banana- and cacao-exporting country into an oil-producing nation. This predominantly rural society, where hacendados controlled rural cultivators, saw the weakening of the hacienda system, high levels of urbanization, the growth of the state, and the expansion of the urban informal sector as well as the working-class and middle-class sectors. Until approximately the 1960s, traditional haciendas were the dominant institutions structuring life for Ecuadorians. The first agrarian census showed that in the 1950s, when most of the highland population (73.8 percent) was rural, large haciendas monopolized more than three-quarters of the total area. The hacienda was also a system of political and ideological domination that allowed landowners, directly or via the mediation of mestizo priests and village authorities, to monopolize power at local levels. The agrarian reform laws of the 1960s and 1970s eroded the social and political power of the traditional haciendas. By 1985, 36.2 percent of the land belonged to large farms, 30.3 percent to medium-sized units, and 33.5 percent to small units. Unfortunately, these agrarian transformations did not put an end to the *latifundio-minifundio* system, and the peasants' third of agricultural land is still insufficient to sustain the majority of the rural population. Nevertheless, such changes did create a power vacuum in the countryside that allowed for the eruption of autonomous Indian organizations and the increasing presence of modern political parties.

Ecuador is currently an urban country. In 1988 urban voters accounted for 75 percent of registered voters. As in other Latin American nations, capitalist development has not resulted in full proletarianization. Moreover, the crises of the 1980s have diminished the number of workers employed in manufacturing by 10 percent: from 113,000 in 1980 to 102,000 in 1986. Industrial workers rely on various strategies to make up for the lack of adequate family wages. Neoliberal adjustment policies have resulted in a drastic decline of real wages, which decreased by almost 30 percent between 1980 and 1985 and at an annual rate of 8 percent between 1986 and 1990. Most workers survive through a wide range of informal activities, such as street vending, domestic service, and self-employment in microenterprises. Official estimates place the informal sector between 40 and 50 percent of the economically active population.

Urbanization and the transformation of the traditional hacienda system were seen as the preconditions for political "progress." With the hope of designing new political institutions and creating a "modern" political system based on party competition, the military government of the 1970s appointed three commissions composed of representatives of political parties, employers' associations, labor unions, and other organized groups. Their goal was to rationalize the party system to avoid the cycle of populism and military coup that had characterized the country's history since the emergence of Velasquismo. The franchise was expanded from 2 million to more than 4 million voters between 1979 and 1988 due to population growth, voter registration drives, and the elimination of literacy requirements.

The plan to create a political system based on regular elections has been somewhat successful. Ecuador is experiencing its longest phase of elected civilian regimes to date. From 1979 to the present, presidents of different ideological persuasions have succeeded one another in office. Even so, political parties continue to be weak and numerous. Personalism, clientelism, and populism still characterize political struggles. Political parties, politicians, and politics in general appear discredited in public opinion surveys. The semilegal demises of President Abdalá Bucaram in February 1997, President Jamil Mahuad in January 2000, and President Lucio Gutiérrez in April 2005 revealed that democracy, even in its more restricted definition, has not been institutionalized.

Political elites still view the state as an entity to be either captured, in whole or in part, to be defended against, or both. The Ecuadorian state is booty. Elites are more interested in capturing state resources to build and maintain clientelist networks and increase the pool of patronage resources than in respecting democratic procedures. Civilian regimes, ruling in an economic crisis, have applied neoliberal policies, which have further increased social inequalities and political instability. Thus far, the military has abstained from carrying out a coup d'état. Its respect for civilian regimes, however, cannot be explained by a general commitment to democracy. More likely, the military has been deterred by economic crisis, by the dangers intervention would present to professional unity, and especially by a new international conjuncture. The military is not fully subordinated to civilian rule but maintains a series of privileges and veto powers, which, in apt characterization of the political scientist, Brian Loveman, make Ecuador at best a "protected democracy."

The sobering reality of Ecuador's political system is that common citizens and political elites typically do not behave according to the expectations of the modernizing intellectuals and politicians who designed the new political institutions. Instead of reflecting on the failure to fully realize this (restricted) conception of democracy, these intellectuals and politicians have constructed images of the antimodern populist "other." Populist leaders and their followers have been constructed as outsiders to the rule of reason and democracy. Populist followers are told that instead of shouting in public plazas in response to demagogues, they should "rationally" consider how to vote in the solitude of their homes. A quixotic task indeed, but one that nonetheless allows so-called modernizing elites to prescribe how politics should be conducted and reinforces their self-designation as the moral guides of what they term as modern Ecuador. Reflecting global changes in political discourse, neoliberalism has become the new dogma and panacea since the 1992 elections, replacing the modernizing social democratic plan of 1980.

Today, as in the past, populist politics continues to challenge the restricted character of Ecuadorian democracy. Contrary to the interpretations of many politicians and academics, populism is a specifically modern phenomenon. It is a form of political incorporation and of rhetoric that has been present in Ecuador since the eruption of mass politics sparked by Velasquismo in the late 1930s and early 1940s. Given the ways in which existing conceptions of democracy and citizenship silence and exclude the popular sectors, populist followers continue to seek empowerment by staging mass dramas and occupying public spaces in the name of their leader. The continuing relevance of the rhetoric and mobilization style that appeals to "lo popular" has not been matched by a strengthening of citizenship rights. Civil rights are not respected, and neoliberal economic policies have further reduced limited entitlements to social rights.

Plans for democratization, which appeal to supposedly universalistic conceptions of rationality, tend to silence and exclude large segments of the population. Despite elite wishes that the excluded "other" adapt and conform to proper notions of modern and rational politics, these subjects have not accepted such impositions even if defiance has been articulated through the delegation of power to authoritarian leaders. Populist politics presents an important example of how the marginal other does not conform to elitist so-called democratic politics.

Deinstitutionalized Democracy

Felipe Burbano de Lara

Translated by Mayté Chiriboga

During the past three decades, Ecuador has confronted an irony that has plagued much of Latin America. The return to democracy has coincided with political chaos and economic crisis. The sociologist and well-known editorialist Felipe Burbano locates the roots of this "unstable transition" in the precariousness of democratic institutions, the civilian-military relationship, the neoliberal model, and a weakened state apparatus.

In August 1979, Ecuador initiated the return to democracy in Latin America. Ironically, the year also marked the beginning of a long period of political instability within Ecuador. Most recently, the last three presidents elected by popular vote were removed from office before they completed the four-year presidential term. Abdalá Bucaram, leader of the Partido Roldosista Ecuatoriano (PRE), a populist party, was forced from office in February 1997, only six months after having become president. Jamil Mahuad, a popular democrat who held office for a year and a half, followed the same fate. Colonel Lucio Gutiérrez, in turn, remained in office for all of two years and two months. In each case, the downfalls were the result of a combination of social unrest, military intervention, and crisis of governability. Between August 1996 and April 2005, Ecuador had seven presidents.

Ecuadorian politics are currently in a state of "unstable transition" defined by four characteristics: (1) The idea of democracy has not been abandoned, but its definition is subject to intense dispute. Any political intervention, from a strike, to a coup, tends to be justified and legitimized as "democratic." (2) We make use of political liberties—freedom of speech, freedom of thought, freedom to organize, freedom to protest—within a context of institutional precariousness. There is continuous political activity that does not find a way to resolve itself through democratic means, because of which Ecuador lives in an environment of constant conflict, protest, and social unrest. (3) The removal of Bucaram in 1997, Mahuad in 2000, and Lucio Gutiérrez in 2005, weakened the very idea of democratic consolidation. It is an open question as to whether or not Ecuadorians will recover their trust in democracy. The institutional precariousness of democracy coincides, therefore, with an even greater uncertainty concerning the country's political future. (4) The ways in which opposition is exerted has become openly anti-institutional and destabilizing. Disagreements between the opposition and the president quickly become sufficient reasons to request his resignation or to seek his removal. This way of practicing opposition is shared by social movements and political parties alike. Elections now grant little legitimacy to those elected, hence the sudden loss of popularity among newly elected officials.

If despite this rather bleak panorama, we can still speak of a democracy it is because there is no possibility for a military government to assume power as it has in the past. Civilian-military relationships unfold within a much more complex power dynamic. The military intervention in the fall of Bucaram, Mahuad, and Gutiérrez demonstrated the military has resumed its role as dispute settlers between civilians. The three cases make evident that permanence in power ultimately depends upon the will of the military, which in turn contributes to the institutional precariousness of Ecuadorian democracy.

Presidentialism, Political Parties, and Struggles for Power

The purpose of the transition to democracy (1976–79) was to modernize the political system to allow new forms of representation. The project implicitly undertook the creation of new mechanisms of political mediation between state and society. The main innovation was to grant political parties what some analysts have termed "monopoly of representation," a system that forces citizens to affiliate with a political party in order to participate in elections for public office. Political parties were conceived as the foundation upon which the new system of representation would rest. Under the system, political parties had to be ideological parties with an established program and clearly defined principles. They were required to be national political parties—not regional or local—for which they were forced to register candidates in a determined number of provinces. And finally, they had to be parties with a minimum electoral support—5 percent of the electoral vote.

Two ghosts from the Ecuadorian political past, populism and parties of the notables, were supposed to be exorcized. According to those who saw the party system as a prerequisite for the return to democracy, populism represented the manipulation of irrational masses by demagogues. Overcoming populism was considered to be a condition for modernizing political practices and establishing Ecuadorian presidentialism. Traditional political parties—mainly Liberal and Conservative—represent the second ghost. For progressive intellectuals, the Liberal Party expressed the interests of the Guayaquileño and coastal oligarchy, while the Conservative Party represented the interests of the highland landholding aristocracy. Both groups were considered parties of notables, without any major popular support. In order to confront the ghosts of populism and political traditionalism, two new groups emerged toward the end of the 1960s and beginning of the 1970s. These were Democracia Cristiana and Izquierda Democrática.

The entire return to democracy and, later, the dynamics of the democracy itself were marked by tension between traditional and populist organizations and the alleged modern political parties. These embodied two moments of Ecuadorian political history—the past and the present, the old and the new—facing each other during the moment of transition. Ecuador's presidentialist system was based on the principle of "power separation" between the Executive and Congress. The struggle between political parties aggravated all the defects that are usually attributed to presidentialism. Theoretically conceived as a mechanism of checks and balances, "separation of power" in practice translated into a "power struggle." The struggle led to stagnation and deterioration of the political system, and consequently, blocked the process of making and defining public policy. Once combined, immobility and blocking systematically deteriorated the political system's capacity to respond to society's problems. Instead of turning into an arena where social groups processed their conflicts and disagreements, the Ecuadorian presidential system added more conflict to the general scenario of the country.

"Power struggle" cannot be explained outside the political party regime that has operated since the return to democracy. What we have now is a "polarized pluralism" characterized by four to six political parties competing in an election, with the possibility of drawing alliances and sufficient strength to exert political blackmail (leverage). The process is "polarized" because of the ideological-symbolic distance between political parties, in addition to the strong personal rivalry between their leaders. This phenomenon leads to a permanent social and political fragmentation and limits the possibility of achieving alliances in Congress in order to form majorities.

Take, for example, the number of political parties and groups with some degree of representation in Congress. Between 1979 and 1997, the groups with parliamentary representation fluctuated between ten and fourteen. Within the context of such fragmentation, power struggle is manifested by the constant strife between the government and the opposition in order to attain parliamentary majorities. Building a majority in the Ecuadorian Congress is exhausting; it requires the participation of between four and ten different groups. Worse yet, it has been repeated every year from 1979 to 1999. The negotiations inside the political system destroy the capacity for public management of the state since it generally implies a redistribution of the state's power in quotas.

It has not been possible to maintain public policies over time, because they have succumbed to the wavering of precarious and short-lived parliamentary agreements. The precariousness of these alliances is reflected in the instability of the ministers. The first government after the return to democracy (1979–84) had fifty-three ministers who had an average time in office of less than a year. In subsequent periods, the number of ministers with less than a year in office fluctuated from a low of thirty to a high of forty. The most critical areas have been departments overseeing economy and energy; heads roll at an average of six months.

Democracy and Dependency

For Ecuador, the 1982 foreign debt crisis set the stage for the transition to neoliberalism. In 1982 the democratic government was shaken by a series of general strikes, convoked by the United Workers Front (Frente Unitario de los Trabajadores), which struck against the adopted economic measures (i.e., devaluation of local currency, fuel price increases, and the reduction of subsidies). These strikes began what would eventually become a relatively permanent conflict throughout the 1980s between those who defended state support for local industry (the import substitution model) and social services, and those who embraced neoliberal reforms.

As a result, the 1984 elections, the second since the democratic return, marked a decisive moment in the transition process. An alliance between traditional political parties—the National Reconstruction Front (Frente de Reconstrucción Nacional)—headed by León Febres Cordero, leader of the Social Christians, won the election, embraced neoliberalism, and inaugurated a long period of social and political upheaval. Since 1984, Ecuador has lived under a permanent confrontation between attempts to impose the neoliberal model and the struggle to defend the old developmentalist model. Although the country has made significant advances in many aspects of the neoliberal agenda—such as opening the Ecuadorian market, loosening industrial protection, liberalizing markets, privatizing several sectors previously owned by the state, eliminating of subsidies—there are still substantial reforms pending. The incomplete nature of structural adjustment is a product of political disagreements in Ecuador, including the labor movement of the 1980s, the state employee's union throughout the entire period, and the indigenous movement during the 1990s. At times, the military even joined this "resistance block" against neoliberalism.

During two consecutive decades, lack of consensus and constant bickering helped contribute to the disastrous performance of the economy. The percentage of the population without access to a basic food basket—according to World Bank calculations—shifted from 34 percent in 1995, to 69 percent in 1999, and to 75 percent in 2003. If according to the Comisión Económica para América Latina y el Caribe, the 1980s was a "lost decade" for Latin America, for Ecuador the 1990s and early 2000s constituted more of the same.

State Reforms

The weakness of the presidential system has been aggravated by a general weakness of the state as an integrating element of society. Until 1995, the instability was contained by a state supported by oil revenues. Behind the power struggle, the frailty of the political system, and of democracy itself, there still appeared to be a robust state. Ultimately, however, the state machinery— subject to the exhausting pressure of neoliberalism, public spending cuts, and diminishing bureaucracy—has been weakened. Today, we find ourselves with a state that lacks clearly defined public policies or the capacity to implement them. The once prosperous Ecuadorian oil state has become a weakened apparatus without any capacity for political representation and or economic development.

The erosion of the state as a field for political negotiation, as a place for precarious balances, has left a generalized feeling of threat and exclusion, risk and pessimism, which has turned the political field into a setting for violent and anguished struggle for recognition. Today, no social sector finds a clear and safe space for representation within the state, making it virtually impossible to formulate and implement rational public policies.

Indigenous uprising, 1992. (Photo by Lucía Chiriboga, courtesy of Taller Visual)

V

Domination and Struggle

Since 1979, when the military formally returned the central government to civilian rule, Ecuador has become more democratic. The country has gone through the longest phase of civilian regimes to date, and the military has resisted the urge to take over the government. But the path has not been a smooth one. The new democracy saw the resurgence of (old) political practices such as clientelism, populism, and a Machiavellian understanding of politics in which enemies are seen as locked in an eternal struggle. Contemporary politics resemble the past in the cannibalistic attitude of politicians, and in the levels of political stability. From 1996 to 2006 Ecuador has had seven presidents and two Constitutions! Ecuadorians have elected presidents with different styles and ideologies, from the flamboyant populist Abdalá Bucaram (nicknamed "the crazy one") to the Harvard-trained Jamil Mahuad. Neither was able to finish his term before popular unrest brought their presidencies to an abrupt end.

In this sense, Ecuador in the 1980s and 1990s embodied one of the central contradictions of Latin American history during the past quarter century. On the one hand, the outward manifestations of democracy—elections, political parties, public debates, street protests, artistic expression, and so on—have been conspicuously present and in many cases remarkably durable over a relatively long period of time. Politics are charged, dynamic, and at times overwhelming. There is no similar period within Latin American or Ecuadorian history. On the other hand, the institutions of democracy—political parties, constitutions, the various branches of government, and others—remain relatively weak and at times ineffective conduits for channeling and representing political expression. A series of structural constraints, perhaps best understood as some combination of structural reforms and globalization, have not only undermined this turn (or return) to democracy but have made it exceptionally frustrating for the very groups who pushed for democratic reforms as they struggled against military dictatorships, oligarchies, and foreign imperialism.

At various times during recent decades, workers, peasants, indigenous peoples, Afro-Ecuadorians, and even women's groups have established remarkably powerful organizations and movements. New actors with new demands have emerged. Indigenous politicians have won elections and now have an important role in national debates. Indeed, Ecuador's indigenous movement is quite arguably the most powerful in the region. They have not only challenged foreign oil companies seeking to extract profit from their lands, but have gained formal access to the state and have proven that they can bring the government and economy to a standstill. Likewise, labor unions have periodically paralyzed the country's political economy and prevented the implementation of the worst of neoliberalism's excesses. But they have done so within a severely constrained context. Ecuador is undergoing racial and ethnic democratization; old prejudices are being examined and challenged. But economic gains for Ecuador's most marginal citizens have been slow to materialize.

As inhabitants of a relatively small and impoverished country, Ecuadorians have only limited control over their own affairs. Regardless of political ideology, state leaders govern within the context of one of the most burdensome foreign debts in the region, an unpredictable world market, and a continuing need for (and dependence on) foreign investment. This is not to say that Ecuadorians have given up, or that they have been completely unable to negotiate the global world. Many have left for other countries in search of economic opportunity. Others have pushed the World Bank to implement major ethnodevelopment projects targeting indigenous people and Afro-Ecuadorians. Wealthy Ecuadorians have experimented with a range of agro-export crops—flowers, broccoli, and palm heart, to name a few—in order to gain a foothold in the global market. Yet, such experiments reflect a basic fact. There is little room for error. Marginal groups now know that gaining access to state power is no panacea. The Ecuadorian state is not only fragmented, but has limited power to exact the kinds of changes demanded by popular sectors. The temptation to exchange environmental regulations, popular organizations, and even democracy for short-term political order and economic gain is always tempting. Ecuadorians are learning a regionwide lesson: capitalism and democracy are in tension with one another in Latin America.

Nina Pacari, an Interview

Carlos de la Torre

Translated by Mayté Chiriboga and Carlos de la Torre

Nina Pacari grew up in an urban indigenous family in the town of Cotacachi in the northern highland province of Imbabura. As an Indian girl living among mestizos, Pacari experienced racism, but also learned to negotiate the dominant culture while developing a strong sense of ethnic pride. Trained as a lawyer, Pacari went on to become one of Ecuador's most important indigenous leaders, eventually becoming the first indigenous woman elected to Ecuador's National Assembly as well as the minister of foreign affairs under the government of Lucio Gutiérrez.

In September 2004, just after the indigenous movement was expelled from the government of Colonel Lucio Gutiérrez, the minister of foreign affairs, Nina Pacari, explained the short, strange alliance in these terms:

> We were able to do something, despite having an ally who did not fulfill his program, a shortsighted ally who does not even know where he is going. We were able to shatter the stereotype of the incapacity of the indigenous people, and that is an accomplishment. We achieved an important objective; the indigenous people recovered their self-esteem. A second accomplishment was that we positioned the indigenous people at an international level, and this would not have been possible if we had remained at the margins. The third potentiality was the quality of our public work, ethical and visionary, in the Ministry of Agriculture as well as in the Ministry of Foreign Affairs.

Thus ends the interview, a two-hour conversation that provides a window into the world of the first woman and indigenous person to be appointed minister of foreign affairs. Doctor Pacari began the dialogue with details about her childhood.

> Altogether, we are eight siblings: five females and three males, of which five of us are professionals but for one sister and two younger brothers

who decided to become merchants and musicians. We are urban indigenous, and came from the few families, almost the exception, who lived in the urban area of Cotacachi. My father comes from a family of farmers from the Quinchuqui community. My mother, from the Peguche community. My maternal grandparents had settled in Cotacachi, where they set up weaving workshops. When my mother married my father, they settled in Cotacachi. My father improved his economic situation with the weaving business. He had prosperous moments as well as bad times. He did not accumulate for the sake of it, but to give us an education.

Being urban indigenous we lived a double exclusion—exclusion from the indigenous rural world because we did not live in a community, and exclusion from the nonindigenous world. In those times, we were almost the first indigenous students to go to school. My brother and uncle were forced to cut their braids during the first year. By the second year, when they transferred to the Franciscan nun's school, they made their first communion with their complete attire and full braids. [This change] was a result of the parent's struggle. An issue that had a very deep impact during school was a book reading contest, and the school had to be represented by the best student. In those times, I was their best student; nevertheless, I was not chosen to represent the school in the contest. I felt this was racism. It was a world where excellence was not acknowledged.

My father wanted me to become a teacher, and therefore I studied at the San Pablo del Lago School. The indigenous classmates did not mingle with the mestizo world; I got along with them, however. I also felt part of the urban world, which was my background; at times, my indigenous classmates were annoyed at me, and I felt forced to be exclusively with them. I did not agree with this and explained that I also wanted to relate with the *mestizas*. In order for them to understand that I was on both sides, I became part of a dance group with the indigenous classmates. Finally, it was established that an intercultural process is possible. It was a boarding school where indigenous and mestizo students from different provinces of the country "shared" together. This personal experience from our youth taught us to recognize ourselves and share with the different races we have in Ecuador.

At school I was taught history of the Incas, the Puruháes, the Caras; everything was in the past. I asked myself: And, what am I? I am indigenous, I have not died, how is it that they affirm that all has ended? This was a shock to me.

I studied law at Universidad Central in Quito, a very different experience from Cotacachi. I speak for myself, but I experienced more discrimi-

[handwritten margin note: braids symbolized indigenousity]

nation in Quito. For example, at a restaurant, we were not admitted. It was a restaurant along 10 de Agosto Avenue, I don't remember its name, but the four of us were not allowed to enter, and were left deprived of some Chinese rice. We agreed that the reason for this was that we were not carrying books: "We must bring books if we want them to believe that we are students," we said. So we started carrying books and notebooks with us for them to believe that we were students; even though we are still Indians, if we were seen with books, we were perceived differently. In fact, when we appeared before them as students, we were immediately admitted into the restaurant. Then we understood how such situations must be handled.

When riding a bus, we did not speak Spanish. We spoke Quichua, and the people in the bus said to us, "Talk like Christians." We just laughed. I think they must have been annoyed, as we did not take notice or confront them. We just continued as if nobody had said anything.

Once, we went on a trip to Baños with mestizo friends. When it was time to enter the swimming pool, my friends went in first. As we were about to enter, we were stopped: admittance to Indians was forbidden. Auki Tituaña [current mayor of Cotacachi] and my sister Arqui, Auki's wife, were also there. My friend was enraged and complained. The owner came out to apologize and make excuses. Our trip was ruined, so we ended walking around Baños instead.

In 1987, I had to go to a conference. As it turned out, it was the very same hotel where I was once denied admittance. This time, I was welcomed. I explained to the hotel people that I had come to the hotel in such and such a year and I was not allowed in. Naturally, those were other times, other circumstances. There has been a process in which the indigenous people have made themselves known, gained respect, and opened horizons; in general, people have become more sensitive. There is now a new openness as well.

After graduating as a lawyer at Universidad Central, I began to practice law in Riobamba. I was linked to the indigenous movement of Chimborazo; the movement took me in as their member. The communities of Colta and Cajabamba integrated me as a member of their community as well. Since 1989, at their request, I joined the Confederation of Indigenous Nationalities of Ecuador [CONAIE], as a legal advisor to help manage the land and territory administration. I was the first woman to hold this position. At the end of 1995, we became the founding members of Pachakutik together with comrade Luis Macas as president, José María Cabascango as leader of the organization, and me as land and territory leader.

Within Pachakutik there are two paths, two criteria. One is that the indigenous movement is in charge and directs. The other is that the party should be more open, include more social movements, with the indigenous people being the backbone.

How do you interpret the mobilizations and the alliances with the military that ended with the removal of president Jamil Mahuad in January 2000?

The CONAIE Congress that took place in Santo Domingo de los Colorados in 1999 caused much concern among some sectors of the grass roots and some leaders, because of the relationship between Antonio Vargas and elements of the armed forces who were part of the high command. The army provided infrastructure, food, and field stoves for our congress. Second, when CONAIE decided to lead the mobilization against Mahuad, Pachakutik took a relatively subordinate attitude toward CONAIE. Some members of Pachakutik, such as Napoleón Saltos, stated that the same mistake of 1996 could not be repeated; that we needed a new strategy to forge an alliance with the military. My hair stood on end.

Hence, why the alliance with Gutiérrez's party, Sociedad Patriótica, during the 2002 elections?

Several scenarios arose. Our objective was to have common Center-Left candidates. There was a process of dialogue with Izquierda Democrática, but they sustained that we would only be admitted as subordinates. The second scenario was to have León Roldós as presidential candidate and Auki Tituaña as vice-president. But Roldós resigned his candidacy. So we ran alone. When Antonio Vargas became the candidate for Amauta Jatari, the Indigenous Evangelical political party, there were two Indian candidates. Hence, CONAIE, instead of considering that we would both go—thinking not only as Indians, but also as a prospect for society with Tituaña as an influential administrative role model—decided not to endorse any candidate. Therefore, Auki decided not to participate, since he would not go against CONAIE's decision. Consequently, we had to find a mestizo candidate. We spoke with Alberto Acosta, who did not show any interest. We were also talking to the Sociedad Patriótica simultaneously, and an alliance with ten programmatic points was agreed on.

Was there any objection with allying with a Golpista [coup leader]?

For us, the concept of coup d'état does not exist. Our analysis is different. But, despite the fact that he is an ex-military, there was still potential if the program is fulfilled.

Let's talk about your transit through power. Wasn't it a contradiction between a left-
ist discourse, and on the other hand, government practices such as signing an agree-
ment with the International Monetary Fund?

First, you must understand that it was the government of an alliance and
must not be perceived as if it were a single unit. Perhaps, the limitation
was that the programmatic points could fail. In that case, we agreed to
battle from within. Within the cabinet, we felt that the first draft of the
economic measures proposed was absolutely appalling. Not all the measures were implemented, such as the increase of the price of gas. One of
the political costs was that we had to sign the letter of intent with the IMF,
which we could not stop because we were not "within" either the Ministry
of Economy or presidency.

Wasn't that the moment to break the alliance?

I don't think the timing was appropriate. It was not fitting to leave after
only fifteen days in power. We would have been perceived as if fleeing
from political office. And we even thought that we would be perceived as
unable to hold office and govern.

What are you doing now?

I continue with my work at the international level, since I have been in
academics and in the political world for twenty years. For example, I was
invited to go to Mexico by the university; I was invited to teach a seminar
on anthropology in Bogotá, after which I will go to Puerto Rico. I belong
to Confederación de los Pueblos de Nacionalidad Kichua del Ecuador. The
Pachakutik congressional block has requested me to be their advisor. On
women's issues it is the same, either one activity or another. I thought I
was going to rest a little, but I am still intensely busy in meetings, events,
etc. I feel well, working eagerly, always with the same disposition.

Women's Movements in Twentieth-Century Ecuador

Sarah A. Radcliffe

Despite the fact that Ecuador was the first Latin American nation to grant women the vote, the country has not been on the leading edge of Latin American women's movements during the twentieth century. In contextualizing the ups and downs of women's organizing, the geographer Sarah A. Radcliffe stresses the ethnic, regional, and class diversity of Ecuador's women as well as the wide range of issues they have confronted during the past century.

In Ecuador, many different "strands" of women's movements are found as in many Latin American countries, and—as elsewhere—these strands overlap, separate, and form new channels for action over time. One characteristic of Ecuadorian women's movements is the lack of a homogeneous group defined solely by gender. Rather, women are plural and diverse politically, as well as ethnically, culturally, and socioeconomically. In this context, women's movements were established at several junctures throughout the twentieth century, reflecting the changing nature of civil society and relationships between social groups. Moreover, the changing nature of state formations over time provided a constantly changing context for women's struggles and gender relations.[1]

In 1924, Matilde Hidalgo de Prócel registered to vote in Machala on the grounds that the Constitution did not explicitly exclude women from the electorate. Her brave action was not, however, sufficient to guarantee women's voting rights. Although Ecuador was the first Latin American country to give women the vote, it was the conservative government's expectation that they would support the status quo. Despite widespread nationalistic pride in this "progressive" action, it is true to say that progress was made in this case without a clear identification by women with this means of empowerment, and women's vote did not become mandatory until 1967.[2]

Urban and rural women experience very diverse lives, due to occupational structures, and uneven state provision of services, infrastructure, and development funding, as well as to historically rooted patterns of class, race or ethnicity, culture, and language variations. Ecuador's population is around three-fifths urban, the remainder distributed across highly diverse social and ecological rural landscapes in the three major regions. In 1990, 11 percent of women were illiterate, compared with 7 percent of men, with female illiteracy concentrated among older and indigenous women. Women's fertility rates fell dramatically through the century, from 6.1 live births on average in the 1970s to 3.6 in the second half of the 1990s. Currently, over half of Ecuadorian women use contraception despite a conservative and politically influential church hierarchy. Ecuador has low rates of female participation in the labor market, as found in other predominantly rural agricultural Latin American countries, although there are persistent problems in collecting accurate data. In 1999, over one-fifth of women were counted as working, with over four-fifths concentrated in the service sector as more women move from rural agricultural employment into services. Women faced persistent discrimination in the workplace from coworkers and the state. Male bias against female workers was found among trade unionists, while a law requiring workplaces with more than fifty female workers to provide child-care nurseries remained unimplemented. Ecuadorian women's political activities reflect not only class position but also, crucially, senses of identity; embeddedness in a public *and* private world; and the (diverse) gender bias of state, church, and development policies.

Social Movements

In discussing women's movements, we face the problem of a lack of documentation of female activism in early twentieth-century Ecuador. Reflecting continental patterns of struggles for liberalization in the 1920s, Ecuadorian middle-class and elite women voiced their demands for emancipation in the pages of a flurry of reviews. In the 1930s and '40s indigenous and peasant women, including such historic figures as Luisa Gómez de la Torre and Tránsito Amaguaña, were active in ethnic and land-based movements, frustrated at limited liberalization in rural areas. Facing racial and gender discrimination, a Serrana indigenous woman, Dolores Cacuango, struggled successfully for rural schools for Indian girls and cofounded the Ecuadorian Indian Federation (Federación Ecuatoriana de Indios, FEI) in 1945. Although her name is now well known, she was not alone in fighting for a public voice. As class politics became established, women became active in the Communist Party women's group, the Alianza Femenina Ecuatoriana (Ecuadorian Women's Alliance). In this group—as in later student, academic, and union organizations—women struggled with the dominant view that gender interests were secondary to those of class. Nevertheless women continued to act against class and gender domination and, over the middle decades of the century, established secretariats or sections within militant organizations, such as the Working Women's Union (UMT), to deal strategically with political exclusion.

During military regimes in the 1970s women's responses were embedded in a largely rural indigenous society, in which authoritarianism and democratization shaped women's activism. Middle-class women worked within political parties, progressive church groups, and teachers' unions to contest military rule. Another characteristic of the 1970s was the emergence of women's charitable activity, found among the wives of armed forces representatives, politicians, and bankers. "Women's fronts" were established in unions, peasant federations, and neighborhood associations to protest against military governments; yet the specific content of women's concerns were not addressed. Nevertheless, housewives grasped the political initiative by organizing an "empty pot protest" in April 1978.

The real "boom" in numbers of women's movements came in the 1980s, comparatively late in the Latin American context. During these years, women's mobilization continued in part through sections or committees in class unions or social movements, as in the Coordinator of Social Movements and the Pichincha workers' federation. Yet the closing decades of the century were particularly characterized by the emergence of "new" women's struggles, including issues around race and ethnicity, sexuality, and feminism. During these decades, too, women's activism occurred in the context of urbanization, structural adjustment, and increasing income disparities between the sexes.

Throughout Ecuador, women were active in social reproduction and the social construction of urban neighborhoods. While often seen as "mothers' movements," the urban popular women's organizations also often negotiate power inequalities, construct collective identities, and develop critical perspectives on the world, thereby challenging dominant gender representations. Where women's associations emerged in urban neighborhoods, it often resulted from struggles with existing male-dominated barrio committees; women's political practices responded to their own needs and priorities. According to one woman's association in southern Quito, "for progress in our *barrio*, it's important that women and men organize, as working together we can achieve our objectives. But the [neighborhood committee] didn't understand that. They were like dictators; they wanted us to obey them and be under their command."[3] Women's collective actions had the principal organizing strategy of connecting across private-public divisions at the local level. Despite this, through much of the twentieth century, political parties and clientelist networks have viewed women's associations instrumentally, thereby restricting women's options. Low-income women's role as multitasking "micro-entrepreneurs" fails to lift them out of poverty, despite recent attempts to incorporate their activities into market-led development initiatives.[4]

Women's grassroots efforts confronted the specific gendered impacts of restructuring under neoliberalism, and the poverty associated with successive macroeconomic crises and harsh adjustment policies. Groups mobilized to provide day-care centers and enhance women's political engagement. Yet 300 local associations lost government funding for day-care initiatives with macroeconomic restructuring under the neoliberal FISE (Fondo de Inversión Social de Emergencia) program of President Sixto Durán Ballén's government (1992–96). Through the 1990s, neighborhood women's associations numbered some 600 including registered and informal groups, with about 30 in Quito alone. Rural and urban popular women's organizations held their first national conference in the early 1990s, independently of middle-class NGOs. Nevertheless, unlike what occurred in some Latin American countries such as Peru, Ecuador's local women's associations did not forge a national movement, leaving heterogeneous women's groups to create diverse relationships with political parties, NGOs, churches, and local governments.

After decades of clientelism, exclusion, and survival, low-income women often reject politics, viewing it as extraneous to their daily lives. The sharp public-private divide and women's exclusion from "public" activities exacerbate these tendencies. Under restructuring and neoliberal reform, women and households retreat into the private realm, individualizing responses to state welfare reforms and growing income disparities. In the port city of Guayaquil, more and more women have disengaged from collective actions, being forced to "hang on" to a precarious set of survival strategies.

The United Nations Decade for Women, specifically the 1995 Beijing meeting of governments and NGOs, was a key moment for Ecuador's women's mobilization.[5] In preparations for Beijing, Ecuadorian women from some 290 nongovernmental organizations met to discuss the conference themes of "equality, development and peace." The resulting statement prioritized the importance of political action at all levels, as a counter to asymmetrical gender power relations that reproduce discrimination and inequality. Out of these meetings arose the Foro Permanente de la Mujer (Women's Permanent Forum), building on networks built up by CEIME (Centro de Estudios y Investigaciones de la Mujer Ecuatoriana), which advocates active incorporation of gender perspectives into civil society. Peaking in the run-up to the Beijing meeting, the *foro* gained official recognition and had fourteen regional centers working to strengthen local women's organizations. Ecuador's official delegation to Beijing included an indigenous woman, making it relatively inclusionary compared with countries such as Guatemala and Peru. Nevertheless, indigenous women felt marginalized by the sheer scale of the meeting, and by white and Northern women.

In another late century development, feminism resurged in Ecuador. Disillusionment with limited social conceptions of women's interests led to the organization of feminist networks. By the end of the 1980s feminists had held two encounters, demonstrating the emergence of a vibrant and national movement. National feminist networks were often based in a series of independent research institutes such as CEPAM (Ecuadorian Center for Women's Promotion and Action), CIAM (Women's Information and Support Center), and CEEAL (Women's Network of the Latin American Adult Education Council). All were founded in the early 1980s in the context of international support and networking through the UN Decade for Women. Their activities included street protests, International Women's Day marches, and participation in international feminist meetings. Feminist research centers worked to break down barriers of class, race, and ethnicity, permitting dialogue among diverse women. For example, the low-income popular women's neighborhood group "Centro Femenino 8 de Marzo" in Quito ran feminist workshops on issues such as sexuality, domestic violence, employment skills, and the distribution of collectively purchased food. In the *centro* and elsewhere, consciousness-raising methods gave women a voice to express needs and priorities outside the masculine contexts of home, shantytown, and local associations.

Feminist groups are far from homogeneous, however, with different priorities expressed by political and autonomous feminists. "Political" feminists push beyond the "personal is political" slogan, bringing issues of power and gender into the public domain. A 1993 workshop on women's participation examined the political system from a gender perspective, working toward greater attention to feminist and women's issues. The Coordinadora Política Nacional de Mujeres—Women's National Political Coordinator, CPNM—is a network established in 1996 as "an instrument for action and political pressure on the state, political parties and civil society" to transform the country's inequality into equality. It arose from a 1995 meeting of over 700 women from different provinces, who addressed issues such as economic globalization, the feminization of poverty, public ethics, and *machista* national culture. It includes feminists from NGOs, the state, and the popular women's movement, whose agenda is to insert a gender dimension and focus in all fields of political and state activity, to overcome the "ghettoization" of gender themes. Following Beijing, the *coordinadora* worked to establish Andean regional mechanisms for gender equity. As in Brazilian feminist networks, the coordinadora's activities were directed at providing information and expertise to state policymakers. For example, in the Constituent Assembly of 1997 they worked alongside CEPAM, while in the 1998 national elections CPNM members acted as observers.

Through such actions, the coordinadora gained itself a leading position in Ecuadorian women's movements by the start of the twenty-first century.

By contrast, "autonomous" feminists became disillusioned with the state and democratic officials, preferring to use theater and performance as a route to challenging gender expectations and macroeconomic policies. Autonomous feminists worked on reproductive and lesbian rights, and abortion access, analyzing "the cultural construction of politics publicly and privately." Loosely networked through the Feminists for Autonomy group established in 1997, these feminists considered sexuality to be women's essence. Low-income women were also active in issues centered on sexuality. In the coastal town of Machala, sex workers created the Association of Autonomous Workers "22nd June" in 1982. Using devices from strikes to life histories to theater performances, the association fought for women's and human rights, reflecting upon the social, juridical, and health conditions of sex work.

A broad coalition of women's movements acted to inform public opinion about domestic violence issues through the 1980s and 1990s. While acknowledging the specific crisis situation of economic downturn, activists pointed to domestic violence's rootedness in social relations of gender domination. Between 60 and 80 percent of Ecuadorian women at one time experience violence, and in 95 percent of cases aggression comes from husbands or partners. As well as annually commemorating 25 November as "Día de No Violencia contra la Mujer" (No Violence against Women Day), women's NGOs set up legal advice centers. Refuges for battered women and children were established by NGOs, first in Quito and then throughout the country, although provision remains scanty and underresourced.

During the 1990s, Indian and black women organized their own networks to tackle multiple forms of discrimination; their efforts include groups such as the Congreso Nacional de Mujeres Indígenas y Negras (CONMEI, National Congress of Indigenous and Black Women) and the indigenous women's movement. Although only granted the right to vote in 1979 (when franchise was extended to nonliterate people), indigenous and black women were organized locally. The highland indigenous federation, ECUARUNARI, was the first to create a section for women's issues in the late 1970s, and continued to support women's leadership and organization, most recently through the "Dolores Cacuango" Training School. Nationally, the major indigenous confederation, CONAIE, appointed several female leaders, reflecting the active involvement of women in grassroots associations and regional federations. The unprecedented election of Nina Pacari Vega to Congress in 1999 for the Pachakutik Party led to her appointment first as congressional vice-president and then, in 2002, as foreign minister. Alongside racial-ethnic federations, indigenous women established the Movimiento de Mujeres Indígenas, and

Afro-Ecuadorian women the Coordinadora de Mujeres Negras. Individual women work at the intersection of ethnic-racial and feminist movement politics, extending mutual understanding and political ties while establishing international linkages among indigenous and black women across the world.[6]

Lesbian networks emerged in Ecuador during the 1990s, articulated around a Quito-based newsletter *En Directo*, which aimed to "reflect positive and real opinions about gay and lesbian identity and culture in Ecuador and the world." Buoyed by international support, female and male mobilization led to the decriminalization of homosexuality in November 1997. The Constituent Assembly recognized free expression of sexuality, elaborated through secondary legislation. Women's associations mobilized to insert a clause banning discrimination on the basis of sexual orientation in the 1998 Constitution. However, repression of sexual orientation continued, with police violence against transvestites. In this context, lesbian networks work to challenge *machismo* and its female equivalent, *marianismo*.

Does Ecuadorian women's activity represent a new way of "doing politics"? Certainly, Ecuador is characterized by highly heterogeneous and decentered political action across a wide geographical and social landscape. Such diversity comprised the strength of women's movements in the twentieth century, with locally appropriate and highly participatory social and political mobilization. Ecuadorian women's movements put decentralization and participatory agendas at the center of their demands. However, the cost of this way of doing politics has been a slow and unconsolidated move toward unified and nationally organized women's movements.

The State

"It is not enough to describe *a priori* the positive connotations of women's political participation. The relevant question is not whether women participate in politics or not. Rather, how do they participate? Where? Who benefits? What effects do they have? And what consequences does participation have, in a specific political context?"[7]

Through the twentieth century, the Ecuadorian nation-state has established legislative and constitutional provision for women's rights, although women's empowerment has not necessarily been the prime motive for legal reform. Although legal provision appears progressive at the end of the century, an enduring problem has been implementation and conservative social attitudes, despite actions by diverse individual women and collective challenges.[8] Numerically and proportionately, women remain marginal to the operation and staffing of state bodies and functions. In Congress, men outnumber female representatives by 23 to 1 on average, while women comprise only 4 percent of judges and 5 percent of ambassadors. Particularly notable is the absence of indigenous and Afro-Ecuadorian women from the decision-making process. With the application of neoliberal policies, citizenship has been increasingly reduced to economic relations at the cost of social, political, and civil rights, raising the specter of a "remasculinization" of politics.[9]

In the 1984 national elections, women voted for conservative parties in larger numbers than men, although in Quito the difference between men and women was small, and in Guayaquil the majority of *all* voters selected a right-wing candidate in campaigns. Many Ecuadorian women—especially older women, wealthy housewives, and women with fewer years of formal education—forged their identities in relation to patriarchal notions of male authority and competence inside and outside the home, leading them to express conservative political choices during much of the twentieth century. Women who rejected these patriarchal and class-based ideologies tended to vote for alternative candidates in the 1984 elections.[10]

Following global trends, Ecuador began in the 1970s and 1980s to acknowledge women's presence in society and involve women in development programs. The United Nations Convention on the Elimination of All Forms of Discrimination against Women (CEDAW) was ratified in 1981. Under pressure from the Organization of American States during the early 1970s, Ecuador created a bureau to "define and implement policies and strategies directed towards women, taking due account of Ecuador's social, political, economic and cultural characteristics." Programs initiated by women's bureaus over the decades included mother and infant health projects, food aid distribution, and training courses, often in coordination with popular organizations. Framed by a global "Women In Development" policy, these projects were widely criticized by feminists for reinforcing gender stereotypes. With the growing confidence of women's movements, pressure was increasingly placed on the state to address women's issues in development planning and with fewer stereotyped expectations.

Rural women were particularly excluded from the formulation of state policies, due to combinations of race and ethnicity, class, lack of infrastructure and educational provision, and urban bias in politics. Integrated development programs for rural women, such as FODERUMA (Fondo de Desarrollo Rural Marginado) in the 1980s and PRODEPINE (Proyecto de Desarrollo de los Pueblos Indígenas y Afroecuatorianos) in the late 1990s, tended to prejudge peasant and indigenous women's priorities while mobilizing them on behalf of programs that they neither designed nor managed. However, in other spheres, rural women voiced development priorities and trained as development experts (e.g., in the FENOCIN [Confederación Nacional de Organizaciones Campesinas Indígenas y Negras del Ecuador] and ECUARUNARI federations programs).

Against the theory of neoliberal restructuring, the Ecuadorian nation-state underwent a "rolling forward" by establishing institutions for gender mainstreaming. Since 1997, the national women's council CONAMU has played an important role promoting gender issues within the state, with feminist staff wielding considerable interpretive and institutional power. With a staff of thirty-four, CONAMU serves as "the interlocutor of gender and development projects on a national level." It delegates the project management for low-income women to town councils and local organizations. The council has carried out highly innovative work on property rights, and organized the publication of women's rights statements in indigenous languages. Criticized by feminists, CONAMU wrestles with the fact that it is powerful vis-à-vis the women's movement yet relatively power*less* vis-à-vis the state.

Political parties acted as key gatekeepers into national political processes, yet they were historically unable or unwilling to engage with women's concerns, a fissure exacerbated by women's (especially feminists') frequent unwillingness to work with existing political entities. Although a handful of individual women dominated certain political parties, the majority of women were excluded by masculinist expectations and practices. Ecuadorian political parties only rarely appointed women to leadership positions, and numbers of women in secondary posts were small. However, during the 1980s women increasingly appeared as party candidates, with numbers rising among right-wing parties to levels in center and left-wing parties. Women very rarely gained high office, a fact making President Bucaram's 1996 appointment of Guadalupe León, a self-declared feminist, as labor minister, and Rosalía Arteaga, the first female vice-president, an unprecedented—if short-lived—move. Nevertheless Bucaram's government was widely distrusted by women's movements, and political mobilization against his regime contained a clear feminist critique. While political parties remained uneven in their adoption of female-friendly policies, parties began to provide female candidates with training in political skills.

In recent years, a new willingness for dialogue between women and political parties emerged, responding to autonomous women's demands for a revision of party programs from a gender perspective. Cross-party alliances around gender issues were establishing, thereby building, networks through which the demands of women's movements could enter the state. A parliamentary commission on women, children, and the family was founded, as was the Association of Municipal Women in 1988, which represented key moments in women's political networking. The commission became a channel linking women with parliamentary "gender delegates," a network that became significant in reforms concerned with domestic violence (see below).

A significant gain for Ecuador's women's movements in the last century was the Quota Law, established in 1997. The law required that at least 20 percent of candidates be women. Inside the state, important groups including CONAMU coordinated the lobbying for this legislation together with groups such as the Foro Permanente de la Mujer, the Guayas women's movement, and indigenous women. Women's movements lobbied continuously to publicize the quota system, and to retain a gender-equitable interpretation of the law. Together with the gains of the Quota law, the Constituent Assembly of 1998 represented a highly significant political space for diverse women to express their views. It has been estimated that nine-tenths of women's organization demands were incorporated into the 1998 Constitution, as a result of networking and activities during the assembly. Reflecting the prominent position of the women's and indigenous movements in Ecuadorian political culture at the time, the assembly was a key arena within which rights for these groups could be debated. In the Constituent Assembly, a cross-party group of women and men, including Nina Pacari (Pachakutik), Patricia Naveda (an independent), Gloria Gallardo (Social Christian Party) and Gustavo Vega and Enrique Ayala (both Pachacutec), coordinated to push for sexual and reproductive rights. Women's rights were thus furthered in the new 1998 Constitution, reflecting sustained lobbying and information-generating by autonomous and feminist associations, as well as strategic individuals within the constituent assembly.[11]

Women's engagement with the nation-state also shifted at the local level. Through the later part of the century, women in local associations and professional women became increasingly legitimate political actors at *local* levels. The majority of women elected to local government office gained political experience and support in community mobilizations, as in other countries. Women were also more likely to be successful in larger cities, where they adopted issues of women's practical interests rather than feminism as their slogans. In 1988 for the first time, a woman was elected mayor: Elsa Bucaram won Guayaquil through dynastic connections and urban power bases. Nationally, networks of local government women were established to link women across party divides. Following the national quota law, the local election law "2000–1" required political parties' candidate lists to include at least 30 percent women, coming into force for the May 2000 local elections. In this contest, 41.3 percent of lists were female, representing a historic increase from between 6 and 14 percent. However, women found it difficult to be elected: just under 25 percent of elected officials were women, including eight female mayors but no female *prefecturas*.[12]

One issue generating mobilization inside and outside the state was domestic violence. Autonomous women's movement lobbied for measures against domestic violence from the early 1980s, pressing for specialized police stations. Independent women's groups such as CEIMME (Centro de Estudios e Investigación Sobre el Maltrato de la Mujer) and CEPAM were particularly important in this regard, bringing the issue to public attention through media campaigns. Sustained pressure from women's movements involved the presentation of a draft law against domestic violence to Congress in July 1995. Ecuador signed an Inter-American convention to prevent, sanction, and eradicate violence against women in 1995, while in the same year five specialist police stations were established in major towns, charged with reporting cases, initiating legal action, and providing support to victims. In the mid-1990s, these police stations dealt with some 400 cases per day. After lobbying and information campaigns by women's movements, Congress passed the Law against Violence against Women and Families in November 1995, which represented significant changes in that it permitted women to denounce their partners, and ordered public officials to help people affected by domestic violence. Complementing the law, services and facilities were established: CONAMU offered legal advice and created temporary refuges and safe houses, as well as centers for offenders' reeducation. However, women's organizations criticized the law for its inadequate sanctions and the state's failure to give the issue political priority.[13]

Conclusions

"Struggles for citizenship have animated women's movements throughout the twentieth century," not least in Ecuador, argues the political scientist Maxine Molyneux. Women as citizens in twentieth-century Ecuador have made important gains in rights, specifically political rights, but with respect to other dimensions of citizenship their position is contradictory. The majority of Ecuadorian women faced domination and continued to struggle for political subjecthood, full participation, and a progressive range of social, economic, and political rights. Afro-Ecuadorian, indigenous, and poor women in rural and urban areas remained seriously marginalized from decision-making arenas and development benefits. During the last three decades of the century, state restructuring and transformations in patterns of redistribution and welfare left the majority of women poorer, less secure in their workplaces, and more dependent upon—often patriarchal—extended family networks than before.

More optimistically, women reached the "antechamber" of the state by century's end. Quota laws and legislation on domestic violence and sexual rights, together with the establishment of the state CONAMU and the powerful civil society Coordinadora Política, brought about undeniable shifts in expectations of women by civil society, and in women's formal and informal access to power. Women's movements reached a level of maturity and degree of coordination that permitted female—and often feminist—representatives to reach positions of authority in Congress, state institutions, major social movements, and local organizations.

Women's movements in Ecuador worried that they failed to comprise an articulating force with a nationwide capacity for mobilization. Alongside the indigenous movement, the women's movements in Ecuador have arguably transformed political cultures and expectations of women and men over the past twenty years. As the twentieth century closed, Ecuadorian women's movements continued to clamor for women's rights to be respected and expanded. Building on the advances made during the past century, Ecuadorian women of diverse class, racial and ethnic, and geographical backgrounds can stand proud on the shoulders of the women who went before them.

Notes

1. On Ecuador in the Latin American context, see Maxine Molyneux, "Twentieth-Century State Formations in Latin America," in *Hidden Histories of Gender and the State in Latin America*, ed. Elizabeth Dore and Maxine Molyneux (Durham, N.C.: Duke University Press, 2000), 33–81; Nikki Craske, *Women and Politics in Latin America* (Oxford: Polity, 1999); and Jane Jaquette, ed., *The Women's Movement in Latin America: Participation and Democracy* (Boulder, Colo.: Westview, 1994).

2. See excellent historical overviews in Raquel Rodas Morales, "Muchas voces, demasiados silencios: Los discursos de las lideresas del movimiento de mujeres en Ecuador," Documento de Trabajo no. 4, Fondo para la Igualdad de Género de ACDI, Quito, 2002; and Astrid Muller, *Por pan y equidad: Organizaciones de mujeres ecuatorianas* (Quito: FEPP, 1994).

3. The quote comes from Linda Rodríguez, "La política, lo político y la politización de las mujeres," in *Jaque al rey: Memorias del taller "Participación Política de la Mujer,"* ed. Red de Educación Popular entre Mujeres (Quito: REPEM, 1994), 103–16.

4. On issues around low-income women's livelihood and politics, see Amy Lind, "Power, Gender and Development: Popular Women's Organizations and the Politics of Needs in Ecuador," in *The making of Social Movements in Latin America: Identity, Strategy and Democracy*, ed. Arturo Escobar and Sonia Alvarez (Boulder, Colo.: Westview, 1991), 134–49; Caroline Moser, "Adjustment from Below: Low-Income Women, Time and the Triple Role in Guayaquil, Ecuador," in *Viva! Women and Protest in Latin America*, ed. Sarah A. Radcliffe and Sallie Westwood (London: Routledge, 1993), 173–96; and Victoria Lawson, "Tailoring Is a Profession, Seamstressing Is Work! Re-siting Work and Reworking Gender Identities among Artisanal Garment Workers in Quito," *Environment and Planning A* 31(2): 209–28.

5. On the UN meeting and preparation, see general discussion in Marysa Navarro and Susan Bourque, "Faultlines of Democratic Governance: a Gender Perspective," in *Fault Lines of Democracy in Post-transition Latin America*, ed. Felipe Aguero and Jeffrey Stark (Miami: North-South Center Press at the University of Miami, 1998).

6. On indigenous women, see Sarah Radcliffe, Nina Laurie, and Robert Andolina, "The Transnationalization of Gender and Reimagining Andean Indigenous Development," *Signs: Journal of Women in Culture and Society* 29, no. 2 (2003): 387–416. On rural women, see Lynne Phillips, "Women, Development and the State in Rural Ecuador," in *Rural Women and State Policy in Latin America*, ed. Carmen Diana Deere and Magdalena León (Boulder, Colo.: Westview, 1987), 105–23.

7. A. Menéndez Carrión, "Mujer y participación política en el Ecuador: Elementos para la conformación de una temática," Working Paper 4, FLACSO, Quito, 1989.

8. On state-gender relations, see S. Vega, "Replanteando nuestras estrategias de acción política," in *Jaque al Rey: Memorias del Taller "Participación Política de la Mujer,"* ed. Red de Educación Popular entre Mujeres (Quito: REPEM, 1994), 15–337.

9. See CEIMME, *Informe del sector no gubernamental, País Ecuador* (Quito: CEIMME, Quito, 1994).

10. On this electoral history, see M. Prieto, C. Rojo, and R. Rosero, "No sé quien nos irá a apoyar: El voto de la ecuatoriana en mayo de 1984," Centro de Planificación y Estudios Sociales, CEPLAES, Quito. On political remasculinization, see Nikki Craske, "Remasculinisation and the Neoliberal State in Latin America," in *Gender, Politics and the State*, ed. G. Waylen and V. Randall (London: Routledge, 1998), 100–120.

11. On Ecuador, see Rodas Morales, "Muchas voces, demasiados silencios," and on the Latin American context, Maxine Molyneux, "Twentieth-Century State Formations in Latin America."

12. On women's local politics, see Amy Lind, "Gender, Development and Urban Social Change: Women's Community Action in Global Cities," *World Development* 25(8): 1205–24; and María Arboleda, "Mujeres en el poder local en el Ecuador," in *Jaque al Rey: Memorias del Taller "Participación Política de la Mujer,"* ed. Red de Educación Popular entre Mujeres (Quito: REPEM, 1994), 41–72.

13. On domestic violence and sexuality, see Magdalena León, *Derechos sexuales y reproductivas: Avances constitucionales y perspectivas en Ecuador* (Quito: Federación Ecuatoriana de Acción y Educación para la Promoción de la Salud, 1999).

The Galápagos: Environmental Pressures and Social Opportunities

Pablo Ospina

Translated by Mayté Chiriboga

The Galápagos Islands are world famous for their spectacular wildlife and as the natural laboratory that helped Charles Darwin develop the theory of evolution by natural selection. Recognized as one of the world's true ecological treasures, the Galápagos are also a crucial tourist site for a country in desperate need of foreign currency. The historian and anthropologist Pablo Ospina explores this tension between, on the one hand, opening the islands to human observation, enjoyment, and use and, on the other, preserving this magnificent ecosystem.

Located 1,000 kilometers from the Ecuadorian coast in the Pacific Ocean, the Galápagos archipelago includes more than 100 small islands and islets that emerged through volcanic processes about 5 million years ago. The islands are home to around 5,000 species that arrived largely by chance and then evolved in relative geographic isolation. As a result of this isolation, more than 2,000 species are "endemic"; in other words, they are unique in the world.

Attracted by the laboratory-like quality of the Galápagos, Charles Darwin visited the archipelago in 1835 and, ironically, contributed to the region's growing integration into world currents (and hence undermined what attracted him there in the first place). His observation of local plants and animals in isolation helped him formulate one of the most influential theories of modern science: the theory of evolution by natural selection. The thirteen species of Galápagos finches, the variations of their beaks and behavior adaptations, are among the most renowned characters in modern science. The archipelago was declared a national park in 1959, in commemoration of the centenary of the publication of *The Origin of Species*. Darwin's visit, along with the islands' spectacular beauty, helped turn the region into a tourist attraction during the post–World War II period. Today, some 100,000 tourists visit the islands every year.

The human population of the Galápagos Islands is less famous but had an enduring impact on its wildlife. During the Spanish colonial period the islands were havens for pirates, and subsequently became a refuge for whalers and fishermen who decimated entire populations of tortoises and sea lions for the extraction of oil, meat, and fur. Beginning in 1832, Ecuador attempted to colonize the islands permanently. Floreana, an island at the south of the archipelago, which had fresh water, was the first to be occupied by settlers. It is likely that this small Ecuadorian colony, which Darwin found three years later, prevented the British from claiming sovereignty and allowed Ecuador to preserve its claim.

Ecuadorian efforts to colonize the islands were carried out by "enterprises" directed by audacious and violent men, obsessed with wealth but also with the intention of developing a new world in isolated, hostile lands. After several failures, the first "successful" settlement took place in San Cristóbal, the island farthest east; toward the end of the nineteenth century, a small sugar plantation was established on the island. Some time later, Isabela, on the extreme opposite side of the archipelago, was settled in order to exploit and export wild cattle and the oil of giant tortoises. Santa Cruz, an island located in the geographic center of the archipelago, was the last to be permanently settled by a civil colony, this time by a group of Europeans settlers attempting to create a "new world." The basic structure of human settlement was finally completed during the Second World War, when a North American military base was built on Baltra Island, north of Santa Cruz (in 1946 this base was turned over to Ecuador).

The current human population of the Galápagos is relatively small, around 18,000 people in 2001. Although part of a relatively poor country, the province of Galápagos, officially created only in 1973, has social indicators noticeably higher than those of continental Ecuador and relatively good public services. Although poverty has not been completely eliminated, the islands have only 2 percent unemployment. Life revolves around urban ports, and most people are wage earners connected somehow to the tourist industry.

Given the relative prosperity, it is not surprising that migration to the islands has increased since the 1970s. During the 1980s and 1990s, the population of the Galápagos grew at more than twice the rate of the country as a whole. Equally telling, in 1998 only a third of the total resident population of the islands was born in the province.

Environmental Challenges

People are engaged in four basic activities on the islands. Each threatens the region's delicate ecosystem in various ways. The first, agriculture, although limited largely to the production of food for the island's small population (as well as some cattle and coffee for export), has served to introduce numerous plants, insects, and exotic animal species that are not natural to the islands and have in some cases resulted in uncontrollable plagues. For example, the guava tree (*Psidium guajava*) has invaded practically the whole humid zone of southern Isabela, displacing not only native species but replacing entire ecosystems as well. Animals turned wild, such as goats and bulls, devastate giant tortoise colonies on almost every important island. The expansion of blackberries in the humid zone of San Cristóbal threatens nests and the re-production of endemic bird species such as the Galápagos Petrel (*Pterodroma phaeopygia*). In addition, the absence of local production of adequate food sup-plies requires importation from the continent, thus increasing the danger of introducing new seeds, insects, and diseases.

Fishing is a second trouble spot in terms of the ecosystem. Asian and North American demand encourages the extraction of certain species, such as lob-ster (specially *Panulirus penicillatus and P. gracilis*), sea cucumber (*Stichopus fus-cus*), and shark. It is estimated that by the year 2001, the local Galápagos fleet had fished at least 395 tons of fish, 66 tons of lobster, and more than 2.6 million of individual sea cucumber. International and national fishing fleets also com-pete for tuna. The main threat is not so much quantity as the fact that fishing efforts are concentrated on such a small number of coastal species.

Efforts to control fishing do exist. The Galápagos Marine Reserve, which excluded industrial fishing within forty miles of the islands' perimeter, was created in 1998. In 2001, the Galápagos Marine Reserve was declared a Heri-tage of Mankind by the UNESCO World Heritage Commission. The Marine Reserve's policies are defined by a governing board in which fishermen, tour-ism operators, conservation organizations, and the Ecuadorian government all participate. It is based on the principle of shared decision making in which local organizations and public institutions acknowledge, manage, compensate, and find limits for their varied interests. The process had a late start and ap-prenticeship is slow, but it is a necessary experience that aims at integrating local populations into the region's management. Without strong stakeholders, whose long-term interests can be maintained, it is difficult to imagine how the islands will be defended and preserved over the long run.

Besides agriculture and fishing, a third major activity on the islands is tour-ism. Tourism was stimulated after Galápagos National Park was declared in 1959, again with the establishment of the Charles Darwin Scientific Station (1961–64), and then more dramatically since the 1970s, as tourism became a ma-jor source of foreign revenue and as a way to fund the island's preservation.

Two-thirds of the islands' economically active population is involved in activities related with tourism. It is estimated that *local* annual income from tourism is close to 40 million dollars annually, while the country as a whole may receive at least 130 million dollars each year. More than eighty vessels offer guided visits to more than 90,000 visitors every year, of which close to 70,000 are foreigners, mostly North American. Tourism is highly regulated from an environmental standpoint. Nevertheless, some islands (or spaces) are overburdened with visitors. This causes congestion problems, path decay, and disruption of animal colonies.

In reality, the negative environmental effects of tourism are primarily indirect, and the situation is severe. Because tourism sustains the island's economy, it assumes continued growth, which in turn means more products and people are brought to the islands every year. Human migration, for its part, implies greater connection with the exterior world (the need for more trips, airplanes, cargo vessels, food supplies, etc.), therefore generating a greater risk for the introduction of exotic species that disturb the islands' ecosystems and jeopardize their existence.

The Galápagos Islands' fourth basic use is conservation. The islands are an object of scientific attraction, conservationist pilgrimage, and worldwide journalistic interest. The Galápagos National Park's annual management budget was slightly under 7 million dollars in 2003. If we add the Charles Darwin Scientific Station's budget of approximately 5 million dollars annually, and an array of additional conservation projects managed by agencies run partly by the state, we have a gross investment in conservation of slightly over 14 million dollars annually. By the year 2001, it was estimated that more than 400 people worked on the islands in the two main conservation institutions.

The most dangerous source of contamination on the island is that which people bring daily from the continent: *exotic species*. In time, insect species, seeds brought involuntarily, and diseases (viruses, bacteria) associated with persons, plants, and animals become fundamental health hazards that endanger the existence of the islands' ecosystems. The Galápagos Islands' distinctive characteristic and importance derive precisely from its genetic isolation. Continuous trips to and from the islands rupture the million-year isolation on which the singularity of the archipelago depends.

Environmental Conflicts and Social Challenges

From the point of view of environmental conservation, the need to build an efficient inspection and quarantine system is undoubtedly the first priority. This, in turn, depends on local stakeholders finding a compromise between the defense of their economic interests and the conservation of the resource they depend upon.

Toward this end a Special Law for Sustainable Development of the Galápagos was approved in Ecuador in 1998. The law defined a principle and a procedure. The principle was that the conservation of the Galápagos ecosystem would only be possible if local inhabitants participated in the prosperity and the decision making surrounding environmental management and development. The procedure consisted in organizing two institutions to define and apply development and conservation policies: the Inter-institutional Authority for the Management of the Galápagos Marine Reserve (Autoridad Interinstitucional para el Manejo de la Reserva Marina de Galápagos) and the Galápagos National Institute.

The special law was itself the product of political conflict among three local "stakeholders": tourism brokers, local fishing cooperatives, and environmental organizations. The Ecuadorian government responded to these conflicting pressures by declaring a commitment to both conserve and develop the islands. Once the law was passed, it marked an important change. The ongoing conflicts and debates moved from the street and parliament to institutions born from compromise in which all the key protagonists had a stake. This has meant—for better or worse—greater local control over the islands. It has also forced locals to ask tough questions: What might the Marine Reserve Management Plan look like? What fishing methods should be allowed? What types of tour vessels are permitted? What restrictions should be placed on migration? How can employment needs be met? These are pragmatic questions with complex answers. Nature and its protection are not only a real issue for stakeholders, but also a complex set of problems around which all participants must take a stand, define a position, and develop policies. Environmental issues may not be left apart, forgotten, neglected, or ignored. Too much is at stake for local and world history.

Emerald Freedom:

"With Pride in the Face of the Sun"

Norman E. Whitten Jr.

Located in the northwestern corner of Ecuador, the province of Esmeraldas is one of three "black" regions in Ecuador and home to the majority of the country's Afro-Hispanic people. As the anthropologist Norman E. Whitten Jr. demonstrates, Afro-Hispanic Esmeraldians have successfully struggled to not only survive but to create a space for black people within a nation that has frequently ignored or denigrated "blackness."

Esmeraldas, so named for its three-tiered canopied rainforest in northwest Ecuador, became home to self-liberated African and Afro-Hispanic people in the mid-1500s. Different groupings seized their freedom in the north and south of the province after fortuitous shipwrecks, intermarried with indigenous people, became the dominant force in the Emerald Province, and resisted all attempts by the Spanish military and the Roman Catholic Church to subdue and subvert them. In 1599 direct descendants of one grouping of the original maroons, fifty-six-year-old Don Francisco de Arobe and his two sons, Don Pedro and Don Domingo (ages twenty-two and eighteen respectively), journeyed to Quito to pay homage to the Spanish Court. Their portraits were painted by an indigenous artist, Andrés Sánchez Gallque, in a magnificent work entitled "Esmeraldas Ambassadors." Today, a restored version of this painting hangs in the Museo de Américas, Madrid. The historian Kris Lane captures the elegance of these Zambo lords in this manner:

> The men's noses, ears, and lips are studded with strange crescents and balls and tubes of gold. Beneath starched white ruffs flow finely bordered ponchos and capes of brocaded silk, their drape lovingly rendered by the painter: here a foil-like blue, there bronze, now bright orange against velvety black. Only don Francisco's poncho appears to be woolen, perhaps fashioned from imported Spanish broadcloth. The three are further adorned with matching shell necklaces, and don Francisco holds a supple,

black felt hat with a copper trim. Don Domingo holds a more pedestrian sombrero . . . and all three appear to be wearing fitted doublets of contemporary, late-Renaissance European style. These are all but hidden, nestled beneath flowing Chinese overgarments, which are, in turn, cut in a distinctly Andean fashion.[1]

Over four hundred and sixty years have passed since the first moments of *cimarronaje* (*marronage,* referring to maroons, self-liberated black or indigenous people) in Esmeraldas, and over four centuries have gone by since the aesthetic moment of magnificent representation of three of the elite of the earliest Afro-indigenous American republic. Through three hundred years of colonial rule that featured European-dominated gold lust, slavery of indigenous and African peoples, and a shift from a Renaissance to Baroque ethos, Afro-Hispanic Esmeraldians endured. They fought in the wars of liberation and later in the Ecuadorian Liberal Revolution. In the twenty-first century, as in previous centuries, they regard themselves proudly as the true Christians of Ecuador. They manifest some of the most Spanish and the most African music and storytelling in the Americas, and they are among the poorest people in contemporary Latin America.

Blackness in Ecuador

During the conquest and colonial era the Spanish divided up the people of their vast empire into two republics: that of the Spanish, and that of the *indios*. No place was ever created under colonial rule for black people, *los negros*, nor was a construction of blackness, *lo negro*, recognized. Afro-Latin American people created their own niches, environmental adaptations, ideologies, and cosmologies (figure 1). Among the core features of blackness in Ecuador, as in Colombia, Venezuela, and elsewhere in Latin America and the Caribbean, is the enduring emphasis on *freedom*. One is either free or not. There is no middle ground.

Three regions of Ecuador have been characterized as "black" from the colonial era to the present: the Province of Esmeraldas, in the rainforested and canopied coastal zone of the north; the Chota-Mira River Valley region, which undulates through the low Andean *montaña* slopes, also in the north; and the Catamayo Valley of *el austro* in the south of the country, where Amazonian and Andean piedmont regions are conjoined.

The first emerged in bursts of self-liberation in the mid-sixteenth century, just as the colonial Royal High Court (*audiencia*) of Quito was establishing its territory. The other two began with violent enslavement of African people by Europeans in the late sixteenth to early seventeenth century that created

Figure 1. A woman from the Chota-Mira Valley region selling food to travelers en route to San Lorenzo, 1963. (Photo by author)

two (of many) very different economies within the large and highly diverse Audiencia de Quito: one depended on plantation agriculture, the other on yeoman skills; both were based on the forced labor of enslaved African-descended people and Afro-Indigenous-descended people.

In the Chota-Mira Valley region, the Jesuits were the landowners, exploiters of the decimated indigenous population, importers of enslaved Africans, and owners and overseers of the expanding black slave population from their entry in 1586 until their expulsion in 1767. After the expulsion, enslaved people were auctioned to private *hacendados* by crown authorities. In the southern Province of Loja, black slavery was introduced by the latter quarter of the sixteenth century. Household servants, field workers, and itinerant gold miners from Colombia, Spain, and Africa were brought to the area by individuals. Fluency of intermarriage and migration in this sector led the various ethnicities there to dissipate into the general population by the late twentieth century. Black people exist in some numbers throughout Ecuador, in large metropolitan areas such as Quito and Guayaquil, and in the small Andean city, Ibarra. In the Amazonian region, Coca has a sizable Afro-Ecuadorian population. Nonetheless, most Ecuadorians erroneously associate all black people with either Esmeraldas or the Chota-Mira Valley, even those born and reared for generations elsewhere.

As the concept of Afro-Indigenous peoples, blackness clearly emerged as a national quality spanning coastal, Andean, and Amazonian regions. Its ethnic nationalist expression was called *négritude*, coined initially by the Martinique writer Aimée Césaire. As the movement surged under such cultural rubrics as "the advancement of the black community," and identification of the movement among white and black intellectuals was expressed by the representations *afro-ecuatorianos(as)* (Afro-Ecuadorians) and *afro-latinoamericanos(as)* (Afro–Latin Americans), varied associations between those so identifying and the indigenous movement came into being. By the twenty-first century the most common representations are *lo negro*, and afro-latinoamericanos, and less so *négritud* (Spanish for *négritude*, but with other meanings). As the concept of Afro-Indigenous peoples also became salient in national discourse, the concept of *zambaje* entered the Ecuadorian literary lexicon. *Zambo(a)* (sometimes *zambaigo*), long a term of identity and reference in Esmeraldas, and elsewhere in the Americas, signifies freedom and dignity. It refers to the genetic blending of African peoples with indigenous peoples. The epitome of such blending is historically embodied in the painting of the three cosmopolitan ambassadors and lords from Esmeraldas, described at the opening of this article. Significantly, perhaps, in the restoration of the Museo de Américas' painting, the features of zambaje described by Kris Lane, were transformed to very black, denying thereby the representation and significance of mixed heritage of the Afro-Indigenous *cimarrones*.

To be black in Ecuador is to be stigmatized by racialist and racist attributes, regardless of political power, class, or social esteem. A prominent black congressman from Esmeraldas, Jaime Hurtado González, founded the political party Democratic Popular Movement (MPD), and twice ran for president of the republic. In 1984, he obtained seven percent of the vote and in 1988 he gained five percent. In 1998 he and his two body guards were brutally assassinated in front of the legislative palace in Quito. Subsequent and to-date unfounded accusations of his alleged linkages with the Revolutionary Armed Forces of Colombia (FARC) were made and the Ecuadorian military occupied the black areas of the interior of Esmeraldas Province, especially the Ónzole River region. This is a region where Afro-Ecuadorians had recently been granted legal rights to land they had worked since the mid-sixteenth century. During this occupation an association was made between an unconfirmed accusation of a prominent congressman's involvement with radical Colombian politics, and an Ecuadorian region known for its "blackness" and its "remoteness." In the face of this military action, publicly espoused Blackness, as ideological *négritud*, retreated into local and regional discussion groups.

Many Ecuadorians express displeasure with the existence of black movements of self-assertion and often deny that Afro-Ecuadorians themselves ever asserted cultural constructs of blackness prior to the indigenous movement,

which erupted in 1990 with the first Levantamiento Indígena [Indigenous Upris-
ing]. Black pride, however, has long existed, side by side with self-deprecation.
Offered below is a poem, written by the late *esmeraldeño* Nelson Estupiñán Bass
in 1954—more than fifty years ago—to move the reader to a level of cultural
appreciation of, and pride in, blackness and enduring freedom in the face of
oppression:

Negro, negro renegrido,
negro, hermano del carbón,
negro de negros nacido,
negro ayer, mañana al hoy.

Black, black, blackened
black, brother of charcoal,
black of blacks born,
black yesterday, today, and
tomorrow.

Algunos creen insultarme
gritándole mi color
más yo mismo lo pregono
con orgullo frente al sol:
Negro he sido, negro soy,
negro vengo, negro voy,
negro bien negro nací
negro negro he de vivir,
y como negro morir."

Some believe they insult me
mocking my color
but I myself proclaim it
with pride in the face of the sun:
Black I have been, black I am,
black I come, black I go,
black real black I was born
black black I must live,
and as black must die.[2]

There can be no doubt about the affirmation of the identity of blackness in
this poem—*negro soy, negro voy*—it is first person, publicly personal, declara-
tive, poetic, and moving.

Esmeraldas: The Emerald Province

The land of Esmeraldas, and its free Afro-indigenous population, is the primary focus of this essay. But, in addition, Esmeraldas is shown to be a cultural system in a wider political-economic and cultural-ecological matrix that
ranges northward into Colombia.

Christianity pervades the cosmology of the *afro-esmeraldeños*. Some aficio-
nados of Afro-Americana and other scholars and activists are bothered by the
self-assertion of black people in this area that they are true Catholic Christians,
people who resisted subversion by the imperialism of the Roman Catholic
Church and resisted the ideology and praxis of inquisitorial curates. Esmeraldians nonetheless cooperate with priests, nuns, and brotherhoods who show
respect for their beliefs and practices. *Respect* is a key to understanding the
resilience of black people of Esmeraldas, as elsewhere. Those who respect the
people and their customs may move freely in and out of the Afro-Esmeraldian

world, but those who seek to deprecate or humiliate their persons and their lifeways may find people there to be uncooperative and unresponsive. Respect and freedom are clearly tied together in the twenty-first century as in the sixteenth through the twentieth. I say this at the outset so that the reader will appreciate the richness of cosmology, and not dismiss Afro-Ecuadorian culture as "assimilated" because of its Christianity.

CULTURAL POETICS

A predominantly male expression of cultural dynamics is that of the *décima*, a Spanish oral and written literary form common to Afro–Latin American regions of Latin America, and pervasive in Esmeraldas Province. Below is an example of part of a décima recorded by Juan García (1988), an Afro-Esmeraldian intellectual and activist from San Lorenzo, northern Esmeraldas:

El sol se vistió de luto,	The sun went into mourning,
la tierra se estremeció,	the earth began to shake,
las piedras lloraron sangre	the stones cried tears of blood
cuando Jesús expiró	When Jesus expired.[3]

The title of this décima is "The Passion of Christ." It falls into the cultural realm of *lo divino* (the divine), a heavenly zone accessible only through women (that contrasts with *lo humano*, the rest of the universe, including earth and hell). Although only men—usually those who are not literate—compose, memorize, pass down through generations, and recite décimas, women sing them during hymns of praise, and male singer-leaders of marimba bands utilize them in their sung music. They often constitute the poetic structure of riddles, and are a source of pride, reverence, and secular amusement throughout Esmeraldas, as in other sectors of the Pacific Lowlands of Panama, Colombia, and Ecuador. Any persons interested in literature and poetry, who are fluent in Spanish and have open minds and rich curiosity, should immerse themselves in this form of cultural poetics. It is one of many windows through which the cultural system of Afro-Esmeraldians may be appreciated and understood. Afro-Esmeraldians are part of Ecuadorian culture, as they have been since the founding of the Audiencia de Quito. They constitute a sector of a multicultural republic that nevertheless witnesses and encounters the rigidity of racist boundaries in thought and in action.

COSMOVISION

Ecuadorian ethnographer Diego Quiroga explicates very clearly key cosmological concepts that undergird Esmeraldian cultural systems: lo divino and lo humano, the domains of the divine and the human. Lo divino is far away and hard to reach. Indeed, only women can open the portals to lo divino, where God, Christ, Mary, saints, virgins, angels, and other powerful and benevolent figures reside. Lo humano is right here and right now, and its history extends back through times of terror, strife, and travail. All humans—men, women, and children—must live in the here and now with the history of exploitation and resistance, the multiple consequences thereof, and carry on their lives in the face of the kinds of development that produce wealth for the very few, and poverty for the many. Not only people live through their life cycles in the time-space of lo humano. Dangerous spirits, called *visiones* (apparitions), such as La Tunda, El Riviel, La Viuda, La Candela, El Hombre sin Cabeza, and *los duendes*, all dwell here too, as do those who have access to them and other forces of evil, such as the witches (*brujas*) and sorcerers (*brujos*) or conjurors.

The evils of contemporary life configure around the Christian figure of the devil (*el diablo, el gran demonio, el mismísimo*) often perceived to be a white, powerful *hacendado* or politician who binds women and the poor to his will. Living people may make a Faustian deal with el diablo for sterile wealth in this life, in exchange for the loss of one's soul and an eternity in hell after death. In reflecting on developmental processes, the accumulation of wealth, and the growth of capital, people of this region sometimes say that "en Es- meraldas ahora el diablo está en nosotros mismos" (now in Esmeraldas the devil lies within ourselves). Quiroga writes poetically about these phenom- ena that provide resources for what he calls "a system of critical thought" in contemporary Ecuador, a system that is used by Afro-Ecuadorian people (and others) in all walks of life to reflect on and express the phenomena of modernization, development, and racism that envelope and threaten their lifeways:

> In the new millennium there is a clear relationship between the forces and images of the *humano* and the processes of globalization and modernization. Nonetheless, care must be exercised. The spirits and apparitions that now seem to serve as devices of symbolic mediation have been around for a long time. In an effort to fit a paradigm based on the dichotomies modernity and capitalism, subsistence and accumulation, man and woman, globalization and the local economy, some authors may ignore the social complexity and cultural reflexivity implicit in these multivocalic mythical figures.

A diagram of the Afro-Esmeraldian cosmos (see figure 2) helps us follow the conceptual system that provides an inner set of cultural expressions rang- ing from daily talk to prize-winning literary virtuosity. This system consti- tutes the core of Afro-Esmeraldian culture, setting it off as distinct, and yet binding it to enduring *ecuatorianidad*. In the Afro-Esmeraldian cosmos the

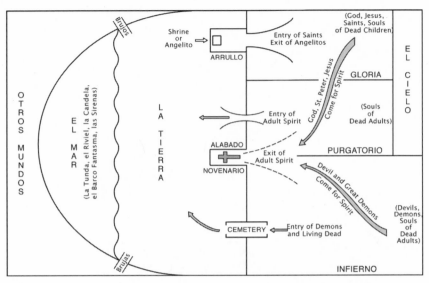

Figure 2. Afro-Esmeraldian cosmos. Drawing by Laird Starrik. (Courtesy of the author)

divine realm is that of the upper-right quadrant that includes heaven (*gloria*) and purgatory (*purgatorio*) in the sky. Otherwise the realm of other worlds, the sea, the land, and hell is of the human realm. To appreciate Afro-Esmeraldian culture in this sector of the lowland black Ecuadorian world, some characteristic ritual systems must be described. They include the secular ritual of the marimba dance of respect (*el baile marimba*), and the sacred rituals of the *arrullo* (song of praise), the *chigualo* (wake for a dead child, which includes the performance of *arrullos*), and the *alabado* and *novenario* (wake and second wake for a deceased adult). The secular ritual features male/female competition over the initiation of rhythms and dance patterns and the behavior of participants. In the public cultural performance of *la tropa* (military troop or troops) that begins the Tuesday or Wednesday before Easter and ends Easter day, this entire cosmovision becomes manifest in sustained ceremony. La tropa features both sacred and secular rituals of communal restoration and affirmation of cultural endurance as Christians and, perhaps in some areas, as free maroons.

THE MARIMBA DANCE

Also called the *baile de respeto* (dance of respect), the marimba (xylophone) dance is held in rural and urban areas. In Colombia, and previously in Ecuador, this was called the *currulao* and was and is performed in the Pacific Lowlands from Buenaventura south to Muisne. But today in Ecuador many

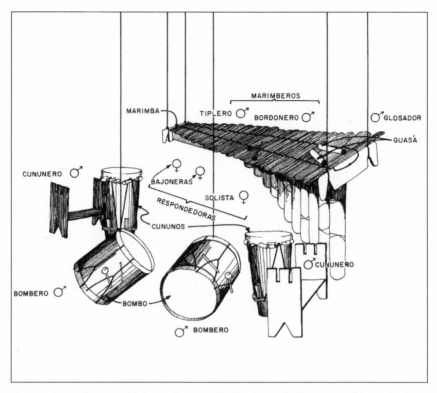

Figure 3. Marimba ensemble, 1970. Drawing by Laird Starrik. (Courtesy of the author)

performers deny that they would use the term *currulao*. Since the mid-1970s the marimba dance has become a provincial cultural focal point of modern Esmeraldas, with bands traveling nationally and internationally to festivals and competitions. The bands are usually composed of two male marimba players (*marimberos*), one of whom is a composer and singer (*glosador*); two base-drum (*bombo*) players, who follow the lead of the *glosador*; and two conga drum (*cununo*) players (see figure 3, above).

In counterpart to these musicians and percussionists are two (sometimes three) women, called *respondedoras*. They sing in response to the glosador and provide another rhythm with their *guasás*, which are bamboo tube shakers with hardwood (palm) nails driven into their bodies, and filled with black beans and maize to give a rainlike sound, *sheeee, sheeee*. Women control the two *cununeros*, who play conga drums. The two *marimberos* and two *bomberos* on one side, and the two women and two conga players (*cununeros*), on the other side, constitute an antagonistic and dynamic musical and percussive dialectic that generates the most African music in the Americas. No saints,

Figure 4. Shrine to San Antonio, San Lorenzo, 1963. During the *arrullo* this saint descends into the room with the shrine when bidden to do so by women. (Photo by author)

deities, demons, or tricksters enter the sphere, nor are there possession or trance states, which is why I call it a secular ritual. La Tunda—the body snatching seductress and fear creature of swamp and forest—approaches the house called *casa de la marimba* during the respect dance, but is driven away by the sound of the bombos.

Although the marimba dance used to be quite self-contained, over the last quarter century many transformations have occurred, including endeavors to incorporate Afro–Latin American and Afro-Caribbean dance music and rhythms while maintaining the basic repertoire of genres, the most common of which are called the *bambuco, caderona, agua larga, patacoré, juga (fuga), caramba,* and *andarele.* There is now one marimba school in South Quito, which was invited to play at the inauguration of the new President of the Republic in the Atahualpa Olympic Stadium on February 20, 2003. As the marimba band played a bambuco, commandos parachuted from Air Force planes into the stadium, one of them carrying Miss Ecuador 2002 as a "passenger." In San Lorenzo, northwest Ecuador, where there is another marimba school, the marimba has become part of some celebrations of the Catholic Mass. Sex or gender roles have shed some of their polarity over the past quarter century and one may now find men playing guasás and women playing cununos. But the structure of gendered musical roles endures.

Figures 5 and 6. End of the chigualo. Inebriated participants take the tiny corpse to the cemetery on the Río Santiago. (Photos by author)

ARRULLOS TO SAINTS AND VIRGINS AND
THE CHIGUALO FOR DEAD CHILDREN

African rhythms also dominate the songs of praise to saints and virgins, and in the *chigualo* where arrullos are sung and performed (figures 4 through 6, above). The sacred ritual contexts of arrullo and chigualo are initiated and

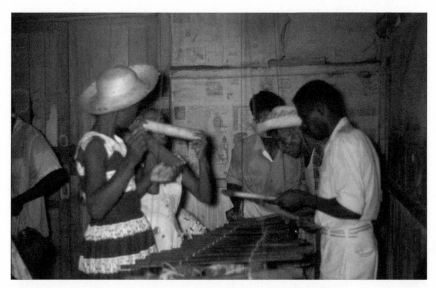

Figure 7. A marimba music ensemble, San Lorenzo, 1963. (Photo by author)

maintained strictly by women. They decide when and where an event is to be held, and they sing, direct both the bombero and cununero(s), and shake maracas. In their songs they open the realm of the divine all the way to heaven, bypassing purgatory. The restless and dangerous spirits of purgatory are kept from the living by the *bombo*, as is the devil, El Riviel, La Tunda, and the multiplicity of demons that would like to become a more decisive earthly force. In arrullo events where death has not occurred, the women open the divine realm to invite saints and virgins to their celebratory activities, and with permission from women, men may make petitions to these celestial beings for luck in fishing, farming, or commerce. The most prominent of saints to come through the gates of lo divino to visit the living is San Antonio (Saint Anthony), patron saint of fishermen and special consort of powerful women.

When the death of a child occurs, a chigualo is performed. The godparents of the little corpse assemble to petition the *cantadoras* (singers) to gather and sing, to open the gates of heaven to the deceased *angelito(a)*, and to locate and petition male bomberos and cununeros to come and perform so that no evil being snatches the corpse. In this context the conga drum is called a *cajita* (little box), and the player is known as *redoblante* (drummer). The coffin for the little child, too, is called a cajita. A chigualo may be held only with women singers and a bombero, but it cannot be held without the singers or without the base drum. The cantadoras open the portals to lo divino, and the bomberos keep evil beings at bay. It is said that the little angel goes directly to heaven, having died before he or she could "sin," there to

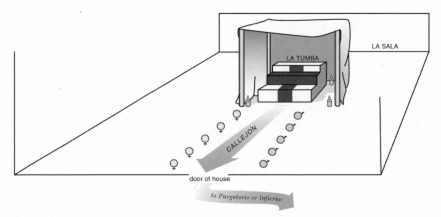

Figure 8. *La tumba.* 1970, Urbana, Ill. Drawing by Laird Starrik. (Courtesy of the author)

live forever with God, Christ, Mary, and the saints and virgins. Although the ceremony of the deceased child has been recorded in medieval Spain, the music itself, like that of the marimba dance, is the most distinctively African in the Americas.

THE ALABADO AND THE NOVENARIO

The house in which an adult dies is precariously balanced between earth, purgatory, and hell. During the wake following death, called *alabado*, and the second wake about nine days after burial, called *novenario*, men and women from the local community cooperate in all endeavors with incoming dispersed relatives. They express equality in their roles, which are jointly oriented to-ward maintaining solidarity of a grouping of kinspeople around the newly deceased person, while at the same time rearranging particular kin ties so that no one can trace a relationship through the deceased. Although much atten-tion is given to kinship by adults in the processes of gathering and commun-ing in this sacred ritual context, relationships of affinity and consanguinity are deliberately blurred. For example, a brother of a deceased man may regard the deceased's wife as his sister during and following the alabado-novenario, or formally broken affinal bonds may be recalled in a relinking of "cousins" to one another. Full cooperation between men and women is expressed: a coop-erative, egalitarian, male-female set of sex-role relationships is enacted as the living solemnly take a position against the dead.

Since no adult is thought to die without enacting sins during her or his lifetime, it is thought that adult souls go to purgatory. Before departing, how-ever, the soul of the deceased passes in and out of the house through windows and doors left open to facilitate its movements. It lingers in the neighborhood until after the novenario. Devils, demons, ghosts, and apparitions come to visit from the common domain of the *humano*. Thanks to the powers of women—as manifest in the lamenting songs—all of whom are *cantadoras* and some of whom are healers (*curanderas*), the realm of the *divino* is open to all, so that saints, virgins, and other divinities are brought from the distant domain to counteract the awful and dangerous powers unleashed by the wandering of sinful souls in the presence of such figures as *el gran demonio*. Women sing of such comings and goings of the soul, of demons, of fear creatures, and of divine creatures, even as living people come and go and join in choruses. Finally, if after nine days people are unsure where the wandering soul of the deceased may be, they enact a ceremony called *la tumba* (the tomb) to dismiss it. A structure (illustrated in figure 8, above) is built in the principal part of the house. Men and women form two rows. Women sing dirges as the soul is forced into the three-step construction that is draped with a black cross, called la tumba. The soul is then forced out of the tomb and into the *callejón* [corridor flanked by participants], and from there out the door of the house into purgatory or hell. As this occurs, women sing:

Te vas y me dejas, solito con Dios	You go and leave me, alone with God
Adiós, primo hermano	*Goodbye*, first cousin.

LA TROPA

This cultural performance is the most dramatic ceremony held in the Ecuadorian Province of Esmeraldas and in neighboring Colombian Departments of Nariño, Cauca, and Valle. It is a forceful enactment of the capture, crucifixion, and resurrection of Jesus Christ, that some take to be an extended dramatic metaphor of the formation of an Afro-indigenous maroon settlement and the resurrection of Christ within it. *La tropa* is enacted during the week leading up to Easter day, and ends with a secular parade, sometimes called Belén, on Easter Sunday. La tropa brings out-migrants back home from Esmeraldas and especially Guayaquil to small villages such as Güimbí on the Güimbí River and Selva Alegre on the Santiago River. Community ties are very important to many out-migrants, who spend considerable sums of money, and take up to two or three weeks from their urban lives, to make their way up the coast of Ecuador, and thence upriver by launch or canoe to attend this important and dramatic communal event.

The La tropa ceremony begins in the fringes of the community as groups of "soldiers" with shotguns, machetes, spears, and knives run off in directed squads to search for the lost or hidden Christ. But they find only the biblical thief, Barabbas. They then march in step on the church. They enter it, march within it, and eventually enact the killing of Christ, his removal from the cross, the reign of the devil on Saturday, the bringing of the forest into the Catholic Church within the black and free village, and perhaps the liberation of the people of the forest and of the true free church from oppression of Crown, Church, and later State. During this ceremony, women sing sacred *alabados* [songs of praise] to Christ and to the assembled "sinners." The tropa formation itself, composed strictly of adult men, march in a stylized manner to a drum beat not used in any other ritual. The stylized manner of marching and walking to and from the church and within the church has been recorded on film and audio tape since the 1940s.

After the enactment of Christ's resurrection on Easter Sunday, women take over the entire ceremony and lead the participants to and fro through main streets, back streets, and house yards to the songs of praise of the arrullos, and to national popular music. This street parade, called Belén ("Bethlehem," and also "bedlam") is led and controlled by women, just as in the arrullos and chigualos. Marimberos, bomberos, and cununeros participate and again are controlled by women, who dance, sing, and shake guasás or maracas. With the beginning of the Belén, the transformation from sacrality and connectivity with the divino to secularity and severance from that realm is instantaneous. Life in the realm of the human—with its myriad of dangers—is fully restored in festivity and joy:

Barrio de los negros	Barrio of blacks
de calles oscuras	of dark streets
preñadas de espantos,	bursting with spooks
que llevan, que asustan,	that carry off, that frighten,
que paran los pelos	that make hairs stand [rise]
en noches sin luna	on moonless nights
Barrio encendido,	Inflamed barrio
de noche y de día	by night and by day
infierno moreno,	dark hell,
envuelto en las llamas	enveloped in the flames
de son y alegría.	of rhythm and happiness.[4]

Political Economy and Cultural Ecology

Esmeraldas as a lowland Afro–Latin American cultural system extends from Muisne, just south of Esmeraldas, through the Departments (states) of Nariño, Cauca, Valle, and Chocó of Colombia into the Darién Province of Panama. In general, the cultural dimensions sketched in this essay are characteristic north to the San Juan River, which flows into the Pacific Ocean at Buenaventura, Colombia. From the San Juan north into Panama the cultural

Figure 9.
A man treks to his small
farm in the forest near La
Boca, 1963. These forests
are being decimated
by legal and, especially,
illegal lumber operations.
(Photo by author)

system configures somewhat differently. Reiterating a point made at the beginning of this essay, Afro-Esmeraldians are among the poorest people in
modern, twenty-first century Latin America.

In Esmeraldas a "boom/bust" economy is characteristic of the system to
which people have effectively adapted. Simply stated, when there is an external or "global" demand for a specific product such as cacao, ivory nut (*tagua*),
bananas, shrimp, or timber (figure 9, above), Afro-Esmeraldians enter the
capitalist market place as laborers and middlemen, and the towns and cities
of the regions become loci for crowded habitation and particular sets of social relations and cultural patterns. When the inevitable "bust" occurs, capital
is withdrawn, commodities lose most of their value, and work for pay is not
available. Then people continue their lives through subsistence activities focused on swidden horticulture of plantains, taro, rice, maize, and in the coastal
zones coconuts, fishing, and some hunting. Since the 1970s, Esmeraldas has
been beset by escalating and utterly devastating logging activities, many if not

Figure 10. A man forages within the mangrove forest between Pampanal and La Tolita de Pailón, 1963. From the 1990s, this ecosystem has been in the process of rampant destruction due to the expanding shrimp farms. (Photo by author)

most of them illegal, and since the 1990s by an explosion of shrimp farms that have ravished the rich mangrove swamps (figure 10, above).

The Pacific Lowlands of Panama, Colombia, and Ecuador is one of the wettest areas of the world. The shifting agriculture of this sector is known as "slash and mulch"; no burning is done. Rainfall is so heavy that although it is part of the neotropics (where Amazonian ecologies are the better known), manioc does not do well and constitutes only a backup root crop. Maize is common and taro is ubiquitous. Nonetheless, over the centuries, black people have adapted so effectively that this sector of South America in the twentieth and twenty-first centuries is as densely populated as any other rainforest region of the neotropics. The point must be underscored that such adaptation and population expansion take place during times of subsistence economic pursuits, as well as during times of participation in the global capitalist expanding economy (figures 11 and 12).

Long part of the scholarship of some historians, literary figures, and anthropologists, the subject of blackness in Ecuador surged into public consciousness in 1992. As Canelos Quichua, Achuar, and Shiwiar indigenous people marched from Amazonia to Quito to successfully claim legal usufruct to their ancestral and contemporary lands, the Afro-Ecuadorian movement surged in its rhetoric of respect and autonomy. Spokesmen and spokeswomen for

Figure 11. The beginning of a new settlement in a mangrove-flanked estuary. (Photo by author)

Figure 12. A woman grinds sugar cane on a sixteenth-century style *trapiche* in Mataje, near the Colombian border, 1963, near Tambillo. In the 1990s, Mataje became a central site for radical right-wing Colombian paramilitary atrocities. (Photo by author)

both movements stressed an end to nation-state nationalist racism, as bound in the concepts of "whitening" (*blanqueamiento*), "blending" or hybridization (*el mestizaje*), and "improving the race" (*mejorar la raza*) of indigenous and black people. A key phrase in these movements, which are, from time to time somewhat intertwined, came to be known by the trope *rescate de la dignidad nacional* (the rescue of national dignity). The solemn affirmation of this figure of speech is that the nation (*el nación*) and the country (*el país*) or motherland (*la patria*) of Ecuador cannot claim a dignity so long as the twin humiliations of racism and corruption work to the detriment of its Afro-Ecuadorian and indigenous people.

Notes

Because of space limitations, ten paragraphs were cut from the end of this chapter, including the entire section on "Globalization and Dominant Forces," which discusses Plan Colombia, the Colombian guerrillas and paramilitary forces, and the situation that led, in 2008, the U.S. State Department to declare northern Esmeraldas unsafe for U.S. travelers. For complete references and footnotes, consult the original and longer version of this article by the same title in *Tipití* 3, no. 1 (2005). In the spirit of sustained collaboration, a number of scholars have shared their manuscripts, ideas, and insights with me over many years, long before their material was published. I have learned much from their works, unpublished and published, and draw extensively from them here. For such collegiality I thank, in particular, Kris Lane, Diego Quiroga, Jean Muteba Rahier, and Padre Rafael Savoia. For helping me conceptualize racialized systems of cultural representation in broad frameworks, I am indebted to Arlene Torres and Dianne Pinderhughes. I thank Kris Lane, Diego Quiroga, Jean Rahier, Sibby Whitten, and Michelle Wibbelsman for a constructive reading of this manuscript.

1. Kris Lane, *Quito 1599: City and Colony in Transition* (Albuquerque: University of New Mexico Press, 2002), xi.

2. Nelson Estupiñán Bass, *Canción del niño negro y del incendio. Canto negro por la luz: Poemas para negros y blancos* (Esmeraldas: Casa de la Cultural Ecuatoriana, 1954), 50, 53. Translation by Norman E. Whitten Jr. and Arlene Torres.

3. Jean Muteba Rahier, ed., *Representations of Blackness and the Performance of Identities* (Westport, Conn.: Bergin and Garvey 1999), 19. Translation by Jean Muteba Rahier.

4. Antonio Preciado Bedoya, *Jolgorio: Poemas* (Quito: Casa de la Cultura Ecuatoriana, 1961), 121–22. Translation by Marvin Lewis.

Suing ChevronTexaco

Suzana Sawyer

*Conflicts between multinational corporations in search of natural resources (and pro-
fit) and indigenous groups in the Amazon have taken on global proportions, involving
human rights groups, U.S. and Latin American governments, the global media, international agencies, lawyers, and even the occasional rock star. As the anthropologist
Suzana Sawyer demonstrates, there is nothing simple about suing one of the largest oil
companies in the world for contaminating the environment and destroying the health
and culture of Amazonian Indians.*

Pablo spoke forcefully as he stood on the flatbed of a large truck seconding
as a stage. His words blared through loudspeakers as he rallied a crowd of
demonstrators to join his protest chant: "ChevronTexaco, ya viste, la justicia si existe." It was October 2003 and approximately 500 Amazonian peasants and Indians were gathered outside the Superior Court in Lago Agrio,
a ramshackle frontier town in the northern Ecuadorian rainforest. Unper-
turbed by the morning rains, men and women, young and old, had traveled
to Lago Agrio to mark what they called "the litigation of the century." Inside
the courthouse, the opening proceedings of a lawsuit against ChevronTexaco had just begun. Filed on behalf of 30,000 indigenous and nonindigenous
Amazonian residents, the suit alleged that Texaco recklessly contaminated
the local environment and endangered the health of local people during its
twenty-odd years of operating in Ecuador.

Carrying homemade placards and swaddled infants, burdened by their
stories and ailing bodies, plaintiffs bore witness—often speaking into the microphone—to the despair that Texaco's oil operations had brought them. Yet
their presence also gave witness to the power of a social movement capable
of both keeping the lawsuit alive and challenging transnational norms of corporate action. Together, marginalized Spanish-speaking peasants and Amazonian Indians demanded that the world's fifth-largest oil corporation be held
accountable for its actions in third world places.

Past the guarded metal gates, on the fourth floor of the superior court, 100 people packed a muggy courtroom. The superior court judge sat behind the dais at the head of the room. In front of him sat the legal teams for the opposing sides, each made up of Ecuadorian and U.S. lawyers. Among the spectators, a collection of plaintiffs listened expectantly, periodically relaying news to the demonstrators outside; foreign human rights and environmental activists watched attentively, if skeptically, to what to them appeared to be highly elaborate and arcane trial proceedings; and national and international reporters set up their video cameras and microphones, while security police and bodyguards watched over the crowd. All focused their attention on ChevronTexaco's chief lawyer as he proceeded, over the course of the day, to respond to the lawsuit and negate all charges.

Legal Wrangling in the U.S. Courts

October 2003 was not the first time the plaintiffs had appeared before a superior court. In point of fact, the hearing in Ecuador was the product of a decade-long legal battle over jurisdiction in the United States. In November 1993, a Philadelphia law firm filed the same class-action lawsuit against Texaco Inc. in the New York federal court for having caused environmental degradation and human illness in Ecuador. The lawsuit alleged (as it still does today) that Texaco made strategic decisions in its New York headquarters to maximize its corporate profits by using substandard technology in its Ecuadorian oil operations. Negligent industrial practices, in turn, the lawyers for the plaintiffs claim, strewed toxic wastes into water and soil systems throughout the region, severely contaminating the environment and jeopardizing the lives of local people.

The lawsuit contended that industrial negligence began in 1964 when Texaco first gained rights to an oil concession in the Ecuadorian Amazon. In 1967, the company—via its subsidiary Texaco Petroleum Company (TexPet)—discovered oil. By 1972, Texaco built the trans-Andean pipeline, connecting Amazonian oil fields with a Pacific port. Over the following twenty-eight years, Texaco produced over a billion barrels of crude, and in the process indelibly transformed the northern rainforest with thousands of miles of seismic grids, over 300 oil wells, more than 600 open waste pits, numerous processing facilities and pumping stations, an oil refinery, and the bare-bones infrastructure essential for petroleum operations. The network of roads linking oil wells facilitated the homesteading of the region by over 200,000 poor Spanish-speaking farmers or *colonos* (colonists). In 1992, Texaco's rights to use the concession ended, the company pulled out of Ecuador, and its operations reverted to the state petroleum company.

Although a number of Texaco's production practices between 1964 and 1992 are questionable, of greatest concern was (and still is) the effect of large, often soccer-field-size, earth-pits. Texaco dug these pits (at least two) along-side each exploratory and production well, and then dumped the sludge, formation waters, and unusable heavy crude that surface during the drilling process—along with the chemical muds and industrial solvents essential for drilling—untreated into these craters. When an oil well was proven to be productive, additional pits were dug at processing facilities where crude is separated out from the waters, sands, and gases also released from the earth. Unlined and open these excavated pits served as holding receptacles for eventual toxic seepage and overflow.

Even during the early years of Texaco's operations, it was standard industrial practice in the United States (and indeed law in Texas, the company's name-sake, since 1919) to reinject highly toxic formation waters and subterranean sands at least one mile below the surface of the earth, and to process chemical solvents until they were environmentally safe. According to the plaintiffs' lawyers, Texaco Inc. chose not to implement this technology in order to cut costs. The decision not to reinject toxic formation waters back into the subterranean strata from which they emerged allegedly reduced the company's per-barrel production costs by approximately $3 and saved the parent corporation roughly $5 billion over the course of its operations in Ecuador.

Although Texaco's practices were sufficiently effective to get and keep oil flowing, they were (and continue to be) harmful to the environment and humans. A growing number of studies document the detrimental and deadly effects of oil contamination on Amazonian populations: they report high rates of intestinal disease, miscarriages, birth deformities, and various cancers. Physical disorders, the plaintiffs argue, are a direct result of environmental contamination. According to them, Texaco executives in New York are ultimately accountable for decisions that condemned many Amazonian residents to living in toxic dumps.

At the time of the initial filing of the lawsuit in 1993, Texaco Inc. summarily denied all charges, claiming complete exoneration and motioning (on multiple occasions) that the case be dismissed from U.S. courts. The multinational corporation contended that a subsidiary-of-a-subsidiary-of-a-subsidiary-of-a-subsidiary was liable for operations in Ecuador and not the so-called parent company. This Texaco subsidiary four-times-removed was legally based in Quito, Ecuador's capital, and it was there, the multinational maintained, that Ecuadorian citizens would have to prove wrongdoing and seek restitution.

Three years after its original filing, the case was dismissed from the New York district court in November 1996. Two years later, in October 1998, the

Second Circuit Court of Appeals reversed the lower court's decision and reinstated the case. Two years after that, in June 2000, the New York district court dismissed the case once more. In August 2002, the Second Circuit Court of Appeals heard the case once more but this time upheld the lower court's decision and ruled that the case should be heard in Ecuador.

Forging a "Class" of Common Injury

Although this was not the ruling that the plaintiffs' lawyers had sought, much had changed in Ecuador between 1993 and 2003. When the lawsuit was first filed in New York, "class action" was a foreign concept in Ecuador. Were a collection of people wishing to sue a corporate entity for industrial contamination under Ecuadorian law, they would each have to do so individually; there was no legal mechanism by which they could sue as a group. Consequently, in order for the New York lawsuit truly to have substance, the "class" of the class action had to be constructed in the minds, hearts, and actions of the *colonos* and *indígenas* affected by Texaco's oil operations.

Forging a "class" was not easy, however. Texaco's operations covered a 400,000-hectare area—approximately three times the size of Manhattan. Colonos living in the area constituted a hodgepodge group of individuals who had arrived in the Amazon at various time periods and from diverse regions. They had no preexisting cohesive identity. To complicate matters more, colonos and indígenas were often quite antagonistic toward each other as a consequence of colonos having largely usurped and homesteaded indigenous lands. Despite the odds, in the early 1990s, diverse colono associations, a handful of urban barrio groups, and four Indian federations worked together to form the *Frente de Defensa de la Amazonia*—the organization that represents the plaintiffs.

During the 1990s, the *frente* emerged as a formidable force in the northern Amazon with the guidance and support of Ecuador's regional and pan-national indigenous confederations and a handful of national and international environmental rights organizations (specifically, Acción Ecológica, the progressive church, Oxfam America, and the Center for Economic and Social Rights). Early actions focused on organizing hundreds of workshops in rural communities to educate people about the lawsuit and the U.S. judicial process, the plaintiffs' legal rights in Ecuador and the United States, and the effects of oil contamination on human physiology and ecological systems. In addition, the frente coordinated direct actions in support of the lawsuit. The plaintiffs and their supporters organized marches and mobilizations, protests and occupations, to pressure the Ecuadorian executive branch to support the case, to lobby congress to enact protective legislation, to boycott Texaco gasoline, and to demonstrate to the corporation and the world the moral righteousness of their cause.

As Luz—a community organizer on the road heading north from Lago Agrio toward the Colombian border—recalled, the frente largely emerged among the colonos by strengthening and extending ad hoc groups of women who began lodging complaints with TexPet in the 1970s. "I remember," Luz said, "traveling to the company clinic when my son was an infant and meeting other women there whose babies were also covered in open sores." These women and their children were among the thousands of Amazonian residents who bathed, washed clothes, fished, and cleaned food in rivers whose waters and sediments reek of hydrocarbons. "Our children kept on getting sicker," Luz continued, "as the toxins and contamination got worse. The doctor told my neighbor that her five-year-old son had leukemia. "That was when we started to organize ourselves." Wastes from oil operations contain known carcinogens that bioaccumulate. And crude oil's most toxic components have been shown to negatively affect the reproductive and cellular development of all life forms. Children in particular are susceptible to many of petroleum's ill effects. Recent epidemiological studies report an increased incidence of skin and intestinal disease and tumors, miscarriages, reproductive abnormalities, and unusually high incidences of cancer in the region—most notably stomach, larynx, cervical, and, among children, leukemia. The neighbor's son died a few years after being diagnosed. Luz's now thirty-year-old son was one of the demonstrators outside the courthouse standing next to a large banner reading "Amazonía Libre de ChevronTóxico."

Demanding Accountability and Exercising Rights

From his ersatz stage, Pablo bellowed to the demonstrators gathered outside the superior court in Lago Agrio, "The hour of justice has arrived." Behind him a huge black banner read "JUSTICIA" in bold lettering. Both Pablo's words and the banner signaled that many—previously wary of Ecuador's judicial system—increasingly believed that the courts might treat them fairly. Although discrimination and injustice still abounded in Ecuador, much had also changed. Throughout the 1990s and into the next millennium, social upheaval rocked Ecuador; the frente was part of this broad-based social action. Between 1992 and 2003, popular groups—often led by CONAIE—pressed for far-reaching social and political changes, rejecting the neoliberal economic agenda which the government had adopted with unprecedented zeal. In addition to ousting three national presidents (Bucaram 1997, Mahuad 2000, and Gutiérrez 2005), this ever-burgeoning indigenous and nonindigenous movement compelled crucial constitutional reforms and legislative changes.

In the late 1990s, intense social pressure compelled the rewriting of the Ecuadorian Constitution. New articles of the 1998 Constitution state that living in a healthy environment is a collective right (art. 86) and that communities must be consulted and allowed to participate in state decisions that might affect the environment in which they live (art. 88). In 1998, Ecuador also signed the International Labor Organization's Convention 169, which recognizes the collective rights of indigenous peoples and their right to demand recompense should their territory or its resources be undermined. But one law in particular passed in 1999 formed the legal basis for the lawsuit when filed in Ecuador in 2003. The Ley de Gestión Ambiental specifically protects individuals against actions that violate environmental norms. And, it allows individuals to file the Ecuadorian equivalent of a class-action lawsuit—an *acción popular*—against entities that have allegedly undermined human health or the environment. Together, these legislative changes made the Ecuadorian court system more sympathetic than ever before to the plaintiffs and their plight.

Circumstances had also changed in the United States. In October 2001, Texaco Inc. merged with the Chevron Corporation. When the new corporation, the ChevronTexaco Corporation, moved its headquarters to San Ramon, California, Amazon Watch—an environmental rights NGO on the West Coast—expanded the U.S. campaign in support of the plaintiffs. The organization flew peasant and indigenous leaders to the United States on multiple occasions. It organized protests in front of corporate headquarters, where the Ecuadorians, carrying a poster-sized faux bill from the "Amazon Rainforest Collection Agency," demanded appointments with ChevronTexaco's CEO. Amazon Watch also organized meetings between visiting plaintiffs and residents of San Ramon. Community and religious leaders from California traveled to the contaminated regions of the Ecuadorian Amazon to see the effects of (now) ChevronTexaco's practices firsthand. With their growing concern, they formed an organization, San Ramon Cares, and have brought local pressure to bear on the corporation that calls their town home. In 2004 and 2005, Amazon Watch coordinated actions with Trillium—a socially responsible investment firm. Having garnered the support of a large state pension fund, they filed shareholder resolutions, and spoke at the annual shareholder meetings to educate stockholders of the lawsuit and actions in Ecuador.

Just as social justice and business concerns in the United States increased public scrutiny of corporate activity overseas, so intriguing developments on the legal front were rewriting the U.S. courts' capacity to extend their power beyond national jurisdiction. When the Second Circuit Court of Appeals decided that the class action should be heard in Ecuador, it made its ruling dependent on certain conditions. According to the plaintiffs' lawyers, because the case they presented was so compelling, the appellate court, in sending the lawsuit overseas, was obliged to circumscribe ChevronTexaco's defense for plausible deniability. The three conditions were (1) that Texaco Inc. submit to Ecuadorian law, (2) that documents obtained during the "discovery" period, which up to then had been confidential, could be used in an Ecuadorian trial, and (3) that the decision of the Ecuadorian court could be enforceable in the United States. In the words of one of the plaintiffs' U.S. lawyers, Cristóbal Bonifaz, "We won a victory when the New York court forced ChevronTexaco to show up [in Ecuador] and comply. Here we have a situation in which an American court forces an American company to appear before a Third World court and comply with whatever comes out of that court."

Many questions remain as to how the ongoing trial in Ecuador will be resolved. As outlined by the corporation's chief lawyer on the first day of the 2003 trial in Lago Agrio, ChevronTexaco (like Texaco Inc. before it) assertively claims that TexPet—not it—is the entity responsible for oil operations in Ecuador. Similarly, the corporation claims that TexPet's operations did not violate any Ecuadorian law and were in accordance with standards used in other tropical countries around the world. And finally, the corporation claims that it or any other entity cannot be sued for alleged activity that occurred between 1964 and 1992 on the basis of a law (Ley de Gestión Ambiental) that was enacted in 1999. Following the Ecuadorian juridical system, laws cannot be applied retroactively.

In response to these claims, the plaintiff's chief lawyer, Alberto Wray, replied:

> Regardless of what name used, regardless of what legal disguise deployed, Texaco caused environmental damages to the Ecuadorian Amazon. And the poison is still there today. It is simplistic to claim it is not. The plaintiffs are not against the exploitation of petroleum. Rather they are against the act of pursuing it aggressively, solely for the purpose of economic gain, and toward that end using production technologies that strewed toxic elements into the environment—which in turn caused harm to the people, fauna, and flora there—all the while knowing that there were less toxic ways of working. . . . We are not asking that any law be applied retroactively. To speak of contaminating elements is not to speak of a myth from the past. We are talking about a present danger that is still harming and causing injury to local people, animals, and the environment, and to you Honorable Judge.

Any final outcome of this lawsuit is surely to be long in coming. When the present trial ends, the losing side will appeal the verdict first with the superior court of appeals in Lago Agrio, and then the Ecuadorian supreme court in Quito. As of Spring 2005, however, the frente—working with a transnational network of U.S.- and Ecuadorian-based lawyers, social justice groups, and environmental rights organizations—has forged a formidable social movement that is transforming the relations between local communities and multinational capital, and in the process setting legal precedent. As the crowd standing on the street in front of the Lago Agrio courthouse affirmed: "Las pruebas te dimos, con eso te jodimos. ChevronTexaco no puedes, con nosotros nunca juegues."

Note

For more in-depth analysis with complete references and endnotes on the circumstances surrounding the legal case against Texaco (subsequently ChevronTexaco and now Chevron), please see Sawyer, "Fictions of Sovereignty: Prosthetic Petro-Capitalism, Neoliberal States, and Phantom-Like Citizens in Ecuador," *Journal of Latin American Anthropology* 6, no. 1 (2001): 156–97; Sawyer, "Bobbittizing Texaco: Dis-membering Corporate Capital and Re-membering the Nation in Ecuador," *Cultural Anthropology* 17, no. 2 (2002): 150–80; Sawyer, "Corporate Sovereignty in a Transnational Lawsuit," *Political and Legal Anthropology Review* 29, no. 1 (2006): 23–43; and Sawyer, "Empire/Multitude-State/Civil Society: Rethinking Topographies of Power in Ecuador and Beyond," *Social Analysis* 51, no. 2 (2007): 64–85. Much (but not all) of the ethnographic material in this chapter appears in Sawyer, "Empire/Multitude-State/Civil Society."

Arts of Amazonian and Andean Women

Dorothea Scott Whitten

Ecuadorians, both past and present, have produced a vast range of artistic expression in terms of quantity, form, and quality. The sociologist Dorothea Scott Whitten provides a useful map for understanding both the works of art—styles, historical context, place of production, and so on—and the artists themselves. In so doing, she pays particular attention to the gendered nature of artistic production within Ecuador's indigenous communities.

Ecuador hosts a treasury of art, writ large, and a treasure trove of arts, writ small. Among the treasury's collections are architectural gems, both colonial and contemporary; eighteenth-century paintings by Bernardo de Legarda and sculptures by his indigenous protégé, Manuel Chili ("Caspicara"); and twentieth-century paintings by internationally known artists such as Eduardo Kingman and Oswaldo Guayasamín. It also includes a vast archaeological testimony to numerous pre-Columbian cultural systems whose artists will forever remain unidentified.

In the treasure trove, travelers may discover a myriad of offerings that appeal to a variety of tastes and pocketbooks. Wood carvings, textiles, ceramics, jewelry, and leather work from all regions of the country find their way to major cities, where they are sold in galleries, shops, open-air markets, and on the streets. Amid handcrafted and machine-made items, the occasional "genuine indigenous artifact" such as a Waorani blowgun, may be found. The histories of these various purchasable, portable arts are sometimes clearly stated, sometimes unknown, and often misrepresented by the merchants. With some notable exceptions, the people who produce these small arts are regionally but not individually identified: finely embroidered table lines and blouses are made by "women from Zuleta," Imbabura Province, for instance; or balsa birds are carved and painted by "men from Pastaza Province" or more recently, "from Baños."

Exceptions to this anonymity include a number of studio artists who work in ceramics, jewelry, painting, or designer clothing as well as a smattering of master craftsmen and craftswomen featured in Cuvi.[1] Two more notable exceptions are artworks that are produced by indigenous women and that are publicly recognized in contrasting ways. These artworks are the ceramics or pottery (here used interchangeably) made by women from Pastaza Province, in Amazonian Ecuador, and paintings by women from Tigua, Cotopaxi Province, in Andean Ecuador.

Although published archaeological research of Amazonian Ecuador is scarce, there is evidence that dates ceramic manufacture here as early as 1500 to 500 years ago.[2] Amazonian pottery impressed early European explorers, particularly Francisco de Orellana and Hans Staden, in the 1500s. Some 300 years later, the British naturalist Richard Spruce traveled through the territory of the Canelos Quichua people of Pastaza and noted the constant use of delicate ceramics, even during canoe trips. On the basis of his field research in Ecuador during 1916–19 and 1928–29 and additional museum research, Rafael Karsten identified the various ceramic styles of indigenous people in Upper Amazonian regions of Peru and Ecuador.[3] He noted the fragility of the clay and added that "certain magical or animistic ideas seem to be associated with the very material used." He thought that the Canelos people in particular brought their ceramic art "to a remarkable degree of perfection."

More recently, Canelos Quichua ceramics have been extensively documented by scholars, and some popular publications give credit to women ceramists of Pastaza. A few galleries and shops in Quito provide general information about the origin and manufacture of the pottery but usually do not identify the potters individually. The artists do not sign their names on pieces, as do potters in the southwestern United States, but they develop distinct styles that are recognizable in design and execution. The work of master potters is admired within their own culture, where it is functional, and by a number of international collectors, for whom it is decorative.

This rich ceramic tradition produces two types of pottery. Smoke-blackened, unpainted wares are made to cook and to serve foods and beverages; sizes and shapes are designed according to specific uses. Decorated wares, beautifully painted with mineral dyes and coated with tree resin, are made to produce and serve *aswa*, the mildly fermented food beverage that is fundamental to the Canelos Quichua diet. Very large jars are made to ferment and store cooked manioc pulp from which aswa is made. The pulp is mixed with boiled water and served in delicate bowls to household members and guests. For ritual, ceremonial occasions, women make a variety of symbolically laden figurines with spouts from which aswa is served. Decorated pottery is far more popular than blackware in shops and galleries. One example of blackware and one figurine are shown here (figures 1 and 2).

Figure 1. Cachi manga, salt jar, by Soledad Vargas, 1986. (Photo by Norman E. Whitten Jr.)

The *cachi manga* (black jar) was made by the late Soledad Vargas of Rosario Yacu, Comuna San Jacinto del Pindo, near Puyo-Pastaza. She learned to make blackware from her mother, who was a daughter of the legendary Shuar shaman and leader "Nayapi" (Javier Vargas), who settled near Puyo in the late 1800s. He was among the men who trekked from the area to brine ponds near the Huallaga and Marañón Rivers, filled cachi manga with slushy, semiliquid brine, boiled it down, and then broke the jars to obtain solid chunks of salt. Soledad Vargas made this jar to inform the outer world of the history of this treacherous trip that took as long as eighteen months to two years to obtain a precious commodity.

The *machin runa* figurine is a representation of the monkey persona stranger from the outside world considered to be a threat or danger to indigenous people. Clara Santi Simbaña, now residing near Puyo, made this oil boss monkey-person (figure 2) during a period of intense petroleum exploration in this Upper Amazonian region. She placed his round head on a body shaped like an edible gourd. One hand shoves the baseball cap back on his head while he shouts orders to his indigenous workers, orders that they understand emotionally if not literally. Clara Santi Simbaña made this image of entrapment and domination to sell to tourists for much-needed money.

In contrast to the ceramics tradition, with its long history and functional base, the paintings of the Tigua area of Cotopaxi Province came into being

Figure 2.
Machin runa,
monkey-person,
by Clara Santi
Simbaña, 1980.
(Photo by Norman E.
Whitten Jr.)

only in the mid-to-late 1970s for purely commercial reasons. Julio Toaquiza is credited as the first person to transfer traditional painting on sheep-skin leather drum heads to rectangular leather surfaces stretched over wood frames. The paintings now hold a prominent place in a vibrant ethnic-tourist arts market and have been exhibited nationally and internationally. There are a number of artists who sell their works through cooperatives, to major galleries and small shops, and directly in open-air markets and on streets.

While painting began as a male endeavor, and still predominately is, in many cases it has become a family enterprise. Wives of painters maintain a strong role in sales, particularly in markets such as the weekend art fair in El Ejido Park, Quito. A dozen or more women have joined the ranks of signed artists—most men sign their paintings—and an unknown number paint wood boxes, trays, and wooden bowls that are usually not signed. Women draw on personal observations and experiences, myths and history lessons, to portray scenes of indigenous festivals, shamanic practices,

Figure 3. Day of the Dead, by Luzmila Toaquiza, 1999. (Photo by Norman E. Whitten Jr.)

domestic activities, and religious celebrations such as the birth of Jesus or All Souls' Day.

A depiction of events taking place on the Day of the Dead (All Souls' Day) was painted by Luzmila Toaquiza in 1999 (figure 3, above). The local priest is visiting an Andean home and is offered a drink by the host. Perhaps the priest has come for the wake of a couple who lie on a mat on the floor; they are covered by a blue blanket, and candles burn on a table next to them. A woman cooks food in large vats over a wood fire. One vat seems to be filled with potatoes, the other could be barley or quinoa, and two more steaming vats sit on the floor behind her. To her left is a pan or tub that holds three *cuy* (guinea pigs) about to be cooked for this special meal. In the center of the picture is a table full of bread dolls, babylike dough figures that the woman has baked and decorated to commemorate departed souls. Three hoes, used to break up hard, arid soil, are carefully tucked into ceiling cross beams. At the back of the room, an assortment of Andean clothing is hung along a rope: a black pleated skirt and brightly colored shawls, men's white pants and a pair of blue jeans, and a pair of fur-covered chaps. This array also includes a long leather rope for lassoing cattle and a double-faced festival mask, called *aya uma* (soul or spirit head).

Figure 4. Amazonian shaman in the Andes, by María Ermelinda Cuyo, 1991. (Photo by Norman E. Whitten Jr.)

María Ermelinda Cuyo, one of the earliest women painters, combined themes of shamanism, ritual fiesta, and history in her 1991 painting (figure 4, above). A well-known shaman from Pastaza, Domingo Salazar, who has traveled and treated patients in many Andean locations, is shown sitting on a simple log seat of power (*banco*) in the midst of a full-blown festival that features colorful masked costumed dancers, musicians, and other participants in Andean dress. From a nearby hilltop four *conquistadores*, the central one holding a book—probably the Bible—observe the ongoing fiesta, while their sailing vessels are anchored in the ocean west of the Andes. In this painting, María Ermelinda Cuyo not only transposed people and settings, but she also collapsed historic and geographic time and space into a dramatic indigenous chronotope.

As indigenous women of Pastaza and Tigua successfully market their arts to consumers and collectors, they may gain not only economically but also, perhaps, well-deserved recognition as individual artists and as participants in contemporary Ecuadorian society.

Notes

1. Pablo Cuvi, *Crafts of Ecuador* (Quito: Dinediciones, 1994).
2. Pedro Porras Garcés, *Investigaciones arqueológicos de las faldas de Sangay* (Quito: Impresión Artes Gráficas, 1987); Patricio Moncayo, "Archaeological Patrimony: Ecuador's Ama-

zon Region," in *Amazon Worlds: Peoples and Cultures of Ecuador's Amazon Region*, ed. Noemi Paymal and Catalina Sosa (Quito: Sinchi Sacha Foundation, 1993), 188–90.

3. Rafael Karsten, *The Head-Hunters of Western Amazonas: The Life and Culture of the Jibaro Indians of Eastern Ecuador and Peru*, Commentationes Humanarum Litterarum 2 (1) (Helsinki: Societas Scientiarum Fennica, 1935), 99–100.

The March against Neoliberalism, Quito, 1986. (Photo by Lucía Chiriboga, courtesy of Taller Visual)

VI

Cultures and Identities Redefined

During the last decade of the twentieth century, commonly held beliefs about the meanings of nationhood—What is means to be "Ecuadorian"—were challenged and redefined. With the peace treaty resolving the long-standing border dispute between Ecuador and Peru now signed, Ecuador could no longer rely on anti-Peruvian sentiment to bring the nation together. Likewise, the dubious notion that all Ecuadorians are "mestizo" was definitively shattered by indigenous and Afro-Ecuadorian movements. The Ecuadorian nation is now popularly understood and legally codified in the 1998 Constitution as multinational and multiethnic. Ecuadorian confidence was then eroded by the generalized economic and political crisis of 1999–2000, which ended with Ecuador surrendering its national currency, the sucre, by adopting the U.S. dollar. Dollarization, in turn, has opened economic opportunities for Colombians and Peruvians to enter the country and earn U.S. dollars, a process accelerated by the Colombian civil war and the resulting flow of refugees into Ecuador. All the while, Ecuadorians are leaving the homeland in growing numbers. Ecuador exports immigrants to the United States and Europe while importing cheap labor from neighboring countries.

These events and transformations are not without their contradictions. Take international migration, for instance. It often reinforces nationalist sentiments among those traveling to other countries while at the same time ensuring that many migrants and their children will never return "home." Transnational identities such as Ecuadorian American or Spanish Ecuadorian are now commonplace. At the same time, such immigration often makes life possible back in Ecuador. As in many other Latin American nations, remittances from immigrants have become one of the most important sources of revenue and foreign exchange within Ecuador. More and more families there are highly dependent on money from abroad to sustain life.

Migration has also exposed white and mestizo Ecuadorians to the realities of racism elsewhere in the world. Relatively white and wealthy Ecuadorians find themselves racialized as nonwhites in the United States and Spain. In the United States, Ecuadorians cease being Ecuadorian altogether as they are defined as "Hispanic" or even "Mexican." In Spain, Ecuadorians often find themselves as a source for cheap labor in agroexport agriculture and racialized as docile workers. The long-term impact of labeling Ecuadorian immigrants as an inferior and unequal "Other" remains unclear.

The Ecuadorians who perhaps best exemplify the global nature of changing identities and livelihoods are the indigenous people of Otavalo. Remarkably successful as a group, Otavaleños have been pioneers in seasonal traveling to sell their crafts and perform Andean music all over Europe and the Americas. The globalization of their culture due to migration abroad and the continued influx of tourists into Otavalo have brought a reinforcement and redefinition of indigenous identities. Otavaleños have chosen to preserve and even market their ethnicity, despite that the meanings of who is indigenous and what is indigenous culture are up for debate. Some young Otavalos are combining traditional cultural traits, such as male braids or female skirts, with Western symbols of youth culture and markers of status like fashionable and expensive tennis shoes, jeans, and T-shirts. Some are preserving and reinforcing their language, while for others to be indigenous does not mean speaking Kichwa. Many no longer see themselves as (nor are) peasants, and transnational migration has transformed them into the most cosmopolitan of Ecuadorians. All of these transformations have made the small city of Otavalo a unique place in Ecuador. It is perhaps the only city where indigenous people are buying prime real state from whites and mestizos. Moreover, it is the only place where some young mestizo males use indigenous dress in order to improve their sales in the tourist market and to have a better chance of seducing "gringas." At the same time, as Colloredo-Mansfeld's piece demonstrates, Otavaleños' embrace of the world market has been a double-edged sword.

The creation and empowerment of indigenous and black middle classes, and their visibility in spaces formerly restricted to whites and mestizos, have also brought to the fore the reality of Ecuadorian racism. Until recently, elites, as well as common folk, denied that racism was a fundamental feature of Ecuadorian society. It was often left to foreign scholars and observers to document what most Ecuadorians refused to acknowledge: the widespread presence of institutional and interpersonal racial discrimination. The increasing awareness of racism and of the need to fight against it has politicized indigenous and Afro-Ecuadorian organizations.

Struggles against racism have oscillated between demands for human and democratic rights and corporatist arrangements with the state. Some claims of indigenous and Afro-Ecuadorian organizations have focused on police brutality, and have pressed local authorities to follow laws that recognize the equality of all citizens. Other demands have sought the inclusion of the leadership of these movements into the state apparatus as representatives of all indigenous or Afro-Ecuadorians.

With the help of foreign donors, the state has been able to channel resources to groups of women, indigenous peoples, and Afro-Ecuadorians. The World Bank, for instance, in the late 1990s gave $40 million to ethnodevelopment projects for indigenous and black people. Some European states have funded development projects for indigenous people, and different nongovernmental organizations are targeting indigenous groups and to a lesser extent Afro-Ecuadorian groups.

Through the National Confederation of Indigenous Nationalities (CONAIE) the indigenous movement has been partially incorporated into the state. Indigenous organizations, for example, managed a program of literacy in Kichwa and other indigenous languages in the government of Osvaldo Hurtado (1981–84). CONAIE has administered bilingual education programs since the government of Rodrigo Borja (1988–92). It has even influenced an official change in Ecuador's national identity to "multicultural," declared in the country's 1998 Constitution.

Given the success of the indigenous movement, some Afro-Ecuadorian activists are following their strategies to negotiate with the state. They are presenting themselves as a nation that has occupied an ancestral territory and that has an autonomous culture. They are demanding state recognition and protection of their lands and resources to rescue and develop their culture. It is an open question as to whether struggles for distinction and cultural recognition will contribute to, eradicate, or diminish social inequality between different ethnic groups.

Indigenous and Afro identities are in constant flux. Even though leaders continue to argue that indigenous and Afro identities are fundamentally rural, not everyone is in agreement. According to the 2001 Census, 40 percent of Afro-Ecuadorians live in cities, and 12 percent of the indigenous population live in Quito and Guayaquil. Agriculture is neither their main source of income nor of employment. In some cases, such as Otavalo, corn production is becoming a symbol of ethnicity more than a source of income.

The possibilities for further democratization of culture, ethnicity, and society are present in Ecuador. At the same time, the struggles are not easy ones. Political and economic elites continue to threaten democracy. The difficulty of finding a path of national development that includes marginalized sectors of society remains Ecuador's greatest challenge.

National Identity and the First Black
Miss Ecuador (1995–96)

Jean Muteba Rahier

How can a black woman represent Ecuador? And how could the first black woman to ever participate in Miss Ecuador win the pageant? As the anthropologist Jean Muteba Rahier shows us, these simple questions move us quickly into larger and more complex issues of racism, national identity, blackness, and gender. This was no ordinary beauty contest.

Since the beginning of the republican history of the country, the white and white-mestizo elite has reproduced an Ecuadorian ideology of national identity which proclaims the mestizo as the prototype of modern citizenship. For the purpose of the present discussion, mestizo is defined as a "mixed race" individual who has both European (Spanish) and indigenous ancestry, a child of the Old and New Worlds.

For Erika Silva, two myths provide the ground within which the ideology of "Ecuadorianness" takes root. The first one, the "Myth of the Dominion on the Soil," has to do with territoriality. It presents Ecuador as a country rich in natural resources, with a varied environment blessed by nature. It also emphasizes the "crazy geography that the indigenous people could not dominate." Only the Spanish conquistadors were able to vanquish the rebellious nature from their initial settlement in Quito, from which they launched their enterprise of discovery and colonization. Numerous texts from Ecuadorian historiography and literature mythify Quito as the "heart of the mother country," "the hub," the command center of national life and history.

The second myth is the "Myth of the Vanquished Race." The various Ecuadorian indigenous communities constitute a vanquished race because they were the victims of a triple conquest: the conquest of geography, the conquest of the Inca, and the Spanish conquest. The latter conquest, "by defeating them, brought the possibility of the emergence of the nationality, because it gave birth to a new product: the mestizo, viewed as the unique and genuine

son of the land of the Americas." *Mestizaje* is understood as the very beginning of Ecuadorian history. It is the essence of Ecuadorianidad.

These myths are based on a belief in the indigenous population's inferi-
ority and on an unconditional admiration and identification with occidental
civilization. The Spanish conquest opened the road of national resurrection.
As Norman Whitten indicated when he explained the significance of the process of *blanqueamiento* in Ecuadorian society, this ideology of Ecuadorianness
as a "mestizo-ness" does not suggest that the white is "Indianizing" himself
but, on the contrary, that the Indian "whitens" himself racially (*métissage*, or
"race mixing") and culturally.

In this imagination of Ecuadorianness, there is logically no place for blacks;
they remain invisible. Afro-Ecuadorians constitute the ultimate Other, some
sort of a historical aberration, a noise in the ideological system of nationality,
a pollution in the genetic pool, the only true alien, the "noncitizen" par excellence; they are not part of mestizaje.

Miss Ecuador 1995–96

On the evening of November 9, 1995, in the Theater Bolívar in Quito, an event
occurred that took everybody by surprise. A black woman born in Quito, the
daughter of two black migrants, an Afro-Esmeraldian mother and an Afro-
Choteño father, was elected Miss Ecuador 1995–96. Her election was a bomb-
shell in Ecuadorian society. During the following weeks, the issues of racism and
national identity were passionately debated in the press (see figure below).

The decision of the pageant jury provoked strong negative responses.
"¿Como así una mujer negra va a representar al Ecuador?" (How can a black
woman represent Ecuador?). The first time a black woman participates in
the Miss Ecuador beauty pageant, she wins and becomes a symbol of Ecuadorianness for a year! To explain this aberration, a rumor circulated: the jury
had decided to elect Mónica Chalá because the next Miss Universe contest, at
which the new Miss Ecuador would represent the country, was to be held in
South Africa. Therefore, to augment Ecuador's chances to win and to please
Nelson Mandela, his government, and the Miss Universe jury, they had chosen the black candidate. The possibility that she had been elected because she
was the best contestant was not raised, because of the weight of the unease
and anxiety provoked by what was seen as the awkwardness of the situation:
a black woman as symbol of Ecuadorian femininity. This position was until
then exclusively occupied by young women whose racial identity and physical features could unequivocally celebrate white-mestizo-ness as the standard
of beauty, in accordance with the hegemonic ideology of mestizaje.

Miss Black
Ecuador on the
cover of *Vistazo*.

The election of Mónica Chalá made the edifice of the racial order tremble. People who usually did not regard the Miss Ecuador contest with interest, academics for instance, were brought into the discussion. An article by Jaime Bejarano in *El Comercio* (the major daily news of Quito) on November 21, 1995, expresses the malaise among whites and white mestizos caused by Mónica Chalá's election. Its tone reveals the strong intention of whites and white mestizos to domesticate Chalá's crowning by attenuating its defiance of the official ideology of national identity and by manipulating the significance of her election in order to reaffirm the validity of the official imagination of Ecuadorianidad. The author refers to Mónica Chalá's blackness and beauty in contradictory ways. On the one hand, he celebrates the ideology of mestizaje. On the other, probably because he wanted to present himself as a tolerant person capable of detecting aesthetic qualities in other "races," he explains the beauty of the "black Venus" by her "noncontaminated race," that is, by the fact that she is dark-skinned and that she has not been polluted by "race mixing."

A tall and curvy young woman of the black race triumphed in a national beauty contest . . . The actual interracial consensus, although it is only in the matter of aesthetic appreciation, cannot be but the result of an acknowledgment by the majority that Ecuador is a crucible of a variety of pigments, oversubtle mixture of ancestral lineages, amalgamated in a symbiosis with diverse epidermic contributions from other continents. . . . The silhouette and features of Mónica go beyond the frivolous and prosaic concept (of "sexual symbol"). She transmits, with her own radiation or os-mosis, an ingenuous gentle breeze that her race, still virgin from external contamination, keeps original and without damage. . . . Mónica Chalá is a Venus of ebony and jet, of the ones engendered by the nights of the full moon, conceived when the light shines in the penumbra.

Various black political activists and black public figures, such as soccer and basketball players, joined by progressive nonblack sectors of society, made statements reproduced in the press in support of the jury's vote. They also condemned the racism behind the comments that questioned Mónica Chalá's election. During an interview published in a November 9, 1995, article of the newspaper *Hoy* entitled "No soy menos ni más que nadie por el color de mi piel," "I Am neither Lesser nor Better that Anybody Else Because of the Color of My Skin," the new Miss Ecuador did, in a sense because of her "race," jus-tify her new symbolic position. It was something that, of course, none of the previous beauty queens ever had to do.

Beauty contests provide the space where a national, regional, or local group reemphasizes the values, concepts, and behaviors which it considers funda-mental for its sense of itself and its survival. "The beauty contest stage is where . . . identities and cultures can be—and frequently are—made public and visible." That is the reason why they are of great interest for the ruling elites who usually organize them. These elites create and maintain their hege-monic order through the manipulation and display of the female body.

By definition, beauty contests can also be controversial and provide a space for debates, discussions, and negotiations. That was the case of the Miss Ecua-dor 1995 contest. The controversy provoked by the election of Mónica Chalá was exclusively caused by her skin color, or "racial features." When looking more closely, one can understand that in fact all of the other aspects of her persona fit the format of the perfect woman for the role. The jury's decision makes sense because her personal qualities made her suitable for the position. Their vote must be understood within the context of greater transnational influence in postmodern Ecuadorian society.

If it is true that the decision of the jury denotes a certain tolerance of black-ness, it is no less true that what Mónica Chalá's election celebrates are neither the values of the Afro-Ecuadorian traditions found in the periphery of the national territory nor the qualities of the average and usually poor black woman. On the contrary, it is quite clear that her election proclaims the standards and values of postmodern Ecuadorian society, which are strongly influenced by transnational ideals produced in the postindustrialized societies of western Europe and North America. In these powerful centers of production of televisual and cinematic images, the black female body is as much commodified as the white one. It is not invisible anymore. There is no television transmitted fashion show, for instance, without black international models. And in the MTV and VHI music videos that are received 24 hours a day through cable in Quito and Guayaquil, the visual presence of black women entertainers is quantitatively equal to, or even, in certain shows, greater than the presence of white women. The strong success of black artists on the "world music scene" ensures a firm presence of blackness in the transnational musical and televisual images consumed in Quito and Guayaquil. The black body, and most particularly the feminine one, is now a medium (when it respects ideal measurements and profile) used to proclaim an international standard of beauty that includes racial diversity. From an Ecuadorian perspective, the foreign origin of these images confers on them some sort of respectability, a fashionable quality, and eventually presents them as models to be emulated. Thus it is not surprising that, in Ecuadorian television circles, specific black women with "good manners" and some education and with the appropriate body type (tall and skinny) can be seen as being à la mode.

The growth of transnational influences in urban Ecuadorian society during the past 20 years may be observed in the Ecuadorian television market. Since their creation, the television stations have provided an opening to the rest of the world. They adopted the American style of television, and their programs, which are frequently interrupted by commercials, often consist of retransmitted American (and secondarily European) entertainment or news shows translated in Spanish. In these television series (e.g., *The Cosby Show*), blacks can be portrayed in a position quite different from the point of view of the Ecuadorian racial order.

In the early 1990s because of the creation of a television cable company, the Ecuadorian stations began to compete more and more with foreign television channels. Every year, cable television expands its number of customers in Quito and Guayaquil. Most of the white and white-mestizo families are connected to cable, which gives access to more than 60 channels, mostly from the United States but also from France, Germany, the United Kingdom, and the Netherlands.

Furthermore, the white and white-mestizo elite, which controls the national industries, sometimes socializes with the American and European managers. Most of them obtained a degree from a U.S. university, where they still send their children (mostly their sons). They visit the United States (Miami, in particular) relatively frequently to take care of businesses and to receive health care.

National beauty contests, which usually constitute only a step toward the participation in the Miss Universe beauty pageant, are occasions when regional, national, and international influences can eventually conflict. Each election of a national beauty queen is the result of a negotiation between these different sets of values and preoccupations. The fact that the contest for Miss Ecuador 1995–96 was organized by one of the most successful Ecuadorian television stations, the Quito-based Ecuavisa, certainly illuminates the understanding of the contest (and of the crowning of Mónica Chalá, for that matter) as the result of such a compromise between regional, national, and transnational norms and ideals.

In 1995 the Miss Ecuador jury was composed of seven members: Yolanda Torres, an Ecuavisa producer, as the jury's president; Jamil Mahuad, Quito's mayor (who later became Ecuador's president); Gogó Anhalzer, clothing and jewelry designer; Gustavo Vallejo, president of the Ecuadorian Association of Advertisement Agencies; Lucía Fernández, ex–Miss Ecuador; Scott Jeffrey, executive of event sponsor Colgate-Palmolive Ecuador; and Marisol Rosero, actor and television show host. With the exception of the Colgate-Palmolive executive, who is a (white) U.S. citizen, all the members of the jury were, as is always the case, Ecuadorian whites or white mestizos. They resided in Quito or Guayaquil. They could all be included in the group of urban citizens who are more actively engaged in the transnational economy of goods, money, and ideas, and who probably studied television, communications, public relations, business, or another discipline in a U.S. university.

The election of Miss Ecuador follows the international format of national beauty pageants as they are performed elsewhere. Before the night of the contest, all the candidates spent some time with the organizers in order to rehearse the various performances of the competition. The afternoon of the contest day, they were all interviewed by the judges, one by one. Later, during the show transmitted live on Ecuavisa, the candidates paraded several times, dressed in various outfits: cocktail dress, "typical dress," swim suit, and evening gown. Between parades, they briefly responded to questions about their backgrounds, their personalities, and their plans for the future.

To participate in the Miss Ecuador contest, a young woman must first find, or be approached by, one or several private businesses that will sponsor her and that will take care of the expenses of her candidacy. She will then register with the organizing committee, as a representative of the province in which the city where she resides is located. One province may present more than one candidate. Since the contest is an event that mostly involves white and white-mestizo urban citizens, the provinces where the most important urban centers (Quito and Guayaquil) are located, Pichincha and Guayas Provinces, respectively, are usually represented by more than one candidate. The large businesses that can afford to be sponsors are established in these two cities. In the history of the contest, most of the elected beauty queens have been from either Pichincha or Guayas.

Mónica Chalá was born in Quito, the third of six children, to two black immigrants who came from the two traditional black communities of the country. Because she was born and living in Quito, she was one of the two representatives of the province of Pichincha. This was a point in her favor because of the regional bias that characterizes the Miss Ecuador contests in favor of Pichincha and Guayas. Claudia Acosta, queen of the third largest city, Cuenca, was convinced that "a similar black woman would not have won if she was representing the province of Esmeraldas or any other province, because of the regionalism."

Mónica Chalá's personal history presented a series of other advantages. She was already known in the urban public sphere because she is the sister of national athlete, Liliana Chalá, who represented the country numerous times at international sports events. With her sister, Mónica had previously participated in fashion and modeling shows and had registered in a modeling school in Quito. Before participating in the contest, she had done a television advertisement with Ecuadorian soccer hero Alex Aguinaga for a national bank. It was after the production of this advertisement that some people (she does not state whom) proposed to her that she participate in the Miss Ecuador contest. She was delighted by the idea. According to the international and corporate standard of feminine beauty, Mónica Chalá has the physical characteristics expected from young women who want to succeed in modeling (tall and thin). She is aware of the market value of her body and takes her modeling career seriously.

Very understandably, she interpreted her election as primarily the story of personal and familial success. If she became Miss Ecuador, she rightfully said, it was primarily because of her work, her determination, her efforts, her personal qualities, and not because the next Miss Universe contest would be organized in South Africa. In various interviews she insisted on the victory that her election represented for black and indigenous people. But her political ambitions stopped there. She never chose to speak as a representative of Afro-Ecuadorian people. She did not attempt any critique of the racial order or the economic and political processes that work to produce the discrimination from which the bulk of Afro-Ecuadorians suffer. Her strongest idea about what a "good Miss Ecuador" should do seems to have been avoiding making waves. She was more preoccupied by "representing Ecuador as a whole" than echoing Afro-Ecuadorian voices. She received specific indications from Ecuavisa not to do so. The blackness with which she identifies is not the rural Ecuadorian blackness, which is totally foreign to her, but the blackness of international fashion shows, of MTV and VH1, the blackness of Janet Jackson and Whitney Houston, of Naomi Campbell and Iman.

Black political activists have mixed feelings about Mónica. On the one hand, they appreciate the affirmation of black presence that her election proclaims to Ecuadorian society and to the rest of the world. On the other hand, they resent Mónica for not identifying more with the Afro-Ecuadorian communities and their political struggle. On the night of her election, some say, she only spoke about her wanting to represent the entire country, "as if she was preoccupied with minimizing her blackness." Her most important message seems to have been that it is not because you are black that you cannot participate in modernity. She strongly identified with urban culture and never mentioned Afro-Choteño or Afro-Esmeraldian cultural traditions and histories of exploitation and resistance. Fundamentally, they resent her lack of rebellion against the processes of domestication which she has undergone.

Her election came as a surprise to most Afro-Ecuadorians, particularly to those who live in rural areas. Before the contest, she had not been in touch with the black organizations. Most blacks did not even know she was competing. Her victory was not directly theirs since they had not been involved in her candidacy.

When I left Ecuador in January 1996, there were some plans by black leaders to try to use Chalá as a public figure to give more notoriety to their struggle. They were talking about the organization of various events in Esmeraldas Province and the Chota-Mira Valley to which they would invite her and the press. The only question was: Will she accept the invitation? When I returned to Ecuador in November 1996, I found out that she had declined all offers.

If it is true that the election of Mónica Chalá expresses a greater tolerance toward blackness and black presence in urban Ecuadorian society, the sort of postmodern multiculturalism that can be observed elsewhere, the story of her crowning does not fundamentally contradict important aspects of the Ecuadorian racial/spatial order. It demonstrates how the subversive fact of her election has been defused. The jury's decision, although opposed by many non-Afro-Ecuadorians, celebrates a form of domesticated blackness which does not really threaten the values of national society and the racial/spatial order, unlike the blackness of rural areas or the blackness found in various black political activists' discourses. The validity of the ideas of progress and development that spatially structure the national racial order was not questioned by Mónica's triumph or by Mónica herself. Despite her black skin, she identified neither with the traditionally black places in the periphery of the national space nor with the hardship experienced by the black migrants in Quito.

The domestication of Mónica Chalá by white-mestizo society also involved treating her as a second-class beauty queen. On April 18, 1997, for instance, the night of the election of her successor, Mónica Chalá and her mother were relegated to seats on the fourth line, with the rest of the audience, in contrast to what had been done in the past with previous queens, who had been much more actively involved in the shows celebrating the designation of their successors. She was invited on the podium only a few minutes before the crowning of her successor.

The Miss Universe contest at which she participated did not take place in South Africa but in Las Vegas. For that setting, she underwent a change of look, which she had maintained until recently. She straightened her hair and wears tinted contact lenses, which transformed her naturally dark brown eyes to a light almond. This change of look is the embodiment of her domestication. It evokes the national ideology of blanqueamiento within the globalizing framework of mestizaje.

Ecuadorian racism is alive and well.

Note

For complete references and bibliography, please consult "Blackness, the Racial/Spatial Order, Migrations, and Miss Ecuador 1995–96," *American Anthropologist* 100, no. 2 (June 1998): 421–30.

Ecuadorian International Migration

Brad D. Jokisch and David Kyle

One in ten Ecuadorians now live in other countries, most notably the United States and Spain, and as a group they send back almost $2 billion a year to Ecuador. Although the origin of this movement dates back decades, most migrants left Ecuador within the past quarter of a century, with the great majority leaving after 1990. This contribution, by the geographer Brad D. Jokisch and the sociologist David Kyle, examines the how, why, where, and who of Ecuadorian overseas migration.

Two blocks from Cuenca's main plaza (Parque Calderón) is a store named "Quishpe Express." The owners advertise it as an "international mail service" and list New York, Chicago, and Minneapolis as the destinations for postal goods. The sign above the door—suggestively painted in red, white, and blue—boasts delivery of local food, medicine, documents, liquor, and guinea pigs (*cuy*) in two days. Newark, Ossining (New York), and Minneapolis are added as other U.S. destinations, as well as Spain and Peru. Cuencanos do not even notice these parallel post offices anymore; there are hundreds in Ecuador—even small towns have branch offices. Tourists from the United States may not notice the store, but if they understand its purpose they may feel that it is not the "real" Ecuador, not the exotic Andes they want. They may even feel contempt for people who left such a beautiful place, and they assume that greed must have motivated the migrants who receive these goods. Other multipurpose agencies can be found in the same neighborhood. Delgado Travel, for example, offers services to migrants and their families; most of their business originates in the United States where migrants send money, letters, videotapes, and other goods to the offices in Ecuador where family and friends retrieve the materials.

What makes Quishpe Express noteworthy is that it illustrates the evolving geography of Ecuadorian migration and Ecuador's integration into the global economy. New York and Chicago were the first destinations of migrants from this region and eventually Ecuadorians moved to Minneapolis and even to the suburbs of New York, such as Ossining. In the late 1990s, Ecuador experienced a mass migration to Spain, of more than half a million people. They have since become the largest immigrant group there. The Peru sign hints at a more recent peculiarity in Ecuadorian migration; Peruvians now immigrate to Ecuador because they can earn higher wages and some can make their way to the United States through Ecuador. Even the name Quishpe suggests the ethnicity of many of the migrants. Quishpe is a Quichua word, the most commonly spoken indigenous language. The name is common among native Ecuadorians and among people referred to as "cholos," or mestizos who have been economically deprived, poorly educated, and otherwise occupy a low socioeconomic position.

How did international migration become so important to this country of 13.4 million people? At least 1.5 million Ecuadorians (11 percent) live overseas, mostly in the United States and Spain. As a group they send home (remit) more than $1.7 billion annually, which is equivalent to roughly 5.5 percent of the country's GDP. Remittances are more important than tourism and even banana exports (Ecuador is the world's largest exporter of bananas); only petroleum exports bring more money into Ecuador than remittances. The United States Census Bureau estimated that in 2003 between 400,000 and 500,000 Ecuadorians lived in the United States, although determining an accurate figure is difficult because thousands of Ecuadorians arrived without legal permission. Ecuadorians are heavily concentrated in metropolitan New York and constitute one of the largest immigrant groups in New York City. As many as 90,000 Ecuadorians live in the borough of Queens, with a concentration in the neighborhoods of Corona and Jackson Heights. A similar number of Ecuadorians can be found in Spain; the government estimated that 491,800 Ecuadorians lived there in 2005. Smaller populations live in Italy, the Netherlands, France, and Canada. More than one million people rely directly on the remittances that return to the country. Ecuador is not, however, only an emigrant country, sending thousands abroad annually: in the past five years, it has also become an immigrant country. Ecuador's dollarized economy has attracted not only Peruvians, as mentioned earlier, but Colombians, and a smaller but growing number of Chinese.

Migration to New York

In 1974, Geographer David Preston remarked that when he was working in rural Cañar, "Seldom a day of fieldwork went by without one person being encountered, even casually by the road side, who had recently returned from a spell in New York or Chicago."[1] Preston was working in mestizo agricultural communities (cholos) where most families cultivated small plots of land devoted to subsistence agriculture, wove straw hats (Panama hats), and had a history of domestic migration to Guayaquil, the coast, and the Oriente (eastern lowland provinces). Since the 1840s Panama hats had been woven by peasants and exported to the United States through importers in New York. The collapse of the Panama hat trade during the 1950s and the subsequent regional economic depression proved critical for Ecuadorian emigration. Men from Azuay and Cañar literally followed the Panama hat trail to New York. These early migrants began a rural-to-urban international migration stream and paved the way for other family members to join them in New York, initiating what would become a mass migration during the 1980s.

International migrants commonly have multiple reasons for migrating. Usually, there are structural reasons, such as an economic crisis (the collapse of the Panama hat industry) and personal reasons such as a desire to build a house, get out of debt, join a sibling or spouse, or even escape sexist cultural norms or domestic violence. Invariably, however, Ecuadorians depart with the intention of returning, hopefully with enough money to afford necessities and some luxuries that few jobs in Ecuador permit. This plan to return strongly influences their behavior in the United States, although the reality of their lives undermines their ability to act on this desire.

Ecuadorians have exploited a variety of methods to get to the United States surreptitiously. Many early migrants (before 1985) flew legally to Mexico and then crossed the U.S. border with the help of a coyote—a smuggler of people. In the early 1980s, the trip was generally not very dangerous or expensive, especially if the migrants could obtain a visa to Mexico. Approximately $1,200 was necessary, and the likelihood of arriving was good. Some migrants paid forgers for falsified U.S. visas or substituted photos on passports with legitimate visas. If the forged documents worked, then the trip to New York lasted only one or two flights. To finance the clandestine trip, some migrants sold land or livestock, but more commonly migrants borrowed money from *chulqueros*, usurious money lenders, at 4 to 8 percent monthly interest, and used the family land, house, and other valuables as collateral.

During the 1990s the trip to the United States became increasingly expensive and dangerous, and the business of smuggling became more underground and complex. The demand for Mexican visas was greater than the supply; many Ecuadorians were forced into traveling to Central American republics and border-hopped their way to the United States. Coyotes usually arranged for migrants to meet another coyote in the intermediate country, who passed them along to the next coyote, until they arrived in New York. Migrants commonly give half of the money to the coyote in Ecuador, and a family member delivers the other half once the migrant arrives and phones the family member with the news of arrival. If all goes well, migrants can reach their destination in two to three weeks, but sometimes the trip can take a month or longer. The cost of migrating illegally increased from approximately $6,000 in 1995 to over $13,000 in 2005. Coyotes now offer would-be migrants the opportunity of three attempts for the same price. If a migrant is detained and deported along the way, then he or she can make up to three tries. Although more migrants have been caught en route in the past five years, we calculated in one community that since the late 1980s fewer than 1 in 5 were caught by migration officials in Mexico, the United States, or a Central American republic.

Economic Chaos and Destination Spain

Just as the Panama hat collapse of the 1950s was the catalyst for migration to New York and the economic crisis of the early 1980s transformed the migration into a mass migration, the economic and political crisis of the late 1990s created a radical reorientation of Ecuadorian migration. After fighting a costly border skirmish with Peru in 1995, Ecuador suffered five presidents in five years (1996–2000) and descended into what may be its worst economic crisis ever. A disastrous El Niño in 1997 and low petroleum prices were followed by hyperinflation and a banking crisis caused by corruption at the highest levels, prompting President Mahuad to freeze bank accounts. By 1999 poverty had risen to over 40 percent and the GDP fell to the level of the foreign debt. Ecuador eliminated its currency, the sucre, and adopted the U.S. dollar in 2000, and was forced to accept harsh austerity measures from the International Monetary Fund. Ecuadorians responded to the economic and political crisis by continuing to migrate to the United States, but more important, a mass exodus to Spain ensued. Led initially by women, thousands of Ecuadorians per month flew to Spain, posing as tourists, and entered the country to look for work. In 1998 it is likely that fewer than 10,000 Ecuadorians lived in Spain. By 2002 as many as 200,000 resided in Spain; the number doubled again in less than three years to reach over 500,000 in 2005. In 2004–5 Spain offered an amnesty to immigrants living without proper documentation, and more than 140,000 Ecuadorians had their status converted from illegal to legal. Ecuadorians are either the largest immigrant group in Spain or a very close second to Moroccans.

A disproportionate percentage of Ecuadorians living in the United States originate from the southern highlands surrounding Cuenca, but the Spain-bound migrants lack such geographic concentration. Migrants have departed from all provinces, though it appears that Quiteños are overrepresented.

During the latest crisis, Ecuadorians, especially those from Azuay and Cañar who had family members in the United States, continued to go to the United States, but the increasing difficulties of traveling through Central America or flying directly to Mexico pushed the migrant route onto fishing trawlers. In March 1999 the U.S. Coast Guard discovered the maritime route by intercepting a trawler loaded with migrants bound for Mexico. Since then, the USCG has intercepted nearly 7,000 migrants on boats; in 2002 more Ecuadorians (1,608) were detained by the USCG than any other nationality, including Cubans and Haitians. When a boat is detained, the Ecuadorians are usually taken to the nearest port, usually in Central America or Mexico, not in the United States. U.S. State Department officials fly to the scene and try to identify the smugglers, who will likely be taken to the United States to be prosecuted. The migrants are simply returned to Ecuador.

Although the USCG's mission is to stop both migrants and drug shipments, it is important to distinguish between migrant smuggling and drug smuggling. Drug smuggling may take similar routes through the eastern Pacific and through Central America and Mexico, but it does not appear to be connected with human smuggling. When the USCG intercepts a trawler, it is loaded with human cargo, not drugs. Although a small number of Ecuadorians profit from drug smuggling, only a tiny fraction of the migrants struggling to join friends and family in the United States are connected in any way with drug smuggling.

Both the overland and maritime routes are dangerous and have resulted in dozens of deaths. Some migrants have died in the desert of northern Mexico or Arizona, and boating accidents have taken the lives of other Ecuadorians. The USCG and authorities from other countries have prevented more loss of life by rescuing trawlers in distress. In late May 2005 a Costa Rican fishing boat pulled in its lines to find a bottle that had been tied to the line. A note in the bottle read "Auxilio, por favor, ayúdennos" (Help, please, help us). It had been tied to the line by an Ecuadorian who was aboard a trawler with eighty-seven other Ecuadorians and Peruvians. Their boat had been adrift and taking on water for two days when the fishing vessel alerted Costa Rican authorities, who rescued them. The migrants had been without food or water for two days, and they were afraid that the ship would sink within the next day.

Transnational Limbo between New York and Ecuador

By 1993 "Jesús" had been shuttling between New York City and his hometown in rural Cañar for ten years. He went to the United Sates in his late teens without documentation and spent many years knowing his three children only through videotapes and occasional phone conversations. Jesús had worked hard in the United States; he took English classes and worked in a series of restaurants, eventually becoming a chef. He managed to get residency and citizenship through the 1986 amnesty offered by the United States. His legal status allowed him to return to Cañar annually to see his family. Jesús was living transnationally; he lived in Queens and worked in Manhattan, but spent much of what he earned in Ecuador building a house and taking care of his family. He was adamant that he would not take his family to the United States, but was concerned about whether he could make a living in Ecuador. He wanted to open a small store as other migrants had done, but he needed to earn more money in the United States before he could return permanently.

In 2003 we had the good fortune to meet Jesús in Cañar, home again on vacation. His wife had exchanged her skirt for jeans. His eldest son, "Enrique," was a bilingual honors student proudly displaying his new "Gameboy." Jesús had done what he said he would never do; he had taken his entire family to the United States. His citizenship allowed him to legally sponsor his family's migration. He still worked as a chef, but he now owned a house in Queens, living on one floor and renting the other floors to fellow Ecuadorian immigrants. He was in the process of purchasing another house, a rental. His family had not been back in Ecuador for three years; they returned to visit family and to take care of medical problems. Jesús did not have health insurance, but his dollars were sufficient to pay for health care in Ecuador. His Ecuadorian home was occupied by an in-law. Jesús showed us around his hometown, which was nearly deserted. Like him, most of the community had lived transnationally for many years, but eventually entire families moved north, leaving a community of "modern" houses of brick and cement block that sat empty, in the care of relatives. We asked Jesús why he had changed his mind and taken his family to the United States. He conceded that he had dreamed of returning to open a store, but "mi sueño voló"—his "dream flew away." He told a familiar story of having made numerous trips back to Ecuador, paving the way for his eventual return, but of realizing in the late 1990s that there was no way he could return permanently. The United States had more to offer his family, and Ecuador's economic and political problems made living in his native country difficult and even heartbreaking. Now, he was proud that his children were bilingual and was pleased that they enjoyed being in Ecuador. Unlike many immigrant children who have been socialized in the United States, Enrique was not in culture shock when he visited his grandparents in their small, adobe house with no flush toilet. At least for the moment, the experience was an adventure, even exotic. He was delighted to finally have a pet dog and experience life away from Queens. Older Ecuadorian Americans, born in Ecuador but socialized since their late childhood in the United States (Generation 1.5), typically cannot adjust to life in rural Ecuador, complaining of the slow pace of life and lack of companions their own age.

Generalizing the experiences of Ecuadorians in the United States (or Spain) is problematic. All 500,000–600,000 Ecuadorians in the United States have their own experience, each shaped by structural, cultural, and personal factors. The experiences of a single eighteen-year-old woman joining family in Queens, for example, are distinct from that of a thirty-eight-year-old man with three children. Yet, Jesús's story is important because it captures the volatile reality long-term migrants faced and the set of circumstances in which they made difficult decisions. When Jesús migrated undocumented, he landed in Queens, and like thousands of other immigrants, he got a job in a restaurant. Most Ecuadorians in New York work at jobs like this, in the service sector, washing dishes, cleaning hotels, or even driving pirate cabs. Some jobs are male dominated—such as construction and landscaping—and others—such as sewing in sweatshops—employ more women. At first Jesús lived in a house with seven men from his hometown, saving money and remitting it to pay off his debt. Undocumented migrants typically purchase a falsified green card and social security number, which allows them to present the necessary paperwork to get a job, or they work for cash under the table. Immigrant earnings are variable and sporadic. Migrants may go weeks without a job, but many will work two or three jobs and clock seventy hours per week. The U.S. Census Bureau estimated that between 1998 and 2000 Ecuadorians were earning $11,848 per person, while the Urban Institute estimated that in 1995 undocumented immigrants households in New York City earned about $32,400. Jesús was not making that much during the 1980s while he lacked residency, but he nonetheless was able to remit enough money to improve his family's well-being in Ecuador. One source estimated that in the early 2000s Ecuadorians remitted on average $281 per month, or $3,372 per year.

Like many other migrants, Jesus lived transnationally, maintaining two households. He phoned home, and used parallel post offices and videotapes to stay in contact. He returned home regularly, something that residency made easy. Prior to the 1990s, some undocumented immigrants returned to Ecuador and made the clandestine trip again. The cost of migrating has increased so much that few if any migrants make more than one clandestine trip. Although returning for short visits is not possible for undocumented immigrants now, they nonetheless have an easier time staying in contact with their families. They are able to use the Internet and videoconferencing and even listen to radio programs produced transnationally. A radio service emitted by Delgado Travel allows Ecuadorians in New York and Ecuador access to the same broadcast simultaneously. Delgado Travel's programs, which can only be accessed in New York by a radio purchased at Delgado Travel, are broadcast in five cities in Ecuador. The station carries numerous programs broadcasting Ecuadorian music and soccer games, and twice-a-day news broadcasts from Ecuador followed by news from New York. On the weekends, migrants and Ecuadorians call in to the station and send messages to their loved ones.

The evidence that Jesús intended to return can be seen in the plot of land he had purchased and the house he built on it. The house is a spacious, two-story, concrete block house with a garage. Compared to houses in other communities, Jesús's house is not extravagant. It is a significant departure, however, from his parents' adobe house and was typical of migrants who migrated during the 1980s and had saved enough by the late 1980s or early 1990s to build a "migrant house."

Jesús's story is similar to that of other migrants who gain residency and have financial success. That he can rent out part of his Queens house to Ecuadorian immigrants and purchase a second home for the same purpose demonstrates how he has gone from an undocumented migrant using the services of migrant merchants to becoming a migrant merchant himself. Jesús is likely a good landlord, charging the going rate for rent in Queens, but even so he now profits from migrants who followed him.

By the early 1990s, Jesús faced the reality that he was living transnationally, in contact with but nonetheless away from his family for months or years at a time. He did not want to take them to the United States, but he needed to earn money in New York to support them. The economic and political chaos of the last half of the 1990s made the decision for him and thousands of other Ecuadorians. The corruption, hyperinflation, and dollarization made returning a poor economic choice. He legally sponsored his family's departure, voted with his feet, and ended his transnational livelihood. He made the same decision that thousands of Ecuadorians with residency or citizenship have made.

Migrants who have not obtained residency, in contrast, do not have the luxury of reunifying their families in the United States. Many women, most of whom are mothers past the age of twenty-two, subsequently migrated clandestinely to join their spouse or another family member. The departure of women left the difficult and sometimes tragic situation of children being raised by grandparents or aunts and uncles. Many undocumented migrants living in the United States are living a forced or reluctant transnationalism, remitting money and staying in touch with their family, trying to gain residency but realizing that it may never occur.

Jesús is similar to other long-term migrants in another important way. He still holds out hope that someday he will return. He is certain that he and his neighbors will come back from the United States to retire in the houses they built. When we reacted with skepticism to his comments, he insisted that life in the United States had its advantages but it was also fast paced, crowded, and difficult, something no one would want in one's retirement.

The Future of Migration

During the first five years of the twenty-first century, Ecuadorian migration has once again changed in an unexpected way; Colombians, Peruvians, and a smaller number of Chinese are now moving into Ecuador, transforming it into both an emigrant and immigrant country. Colombians are fleeing a long civil war exacerbated by the U.S.-sponsored "Plan Colombia," which has displaced thousands of people in southern Colombia. Social service offices in Cuenca, set up to assist Ecuadorian migrants and their families, also expend considerable effort helping Colombians obtain refugee status. In the summer of 2003 the existence of thousands of Peruvians living in Cuenca in substandard housing came to light. The Peruvians are taking advantage of a dollarized economy and inflated labor costs in Cuenca, caused in part by the migrant stream that has led so many workers to the United States. The dollars Peruvians earn in Ecuador will go a long way in Peru. Chinese immigrants, many coming from other Latin American countries, are responding to the dollarized economy also, but instead of working as underpaid day-laborers, they have opened retail stores throughout Ecuador, selling inexpensive and imported clothing and other items. The dollarized economy has meant that imports are more competitive, and Chinese entrepreneurs have been quick to capitalize on this economic change to earn valuable dollars.

The recent history of Ecuadorian migration has shown not only that migration can change quickly and unexpectedly, but also that it reflects the multiple linkages Ecuador has with the global economy. Just as the presence of Quishpe Express illustrates the geography of Ecuadorian emigration to the United States and Spain, the presence of Chinese stores on the most prominent streets in Quito (Amazonas), and Cuenca (Gran Colombia) reflects Ecuador's greater integration with Asia. Ecuador now faces the reality that more than 1.5 million of its people live overseas. Some are living transnationally, planning to return—eventually. Others are putting down roots in the United States and Spain, and Ecuador has become for them a vacation destination where family business is attended to and children engage with their parents' culture. How migration will change in the future is unclear, but we can be sure that events beyond the control of migrants—such as the international and domestic policies of the United States and the European Union as well as the rise of China in the global economy—will affect who migrates where and under what conditions. We can also be sure that even as nation-states try to regulate the flow of people, the persistence and creativity of migrants and migrant merchants will continue to complicate our understanding of Ecuador, Ecuadorians, and where exactly they live.

Note

1. David Preston, "Empire and Change: Experience in Southern Ecuador," Working Paper 52 (1974), Department of Geography, University of Leeds, 4.

Cities of Women

Mary J. Weismantel

In the United States, Canada, and Europe, many people believe that gender roles in Latin America, especially among Indians, are far more restrictive than in the north. It has been suggested that this pattern originated in the cultures of the Mediterranean, where Arab and Muslim traditions of secluding women from public view influenced the rural societies of Spain, Portugal, and Italy—and later, the soldiers and adventurers who traveled to the New World. Like most simple ideas about other societies, this picture of gender roles in Latin America has elements of truth, but does not capture a complex social reality in which women sometimes enjoy forms of freedom not found elsewhere. In Andean nations such as Ecuador, the produce markets, in which women dominate and men often are made to feel marginal, provides one such counterexample.

In her influential essay "Democracy for a Small Two-Gender Planet," Mexican anthropologist Lourdes Arizpe surveys a wide range of politically active women, including "Bolivian peasant[s] . . . Chilean trade unionists, mothers . . . in Argentina . . . and the women leaders of the poor neighborhoods and shanty towns in São Paolo, Lima, and other Latin American cities," and finds one underlying commonality: all of these women struggled to gain access to the public life of their societies.[1] Regardless of class, race, or nationality, she asserts, the opposition between a feminine private domain and the masculine outside world is fundamental to the social geography of the continent.

Arizpe goes on to provide an illuminating analysis of political activism at the end of the century; but the gendered geography from which she begins is not as universal as she claims. Her Latin America does not include the long-established dominance of women vendors in thousands of produce markets across the Andes—as well as in some indigenous regions of Arizpe's own Mexico.[2] In Ecuador, men drive the trucks, buses, and taxis that move sellers and products in and out of the market, and they control the wholesale end of the business, where most of the money is made. But by far the largest numbers of people who work in the market are vendors, and almost all of these are women. In the central markets of the city of Cuenca, as well as in smaller surrounding towns such as Gualaceo and Chordeleg, at least ninety percent of the vendors of fresh and cooked foods were women, while female ownership of the prized interior stalls approached one hundred percent. Similar patterns obtain throughout the highlands. Bromley found that eighty-five to ninety-five percent of the retailers of fresh fruits, vegetables, meat, and fish in the highland Ecuadorian markets in the early 1970s were women.[3] Blumberg and Coyler, too, estimated that eighty-five percent of the vendors in the Saquisilí main market in the late 1980s were women,[4] numbers that I can confirm for all of the major markets of Cotopaxi Province throughout the 1980s and 1990s.

That such a large, old, and well-established institution could remain invisible to educated women like Arizpe, allowing her to speak unconditionally of Latin America as a society without public spheres for women, illustrates just how anomalous the market is within dominant sexual geographies. The produce markets take place within large plazas (although in most cities, the local government provides a large, covered building as well); but these are not the only plazas—or the most important plazas—to be found in the Latin city.

Gender is deeply inscribed in the plan of cities in the Ecuadorian highlands, which exalt the difference between public and private. Traditional homes are often walled, turned inward to protect family life within a generous but totally enclosed space. Public life occurs within a city plan dominated by a central square, typically bearing a name like "Plaza de Armas," "Plaza de la República," or "Plaza de la Independencia." Encircled by the palatial halls of government, this central space bespeaks a Mediterranean legacy stretching back to the city of Athens in the sixth century BCE, where the agora was celebrated as the heart of the polis.

The central plaza is designed to present a visually overwhelming image of the power of the state, the glory of the wealthy, and the honor of men. It is clean and barren and masculine, an open space surrounded by the closed and forbidding architecture of state power. In contrast, the produce markets are messy and feminine spaces. Here, rather than the empty formality of the masculine plaza, every available space is filled with impromptu constructions and criss-crossed with ephemeral passageways. In its haphazard functionality and enforced intimacies, this is a public place that mimics the informal spaces of domestic life. And since the women themselves must build their stalls with whatever they have on hand, the architecture, too, is decidedly vernacular: small in scale and open-walled, these structures invite the passerby to look, touch, and taste.

In rural towns, these two different plazas occupy the same space: once a week the market takes over the civic plaza, temporarily re-defining its purpose. In larger cities—where politics are played for higher stakes—civil authorities try to keep the two spaces separate, designating specific squares, streets, and buildings around the periphery of the city as officially sanctioned markets, and sending the police to cleanse the main plaza of vendors and *ambulantes*. Everywhere, public authorities are perpetually at work to contain the constant, organic growth of the markets within spatial and temporal limits, and so to protect the city's public persona.

Public life derives its masculine air of importance, its celebratory sense of dignified display, from its contrast with the secluded existence of its necessary complement: the private world of the family. Market women play havoc with the gender of the city, breaking down this opposition with activities that undermine the plaza's self-importance, making low comedy of high drama. In this plaza, the atmosphere is redolent with the smells of food and cooking, as well as of the refuse heap and the abattoir. The sight of bloody carcasses and dirty potatoes, the loudspeakers extolling Jesus or toilet paper, the bustle of women cooking dinner, washing dishes, emptying the slop bucket—all of these bring the mundane and even the unmentionable into open view.

Experiencing Gendered Space: Men in the Markets,
Women in Town

Women and girls know that public spaces do not belong to them. The teachers and administrators who welcome foreign exchange students to Andean cities inevitably include lectures on gender etiquette among their orientation materials: women should not dress provocatively, go anywhere with strange men, or be seen out-of-doors unescorted after dark. The young women from Europe or the United States who are the targets of these admonitions are uniformly dismayed to find their lives so much more circumscribed than those of their male fellows. None of them, of course, hear anything in these lectures that they haven't heard before—their movements are curtailed at home too. But as they begin to move about Andean cities, they are often taken aback by the speed with which lessons about sexual protocol are enforced by stray males on the prowl. On foot or in cars, idle men entertain themselves by harassing and teasing lone women who pass by; if no one else is in sight, their behavior can quickly turn menacing. Foreign women carry the stigma of sexual wantonness, and so are especially likely targets; but others are at risk too.

Whatever their race, almost all women are vulnerable to some variation on these embarrassments. Some girls may be taught to blame themselves, because "good" women belong in the home; on the street and in the plaza, they feel out of place and ill at ease. They travel across public spaces like moving targets, sometimes hopeful of earning men's admiration, always fearful of attracting their ridicule or abuse. Unlike men, women rarely loiter in public. Like a black man in a white neighborhood, they move quickly, purposefully. I'm only here temporarily, their body language says; I have a gender-appropriate destination.

It is surprising, then, to enter the markets, a public place filled with women, and with women's work. Entering such a contradictorily gendered space heightens one's awareness of one's own sex; it is a different place for men than for women.

The market is made up of individual stalls, row upon row piled with fresh food. Whether the display of produce is simple or elaborate, at its center sits the market woman herself, a rounded vertical form rising from flat rectangles piled with goods. Repeated again and again across the open expanse of the plaza, or under the enormous metal roofs of the municipal market building, the female bodies of the vendors take on an almost architectonic function. Seligmann writes of the vendors in the outdoor markets in Cuzco that

> They occupy crucial space in more ways than one. They spread out their numerous cotton or velveteen skirts and wares around them and sit, ignoring the uproar of crowding, often covering their faces from the sun with their hats, which have tall, white, stovepipe crowns and wide black or colored bands. Their earrings flash and glitter in the sun.[5]

Stationary in the midst of the tumult, these are the pivotal figures who give the market its shape and purpose. This public visibility of the female form, on display not to give men pleasure but for other purposes entirely, presents a symbolic inversion of the dominant sexual order that some men find profoundly unsettling. Constrained by the bold gaze of a myriad of women, they find themselves momentarily bereft of a hitherto unquestioned privilege: the freedom to move about in public with relative unself-consciousness. The sight of so many women so completely at ease in a public sphere of their own making creates a corresponding unease in some masculine visitors.

A journalist's recent encounter with Bolivian market women shows how some male travelers react. When a female friend brought Eric Lawlor, author of *In Bolivia: An Adventurous Odyssey through the Americas' Least-Known Nation*, to the La Paz markets, he had a series of alarming encounters. His rising sense of panic culminated when he accidentally knocked over a pail of *refresco* [fruit drink] belonging to one of the vendors. "The woman glared with such ferocity," he recalls, "that, before I quite knew what I was doing, I had pressed all my money into her hand and fled."[6]

The most intimidating figures are those of the well-established *vivanderas*, who evince a total equipoise even when confronting wealthy foreigners. Unlike recent migrants and the perennially poor—who trudge down the streets with their merchandise strapped to their backs, balanced on their heads, or held in their arms—these merchants sit comfortably in one place. Since they sell to a regular base of customers, established vendors rarely call out to strange passersby; instead, they wait for their buyers to come to them. In Peru, travel writer Henry Shukman was made more uncomfortable by these older women than when accosted by aggressive younger vendors on the streets outside. When he entered the municipal market building of a small town on the Peruvian altiplano, he was stung by the silent stares of the sellers. They seemed indifferent to him; even their clothing—"absurd, wide, ballerina-like skirts and derby hats"—expressed an apparent unconcern with attracting masculine desire that he found frankly terrifying. Upset by their unreadable expressions as they gazed upon him, appalled by the absence of other men, he hastened to leave. "[T]hey didn't want me here," he writes, apparently astonished at the notion.[7]

Entering the markets with hesitation, such foreigners leave with the uncomfortable sensation that people are laughing at them. This uneasiness can translate into a suspicion that one has been fleeced: accusations of financial chicanery abound, even when, as is often the case, prices are fixed. In 1997, after my traveling companion, Stephen, and I had been in Cuenca, Ecuador, for some weeks, he encountered an American acquaintance leaving the 10 de Agosto market on Christmas Eve. My compadres had introduced Stephen to the pleasures of eating fresh fava beans in Zumbagua, and he in turn had encouraged this man, a retired engineer with wide-ranging interests, to try some favas himself. When Stephen met up with him, the engineer immediately launched into a long harangue about his frustrating experiences in the market, which his daughter, who had spent many years in Latin America, tried in vain to stem. The vendor, mindful no doubt of governmental price controls, had refused to bargain with a stranger. "But I had just seen her giving one of her regular customers a better deal," he fumed.

"Dad," responded his daughter hopelessly, "It was only a thousand sucres' difference—that's less than twenty-five cents."

"That doesn't matter," he responded through clenched teeth. "It's the principle of the thing. She was making a fool out of me, and I wasn't going to stand there and take it. Not with everyone staring at me to see what I was going to do next."

When he stopped to buy beans, this tall, gray-haired Midwesterner undoubtedly attracted attention, speculation, and commentary. Tourists often come to the markets to gawk, but—having nowhere to cook raw products, and fearing to eat the cooked items—they rarely make a purchase. Local men, too, can find shopping in the markets unnerving—and so do women, when they come from a different social class than the sellers. A very wealthy

Ecuadorian woman told us about going to a well-known market for a lark. She and a girlfriend descended upon a woman selling apples, and asked to know the price; but the woman refused to sell. "Well, at first I was going to get angry, but then I realized—poor little thing, it was early in the day and she was afraid we would buy all her stock. Then what would she have done? It's not as though they go there to make money, you know. Sitting there all day with her apples was all that she had in the world to do."

Our Quiteño taxi driver, Julio Padilla, listened to my retelling of this story with interest. "I know exactly what happened," he said. "I've often seen it. Those rich women, they walk in there like they own the place, and start demanding the price of everything. But they don't even listen to the answer. They just throw down some money, grab what they want, and walk away. The women working there can't stand them; that's why they won't talk to them."

The emotional experiences and interactions in the market, then, are affected by class as well as by gender. A man like Julio has immediate sympathy for women who, like himself, struggle to keep their dignity in the face of upper-class arrogance. And market women are happy to sell to, talk with, and occasionally be seduced by the working-class men whose jobs bring them into the market. But there are limits. Men who share the vendors' working-class identity navigate the markets with greater ease. A few men work as vendors themselves, selling side by side with the women. The truckers and taxi drivers who ferry vendors and their products to and from the markets are also at home there, eating and drinking in the markets every day, and entering into familiar relationships—including love affairs—with the women. The same is true of the wholesalers, bakers, restaurateurs, and other men who do business with market women on a regular basis.

I have occasionally witnessed an awkward scenario when a young market seller's boyfriend makes himself too much at home. The girl sits at her stall, but is unable to sell because the young man is sitting on her lap. He affects an air of defiance and possessiveness, throwing his arm around her neck or clasping his hands around her waist. She looks alternately miserable, ashamed, and angry, or all at once. Work comes to a halt in the stalls around her, as older women stare disapprovingly and girlfriends giggle. He is acting inappropriately, but it is she who will pay the price: she cannot sell until he leaves, and her reputation as a serious vendor has been greatly diminished in the eyes of the older women she longs to impress.

These young women are struggling to get established in a very different workplace than their middle-class peers. In the global society occupied by the professional classes, it has become a commonplace to speak of women's success in entering traditionally masculine spheres of business and politics. But the inclusion of women—and non-whites—as full-fledged members of such communities remains tentative and incomplete, giving rise to a popular discourse about glass ceilings and a legal wrangle over hostile environments. These architectural metaphors are apt: the buildings erected by governments, banks, and corporations are white male spaces, within which femininity and non-whiteness are stigmas that mark the interloper. Radcliffe and Westwood were taken aback by the geographical specificity of one common response they received when asking residents of Cotopaxi to describe whites: "Ah, yes, those are the men in the offices."[8]

In the produce markets, it is well-to-do white men who feel peripheral. Shukman complained bitterly of the inhospitableness of a place which, despite being "the center of Cholo life," consigned men to "hover in the dimness outside" (1989:138). The women who work there, of course, have a very different point of view: to them, the market is not only a home—and a workplace—but also a refuge from the inhospitableness of the rest of Andean social space, where men dominate and women must submit. In actuality, the markets, too, are largely constrained and controlled by men, especially the municipal police, whom market women fear. Nevertheless, the markets create a social realm so different from the world outside that it has given rise to rumors and myths that within the patriarchal heart of the Andes lies a secret, "matriarchal" society. And indeed, the markets have long been a refuge for women fleeing domestic violence, whether at the hands of fathers, husbands, or employers— and for women who, for whatever reason, choose not to marry at all. The image of the market woman is of a single mother raising her children without the help of a man. This is far from reality—many women are happily married, or live with boyfriends or male partners, and some suffer brutally violent or abusive relationships for many years. But although far from a matriarchy, the households that surround the markets do reveal an array of marital and child-rearing arrangements that belies the image of highland Latin America as a world where all women are married, and all husbands rule the roost.

Market and Home: Interdependent Spheres

The world of the produce market, then, is the opposite of the secluded life of the home: a public world of women without men, living and working in the streets. The only problem with this picture is that the street market is less an antithesis to the domestic kitchen than its raucous twin. The public market exists in close economic symbiosis with the unseen interiors of the private homes that surround it, and which it daily provisions. The home and the homemaker are the market to which produce vendors sell their goods: the world of the plaza exists to provide services for the domestic sphere. "Casera, casera," shout the market women to potential customers: "homemaker, homemaker."[9]

Visitors from other countries are often charmed and surprised by the incongruous domesticity of scenes in the market: a man sits at his sewing machine, ready to patch your trousers or catch up a fallen hem; a woman spreads a wooden table with a bright-colored plastic tablecloth, and offers to sell you anything from a Coca-Cola to a four-course *almuerzo*, complete with dessert. Nor is this commercial domesticity a mirage: workmen and students cultivate special relations with particular market women, eating at their stalls day after day, taking comfort in the familiarity of the woman's voice, her steady supply of gossip, and her knowledge of their particular tastes and appetites. Real and fictitious family relationships abound. Some customers are distant relatives—perhaps the son of a country cousin, sent to the city to attend high school with a strict enjoinder to eat all his meals "donde su tía" [where your aunt is]. No one who eats at a particular stall for any length of time remains a stranger; regular customers are inexorably drawn into the domestic dramas between the women who work there, and are ruthlessly—albeit sympathetically—interrogated about their own lives and kin.

Cooking is not the only housewifely work that market women do. Like women who shop for their families, they bring the products of male producers and wholesalers into a feminine realm where these can be transformed into meals for individual families. Vendors break down bulk quantities into smaller portions; shell beans and peas; peel fruit and vegetables; chop herbs and grate onions. They even make small ready-to-cook soup packages, filled with combinations of raw legumes, herbs, and vegetables in exact proportions. Many stalls feature a single product offered in every stage of preparation, from unpeeled and dirty, to washed and sliced, to cooked and ready to eat.

Up in the high, cold mountain town of Zumbagua, Heloisa Huanotuñu's *trago* shop is a case in point. She buys contraband cane alcohol in large quantities from the men who bring it up from the western jungle by mule and llama train. The little caravans arrive at her home in the early hours of the morning, and she and the men pour the alcohol from saddlebags into big plastic containers that once held kerosene. Customers occasionally buy entire barrels of the stuff for parties, or to bootleg over the mountains for resale in the white towns down below in the Interandean Valley. Most people bring smaller containers—gallon jars, empty liquor bottles—that get filled by a hose and closed with a fragment from a plastic bag. As the morning wears on, other customers appear looking for a shot to be consumed on the spot. Heloisa or another family member is ready to oblige, siphoning the liquor directly from a fifty-gallon drum into a small glass.

If work done in the market strikes economists as somehow too informal, too feminine, too unimportant to be recognized as productive, it is at the same time too commercial in nature to be properly domestic. The same activities, done inside the home, do not count as labor at all; in economic terms, they become invisible. But if it is difficult to quantify, the relationship between work done inside the house and food preparation done for cash matters. For housewives in Ecuador, the existence of inexpensive market labor radically re-shapes the work load within the home. Women come to the market to buy big quantities of corn already cooked into *mote* for a family dinner, or a little bag of it with hot sauce on top for immediate snacking. They may purchase a whole cooked pig or a single slice of roast pork. Enormous wheels of *panela* [turbinado sugar], dark and strong-smelling, wrapped in banana leaves, are sold in some stalls; but the vendors are happy to divide a wheel, or even to cut off a little chunk to eat like candy as you walk around.

Histories of the American consumer describe the advent of ready-to-eat foods as a recent innovation made possible by enormous technological advances. The willingness of working women and their families to eat prepackaged food, or to dine in restaurants, is described as a fundamental change in twentieth-century social life. Arizpe describes a pernicious penetration of the capitalist market into Latin daily life, usurping women's traditional functions and leaving them "empty handed." These visions of history are too narrow in both class and geographical perspectives. In Latin America, the presence of the markets with their abundance of precooked foods is old, not new. Some industrial technologies have filtered into the markets: many factory-made foods are sold there; beverage stall counters are lined with electric blenders; some of the small stores ringing the market have invested in refrigerators. But for the most part, this enormous system of provisioning works through the most simple technologies possible: knives to slice and peel, ropes and baskets to carry bundles, cooking pots and wooden spoons to boil and stir. It is human labor that adds value to the products sold there.

Working-class women depend upon the ready availability of meals and ingredients from the markets; in small cities and towns this attitude extends to professional women as well. Traveling the back roads of Cotopaxi Province with a car full of Ecuadorian anthropologists, I was surprised when one passenger insisted that we drop in for lunch on an old school friend he had not seen in some time. Her feelings would be hurt, he insisted, when she found out he had been in the town and had not let her give his friends a midday meal. How, I wondered, could this unknown woman cope with a half dozen unexpected lunch guests? The market provided the answer: our hostess disappeared within minutes of our arrival, then returned to usher us in with fanfare to a dining room laden with local specialties: potato pancakes, roast pork, tomato salad, fresh corn. Beaming, she boasted of knowing all the best market stalls in town; without her, she insisted, we would never have been able to eat well in a strange place.

The willingness of market women to perform any sort of food preparation, and the eagerness of housewives and domestic servants to avail themselves of these services, mediates the boundary between the loving work of
caring for a family, and the paid labor of strangers. Men and children eating a
meal at home consume the work not only of their own wife and mother, but
of other women as well. In order to be the ideal housewife who knows how
to provision her family, women must create and keep good relations with the
women of the market and of the small shops that surround it.

The relationship between a market woman and her customers has its own
arcana. Many a gringa who has lived in the Andes for an extended period of
time recalls with pride her first "yapa": the first time that, as a repeat customer, she earned a little "extra" scoop of flour or beans, poured into her bag
after it had been weighed and the price figured. Market women who sell to
Indians often keep a bag of cheap, brightly colored candies with which they
"yapa" their customers, preferring to offer these treats rather than any of the
more expensive dry goods or produce they sell. The result is a subtle insult,
masked as a kindness: are these candies for the purchaser's children, or is
the Indian woman herself being treated as a child? Why is it that the seller,
pretending friendship, nevertheless insists that Indians—unlike their white
customers—pay full price for every ounce of merchandise?

From the market woman's perspective, maintaining the proper degrees
of intimacy with customers is among the most complicated and delicate of
tasks—and the one that separates an inept from a successful entrepreneur.
My landlady in Zumbagua, Rosa Quispe, operated a cooked-food stall in
the Saturday market there for a while, but gave it up in disgust. "It costs
me more than I earn," she explained to me. "The entire family comes to
the market and expects me to feed them for free, but I have to buy all my
ingredients in Latacunga the day before, and there I pay cash." Successful
market women, too, find the boundary between market and domestic relations impossible to maintain. What distinguishes stall-owners in the Cuenca
municipal markets from amateurs like Rosa is their ability to make profit
out of their personal relationships, while using their commercial ties to benefit themselves and those they care about. For the true professional, the
line between public and private, commercial and familial disappears almost
completely.

In the late afternoons, the 10 de Agosto market is a drowsy place. There
are almost no customers. The big metal doors of the market are pulled down
partway, making the interior dim and cool. Young assistants and relatives
have been sent home; only the older women, owners of the stalls, lounge in
them half-asleep, reading newspapers or taking naps as though in their own
living rooms. They take out their reading glasses, their crocheting, and their

slippers, wrap themselves in their shawls, and prop their feet up on a sack of potatoes or noodles.

If the market is literally a domestic space for these women, whose work brings them there seven days a week from the middle of the night till mid-afternoon, their homes, in turn, become staging sites for commercial and productive operations.[10] Sra. Loja, the *rocoto* [chili pepper] seller, didn't mind that her daughters had not followed exactly in the footsteps of their mother and grandmother. They sell clothing rather than food, and recently began to manufacture some items at home. "They have turned the house into a factory," she remarked with satisfaction.

Heloisa Huanotuñu lives in her trago shop. The counter and shelves, table and chairs serve both as her kitchen and the bar's furniture. Her bed, partly curtained with a sheet of plastic, and the small storage areas above and below it are the only semi-private spaces within the one-room building. Much of her emotional life is centered elsewhere, in the family farmstead up above town, where her brothers and sisters and nieces and nephews live. She spends many hours there, cooking and eating, listening to complaints and giving advice, loaning money and demanding help. But she does not sleep there. She, too, then, has arranged working, sleeping, eating, and loving in ways that cannot readily be reduced to a single dichotomy of public and private.

Today, the produce markets are changing fast, as Ecuador's economy is beset by problems and re-shaped by neo-liberal reforms. On the one hand, poor migrants from rural areas, farm women and men displaced by the collapsing agricultural economy, are flooding urban areas, and many of them end up in the markets, not to buy but to sell whatever they can get their hands on. At the same time, large corporations are opening up chains of supermarkets across Ecuador, siphoning off the wealthy consumers who once sent their cooks and maids to buy at the markets even if they did not shop there themselves. These two phenomena act like a pincers, squeezing once-successful vendors like Rosa Loja, whose profits are eroding and whose future seems almost as uncertain as the ex-farmers who are undercutting her sales. In Cuenca, where she has her stall, the next generation, the so-called "hijos de la pollera" [children of market women and other poor working mothers] are leaving Ecuador altogether in search of new lives in Europe and the United States. When they do, they bring with them memory of those smelly, lively, female places, literal cities of women within Ecuadorian urban space: the produce markets.

Notes

1. Lourdes Arizpe, "Democracy for a Small Two-Gender Planet," Forward to *Women and Social Change in Latin America* (London: Zed Books, 1990), xvi.

2. See, for example, Scott Cook and Martin Diskin, *Markets in Oxaca* (Austin: University of Texas Press, 1976).

3. Ray Bromley, "Market Center and Market Place in Highland Ecuador: A Study of Organization, Regulation, and Ethnic Discrimination," In *Cultural Transformations and Ethnicity in Modern Ecuador*, ed. Norman E. Whitten Jr. (Urbana: University of Illinois Press, 1981).

4. Rae Lesser Blumberg and Dale Coyler, "Social Institutions, Gender and Rural Living Conditions," in *Agriculture and Economic Survival: The Role of Agriculture in Ecuador's Development*, ed. Morris D. Whitaker and Dale Coyler (Boulder, Colo.: Westview Press, 1990), 255.

5. Linda J. Seligmann, "Between Worlds of Exchange: Ethnicity among Peruvian Market Women," *Cultural Anthropology* 8, no. 2 (May 1993): 194.

6. Eric Lawlor, *In Bolivia: An Adventurous Odyssey through the Americas' Least-Known Nation* (New York: Vintage Press, 1989), 31–32.

7. Henry Shukman, *Sons of the Moon: A Journey in the Andes* (New York: Charles Scribner's Sons, 1989), 53.

8. Sarah Radcliffe and Sallie Westwood, *Remaking the Nation: Place, Identity, and Politics in Latin America* (London: Routledge, 1996), 112.

9. For a very interesting discussion of this term as it is used in the markets, see Edmundo Morales, *The Guinea Pig: Healing, Food, and Ritual in the Andes* (Tucson: University of Arizona Press, 1995), 34–35.

10. The worsening economy has lengthened the days and hours that these women work, a subject of much bitter commentary among them. They envision a proper work week in which one rises early, but finishes early, and in which most women can take Sundays and holidays off; but by the late 1980s, they worked endless long days, afraid to miss out on a single purchase.

Traditional Foods of Ecuador

Noemí Espinosa

Translated by Mayté Chiroboga

Ecuador is known for its fantastic fruits, wonderful seafood, numerous varieties of potatoes, and wide range of regional and national dishes. The country's most famous dish is, without a doubt, ceviche, *a seafood dish (made up of some combination of shrimp, prawns, fish, or squid) that is marinated in a sauce and often topped with popcorn. The country's specialty, however, is soup. Ecuadorians take soup seriously. Virtually all lunches and dinners come with soup as the first course, followed by a meat dish accompanied with rice and salad. Below are a few recipes to get one started.*

Quiteño-Style Shrimp or Prawn Ceviche

INGREDIENTS

  2 pounds shrimp or prawns
  2 tablespoons lemon juice

INGREDIENTS FOR SAUCE

  1 cup orange juice
  1/2 cup tomato sauce (ketchup)
  1/4 teaspoon Ajinomoto (MSG, optional)
  1 tablespoon vegetable oil
  1/2 teaspoon sugar
  salt, pepper, and ground hot chili-pepper sauce or Tabasco sauce to taste

ACCOMPANIMENTS

  1 large red pickled onion (To pickle onions: add salt to the onions and scrub
      them thoroughly, rinse twice with boiling water, add lemon juice, and
      season with salt and pepper to taste.)
  1 sprig of parsley, and parsley leaves for garnish

a stalk of celery, a spring onion

white bread rolls, popcorn, fried peanuts, *patacones* (fried plantain), *chifles* (fried plantain chips)

PREPARATION

1. Wash and clean the shrimp or prawns. Cook them in boiling water for three minutes with the salt, lemon juice, celery, and spring onion. Strain and let cool.

2. Prepare sauce for the ceviche by mixing tomato sauce, orange juice, Ajinomoto, oil, sugar, salt, pepper, and ground hot chili-pepper to taste.

3. Serve shrimp or prawns in deep dishes. Pour sauce on top, and garnish with pickled onion and parsley leafs. Accompany with rolls, popcorn, fried peanuts, patacones, chifles, and chili-pepper sauce or Tabasco sauce.

NOTE: This dish may be prepared with mushrooms or hearts of palm alone, or mixed with shrimp.

★ ★ ★

Coast Style Shrimp or Prawn Ceviche

INGREDIENTS

2 pounds shrimp or prawns
   lemon juice
2 or 3 tablespoons oil
2 medium-sized, peeled, seedless chopped tomatoes
2 small chopped red and green bell peppers
1 large pickled red onion (see instructions above for pickling onions in Quiteño-style recipe)
2 tablespoons finely chopped cilantro
1 tablespoon finely chopped parsley
salt, pepper, and ground hot chili-pepper sauce or Tabasco sauce to taste
1/4 teaspoon Ajinomoto (optional)
1 celery stalk, 1 spring onion

ACCOMPANIMENTS

> white bread rolls, popcorn, fried peanuts, patacones (fried plantain), chifles (fried plantain chips), and pickled onion

PREPARATION

1. Wash and clean the shrimp or prawns. Cook them in boiling water for three minutes with the salt, lemon juice, celery, and spring onion. Strain and let cool. Reserve stock.
2. Prepare sauce for the ceviche by mixing tomatoes, bell peppers, red onion, parsley, and cilantro. Season with hot chili-pepper sauce or Tabasco sauce, Ajinomoto, oil, salt, pepper, and the stock in which the shrimp or prawns were cooked in (the amount needed to achieve proper sauce).
3. Add shrimp or prawns to sauce and let stand for at least an hour.
4. Serve in deep dishes. Garnish with pickled onion and parsley leafs. Accompany with rolls, popcorn, fried peanuts, patacones, chifles, hot chili-pepper sauce or Tabasco sauce, and tomato sauce.

* * *

Basic Hot-Chili-Pepper Sauce

INGREDIENTS

> 6 large chili peppers
> 1/4 cup water
> 1 stalk spring onion
> 1 sprig parsley
> 1 tablespoon salt
> vegetable oil

PREPARATION

1. Wash chili peppers, and chop and place them in blender. Add water, spring onion, parsley, and salt. Blend well and strain.
2. Add several drops of oil.
3. The chili sauce is ready for seasoning any type of foods such as ceviches, sauces, meats, poultry, etc.

*Locro de Queso (*Potato Soup with Cheese*)*

INGREDIENTS

8 Idaho Potatoes
2 stalks spring onions
1 garlic clove
2 tablespoons lard, oil, or butter
1/2 to 1 cup milk
1/2 cup grated fresh white cheese or Philadelphia cream cheese
   salt and pepper
1/4 teaspoon finely chopped oregano, cilantro, or parsley

PREPARATION

1. Peel and wash potatoes. Cut 6 of the 8 potatoes in three parts each, and chop the remaining 2 in small squares.
2. Place lard, oil, or butter in a pot. Add finely chopped onion and garlic, salt, and pepper, and sauté for a moment. Add small potato squares, strained. Stir for approximately five minutes. Add remaining potatoes.
3. Add boiling water to cover the potatoes. Cook until the locro thickens and potatoes are thoroughly cooked.
4. Add milk and cheese and let boil once at medium heat, stirring constantly so the soup does not curdle. If too thick, add boiling water a little at a time. Add seasoning, and adjust to taste.
5. Serve immediately accompanied by avocado wedges (optional) and hot chili-pepper sauce.

★ ★ ★

Pristiños

INGREDIENTS FOR DOUGH

1 cup cream
1 egg yolk
1 teaspoon salt
amount of flour needed to form a soft dough
1 teaspoon baking powder

a few drops vinegar

sugar syrup made from brown sugar (Place 1 pound brown sugar in heavy
saucepan with 1 1/2 cups water and a cinnamon stick. Let it simmer at
low heat until thickened; strain.)

PREPARING THE DOUGH

1. Mix all ingredients (except the sugar syrup) to form dough.
2. Vigorously knead and beat the dough against the table.
3. Let the dough stand without refrigerating for 30 minutes or more.
4. Spread the dough thinly and evenly over a floured surface. Shape the
   pristiños by cutting strips 5.5 to 6.5 inches wide by 1 to 1.5 inches wide,
   make small cuts at the edges, and join the ends together.
5. Deep-fry the pristiños in plenty of oil at medium heat until golden. After
   removing from oil, place the pristiños on absorbent paper towel.
6. Serve accompanied with warm brown-sugar syrup.

★ ★ ★

Oven Roasted Pork Leg

INGREDIENTS

5 to 6 pounds leg of pork
4 cups beer
4 garlic cloves, minced
2 red onions, chopped
2 stalks spring onions, chopped
1 tablespoon cumin
1 teaspoon hot-chili-pepper powder
1 teaspoon thyme
1 teaspoon oregano
1 tablespoon lard
salt and pepper

ACCOMPANIMENTS

sour and sweet sauce (recipe below); potato patties; and lettuce, tomato,
and avocado salad

PREPARATION

1. Blend 1 cup of the beer with the garlic, onions (both), hot chili peppers, cumin, thyme, oregano, lard, salt, and pepper. Season the leg of pork with the mixture and let stand for at least twenty-four hours. Poke and bathe the leg with the mixture frequently (it is best to place the seasoned leg within a thick plastic bag for two or three days, to avoid bad odors in the refrigerator).
2. Preheat oven to 450° F. Remove leg from seasoning mixture. Reserve mixture. Place leg in a baking pan. Roast until golden on all sides. Decrease oven temperature to 350° F and pour reserved mixture and remaining beer over the pork. Roast until meat is thoroughly cooked but not dry. Roast 35 to 40 minutes for each pound of meat.
3. This dish may be served hot or cold, thinly sliced, or in thick chunks.

★ ★ ★

Sour and Sweet Sauce for Leg of Pork

INGREDIENTS

2 tablespoons water
3 tablespoons lemon juice
1 tablespoon white vinegar
3 to 4 tablespoons brown-sugar syrup
1 tablespoon blanched hot chili pepper, finely chopped
1 tablespoon parsley, finely chopped
1 tablespoon fresh cilantro, finely chopped
2 cups finely chopped tomatoes
1/2 cup feathered red onion
1 tablespoon vegetable oil
salt, pepper, and hot chili pepper to taste

PREPARATION

1. Mix all ingredients, making sure the brown sugar dissolves completely.
2. Check seasoning, and adjust as necessary. Serve the sauce in a separate dish.

Globalization from Below and the Political Turn among Otavalo's Merchant Artisans

Rudi Colloredo-Mansfeld

Few tourists leave Ecuador without visiting Otavalo, Ecuador's most famous indigenous market. World-famous for their weavings and other wares, Otavaleños have long been held up as "successful Indians," praised both for their economic success and cultural pride. The anthropologist Rudi Colloredo-Mansfeld looks beyond this simple vision by situating the Otavalo economy within the broader context of state policies, national politics, and global markets.

On Tuesday, 22 May 2001, *El Comercio* ran the headline "La renta de hijos es común" ("The renting of children is common") on the top of the front page, accompanied by the line "la zona de Otavalo registra una alta migración infantil" ("the zone around Otavalo has registered a high ratio of child migration"). As the paper's "story of the day," it reported that nine teenagers from rural indigenous communities "were discovered working as slaves" of a prosperous Otavaleño merchant in Uruguay. Peddling goods twelve hours a day, they received only a plate of rice daily and $20 a month in wages. The mistreated youths had departed Ecuador after *carnaval* had ended (February). Their parents, though, first heard of their offspring's misery in mid-May and enlisted the support of international organizations, the state, and indigenous groups to secure the return of their kids.

Perhaps just as disturbing as the image of migrant Otavaleño slaves was the purported misery that compelled parents to send their children off. "Poverty obliges youths to look for work abroad," the paper reported, going on: "It is a common practice in the Otavaleño countryside. Rosa María Viñachi does not understand well where her daughter went. But the monthly $40 appears to her as a good quantity in the face of the lack of work and nine, of her twelve, children that she has to maintain." Here is globalization's dark side. A desperate woman sacrifices the well-being of one child in a distant country so that others may live at home. Nor is Viñachi's plight easily dismissible as that of an uneducated peasant. In the unrelated "photo of the day" which ran below the story, the backs of thirteen men and women are seen crunched together at the bars of the gates of the Spanish consulate. On the other side a lone woman stares at the visa seekers, her indifference underscoring the remoteness of economic opportunity. The Otavaleña Viñachi and her children thus offer a parable, not of Indian backwardness but of "globalized" hardship—the Ecuadorian who sees no future at home yet finds enslavement abroad.

Otavaleños used to star in brighter narratives. For decades, political elites, academics, and reporters praised their industriousness, material progress, and cultural pride. The *Los Angeles Times* touted Otavaleños as "Shuttle Capitalists" in 1993 (14 November, 30). The article noted that men and women from Otavalo were selling wares in Los Angeles, Frankfurt, and Tokyo: "They are the international sales brigades of an Andean capitalism that has elevated Otavaleños to an affluence never before attained by Latin America's indigenous peoples since the white conquest of the New World." Even in 2001, *El Comercio* ran an article about Otavalo that trumpeted, "Business is part of their life" and claimed, "In the last four years, the indigenous people inclusively are entering into activities such as cyber cafes, tourism, and export companies" (29 May 2001, A7). The stories of exploited youths working abroad for a pittance taint such tales of progress. The question now arises: Why has Otavalo's export capitalism unraveled at the moment when globalization was supposed to benefit precisely this sort of international, free-market, self-directed development?

Otavalo's predicament lies in the grave difficulties that a global economic order engineered by international capital markets and transnational corporations creates for the specialized, distinctive regional enterprises of communities. Put another way, Otavaleños show the fallout that happens when globalization from below butts up against globalization from above. Top-down integration promises growth through "market forces, international competition and a limited role of the state in economic affairs" in the words of a former World Bank economist.[1] However, it frequently delivers its opposite. Privatization, currency devaluation, and fiscal austerity result in bankruptcy, unemployment, endless debt, and a bitter backlash against free-trade policies. Thus in one of the ironic twists of an era that supposedly promised less political interference with the market, small-time capitalists such as the Otavaleños must do something most have spent their life avoiding. They now divert their efforts from their business to politics. They take to both the streets in popular protests and to the hallways of government in order to reestablish conditions that would allow them to earn a living.

Globalization from Below

A highland Quichua people with agricultural roots, Otavaleños are notable not just for their business acumen and cultural pride, but for the substantial changes in residence and occupation that they have both initiated and adjusted to. Otavaleños number about 70,000, the majority of whom live in the province of Imbabura, about 120 kilometers north of Quito in a green, lake-filled valley divided by the Pan-American Highway. The tourist-attracting Otavalo textile trade became entangled in international markets early in the twentieth century, when artisans "reverse-engineered" European imports and wove Scottish tweeds on Andean back-strap (those tied around the weaver's waist) looms for urban Ecuadorian markets. At midcentury, textile tastes changed. Otavaleños found fewer buyers for their *casimires* (imitation tweeds) but discovered new interest in ponchos and other articles that met demand for ethnic arts. By the 1960s merchant-artisans worked sales territories that stretched from Lima through Quito and Bogotá to Caracas, with the most well connected making it to New York to sell wares. Travelers soon turned into settlers, and in the 1970s and 1980s expatriate communities with membership numbering in the hundreds took root in Colombia, Venezuela, Holland, Spain, and the United States.

By the early 1990s, even the most domestic of industries, such as the production of *fajas* (belts) for indigenous women of the sierra, had their fortunes shaped by transnational concerns. Commercial production of fajas began in 1978 in a community called Ariasucu. It grew quickly so that by the mid-1990s, almost half of the community was involved in faja manufacture. Close to twenty households had expanded production beyond their capacity and required piecework weavers. These laborers were boys and girls from throughout the community, weavers who reinvested their small savings in export tourist crafts. Indeed, in 1994, three of the nine youths later stranded as street peddlers in Uruguay began their working lives as faja weavers in Ariasucu, acquiring the resources they would need on just such a sales trip.

Concentrating on local production, however, can underplay Otavalo's real global habits. While manufacture anchors the economy, marketing has given it its worldwide pulse. Otavalo's marketplace is not only Ecuador's third most popular tourist destination after Quito and Guayaquil; it is a crossroads for artisan wares from throughout the country and continent. Woven and embroidered products from other Ecuadorian communities, including Zuleta, Salasaca, Salcedo, and elsewhere find their main outlets here. From abroad, Panamanian molas, Bolivian cloth, Guatemalan belts, and Peruvian sweaters sit in tall stacks in most Otavalo wholesale outlets.

In an era of Nike swooshes, Microsoft Windows, and other juggernauts of corporate capital, Otavalo's face-to-face, craft capitalism—so clearly anchored in the rich, cultural setting of a historic Andean market town—cuts a dashing figure of alternative development. Antiglobalization activists hunger for such cases. Colin Hines, the former head of Greenpeace's International Economics Unit has written a book *Localization*, promoted as a "manifesto to unite all those who recognize the importance of cultural social and ecological diversity for our future and who do not aspire to a monolithic global consumer culture" (back cover).[2] In his vision, people must develop policies that "increase control of the economy by communities and nation states. The result should be an increase in community cohesion, a reduction in poverty and inequality and an improvement in livelihoods, social infrastructure and environmental protection and hence an increase in the all-important sense of security" (5). Nationally, Ecuador's indigenous leaders anticipated these ideas. For a decade, the indigenous movement led by CONAIE (Confederación de Nacionalidades Indígenas del Ecuador) has pursued a Model of Planned Communitarian-Ecological Economy that takes household-based enterprise, which is the basis of Otavalo's economy, as a cornerstone.[3]

In reality, though, Otavalo does not jibe with the localist alternatives. Yes, the handicraft trade upholds place and tradition. But the social result is not the cohesive community that bottom-up development supposedly promotes. Rather, it is a specialized, economically polarized world that rewards dynamic innovation and entrenches deep inequalities. This is a town that offers wares simultaneously to a merchant who ships containers of merchandise to Chicago and the United Arab Emirates and a peasant-weaver who barters cooking oil for wool on donkey-back in provincial settlements. Whatever this variety may do for economic sustainability, it aggravates class divisions and creates distinct worldviews and interests. When I conducted interviews in 1994 in Ariasucu, an anxious young father came to visit me to request that I ask my laptop if his eight-month-old daughter, sick with diarrhea, would live or die. In 2001 while doing interviews in downtown Otavalo, I met a young man who used his own Dell laptop computer to get his sweater designs off his desktop computer and into the memories of his family's $75,000 knitting machines (they have three). While seemingly an anecdote of progressive change—the mystical box of Western knowledge becomes the native's tool—this story says more about a rapidly diverging society.

If "globalization from above" succors transnational corporations, macroregional trade pacts, and speculative capital, and "localization" promotes community-directed economies, diversified local industries, and redistributive social policy, then Otavalo's "globalization from below" is neither. It revitalizes a regional economy through aggressive international expansion of a historic specialty trade, generates ongoing investment in locally controlled production, diversifies careers, and sparks cultural pride. At the same time it produces inequality, turns households into competitive enterprises, and eliminates cultural common ground. And while Otavaleños long ago hitched their fortunes to their own brand of internationalization, it turned out to have a deep flaw. It had no political teeth. When in the late 1990s, the national government began to implement a series of monetary and fiscal policies designed to win back the confidence of the IMF and international capital markets, Otavaleños had no power to fight for the long-term health of their own export economy. The damage has been severe.

Globalization from Above

Having had a long running start, Otavalo's economy only really began to be undermined by economic adjustments in 1998. The administration of León Febres Cordero (1984–88) initiated the "state-izing of neoliberalism" with attempts at deregulation, reductions in public spending, and reinforcement of the Central Bank and strict monetary policy. Later, President Sixto Durán Ballén added an aggressive privatization program to this recipe. However, neither administration advanced reforms that overly affected Otavaleño business. Only with the dollarization—the destruction of the sucre, adoption of the U.S. dollar as Ecuador's national currency, and the concomitant fiscal reforms—did the austerity policies turn macroeconomic conditions sharply against the Otavaleños.

Intended to safeguard worker' earnings (they could earn hard currency without migrating) and investors' capital, Ecuador's massive currency did neither. Inflation during the year of implementation of the plan ran at 91 percent, versus an average of 9.5 percent for the rest of Latin America and 3.4 percent in the United States.[4] The upshot was that in Ecuador, the U.S. dollar was undergoing rapid devaluation even as it maintained its buying power in the United States. Worse still, the government removed subsidies on electricity and diesel fuel. Rising energy costs pushed up all the basic input costs for manufacturers. Given that the majority of goods made in Otavalo are produced on machinery (the mayor and sociologist, Mario Conejo, puts the figure of industrialized production at 80 percent), all these changes badly wrenched Otavaleño business operations.

For Otavaleños, a year after currency and fiscal reforms took effect, "dollarization" had come to stand for the almost unworkable condition of their market. Three factors stood out: falling sales, the new high costs of material and energy, and the loss of the cushion that came when exchanging hard currency revenue to cover their sucre-based costs. Some found solace in having stable prices. Even so, they saw no clear way forward. For instance, we asked one acrylic sweater maker, "Has the dollarization hurt business?' She said:

> There has always been competition, but the merchandise moved faster. In spite of the competition, there were a lot of sales. For example, Venezuela. I had a big market in Venezuela. But with the passing of time, little by little the market dropped. I believe, not only because of the competition but with the prices, one may not be able to compete outside of the country.

For another producer, this new price stability is, in fact, part of the trouble. As he explained: "The problem is totally the dollarization. . . . Before, when it was sucres, I did not complain. When it was sucres, costs could rise and we could still earn. It is not like that anymore. This whole country is damaged." In the face of all these problems, producers seem to be contemplating getting out of the business. Two shops have shut down their sweater knitters all together, one closing the door on over $100,000 dollars' worth of machinery.

Just as orthodox economics would have it, rising factor prices in one nation will create a comparative advantage for another. In this case, Otavaleños' woes have been Peruvians' gains. Since 1998, Peruvians have shifted their sales from their previous Otavaleño trading partners to direct sales outlets owned by their fellow countrymen and women who have relocated to Otavalo. By 2001, at least eighteen Peruvian shops did business in Otavalo. Now importing a broader range of goods because of both their new price advantage and permanent Ecuadorian business outlets, Peruvian wholesalers have cut out a whole segment of Otavaleño resellers. As sales fell throughout 2001, a group of vendors on the plaza drew up a legal petition requesting an investigation into the Peruvian stores with the goal of shutting them down. Over 150 sellers signed the document. The spokesman for the market vendors put the case as follows:

> We have even sent Peruvian crafts to other countries. Unfortunately, in this past year, they have opened many shops. . . . In the past, the Poncho Plaza was good. Now, the market does not even give us our daily bread. Now one earns a quarter of the bread that one gives to our children. For this reason, we are concerned with shutting the stores of the Peruvians.

The petition put the UNAIMCO, a union of artisans who act as the guardians of Otavalo's Plaza de Ponchos, in a bind. Licenciado Quimbo, president of the UNAIMCO, pointed out that Ecuadorian trade policies made it impossible to support the petitioner's primary demands. In a meeting of the union's board members in May 2001, he reminded the other officers that Ecuador has signed the Andean Pact, the General Agreement of Tariffs and Trade, and several bilateral agreements specifically with Peru, all of which opened Ecuador's markets to Peruvians. "How can we throw anyone out?" he asked rhetorically.

Despite a long history of embracing the new—from street fairs in newly capitalist eastern Europe to cyber cafes—the region is losing ground. Young people are especially pessimistic. When I interviewed César, one of the teenage boys UNICEF and the Ecuadorian government worked to have returned from Uruguay in 2001, he related his journey to me: how the bus broke down in Bolivia on the way there, stranding him for a week with no money and little food; how he walked the streets of Montevideo for twelve hours a day and if he did not sell anything he did not eat; and how they slept ten to a room in a bleak apartment on the edge of town. I then asked him whether he would stay in Otavalo, either to weave or sell, or whether he would go and travel again. He replied, "I would go tomorrow." The headline-making misery trumped anything Otavalo had to offer him.

Otavalo's market, of course, has always ridden waves of instability and periodic decline. Whole branches of textile production have lost their profitability in the past. So the question is whether today's problems also represent momentary market loss, one that entrance into some new handcraft line will overcome. Or will austerity programs amplify current market losses, converting them from a temporary setback to a long-term exclusion from the hemisphere's sober new political economy?

Conclusion

Here is the final irony of globalization from above. According to supporters, global capitalism can only survive "with strong and wise leadership" that must "promote international cooperation to establish and enforce rules regulating trade, foreign investment, and international monetary affairs."[5] Free trade is meant to arrive as the carefully implemented next step in capitalism's promise of prosperity. In fact, in Ecuador and elsewhere, the global market comes down as economic triage—harsh decisions about which jobs and businesses will live and die implemented amidst a financial emergency. The coupling of fiscal austerity programs with huge international swings in private investment has put whole nations at risk of being excluded. Trouble begins when conventional wisdom of international financiers, national economic elites, or think tank pundits begins to question the fitness of a place. Falling prey to narratives of economic noncompetitiveness—lack of natural resources, poor education, dated technology, financial instability, or an impaired rule of law—countries have been dropped from market-driven economic development.

In the face of such marginalization, Otavaleño capitalists must voice their own "strong and wise leadership" to preserve the conditions of their trade. And in developing their political influence, they must take on both the integration-at-any-cost policies of politicians representing traditional capitalist elites and the localization alternatives powerfully represented by CONAIE and the mainstream indigenous movement. While the politics of indigenous artisans and the indigenous movement can help build each other, the internationalized business interests of Otavaleños have yet to find a sympathetic home in CONAIE. Consequently, renewed economic vigor in Otavalo depends on the region making political hay out of its accumulated capital, business savvy, and fragmented society that is the legacy of globalization from below.

Otavalo's largest artisan union, the UNAIMCO, has taken on this challenge. Its members have learned there can be no economic solution without political clout. They turned to boycotts and popular mobilization to work out prices for raw materials. Similarly, they make everyday responsibilities of their associations, including training programs, into pressure points on state agencies. Combining an active, involved constituency with effective, high-level state contacts, a powerful artisan association now seeks to be heard on energy subsidies, export supports, limitations on the presence of foreign competitors, and other structural issues of an internationalized, industrialized, handicraft economy. Over time, these efforts may help Otavaleños steer national policymakers toward creating more amenable rules for their extremely competitive game—moving merchandise anywhere on that planet where a bright Andean textile may catch the eye of a potential customer.

Notes

1. See S. Edwards, *Crisis and Reform in Latin America: From Despair to Hope* (Oxford: Oxford University Press, 1995).

2. Hines's arguments are fleshed out in his *Localization: A Global Manifesto* (London: Earthscan Publications, 2000).

3. The political program of CONAIE is set out in its *Proyecto político de LA CONAIE* (Quito: Consejo de Gobierno de la CONAIE, 1994).

4. Wilma Salgado details the ironies and unexpected consequences that accompanied the dollar's adoption in Ecuador in his article "Dolarización: Del vértigo devaluador a la pérdida de competitividad" found in the journal *Ecuador Debate* 2001, vol. 52 (2001): 7–22.

5. See, for example, R. Gilpin's *The Challenge of Global Capitalism: The World Economy in the 21st Century* (Princeton, N.J.: Princeton University Press, 2000).

Pancho Jaime

X. Andrade

The controversial independent journalist Víctor Francisco Jaime Orellana, widely known as Pancho Jaime, or PJ, was born in Guayaquil in 1946 and assassinated there in September 1989. Today, people remember him as a rockero (rocker) and as a political activist. Some see PJ as either a puppet in the hands of populist leaders, or as the last truly honest, independent fighter for popular causes. Equally important, many see PJ as "un verdadero macho" (a true macho man), an honor conferred on him for the ballsy, personal flair with which he denounced political corruption. At the same time, Jaime is widely considered an example of a "style" believed to be common among working-class sectors, one characterized by vulgar, violent language and a disproportionate emphasis on sexual references. The anthropologist X. Andrade leaves it up to the reader to decide.

Pancho Jaime grew up in Los Angeles, where his family had moved in the early fifties as part of the first massive wave of Ecuadorian immigrants to the United States. Jaime, an observant Seventh Day Adventist, was proud of having been a Vietnam Veteran and a participant in the California hippie movement, details in his colorful life history that differentiated him from most of his readers and provided him with a certain status in Ecuador. He presented himself to his Guayaquil readers as a cross between a hippie and a working-class intellectual, appearing in caricature in his own magazines wearing jeans, T-shirt, baseball cap, flip-flops, round glasses, and a ponytail. At the same time, PJ built a bridge between himself and his working-class readers by underscoring his personal experience with poverty and oppression.

While in Los Angeles, Jaime worked an endless series of odd jobs, such as dishwashing, selling newspapers, and cleaning restaurants and service stations. Nevertheless, he earned a technical degree at a community college. In the 1970s, he got involved as the music editor of *L.A. Touch*, an adult magazine devoted to pornography and the hippie lifestyle. According to PJ, shortly after the beginning of his career as a journalist, his luck changed dramatically. He claimed to have found a large sum of money that he used to return to Guayaquil, where he lived for the remainder of his life.

Promoting rock music was Jaime's top mission on his return, and in so doing he acquired local celebrity. His knowledge of North American pop culture and his hippie experience became the symbolic capital that he exploited in the course of various enterprises. His first publications were devoted entirely to music and emerging bands. By the time PJ started criticizing the music industry for its discriminatory practices toward local bands, he had already toured with his own group, Texaco Gulf, and opened the city's first rock discotheque and "head shop." Jaime's notoriety spread further through his stint at a radio station, where he worked as a DJ under the professional name *La Mamá del Rock*.

Although the tone of Jaime's allegations against the music industry became increasingly virulent in the final issues of his early magazines, his jump to a more clearly political form of journalism was the direct product of a violent incident with local police. During November 1984, PJ was tortured and incarcerated. His torturers, government officers, made him eat both his hair and his paper and then broadcast a photograph of his bloody, disfigured face on national television. This episode occurred during León Febres Cordero's ultraconservative presidency, a time when Jaime had begun printing a tabloid, *Censura* (here translated as "Censured" rather than "Censorship," in reference to PJ's constant subjection to state terrorism). In the years that followed this episode, Jaime was on several occasions tortured by local authorities, kidnapped by government agents, and was even once illegally incarcerated for several months.

In defiance of his torturers' threats, to which he made frequent reference in his magazines, PJ spent the rest of his life speaking out. Throughout Febres Cordero's regime (1984–88) and the first year of the presidency of the social-democrat Rodrigo Borja (1988–92), PJ published approximately thirteen issues of *Censura* followed by twenty issues of *Comentarios de Pancho Jaime*.

Although the format of the publications gradually changed from that of a tabloid newspaper to a magazine, the main feature added over time was the use of crude caricatures instead of photographs. Advertising, always marginal, gradually disappeared altogether, although Jaime did occasionally publish propaganda from friends, and populist and leftist figures. The magazines were printed on cheap paper, the colored ink reserved only for the cover. They consisted on average of forty pages, which included approximately thirty articles and an editorial page about current political developments. Generally speaking, each page had at least one illustration, most often a single cartoon. Sometimes, articles were accompanied by reproductions of original documents, such as letters or certificates, offered as proof of the veracity of the contents. The small typesetting and crowded layouts created the impression of each page being packed with information. The saturation of space was due in part to economic constraints, a limitation that Jaime frequently lamented in his writings. More importantly, the narrative structure itself created a space-consuming effect. For instance, entire pages were filled by only two or three paragraphs. Each paragraph was composed of several sentences, not necessarily about related topics, but that were somehow intertwined to form a continuous, single account. Jaime possessed a fair level of orthographic expertise, but his grammar and punctuation departed from the standard.

Estimating the numbers of readers is difficult. First of all, it is hard to determine the actual print runs. There are no laws in Ecuador that require even registered publications to disclose the number of copies sold, and PJ's magazines were never officially approved for open distribution. The estimates of the ex-collaborators I interviewed fluctuated between 8,000 and 18,000 copies, both impressive numbers in the case of Ecuador. Second, the circulation of the magazines increased as they were photocopied, borrowed, or transmitted via networks of gossip in public offices, educational centers, and neighborhoods all over the city. Although Jaime targeted local bureaucrats and politicians, and mostly male working-class audiences, the widespread consumption of his magazines suggests that there was a far more diverse readership that included male and female, upper- and middle-class readers.

Jaime's works were sold primarily in downtown Guayaquil, the financial and administrative center, as well as an important meeting place for all social classes. Members of a local association of disabled persons, who in the last few decades have dominated the selling of lottery tickets and newspapers, were eventually recruited to distribute the magazines at the height of the publication's popularity around 1987. Vendors advertised the magazines on the sly by whispering to potential or well-known clients as they passed by in the streets. Even to this day, Jaime's work retains a following among Ecuador's urban classes.

Big Angel, My Love

Javier Vásconez

Translated by Will H. Corral

Javier Vásconez is one of Latin America's literary lights. Born in Quito, he grew up in a world of books and travel. Educated in England, France, Spain, the United States, and Ecuador, he has traveled widely, and his extensive writings reflect an energy that comes from his travels. The following was written in 1983.

It pleases me that my memory disappears from men's memory.
—Marquis de Sade

Big Angel, my love. Yesterday, when I looked at your rice-dusted face, your angelical clown face, livid in your casket, I didn't feel like doing anything, least of all crying at your feet Jacinto my love, least of all . . . Your relatives followed every one of my steps with fixed eyes. Once again, their lies, deceit, and hypocrisy reared up when they dried their tears with silk handkerchiefs. But you, for whom the sense of history passed between your legs, what did you care? Now you are the Big Angel in an altarpiece, a bit of the city's history. But you are not the prick you used to be, Devil of an Angel you. You have turned out to be a traitor despite yourself. That is why I wasn't able to leave some violets at your feet, nor the tuberoses that decorate your forehead in my memory, or even a rose or a poor lily that would stain your bride's gown. Afterward, everything happened in a different way. Angel with a hooker's rosy blush, it saddens me that your penis is in torment in Petrona's hands. You, devil who have definitely lost your trumpet. What was it to you? An angel broke into a thousand pieces when your misfortune was born, the guardian angel of your poor childhood. I know that you then fed your curiosity by feeling the dark hole of an adolescent, the enchanted ring, that place which you would later go over, day by day, with your evil tongue. Anal archangel, God's eye blessing its vices, what was it to you? You have been the She-Devil in the abyss of Alameda Park during those nights when a man kicked to death appears, in the hell of this prudish city. You have been the machine that teases your sodomite wool, your scathing tongue in my body. Now, on the other hand, you are the Angel of Light, a third-rate angel since you wander softly among silk flowers like Chagall's brides, while your funeral proceeds with an adoring rhythm. No, Big Angel, I wasn't capable of putting those violets at your feet. Too many people would have sobbed, repeating endlessly that you were better off dead. It was better for you to be a beast rather than a sinner. Why pretend if during your whole life you have been nothing but a source of scandal for them? Why get upset if they will never have enough courage to vomit on your tomb? As much as they may try to make an Angel out of you, a Saint Sebastian or whatever, they never will. I think you won the game, although it is not so. Old man Castañeda, whose cynicism was well known in the lobby of the Majestic Hotel, remarked next to me: "Poor Jacinto, he was a faggot, but a faggot with a lot of class. That is what we need to distinguish us from others, a lot of class in everything. . . ." But upon noticing your sister's defiant gaze he preferred to save his comments by fixing the monocle on his tiny eyes. Stumbling briefly, an angel went through the grayish light that lit up the hall. A moon gleam burst suddenly: the musical clocks, the decorations inside an Oriental cabinet, the silver fish on the table, the leather bound books, they all burst at the same time with that angel's passing through the glass. Your body looked like an inventory of knickknacks, an inventory of fantasies that Petrona has decorated with the determination of a cook. Resting on chrome paper moons you had the ridiculous look of someone who is waiting, hoping for the sanctity that only Petrona's love has been able to offer you. Devil of an Angel, you have died as you should have, corrupting schoolchildren in a neighborhood movie house. Angel remnant, you have died vomiting blood in an adolescent's lap. Were you looking for God in the dirty pants of the one who stabbed you? I can't believe Big Angel, because the idea of God was the only one that you could not forgive in people.

Yesterday I saw your angelic face in the middle of the coffin, a face that in the darkness of the hall became confused with those of all those saints who are too beautiful to be saints. They are too rude, aggressive in their gold leaf frames, like your relatives' coin collecting. They were more demons than angels. They disemboweled your funeral with greedy eyes, deliriously raiding your belongings at every instance. Their lustful complacent faces seemed to sprout from the interior of a cathedral. Your company perverted itself through doubtful devices in the gold bathed and colonial La Compañía church. An Archangel showed his organ about to explode: an acolyte like me in nights of horniness. From Saint Sebastian's chest caverns and bloody sites in which to place a phallus opened up, a place to go over with a pumice stone and invent God's finger after each pleasure spasm that I received with your divine grace. Devil of an Angel, you have turned your death into a *santería* ritual. Inveterate sodomite in Paris or Rio de Janeiro, patron of darkness, you have turned your life into a relic of vices. What do you care, if the saints watch over you from their shelves with glassy tears? What's the difference if you are dead? Ah, life cannot be only memories. But from the paradise of my memories I can barely make out those saints in the darkness. The face of an exterminating angel appears amidst the fog dominating the dreams of your childhood. The face of a prudent virgin disappears with the mist while you are about to spill the fruit of your pleasure with the haste of a cursed child. The face of a youth whose handsomeness will captivate you appears in your dreams, while you remember some faces dancing to the rhythm of the shadows in the carnival of mirrors. Suddenly, you, the rapist Angel appear, you who never penetrated the twists and turns of misery because there was always a hungry little love, a desolate cherub to flagellate you, the one that my penis would stubbornly enter and furiously push your vital eye, your sweet star, your rose with the fart smell; your compass asking, demanding, and screaming for a bigger tower in the convent's atriums, in the public restrooms, in the humid hallways downtown, in parks, in notaries' offices, in those cheap hotels that you undoubtedly frequented carrying a walking cane, hat, and white silk scarf to protect yourself from tactless gazes.

Big Angel, my love, you have deceived yourself, because that is how your parents wanted to see you, reduced to being the seraphic figurehead of a coffin. Those pot-bellied diplomats that frequented your house, those ministers maddened by the alchemy of power, those men with coats of arms and brilliantine that you so abhorred, will finally breathe. Journalists will also breathe easily. You won't be causing more scandals. You won't be the midsummer dissolute on rainy nights. You won't be able to revolt, nor howl in front of your mother's portrait. Your family will give a sigh of relief. Big Angel, my love, you are dead. But I will never forget the magnetic smell of your semen, like pearls on the saints' faces, like tears. You, on the other hand, will always tremble looking in my hand for the very depth of your being, two in one, like Russian dolls. Big Angel, I will prolong your life with the storm of my orgasm. You will not die in my memory; nor will I ever forgive you. With a butcher's abandon I will spill blood vapor on your back, I will look for your thighs in my bitter loneliness, and your rump will purge my vengeance every time that my nails attach themselves like butterflies to the dreams that still lie in waiting and break my will today. You will grow up bent under my body, and my rancor will grow when I recall your wonderful penis, your abundance spilling over my anatomy texts, ignoring my worries because you didn't care whether I studied or not, or if I had enough money for the boarding house. But we will undoubtedly grow together, Big Angel. I am your faithful servant, even though your relatives curse my presence. What can I do

Big Angel? They deserve only my disdain. I am now a tranquil man, lonely, who smokes in the middle of the night. I am a tired man who has been forced to cross the city with a violet bouquet in order to pay tribute to your family. What can I do Big Angel? I am also getting old, with my red slippers, without a family that will accept me as I am. It does not cost anything to remember, not even a cup of coffee. All these years I have been amassing a variety of scissors, straight razors, old silver tongs, syringes of different sizes, jars full of blood, loose blood wrapped in humors, clotted life, secretions that have been fermenting in my basement. I treasure all kinds of flies next to me, for the benefit of others, flies that buzz over my head from time to time with the feeling of tender death. Every morning I rip the world apart with my hands, with my pliers, with my scissors. I don't listen, I don't want to listen to those women's screams or their pain, although they frequently remind me of your screams, your howling in front of your mother's picture. I give birth to cadavers in the basement's darkness, while outside the city burns up in turquoise, with the color of rubies on top of church belfries, with yellow damasks that explode on top of the walls. . . .

I should have started from below, way below. What could I do, after meeting you, Big Angel? I curse the moment in which I read your ad: "Wanted. Young secretary, fairly cultured, capable of organizing a library." I should have started from below, organizing your life. With a poor slob's patience I withstood your charges, your blatant blackmail of my schooling, your angel's sobs begging me for forgiveness. Now, I give birth to jellylike dolls that seem to come from your saints' blisters. Otherwise I am your intimate diary: fantasy keeps a truth that is incompatible with reason. But your fantasy limited itself to causing ravages, nothing more. You accumulated so many pretensions. You dreamt about putting it all in words: you who were never able to put two words together on paper, nor could even draw a line—a drawing that would have been your most secret wish, since you only knew how to draw, that is, destroy your voracious cock in my body. Now your relatives conspire against your anger, against your lack of memory. Challenging goodness was always your billiards, your Russian roulette, or your king of hearts. You preferred wickedness to the monotony that they wanted for you. Your San Juan apartment became famous. Famous were also your creams that smelled like elephant semen, the movies you brought back from every trip, your leather whips, your penises incrusted with porcupine spines at the tip, the spurs with which you wanted to conquer the world. Same for your immense crucifix, in which you alternated in the role of centurion with that scary painting of Christ of the Sorrows. Devil of an Angel, I paid the price for your burning fantasy. It was there that I became what I am: a quack who explores your virgins' vaginas day by day. Bleeding virgins has been my occupation for years. Every day increases my hatred of the rootless horn on which your beautiful Virgin of Quinche rests her chastity. To hell with chastity, since I make it with my tongs. I abhor the whorehouses that smell like vestries, the churches that look like whorehouses. I will always abhor the obscene gesture that seems to be hiding behind your mysterious Virgin of the Finger's celestial cloak. The only image I have left of that sensual and pro-vocative virgin are her big breasts hiding a red glass heart, a heart in which your relatives stupidly try to drown their sorrows year after year. I will detest my whole life your aggressive Virgin of the City's capacity to dissolve like an archangel in the shadows of the nearest alley. She rules with cement wings during the day, like a twilight whore who visits her house's lower floors at midnight. I detest all those virgins who roam the city like ghosts, exhibiting their privates, covering their great imprisonment with fool's gold. No sooner has life ceased within you when they start weaving silently the veins in their wombs. There is no possible pardon or solution. Nevertheless, I drink the blood those virgins let out, thus feeding the thirst of my basement and its smelly pits. From all those whores, from all those fillies who inhabit the city's altars, the decent homes as you call them, with the taste of death I gladly ac-cumulate the coins and bills that justify my misfortune. I curse the moment I met you, Big Angel, for it was then that my affliction was born. I damn your ominous influence, even though it is now too late. I curse the day in which, for the first time, I put my hands on a woman's womb, since that woman could have been my mother.

Suddenly, Big Angel, I had the absolute certainty of the deception, a cer-tainty that would later be confirmed. Now you appeared in front of me, like a sad sketch of an angel without contours, next to the candles that lit your wings with splendor, in your coffin lined with red velvet. You are a withered angel in the twilight, but a celestial spirit after all. You advertised yourself like the fleeced Angel you never were. They have beaten you by using Petrona. How could I not notice the deception Big Angel? Petrona has diminished your vanity by going over your eyebrows with charcoal, by putting geranium pet-als on your cheeks, and by adding pieces of mirror to the coffin's walls. The rice powder erases your past. You also smelled like frankincense or old paper that a hearth consumed at your feet. You emitted the smell of a fine dead body. Whatever you say I can't stay here, my Angel draft in your splendid catafalque, tear in my memory. I then understood that my flowers didn't have a place in the garden that Petrona had planted around you. It gave me a bad feeling to see you that way. I felt like blowing away that warm air which hovered over the room like ashes. Draft of an Angel mortified by the rouge they had put on you, that's what you were Jacinto, my love. It was so sad, so sad. . . . You will never be the fearsome Jacinto to your relatives, or Jacinto the child to Petrona. Rather, you will have finally reached a privileged position in that paradise of saints that decorates the walls of your house. Disguised, you have been defeated one more time. That is why you are afraid of masks. Years ago your mother had disguised you as a Fish Damsel, so you could dance with the lightness of carved crystal in front of her guests at the Rue de Cirque, or in the downtown house. While you kept rising to the rhythm of the piano you heard, completely humiliated, lots of applause from those who feigned accommodating your mother's wishes. Dressed up during your childhood because of your dead little sister, you would soon understand that there is a mask behind every face, the mask of a stepfather transforming himself into a demon, a future faggot in every boy. Since you had been defiled a long time ago, what was the difference then in defiling your mother's portrait? One night, staggering on the stairs, you said to me come on Julián, let's go pray before the school's Our Lady of the Sorrows. After that sojourn I suspected your bitterness had been accumulating for a long time. I learned so many things with you Big Angel. . . . I learned to be a scoundrel. I remember you drew bodies in the air with your hands, but above all you wanted to pray for a little while. . . .

You put your mother's portrait on top of the Our Lady of Sorrows painting, knelt like a supplicant, while at the same time you screamed come on Julián. You then lowered your pants, spitting at your mother. She was looking at you from the Place de la Concorde in an old yellowing picture that said "for my adored Jacinto, his sorrowful mother," and your moaning started then. You asked for it my love with a feverish and booming voice, always spitting, throwing spittle at your mother's portrait. In a dubious conception, you wanted me to consume you through the back. While combing my penis you wanted me to let go, demanded that I kill you. Suddenly—as I continued arching my back and torturing my cutlass in your Magellan strait, both of us maddened by a blasphemous embrace, with my entering very slowly as I drove my hand bell deeper into your very tall belfry—in the dawn of my agony, which was also yours, I found your hands gesticulating, composing tears that rolled like pearls. Fresh black pearls rolled on Our Lady of Sorrows' cheeks. Those pearls rolled and completed the miracle. I don't remember anything after that. I stopped thinking for a moment, stopped being myself, when you fell to the floor Big Angel. I later suffered the attack of your damned mockery for many days, calling me naïve, a miracle-worker who discovers miracles in religious pictures. Is that how it happened Big Angel? Storytelling is a way of aborting words every morning, abundant words, if words allow themselves to be aborted with a simple scalpel cut. Is it true Big Angel? Now that you are dead perhaps my memory mirror reproduces the events and your beatific face poorly. Perhaps my image memory is always moving forward like a river, unwilling to stop the water flow or water itself with my hands. Big Angel, could that be why my time memory debases, enhances, and ultimately enslaves your words, your words that will be never more? I am your faithful servant, but I am not sure I am your faithful story-teller. Storytelling is an acrobatic leap that is beyond my reach. What else can I tell you? Big Angel, my love, I finally deposited my violets at your feet when I gazed at your rice-powdered face, after so many hours of waiting. I deposited the flowers, hesitating at every step, while the servants slid behind me carrying silver trays with the smell of freshly roasted coffee. When they walked they removed the room's lukewarm air, taking out sugar with sil-ver teaspoons before serving the coffee. At that moment your sister moved away from old man Castañeda, outlining a fleeting gesture in the air. With small steps he walked toward the coffin. It was five on the wall clock and a rooster crowed in a yard next door. Old man Castañeda lit his pipe, whose pine fragrance reminded me of the woods that grow on the moors. That is how everything turned into a smoke mirror that dusk filled with mourning and the smell of incense, which came in swirls of silk under the dresses, with a chorus of condolences. You Angel of floating smoke. Angel Mist who has dissolved in the city's memory. Your sister was next to me. She tried to make me understand—behind a shawl that partly covered her face, half-closing her eyes with pride—that the old bitter feelings subsisted. I was still the worst of the swine. Later, adopting a suspicious attitude, as if she wanted to separate me from the rest of the people, without saying anything she handed me a package wrapped in silk paper.

What could I do Big Angel? I decided to leave before night fell like a bat. I crossed shutters; wooden gates cracked by the daily hustle and bustle; steel railings that resembled embroidery; yards that smelled like lemons; long and deep hallways, black like the corridors that the city gave shape to outside. I received the wind on my face with relief, almost happily, and the drizzle that broke up on the roofs, the pavement and on the cars that passed by me. You are left behind, Angel of smoke. Back there you were already a bit of memory. I crossed streets, squares, and desolate avenues. I moved on without thinking, taking any alley instead of following my usual route. I walked quickly, as if afraid of missing the bus, the last bus, slowing down only before each lit shop window, before the smell of urine, touching the package in my pocket at every moment. I walked leaning against the walls, soiling my suit, suspecting that the crime was on the other side of the street, the murderous angel who would change the course of my life. I went into a tavern and asked for a beer, noticing the pillaging eyes with which the waiter watched me. I asked for a scissors, a sharp knife, something that cut. I asked that the drunks be quiet, that they leave me alone while I opened the package, while I watched with horror how that pathetic guffaw came apart, biting unevenly, your dentures falling with the rhythm of maracas in the middle of the table, your dentures guffawing during the fall, perhaps during your whole life. I once asked for a child's smile, a bit of tenderness. What I found instead was a dead man's bellow in the palm of my hands.

But you, what do you care, Big Angel, if they even took away your smile?

Nature and Humanity through Poetry

María Fernanda Espinosa

María Fernanda Espinosa was born in Spain in 1964, while her father was a law student at the University of Salamanca. Eventually, her family returned to Ecuador, where she earned a B.A. in linguistics at the Catholic University in Quito and then an M.A. in social studies at the Facultad Latinoamericana de Ciencias Sociales. For the next five years she worked for Fundación Natura, an organization dedicated to the study of the socioecology of indigenous peoples from the Ecuadorian Amazon while also serving on the Intergovernmental Panel for Forestry at the Commission of Sustainable Development at the United Nations. One of a new generation of women writers, Espinosa's poetry often combines abrupt juxtaposition of vivid jungle images with neoromantic themes. A writer of immense talent and promise, Espinosa constantly reminds us of the daily, surprising vicissitudes of life and the hope for the future.

> *Los hombres Xingú*
> *tienen pájaros en la cabeza*
> *en las canillas*
> *se mueven como garzas*
> *en meneo de lanzas*
> *como grilles en péndulo*
> *la segunda piel del tatuaje*
> *les hace caimán negro, puma o tigre*
> *se ponen doble vuelta de cinta*
> *en los cuellos de granito*
> *hacen danzas como el amor*
> *entre el humo y los charcos*
> *son abrazos agua especies*
> *hombres ave*
> *hombres ceibo*
> *con la conciencia sin jaula*
> *vuelan a ras de selva*
> *a ras de tierra*

Xingú men
have birds on their heads
on their shins
they move like herons
like quivering spears
like crickets on a pendulum
the second skin of tattoo
makes them
black alligators, puma or tiger
they put on double rows of ribbons
around their granite necks
they dance like they make love
among the smoke and pools
they embrace water species
bird men
men of silk-cotton trees
with cageless consciences
flying level with the jungle
level with the earth

el baño de las nutrias
es cascanueces bajo la cascada
movimiento simétrico del trigo
espaldas sobre la superficie del agua
esperando la copula
dientes en los dientes
abrazo de aletas y serpentinas
temblor apresurado
beso entre barbas
y un extraño descanso
para siempre
en las lunas llenas
y los estribos acuáticos

the bath of otters
is nutcrackers under the cascade
symmetry of moving wheat
splayed back on water's surface
waiting for sex
teeth to teeth
limbs coiled in embrace

hurried shudder
kiss among hair
and resting deathless moments
always
in full moon
in aquatic roots

En que orilla de grava
se filtraron tus dedos
silencios manuales delatan tus largas travesías
por esteros poblados de imágenes y caracoles
entre líquenes desnudos
y mantos grises
estás al otro lado del nogal
y los estambres de flores
ausente en tu propio trajín
de ciervo en páramo
heredero de quebradas y murallas
antorcha y ceniza de todas las palabras

On what gravelled shore
your fingers were filtered
manual silences denounce your long crossings
through estuaries populated by images and seashells
among naked lichen
and gray cloaks
you are on the far side of the walnut tree
and the stamens of the flowers
absent in your own chores
of deer in moorland
heir of ravines and ramparts
torch and ash of all words

Las esperanzas están permitidas
si no estropean la estética del tiempo
cuando se ama
la paz del cuerpo muere
se pierde el sueno para siempre
la voz se teje despacio
voz que consiente
espera
recrea

después de amar vuelve la paz
se va la voz
queda el tatuaje:
permanencia y angustia
se quiebra el resto
plaza
cielo
selva

Hopes are allowed
if they do not mar time's beauty
when we love
the body's peace dies
forever we lose sleep
the voice slowly weaves
voice that consents
hopes
re-creates
after love comes peace
the voice fades
the tattoo remains:
permanence and anguish
shatters what is left
plaza
sky
jungle

Romar tus filos
desatarte las manos
para amar
mitad agua
mitad viento
crecidos
en bicarbonato
revivamos en la sombra
en los árboles desnudos
en el mar
que se escapa y vuelve incesante
a mojarnos los pies
a espantar los sueños
más allá de la magia
encuentro tus camisas

repienso
y vuelvo a firmar mi pacto
para llegar a tu espejo
cuerpo
pájaro

To blunt your edges
to untie your hands
to love
midwater
midwind
swollen
in bicarbonate
let's rise again in shadow
of naked trees
in ocean
always fleeing and returning
to drench our feet
to drive away dreams
beyond magic
I find your shirts
I think again
and return to sign my pact
so to see myself in you
body
bird

En esta noche de tumbas y ojeras
he soñado todo
confundido historias y vida
En la imaginación
el mar y el lago tienen las mismas aguas graves
como el eco del ritmo es el mismo ritmo
En las brasas ardientes de la playa
veo cuerpos y estrellas
la música se siente nueva y fresca
y nueva cada vez
en las mascaras se dibuja
una expresión de nostalgia inventada
En esta noche de insomnio
he soñado todo

confundido todo
he vivido fantasmas magias y miedos

In this night of tombs and heavy, sleepless eyes
I have dreamed
confused stories and confused lives
In imagination
sea and lake have the same dark waters
as the echo of rhythm is rhythm
In the splintered embers of the beach
I see bodies and stars
the new music refreshes
and each time
in the masks an expression
of invented nostalgia sketches itself
In this night of insomnia
I have dreamed everything
confused everything
I have lived phantoms magic tricks and fears

Más allá de tu cuerpo
espacio
el arco iris que conspira a tu espalda
te cubre de miedo
te conduce torpe
invisible y sombra
quiebra tu halo mágico y tus manos
te acosa y te aborda incesante
carcome
el mito de la palabra
cántaro y piel
ya no espero que revivas
ni que se haga el milagro y te transforme
prefiero la memoria
robar tiempo
tender puentes

Far away beyond your body
space
the rainbow
plotting behind your back

clothes you with fear slowly leading you
unseen shadow
shattering your mystic halo and your hands
ceaselessly hounding and accosting you
gnawing
the myth of the word
urn and skin
I no longer hope for your resurrection
or your miraculous transformation
I prefer memory
to rob time
to extend bridges

"Simple People"

Barry Lyons, with Angel Aranda and Dina Guevara

In many respects, land-poor peasants such as Dina Guevara and Angel Aranda are the backbone of Ecuadorian society. They feed themselves and much of Ecuador. In the following, an account taken by the anthropologist Barry Lyons, Señora Dina and Don Angel recount their struggles as peasants and sharecroppers in Ecuador's central highlands. As is the case for so many of Ecuador's farmers, the peasant struggle is primarily one for land—to obtain enough land of a certain quality to be able to survive from one year to the next. It is a struggle that necessarily puts them into conflict with local elites and the Ecuadorian state, and one that is characterized by profound precariousness and insecurity on an almost daily basis.

The rich say [of people like us], "They are simple people" because we are serving them. But it's not because we are fools. We realize everything that's happening.
—Dina Guevara

On a sunny afternoon in 1981, the day after arriving in the village of San Ramón that would be my home for the next two years as a Peace Corps volunteer, I wandered up the inlaid-gravel road to explore. The hills and mountains to my left and across the valley to the right were covered with a patchwork of green pastures and fields of ripening corn, wheat, and barley in various shades of yellow and brown. A breeze occasionally rustled the corn and moved as a wave through the wheat and barley. As I approached a house, a woman came out to the road and invited me inside, where she served me a snack and, together with her husband, began to tell me about life in the village. Their children arrived home from school—the oldest son, who would soon graduate from high school; two daughters, also in secondary school, one of whom stood in a corner and looked at me with a pretty smile; and a little boy in primary school.

So began an enduring friendship. Señora Dina and Don Angel became my main teachers about what it was like to be land-poor peasant farmers. Their older son, only two years my junior, initiated me into the world of young people's romantic intrigues, inviting me along with him to serenade his girlfriend (now wife). The little boy was my "tag-along" companion on trips to town. For a while, the two daughters were both like sisters to me, but years later, when she was working as a school teacher and I was back in Ecuador as an anthropologist, I married the young woman with the pretty smile.

San Ramón is in the middle Chimbo River valley of Bolívar Province in the central highlands. This has long been an area of mainly Spanish-speaking, mestizo peasant farmers. Prior to improvements in roads made in the mid-twentieth century, transporting agricultural products on mules and horses between the coast and the highlands for barter and sale was a prime occupation along with farming. The dramatic contrasts between aristocratic landlords and Quichua-speaking Indian laborers that historically characterized some areas of the highlands were absent here; local social divisions were not immediately obvious to a superficial observer in 1981. Yet land was far from equally distributed. The Aranda Guevaras helped me understand how the village was divided between *ricos* and *pobres*, "rich" and "poor." Poor villagers generally subsisted by sharecropping land belonging to the rich. The landowner supplied the land; the sharecropper provided all the agricultural labor while also serving the landowner in other tasks; and the two divided the harvest in equal parts.

Don Angel shared with me his childhood memories of a landowner who would ride by his house at night on horseback rudely shouting orders for the next day at his father. Dina Guevara would sometimes break into tears when she recalled working as a servant girl in a wealthy lady's house. As a young couple, Don Angel and Señora Dina took up residence on a thirty-hectare farm down by the river, a large enough estate by local standards to be called a "hacienda." The landowner lent them a house near another family of share-croppers, and the two families performed daily chores for the landowner. When their first child was seven years old, they left the hacienda and moved up to the house by the road, closer to the village school—at the cost of a beating Don Angel received at the hands of his former *patrón*. Don Angel had built this house as a young man on a small plot belonging to his family. He planted corn on the slopes around and below the house, but in order to make ends meet, he continued to sharecrop. Now he made arrangements with three to five landowners each year instead of being totally dependent on just one.

In the mid-1980s, while studying anthropology, I returned to Ecuador several times to tape-record life histories and dialogues with Don Angel, Señora Dina, and other villagers. I planned to assemble these together into a book, a project I have taken up again just recently. In these excerpts, Don Angel and Señora Dina talk about some of their childhood memories, their experiences as sharecroppers, the choices they made in raising their children, and their view of the world. (All translations by author.)

Looking for Land

In one corner of the plot by their house, the Aranda Guevara family had planted some rows of cabbage. I found Don Angel there one June morning, weeding the plantings with a hoe. He rested his hands on the top of the hoe handle when we began to talk.

I wanted Don Angel to describe the cycle of agricultural tasks that mark out the life of a peasant farmer: the search for a plot to work and then its preparation, planting, weeding, and harvest. I thought I might alternate the phases of the agricultural cycle with the different stages of Don Angel's and Señora Dina's lives in the book of life histories I was working on. For those of us who live in the city, the image of rural life as a repetition of cycles in harmony with the rhythms of nature evokes nostalgia. I feel that nostalgia now as I write. I am sitting at a desk in my study in Michigan, but I remember what I saw and felt as I spoke with Don Angel: the black earth beneath my feet, the open air, the still green cornfields around, the bright sun that announced the beginning of the dry season and the approach of the harvests.

I never did obtain a complete description of the agricultural cycle. My conversation with Don Angel remained focused on the main thing he worried about as a sharecropper, the worry that guided his actions throughout the year: the need for land to work. If there was a cyclic repetition in this conversation, it was the struggle, year after year, to obtain a plot to work. Don Angel explained what a land-poor peasant had to do so that the landowners would allow him to work the land "on half-shares" and some of the thoughts and memories that would come to him when he was short of land to work. Every year, he faced the temptation of becoming discouraged and giving up in this struggle. It seems his father had given up, and Don Angel suffered the consequences; now he thought about his children and did not want to repeat the same story.

Don Angel began with an explanation of how he and his wife planned their household economy each year:

> Here we have this little plot to work, and also, in Tacaló, another plot of our own that amounts to one *cuadra*. This one must be one *solar*.
>
> In Tacaló and here, we plant corn for food. For grain to sell, we sharecrop. This year we are sharecropping with Don Luis, Don Mesías, and those Yánez sisters. We have fields to sell in the corn-on-the-cob stage, or alternatively, it can be left on the stalk for harvesting later, and then we sell it as dry corn to buy other grains and other things in the market.

So, this year they gave us three plots to sharecrop. Once we have that much, we don't worry; it's enough to support the household.

You have to ask for land in advance. Otherwise, other people ask first, and when it's time to start working the land, there's no more left. They all have their plots given to others. So therefore, already in July, you have to walk around asking people to do the favor of giving a plot to sharecrop. And you have to serve them, above all. You have to go lend a hand to try to gain their goodwill. The person who goes to lend a hand first—that's the one who gets the plot to plant. And you have to continue lending a hand; otherwise the following year they take it away.

BL: *And in that period of asking for plots, how do you feel? What are your thoughts, when you haven't yet gotten land to work?*

Well, for example right now, since Don Luis says he's going to sell the land that we worked this year, and the other one already said he's going to change sharecroppers, we have to look elsewhere. So, for sure, you think and think, "What are we going to do? Who[m] can I ask for land to work? If I don't work enough land, it won't be enough to support the family the whole year. And to keep the kids in school, all that. This year it's time to put another one in high school. . . ." You think about all of that, right?

And sometimes you blame your parents. You think they didn't think about things; in the old days, land was cheap, and they didn't buy any. . . . But at the same time, well, you realize, "No. If they didn't have anything to begin with, they didn't have a way to make money to buy land, either."

So sometimes I'm here sitting, thinking, "What should I do? What can I do in order to have the things we need and see to my children's needs? So that they too later on won't be blaming us."

That's why I think sometimes you see me, and maybe you say to yourself that I'm angry. Because I get a bit sad; I'm leaning on the railing, or I go out and stand in the street. Or sometimes I come down here, to forget a little bit the sadness that I don't have land to work. It's not because I'm angry or anything.

The fact you have to go around trying to find land to work, it's a bit tough. It makes you think about poverty. You say, "*Carambas*, maybe it would be better not even to work at all." [*Laughs a little.*] But at the same time, you think, "No. Even worse, if you don't struggle and find land to sharecrop, there won't be anything. And then even the children will become resentful that there's not even food to eat." Just like me, before, with my parents, when I was in school, there wasn't even breakfast. There wasn't a grain of boiled hominy corn. Early in the morning I got up, I put on my shirt; I went down to the school and sat and sat on the wall around the church. Already at six o'clock I would be sitting there. So then I didn't have energy to learn anything. Sometimes it seemed that sleepiness got the better of me . . . [*Laughs.*]

I didn't learn anything, because I didn't even have pants. I had one pair of pants that I had to wear until it was dirtier than this one that I've gotten dirty here while working. And all of this torn, behind. So I was ashamed to go to school, because my classmates criticized me and said, "Why don't you fix your pants?" And I came home from school, and what was there to eat? It was tough.

So because of that I thought, "It's better for me to leave school and go to work as a servant." So I was a servant for Don Secundino.

Don Secundino told me, "Find a plot of land to work. That will be a good thing for you later on. Even if it's [by working] as a sharecropper, grain will come into the house, at least half [of the harvest]. That's what you have to start learning," Don Secundino said.

He taught me, "That's what you have to do for later, when you become a young man. Some day you'll form a household. And what will you do if you don't work the land? A person can get used to working just as a day-laborer. And the daily wage won't be good for you all the time," he said. "The daily wage is something you can earn when you're healthy. And when you get sick, you won't have a wage, because you can't go earn it. So then, where are you going to get money? But if you sharecrop, you'll have grain; you can sell it, or at least you have it to eat. But a day wage is no good," he said. "Learn to work the land. You have to struggle in life, so that some day you'll have something, for later on," he said.

So, hearing what he said, I began to work. Now it makes me worry when there isn't enough land. It seems there won't be any food. So I have to go around and find land to work. . . .

So that's how I've suffered . . . I've gone around as a sharecropper, serving the landowners more than anything. And I haven't progressed myself. I say to myself, "Maybe they'll say it's because I'm lazy, 'that's why they haven't come to own anything.'" That's not it, but, you see, in the old days, more than anything you had to serve the landowner, and the result—the profit—there was hardly any for you. At most there was food to eat, and that's it. But grain to sell and make money, no.

You couldn't work a lot of land because you had to serve them. For example, this time of year when there's fodder to cut, they made you go and cut fodder for their animals, . . . at least two days a week. . . . And what they paid you in those days, when I first learned to work, was two *sucres.* . . .

And in the old days, to sharecrop, you always had to give a gift-offering. The landowners had the custom of asking for it. They would say,

"And what about the hen, the gift-offering?" Every wealthy person was like that. It wasn't a matter of our goodwill, something that out of gratitude you go to give it to them. No: they asked for it, they made you. Otherwise, "I'm not giving you the plot. So-and-so already came with guinea pig," or "a hen and a basket of tortillas," they'd say. So they took away the plot.

And now, it's almost the same as before. Because there isn't enough land to work, and the land is tired. It doesn't produce much. So . . . you think about how to live. And you arrange to work a lot of land so there will be something; otherwise, there won't be enough.

The Gift-Offering (El mediano)

Here, Don Angel shares some other childhood memories, and he and Señora Dina draw a contrast with their own children's developing awareness. I have arranged these passages in a poetry rather than prose format to help the reader "hear" the pauses and tones they used to convey images and feelings.

THE OFFERING, I (ANGEL ARANDA)

I.
We saw, you understand?
In the house, our parents prepare
a whole lot of cheese-stuffed tortillas.
Big baskets, full of tortillas.
There they put them.
    Put in some four guinea pigs.
    A baked chicken they put in.
And for us
of the guinea pigs, they would give
    "so that you get a taste"
they'd give the feet.
Roasted, the little feet.
And of the chicken, the intestines.
They'd prepare the "gizzards," that's what it's called.

They'd cook that to eat in the house.
Well, all the good meat
it turned out all that
was for the landowner
to go give him
arrive at his house with that.

So, they hand him the offering.
So then, he takes it.
So then, finally, they have the face to beg
to say,
    "Do me the favor
    for another year the land, to plant."
But as a little kid, one didn't know that.
No, one did not know.

II.
In the old days, parents weren't in the habit
of teaching what, why
they're preparing the chicken, the guinea pigs.
And making tortillas.

For example, now she says
if she's making some tortillas,
she says it's
    "to serve with some coffee
      for the whole family."
If she's going to slaughter a chicken
she explains,
    "It's to eat here, for all of us."
So the little kids are more—
more advanced in their knowledge.
In the old days, the old people didn't explain.
They wouldn't say what it's for, nothing.

We would be watching
as they prepare the chicken, the guinea pigs,
    and toast the tortillas.
And we'd watch
as they put the tortillas in a basket,
and put the chicken and the guinea pigs in a basin
And they'd cover it with a plate.
    And they'd leave the house.
      And we wouldn't know where they went, nothing.

One child would say,
"Where are they going to give away the tortillas?"
Well, the other would answer.
He would say,
    "I don't know."

THE OFFERING, 2 (DINA GUEVARA)
But now
> This year, for the Yánez sisters
> we'll have to buy a chicken to give them.

My son, who is still little
He says,
> "Sure, let's buy it
> and eat it ourselves!
> Not give it to them.
> You're working the land for them
> spending so much
> On top of that, you're going to give them
>> a chicken, a chicken?"

He doesn't want that.

"It's time to forget the old people's ideas," he says.
He doesn't want that.

Raising Children

The village elite in San Ramón began to send their children to secondary school in nearby towns and then, in some cases, to college in Guayaquil or Quito, by the mid-twentieth century if not before. When Don Angel and Señora Dina's first child finished primary school in the early 1970s, though, that was about as much education as a child from a poor family was expected to get. Wealthier villagers told them they would not be able to afford to put him in secondary school, pointing to the cost of school uniforms, books, and other expenses. Their son's teacher, however, told them he was a talented student and encouraged them to try.

> DG: We set ourselves to work and put the children through school, so that they can work and earn a living. We decided beginning with our first child to give him a primary and secondary education. . . . Because we don't have lands to leave them as an inheritance.

> BL: *If one of your children wanted to stay here and work as a farmer, would you rather they do that or look for a job somewhere else?*

> DG: I would prefer they look for a job, because that's why we've put them in school. Because we ourselves go through life feeling tired of suffering in this way as sharecroppers, working for so many landowners who, if one is bad, the other one is worse. . . .

Even if they go far way, what can we do? . . . We've given them a start so that they wake up and know how to think, not like us, we don't know any school-learning. . . . What makes us think is our suffering. . . .

That's why we want them to know something and go to the city to work and hopefully live better than we do. . . . They are completely aware of how we suffer, how the landowners insult us, all that. . . . I have told them, "Village life is bitter. It is a terrible suffering."

Reflections

I also wanted to know Dina Guevara's and Angel Aranda's thoughts about some deep philosophical questions concerning justice and injustice. Their responses were grounded in their everyday experiences of generosity and mutual aid among poor villagers and the moral assumptions such experiences helped sustain. They contrasted their notions of morality, centered on the obligation to respond to others' needs, with the behavior of wealthier villagers.

BL: *How do you think things should be? What would a just world be like?*

DG: Well, a just world would be if everything were equal, instead [of the way things are now] . . . so that everyone has their food and what they need to live. That would be better so that nobody would suffer—or if they suffer, they suffer the same. But that doesn't exist now; instead, the rich become richer. And now, the poor person becomes poorer, and that's it.

BL: *But you think everything should be equal, even if it means taking away from those who have things?*

DG: Even so. Sure, even so. Every poor person needs their daily bread. Don't you see, for example, in *carnaval* or some fiesta, you slaughter a pig . . . well, for my part, if I don't share with all my neighbors, I'm not satisfied. So it would be best if everything were equal. . . .

BL: *Do you think it's possible for that to exist some day?*

AA: The world will end before there's equality. . . .

DG: Well, there can be equality . . . in the sense that a poor person who thinks about how they have suffered, if some other poor person comes and says, "Look, sell me" something, you feel happy to give it to them. You give them at least a little bit, what you have. That's the only way.

BL: *That is, equality among the—*

DG and AA: Among the poor ourselves. . . .

DG: We have planted cabbage. . . . Some friend comes and says, "Sell me some"; if it's a friend who has done me a favor sometime, or has given me something, or I see they're lacking, well, I give it to them. . . . We would go with loads of cabbage to [the market in] Chimbo. We couldn't sell it. Well, there are old people, there are poor people, there are friends; so I've given it away. . . . And when I'm lacking [some onions or squash], they [some neighbors who are poor] have seen that I don't have it, and so they have given me some. So you realize that among poor people, people recognize [one another's needs].

But with the rich, no. Money is everything. . . . I think they won't even give away a glass of water for free. The rich don't care about good will (*voluntad*); the rich aren't about to say, "since this person is lacking," or "this is a poor person, we have to give it to him." Not at all. They're like this: If you pay him so much, he sells it; if not, he doesn't sell it. . . .

For example, someone from somewhere else comes and asks for lodging. . . . You realize that they're hungry, their stomach is empty, and you have to give them something to eat. But with the rich, it's not like that.

Right here, . . . if some indigenous man or woman goes to ask [a wealthy neighbor] for charity, he says, "You're young. Why don't you work?"

I realize that even if you work, . . . [the harvest might fail]. Supposing [this year] we hadn't harvested anything at all, what would we have had to do? Ask for charity, even if we're young. And the same thing happens in other places: a frost falls on the grain, the potatoes. With good reason, they have to go and ask for charity somewhere else.

That's why I say here, *never, ever* should one deny charity. Because if God does not deny charity to us, nor do we have any reason to . . . deny God's charity. Just as [God] gives to us, we have to give. If [someone asks] a favor, it's because they need it. Not for nothing. . . .

As I say, there's good will and charity (*voluntad y caridad*) between poor people, with another poor person, but with the rich, everything is based on money. If you have the money, you can go ask the rich for something. If not, forget it. . . .

BL: *Why does God allow people to treat other people [badly], or allow some to be rich and others poor?*

AA: I don't know. [*Pauses.*] That is, they just get that bad idea of harassing the poor sharecropper. . . . And the poor person is forced to do what the landowner says in order to have the plot. . . .

God has given us this light of day, He, so that we should work. And not so that we would be ordered around by the rich. But the poor person, like it or not, has to get used to the rich ordering him around.

Postscript, 2004

The Aranda Guevara children, well aware of their parents' bitter experiences as sharecroppers and the sacrifices their parents made to feed them and buy their school supplies, excelled in their studies. In 1990, the last of the four graduated from high school. None were able to find jobs that would allow them the means and time to pursue a higher education in the city. The ongoing expansion of primary education did create new teaching jobs for high school graduates in some parts of the country. Getting a job close to home in the highlands or near urban centers, however, required having well-placed connections, money for bribes, or a willingness on the part of women to give sexual favors to Education Ministry officials. Lacking any of these, one by one the Aranda Guevara siblings took jobs as schoolteachers in remote Amazonian settlements. They took classes by correspondence and during vacations to obtain higher degrees. Eventually the two sons managed to obtain transfers to teaching positions in the central highlands, closer to home.

All four of the children are married, and Don Angel and Señora Dina have nine grandchildren (with one more on the way at this writing). Angel Aranda and Dina Guevara have managed to buy a little more land, and now that their children are grown and self-supporting, they no longer have to sharecrop to get by. They can rightly take pride in their hard work that allowed the children to complete secondary school and pursue teaching careers. The children do not have to endure the petty humiliations and year-to-year insecurity of a sharecropper. The three who remain in Ecuador do contend with their own frustrations and economic insecurity: the Education Ministry sometimes fails to pay schoolteachers for months at a time, and in any case salaries are too low for them to support their families without continually seeking extra sources of income on the side.

The Aranda Guevara family's story exemplifies continuing trends in San Ramón and similar villages, as rural youth and even some adult former farmers increasingly view agriculture as an unviable occupation. Low prices for corn in recent years, apparently an effect of national and international policies associated with neoliberalism and globalization, have only intensified the pressures to leave. San Ramón has lost perhaps half of its population since I was a Peace Corps volunteer there in the early 1980s. Most youth abandon the village in their teens or early twenties. Some go wherever they can find jobs as schoolteachers; others to work or continue their studies in Guayaquil or Quito (and a few recently have made their way to Spain or the United States).

They return for carnaval and the village's patron saints' fiestas, during which otherwise empty houses briefly return to life, motor vehicles force horses and cattle to the side of the road, and old schoolmates and cousins renew their bonds. The sons and daughters of landowners and sharecroppers, encountering one another on paths or in the village store, speak easily of common school memories and similar experiences outside the village. Some sharecroppers' children have managed to rise higher on the social ladder than some landowners' children through their talents, hard work, or special skills in making useful connections. Still, nobody forgets old differences in family wealth and status; those with elite surnames and (what generally goes along with that) "whiter" features often continue to consider themselves "better" than their peers. Those differences had a lot to do in general with who became lawyers, engineers, or prosperous businessmen in the cities and whose options were more limited to menial jobs in bakeries, factories, and domestic service, or to teaching careers that began in remote one-room schoolhouses like the Aranda Guevara children's.

Given the shortage of labor, those from land-poor families who have remained in San Ramón find themselves in a stronger position than before when it comes to negotiating sharecropping arrangements. Señora Dina enjoys telling of an encounter she had a few years ago with a miserly old lady she used to work for as a servant girl. She reminded the lady how the rich used to make the poor beg for a plot of land to work. Now, she said, the landowners had to supply seed and fertilizer and beg the poor to sharecrop for them.

The Writings of Iván Oñate

Iván Oñate

Translated by Alfred Corn and Tabitha L. Combs

Iván Oñate was born in Ambato, Ecuador, in 1948. He was educated in Quito, Argentina, and Spain and is currently Professor in Semiotics and Hispano-American Literature at Universidad Central del Ecuador. Oñate has published numerous books of fiction and poetry, and is widely recognized as one of Ecuador's most creative and talented writers.

THE HOLES IN LANGUAGE
My friends reproach me,
saying that I don't read. That my eyes
don't exhaust
countless lines
in search of what was
or was not given me.
In search of a single
new thrill.
Oh, but they're mistaken,
those friends of mine.
With how much love
I take up books
and slide my hands over their pages
in the early dawn.
It's true
I've reached an age
where I only care to read
the white spaces. Those that shine
like a cool daybreak
over seaside hills.
How much life,

how many stories,
how many fish it fails to catch,
the net of language.
How much sea,
how much delectable forgetting.
—*Translated by Alfred Corn*

IRONY
I, who attacked the future
Who of the world
made an adverse and dried-out landscape
At the last minute
transforming myself into an ecologist
And everything
Because they had felled
a tree
The only tree
where I chose to hang myself.
—*Translated by Tabitha L. Combs*

JAMES DEAN
Sick of you
With lips parched from fever and thirst
one day I awoke
in the most merciless of deserts.
I awoke
With the irremediable wisdom
that within my cadaver
lived a violent teenager
A melancholic animal
inept at happiness.
—*Translated by Tabitha L. Combs*

HOW WHERE WHEN
In the center of a poem
a forest exists
Within it
hides a tree
There
under its shade

(While I contemplate passing
over the river of Heraclitus)
I shall return
to wait for you, in order to Be
Through all the moments
of the eternal return
The poem existing
in the forest's center
under the shade of a tree.
—*Translated by Tabitha L. Combs*

Suggestions for Further Reading

The writings below cover most of the basic themes that have defined Ecuadorian history. The bibliography on Ecuador is extensive, though, so this list is by no means comprehensive, and it favors those works available in English.

I. Conquest and Colonial Rule

Alchon, Suzanne Austin. *Native Society and Disease in Colonial Ecuador*. Cambridge: Cambridge University Press, 2003.

Lane, Kris. *Quito 1599: City and Colony in Transition*. Albuquerque: University of New Mexico Press, 2002.

Salomon, Frank. *Native Lords of Quito in the Age of the Incas: The Political Economy of North-Andean Chiefdoms*. Cambridge: Cambridge University Press, 1986.

Yánez, Segundo Moreno. *Las sublevaciones indígenas en la Audiencia de Quito desde comienzos del siglo XVIII hasta finales de la colonia*. Quito: Pontificia Universidad Católica, 1978.

II. A New Nation

Clark, Kim. *The Redemptive Work: Railway and Nation in Ecuador, 1895–1930*. Wilmington, Del.: Scholarly Resources, 1998.

Kingman, Eduardo. *La ciudad y los otros: Quito 1860–1940*. Quito: FLACSO, 2006.

Pineo, Ronn. *Social and Economic Reform in Ecuador: Life and Work in Guayaquil*. Gainesville: University Press of Florida, 1996.

Prieto, Mercedes. *Liberalismo y temor imaginando los sujetos indígenas en el ecuador poscolonial, 1895–1950*. Quito: FLACSO, 2004.

Van Aken, Mark. *King of the Night: Juan José Flores and Ecuador, 1824–1864*. Berkeley: University of California Press, 1989.

III. The Rise of the Popular

Cueva, Agustín, *The Process of Political Domination in Ecuador*. New Brunswick, N.J.: Transaction Publishers, 1979.

de la Torre, Carlos. *Populist Seduction in Latin America: The Ecuadorian Experience*. Athens: Ohio University Press, 2000.

Hurtado, Osvaldo. *Political Power in Ecuador*. Boulder, Colo.: Westview Press, 1985.

Muratorio, Blanca. *The Life and Times of Grandfather Alonso: Culture and History in the Upper Amazon*. New Brunswick, N.J.: Rutgers University Press, 1991.

Quintero, Rafael. *El Mito del populismo en el Ecuador: Análisis de los fundamentos del Estado Ecuatoriano Moderno (1895–1934)*. Quito: FLACSO 1980.

IV. Global Currents

Becker, Marc. *Indians and Leftists in the Making of Ecuador's Modern Indigenous Movements*. Durham, N.C.: Duke University Press, 2008.

Conaghan, Catherine. *Restructuring Domination: Industrialists and the State in Ecuador*. Pittsburgh: University of Pittsburgh Press, 1988.

Lind, Amy. 2005. *Gendered Paradoxes: Women's Movements, State Restructuring, and Global Development in Ecuador*. University Park: Pennsylvania State University Press.

Miller, Tom. *Panama Hat Trail: A Journey from South America*. Washington, D.C.: National Geographic Society, 1986.

Pachano, Simón. *La trama de Penélope: Procesos políticos e instituciones en Ecuador*. Quito: FLACSO 2007.

Striffler, Steve. *In the Shadows of State and Capital: The United Fruit Company, Popular Struggle, and Agrarian Restructuring in Ecuador, 1900–1995*. Durham, N.C.: Duke University Press, 2002.

V. Domination and Struggle

Bretón Solo de Zaldívar, Víctor. *Cooperación al desarrollo y demandas étnicas en los Andes Ecuatorianos: Ensayos sobre indigenismo, desarrollo rural y neoindigenismo*. Quito: FLACSO, 2001.

Lyons, Barry. *Remembering the Hacienda: Religion, Authority, and Social Change in Highland Ecuador*. Austin: University of Texas Press, 2006.

Pallares, Amalia. *From Peasant Struggles to Indian Resistance: The Ecuadorian Andes in the Late Twentieth Century*. Norman: University of Oklahoma Press, 2002.

Sawyer, Suzana. *Crude Chronicles: Indigenous Politics, Multinational Oil, and Neoliberalism in Ecuador*. Durham, N.C.: Duke University Press, 2004.

Whitten, Norman. *Millennial Ecuador: Critical Essays on Cultural Transformations and Social Dynamics*. Iowa City: University of Iowa Press, 2003.

VI. Cultures and Identities Redefined

Colloredo-Mansfeld, Rudi. *Native Leisure Class: Consumption and Cultural Creativity in the Andes*. Chicago: University of Chicago Press, 1999.

de la Torre, Carlos. *Afroquiteños: Ciudadanía y racismo*. Quito: CAAP, 2002.

Kyle, David. *Transnational Peasants: Migrations, Networks, and Ethnicity in Andean Ecuador.* Baltimore: Johns Hopkins University Press, 2003.

Meisch, Lynn A. *Andean Entrepreneurs: Otavalo Merchants and Musicians in the Global Arena.* Austin: University of Texas Press, 2002.

Weismantel, Mary. *Food, Gender, and Poverty in the Ecuadorian Andes.* Long Grove, Ill.: Waveland Press, 1998.

Acknowledgment of Copyrights

University Press of Florida, 1996). Reprinted with permission of the University Press of Florida.

"Portrait of a People," by Albert B. Franklin, abridged from *Ecuador: Portrait of a People* (New York: Doubleday, Doran Company, Inc., 1948), 261–66. Copyright 1948 by Doubleday, a division of Random House Inc. Used by permission of Doubleday, a division of Random House Inc.

"You Are Not My President," by José María Velasco Ibarra, from *La Crítica* (Santiago, Chile), 2 August 2, 1941, published by the Bureau of the Press of the Ministry of Foreign Affairs of Peru.

"The Wonderland," by Raphael V. Lasso, from *The Wonderland*, limited ed. (New York: Alpha-Ecuador Publications, 1944), 267–70.

"Patrón and Peon on an Andean Hacienda," by Jorge Icaza, from *The Villagers (Huasipungo)*, trans. Bernard M. Dulsey (Carbondale: Southern Illinois University Press, 1964), 148–55. Reprinted by permission of Southern Illinois University Press.

"The Indian's Cabin," by Henri Michaux, from *Ecuador: A Travel Journal by Henri Michaux*, trans. Robin Magowan (Evanston: Northwestern University Press, 2001), 125–27. Reprinted by permission of Northwestern University Press.

"Heroic Pueblo of Guayaquil," by José María Velasco Ibarra, from *Obras completas*, vol. 12a (Quito: Ed. Lexigama, 1974), 32–40.

"Two Experiments in Education for Democracy," by Galo Plaza Lasso, from *Responsible Freedom in the Americas*, ed. Angel del Río (New York: Doubleday and Company, 1955), 68–73. Copyright 1955 by Trustees of Columbia University. Used by permission of Doubleday, a division of Random House, Inc.

"The Origins of the Ecuadorian Left," by Adrián Bonilla, from *En busca del pueblo perdido: Diferenciación y discurso de la izquierda marxista en los sesenta* (Quito: FLACSO and ABYA-YALA, 1991), chaps. 2 and 3.

"Los misioneros salesianos y el movimiento indígena de Cotopaxi, 1970–2004," by Carmen Martínez Novo, abridged and modified from *Ecuador Debate* 63:235–68.

"Man of Ashes," by Salomon Isacovici and Juan Manuel Rodríguez, from *Man of Ashes*, trans. Dirk Gerdes (Lincoln: University of Nebraska Press, 1999), 216–27. Reprinted by permission of University of Nebraska Press.

"Creolization and African Diaspora Cultures: The Case of the Afro-Esmeraldian Décimas," by Jean Muteba Rahier, a shorter version of "Blackness as a Process of Creolization: The Afro-Esmeraldian Décimas (Ecuador)," in *The African Diaspora: African Origins and New World Identities*, ed. Isidore Okpewho, Carole Boyce-Davies, and Ali Mazrui (Bloomington: Indiana University Press, 1999), 290–314.

"The United Fruit Company's Legacy in Ecuador," by Steve Striffler, from *In the Shadows of States and Capital: The United Fruit Company, Popular Struggle, and Agrarian*

Index

Page numbers in italics signify illustrations.

Carlos de la Torre is an associate at FLACSO in Quito, Ecuador, and a fellow at the Woodrow Wilson International Center for Scholars in Washington. He is the author of *Afroquiteños: Ciudadanía y racismo* (2002); *Populist Seduction in Latin America: The Ecuadorian Experience* (2000); *Un Solo Toque: Populismo y cultura política en Ecuador* (1996); *El racismo en Ecuador: Experiencias de los indios de clase media* (1996); and *La seducción velasquista* (1993). He has co-edited (with Felipe Burbano) *El populismo en el Ecuador: Antología de textos* (1989).

Steve Striffler is professor of anthropology and Doris Zemurray Stone Chair in Latin American Studies at the University of New Orleans. He is the author of *Chicken: The Dangerous Transformation of America's Favorite Food* (2005) and *In the Shadows of State and Capital: The United Fruit Company, Popular Struggle, and the Agrarian Restructuring in Ecuador, 1900–1995* (Duke, 2002). He coedited (with Mark Moberg) *Banana Wars: Power, Production, and History in the Americas* (Duke, 2003).

Library of Congress Cataloging-in-Publication Data
The Ecuador reader : history, culture, politics /
edited by Carlos de la Torre and Steve Striffler.
p. cm. — (Latin america readers)
Includes bibliographical references and index.
ISBN 978-0-8223-4352-3 (cloth : alk. paper)
ISBN 978-0-8223-4374-5 (pbk. : alk. paper)
1. Ecuador—History. 2. Ecuador—Civilization. 3. Ecuador—Social conditions.
I. Torre, Carlos de la. II. Striffler, Steve
F3731.E37 2008
986.6—dc22   2008032019